ACTING

MAKE IT YOUR BUSINESS

PAUL RUSSELL

First published in 2008 by Back Stage Books,
an imprint of Watson-Guptill Publications, Crown Publishing Group,
a division of Random House Inc., New York
www.crownpublishing.com
www.watsonguptill.com

Library of Congress Control Number: 2007942904
ISBN-10: 0-8230-9955-5
ISBN-13: 978-0-8230-9955-9

Watson-Guptill Publications books are available at special discounts when purchased in
bulk for premiums and sales promotions, as well as for fund-raising or educational use.
Special editions or book excerpts can be created to specification. For details, please contact
the Special Sales Director at the address above.

First printing 2008

Printed in the United States of America
2 3 4 5 6 7 8 / 14 13 12 11 10

ACTING

MAKE IT YOUR BUSINESS

Avoid Mistakes and
Achieve Success
As a Working Actor

PAUL RUSSELL

Back Stage Books
An imprint of Watson-Guptill Publications
New York

For Sandy,
my mom,
who once dreamt of life upon the wicked stage

CONTENTS

Everything I say is right.

Everything I say is wrong.

There are many conflicting opinions in this industry.
Don't take one person's words as gospel, including mine.
Take what works for you.

—Paul Russell

INTRODUCTION

COWS AND GREASEPAINT

A Journey Begins

Auditions can be hell. And lately . . . hell's been getting worse. In this particular hell, I've endured the following:

> A male actor unexpectedly dropping his pants to flaunt his endowment during an audition (his agent quickly disavowed association with the actor and the endowment).

> An actress, well past the prime of Ms., auditioning for an ingenue, climbing a stepladder as she squealed in song "Climb Ev'ry Mountain." The ladder would do better on its own (I didn't ask how, at her mature age and diminutive height, she carried round town the five-foot-tall metal monster).

> An actor arriving at a Shakespeare audition without a headshot, résumé, or prepared audition material. When asked why he was bare without tools, his response was, "I didn't know I had to bring anything." (Uh-huh. Just stand there and look pretty, and we'll do your work for you.)

> At an audition for a new musical, an actor arriving without a song to sing asked my fellow auditors and me if he could create one on the spot. Benevolent fools, we indulged him (our mistake). The young blond boy in his twenties began an impromptu rap. The gist of his jive?

> "I'm standin' here,
> up on da stage.
> You sittin' there,
> me bein' all da rage."

> The musical he was auditioning for was based on the country-folk songs of Woody Guthrie. Woody ain't no homie.

I've had weapons thrust my way, audition room mirrors smashed near my face, and I've been routinely shouted at in soliloquy. Outrageous acts of emotional and professional insecurity, a lack of preparation, and auditors' senses being assaulted by actors (gripping, yelling, and smelling) are not the only forms of actor self-destruction that I have witnessed. This growing phenomenon of actors annihilating any hope of success (or personal dignity) is also prevalent before and after their time in front of me in the audition room. There's little escape from the increasing madness.

Actors have called me at home on Christmas Day and New Year's Eve asking for auditions. One former celebrity's call pulled me dripping wet from the shower. The 1970s sitcom ex-heartthrob offered to fax me a copy of his Tony nomination from the era of Watergate and polyester musicals as validation of his suitability for a role, for which he was not right (the fax came; he didn't get the audition).

The misguided attempts for attention come not only by phone but also by postal carrier. For over two decades I've witnessed actors wasting far too much money on ineffective marketing-by-mail that makes Valpak appear chic. Actors I've never met send me Christmas cards with well wishes from Christ their Savior, followed by a plea to keep watch for their current erectile dysfunction commercial (if I were Jewish I'd be even more mortified). Along with the Christmas greetings from people I've never met comes a deluge of actor headshot calendars with varying poses to match each month. The more outrageous the actor mail marketing the more likely I am to toss it into the trash. However, on occasion, I've kept misguided actor marketing. Once an actor sent me a cereal box, his headshot on the box front, his credits listed as ingredients on the side, and his video reel plunged deep into the cornflakes. This unique marketing package and contents received my attention. The cereal was tasty, thank you; the actor's video? Never watched it.

Some actors are more blatant in the food bribery ploy. One actress, auditioning for a country-esque musical, baked Rice Krispies treats in the shape of Texas. As she sang, the sticky sweets were presented to us auditors from a small wicker basket festooned with red gingham bows. She didn't get the role. I've forgotten her name, but the li'l ole treats were dang delicious.

Casting personnel are not the only bribed industry participants. An agent, Jack Menashe, owner of Independent Artists Agency and a friend I've known for decades, told me an outrageous story of actor suck-up. Menashe was attending an actors-meet-an-agent seminar (a common nightly ritual on both East and West Coasts where actors without representation hope to attract the interest of agents and become a client). As one of the actors introduced himself, Menashe commented that he admired the actor's fashion sense, particularly the shirt that the actor was wearing. OK, so you're possibly jumping ahead of me and guessing the actor took the shirt off his back and handed it to Menashe. That would have been oh-so-Hollywood obvious, and this actor had keener sense. Several days later the actor arrived at Independent Artists and presented Menashe a newly bought copy of the admired shirt. Does Menashe wear the shirt? Yes. Did the actor bearing the gift of Guess become a client? No.

Bribes, sloppy résumés, résumés without pictures, pictures without résumés, freak-show headshots, Post-it cover letters, audition material not learned, audition material not understood, inappropriate audition material, no audition material, auditioning with props, auditioning with pets (don't ask), audition fashion faux pas, embarrassing audition behavior, actors talking trash behind the backs of others, actor wannabes without training, and offers of intimacy in exchange for advancement—all examples of routine bad behavior that hinders an actor's image within the industry.

The entertainment industry is all about image, image, and image. Oh, and did I mention the industry is all about image? Just like performing, perfecting and maintaining a proper self-image to others is an art itself. Many actors are not capable of maintaining an image that presents them favorably to audience and industry. What's become obvious, and frustrating to me (and my colleagues), is that many seeking to land roles—be it for stage, film, TV, or other media, hoping to work in New York, Los Angeles, Chicago, or regionally—just *don't get it!* What's "it"? The "it" is that there are better and *smarter* ways to becoming a successful, professional working actor.

Actors, like the rest of the human race, all make mistakes. Smart actors recognize their screw-ups, make appropriate alterations, and move forward. Ignorant actors, unable or refusing to see themselves, repeatedly choose missteps that hinder their careers. I should know. I've been on both sides of the audition table. Prior to being a director and casting director, my career in entertainment began as a working actor. Despite luck, talent, and a desire for perfection, I, too, made embarrassing blunders (but I never bribed with baked or dry goods). I recovered and learned from my mistakes. My education began with reluctance. My reluctant schooling began in a pasture of grazing cows.

"You're going to be in the show, like it or not!" Mr. DeMaio threatened. So began my insane and incredible journey into entertainment. Over thirty years ago, at North Warren Regional High School, located in the middle of a cow pasture in northwestern New Jersey, an ambitious choral director pulled a painfully shy adolescent into the ensemble of the school's first-ever musical production, *Brigadoon*. The cows outside peering into the chorus room windows were granted immunity from performing. I envied those cows.

At the end of the show's closing night, that timid adolescent stood at the back of the rural school's cavernous, brick-walled auditorium. Alone. I stared at the show's set on the distant stage. A lingering audience member poked his head into the doorway behind me to offer final congratulations. His flattery, spoken in the past tense, privately signaled that I would no longer have the stage as a refuge from the classmates who pummeled me in hallways and the boys' locker room. I was losing a place where others accepted me for who I was. I was losing my safe haven. Tears welled up in my eyes. I ran down the carpeted aisle and jumped up onto the white, linoleum-tiled stage. I darted behind the towering, twelve-foot-tall, revolving, triangular flats that formed the mythical village of Brigadoon (artwork courtesy of fifth period's "Lessons in Paint"). I collapsed behind the set, sobbing. I was hooked. Bitten. No matter how shy, retreating from the footlights was not going to be an option. From that moment I was doomed, destined to poverty of the pocket but on my way to a wealth of knowledge and experience in the performing arts. How could I say no?

Damn those lucky cows.

After moving to South Jersey, forming a theater company at seventeen, performing in community theater, and about to depart high school, I looked forward to my continuing journey. The next step should have been formal training. This is where I, like many actor-hopefuls, stumbled. I didn't have the grades for anything better than community college. Summer school is how I graduated from Cherokee High School. My diploma was unceremoniously handed to me in early August of 1983, in the school's front office, by a secretary. No cap, no gown, no smiling family photographs. The fault was mine. I pushed away academia and focused far too heavily on the arts, a mistake many actor-hopefuls often make. Besides lacking a healthy grade average, I was also without funds for a respected performing arts program. My family, like many families that spawn actors, couldn't afford the cost of a continuing education. Nor could I. If I had taken after-school jobs that paid instead of pursuing theater that didn't, I would have had choices upon my leaving Cherokee. But I didn't. So like many wannabe actors I pursued the only path plausible to me at the time. I took what little knowledge, talent, and luck I had and tried my best at being a working actor. I was damned lucky. I was also foolish.

From my first professional audition, I began, like most actors, sweating in summer stock. The summer stock schedules were insane. Cast-house mating rituals were often incestuous, and the producers, well, they were just basically bizarre. One such summer stock producer drove corpses to funeral homes by day and staged Neil Simon plays by night. The cadaver-cabbie-country-theatrical impresario had converted a church, adjacent to an embalmer, into a theater. No air conditioning. No windows. Dark. Moldy. Cavernous. It was less a church for a congregation and more a cave for sinners.

An actor's journey takes many forms, mostly none too glamorous. From summer stock I ventured into regional theater and played too much the ham on the dinner theater circuit. Some venues were grand; most were not. I made my dinner theater debut at the short-lived Domino's Pizza Box Dinner Theatre. The pizza-with-a-play venue was located at the world headquarters for Domino's Pizza in Ann Arbor, Michigan. During an August heat wave, in a poorly air-conditioned conference room, pepperoni and cheese pizza was shoveled to blue-haired audiences as actors bottle-danced *Fiddler on the Roof*. I was Motel the tailor. Despite the heat, cheese-scented costuming and having to use the audience bathroom as a dressing room, my fellow cast mates and I were ecstatic to be working in dinner theater. OK, so it was dinner theater with paper plates and an entrée served hot from a cardboard container. But the production was mostly kosher. The pizza definitely wasn't. My love for Ann Arbor continues, but I shudder when passing by an empty Domino's pizza box.

My path evolved into becoming a director and an independent casting director. I jumped the audition table late in life—late being twenty-nine. The jump wasn't instantaneous but transitional. I began to pull away from acting for several reasons. First and foremost was that I knew I was too self-aware to be an actor. I was always watching myself, overevaluating my work. Self-awareness is a trait that every actor *should have* but when that awareness becomes a constant drag on the psyche, with the wheels in your mind spinning endlessly over every minute motivation, action, and response, it's time for you to get off the stage. To be overly critical and self-conscious is death for an actor, but these are great traits for a director or casting director.

Falling into casting was an accident. A summer theater producer I worked for (as an actor) hated auditions. He invited me to sit in on a casting session with him, to keep him company. I was instantly fascinated by the process and hopeful for every actor who appeared before us. But my desire for each actor to succeed didn't overshadow my critical eyes and ears. The producer took note of this, and the next day he invited me back. That invitation to return continued for several years, and I informally became the theater's casting director.

After I cast summer theater for several seasons, my partner, who was then an agent's assistant, told me about an opening for a casting internship at a major New York casting office. The pay was seventy-five bucks per week. He wondered if I would be interested in dropping to such a low-level entry position. I was standing in our then-slum of an apartment in Hackensack, New Jersey, looking at myself in the bathroom mirror while shaving, and I half-heartedly mumbled, "Yeah, what the hell. Why not?" I quickly became one of the oldest casting interns ever.

I worked for a high-profile casting office, but despite the casting director's impressive reputation his office space was definitely low-rent. The ceiling was crumbling. Small pebbles often fell onto our heads as we juggled a handful of Broadway musicals, several national tours, a dozen regional theater clients, and the New York casting for a television network. The landlord had a cat that used our entrance hallway as its litter box. There was no A/C. The windows wouldn't open and the casting associates were smoking fiends. The owner, known in the industry for his abusive temper, was a champion chain-smoker. His near continuous nicotine intake did little to curb his temper. Of all the lessons I learned there, the most important was when to duck.

Not long after avoiding several flying telephones, suffering inappropriate comments bantered about my buns, and denying an indecent request made by my employer for a back massage, I left the casting office that doubled as a litter box. I ventured off on my own to begin Paul Russell Casting. Early on, money (lack thereof) dictated that I continue to work in the casting offices of others. My next two projects as a subordinate were for the same person. After a telephone interview, I began working for an English casting director of high regard, Mary Colquhoun.

Mary, a stout woman with a fondness for flowers and little patience for fools, was a strict disciplinarian. Of her many commandments (and sermons supporting them), her most stringent was that any correspondence sent from her office be written in the Queen's English, as the British Empire, Mary, and God all *favoured*. Before Mary passed, we worked together on two major films that were shot in New York. God love her, here was someone more anal and image-conscious than me.

One day, after all the offers were put out and there was nothing to do but sit and wait for agents to respond, Mary soundly scolded me for not reading a newspaper as I sat. She was appalled and embarrassed that her assistant was sitting at his desk with nothing to do. Her tone was forceful, not friendly, when she instructed me that I should be solving a crossword puzzle, reading a book, or scanning a newspaper. When I foolishly tried to defend myself by saying that at most places of work, such activities were not acceptable while on the clock, Mary stated, "This is not most places." When I returned to work Monday morning, the first thing I heard was Mary Colquhoun's voice coldly coming at me from her office, asking, "Mr. Russell, do you have something to read?" In my knapsack were two newspapers, a book, and several scripts. I was prepped for goofing off.

After the films came television. While juggling my own clients, I once again worked as a subordinate, this time helping to cast the first season of *Cosby*. Not the original, humorous *The Cosby Show* from the 1980s. This was that other *Cosby*, from the 1990s. As I worked, I was actually being auditioned for my position. The casting director in charge was trying me out on a week-to-week basis; despite my track record, I was on probation.

One day we were searching for a male actor in his fifties to sixties who could be funny. The character was a bit of a weasel. My first thought was a quasi-acquaintance of mine, Larry Linville. Larry, then living in New York, had played Major Frank Burns on *M*A*S*H*. When I suggested Larry, my boss, the casting director for a major television comedy on CBS, turned to me and asked, "What's *M*A*S*H*?" She wasn't being coy, cute, or funny. She was serious. She had not one clue as to what *M*A*S*H* was.

Here was a person in charge of casting a highly visible comedy on CBS, the very same network that was home to *M*A*S*H*, one of television's highest-rated, longest-running shows! *M*A*S*H* is legendary TV, and this casting director, older than I, in a position that required extensive knowledge of televised entertainment, knew nothing of it! With reluctance, she finally agreed to meet Larry, but the indignity she put him through was horrible and not unlike what actors continue to encounter today. Every Saturday, she would invite inexperienced actors she had found through ads in the trade papers to audition in a small studio on the West Side of New York. This was an odd practice for a highly visible project like *Cosby*. On one of those Saturdays, Linville, who appeared in numerous films and television series, sat patiently on a metal folding chair, in a humid, crowded hallway among young, inexperienced actors, waiting to be seen. Disgusting.

Larry, who had had a notable career, was being treated as if he had no experience, no value. He should have been shown respect in the form of either being called in for a private meeting with the director or given a straight-out offer for the small, one-time role. Instead he was invited to a general open call. My distaste for the way Larry was treated is not to say that newcomers or nonfamous actors should be treated with any less regard. There should always be courtesy and respect on both sides of the table. Unfortunately there are many casting directors, directors, producers, and yes, actors, who falter at decency.

Once I jumped the audition table I was not only astounded by the behavior of behind-the-scenes industry professionals but also by the mistakes made by actors—bad choices I remembered having made myself during my own acting career. In auditions, actors make more errors than successful choices. Beyond the audition room, many actors are unaware of how to properly market themselves. Actors not only struggle with these challenges but also often suffer from poor networking skills and an inability to work well with others. These problems all come into play no matter what training actors have had. I want to change that.

Academia for the performing arts concentrates on teaching technique. Fine. Only in recent times have some collegiate programs taught actors career survival and how to achieve longevity. The basics. Reality. I applaud those programs. For far too long actors were routinely manufactured by undergraduate or graduate assembly-line-like programs unprepared for how to properly market, brand, and sell themselves. Worse off are the naturally gifted performers who cannot afford the high cost of a formal education. They meander from open call to open call, gambling with their natural talent, hoping for a lucky break.

As a casting director, what I do is nothing more than glorified human resources. Actors and nearly all others in the performing arts are professional job-seekers. Throughout an artist's entire career, the pursuit of finding work (justifying his or her ability and worth) is an interview/audition treadmill that never pauses for rest no matter what level of success and recognition has previously attained. I have empathy for actors, having lived the hell of being a professional job-seeker myself. No experienced industry voice was available to me when I was an actor. I wish I had access to a knowledgeable insider to advise me from behind the audition table. I, like many actors mystified by the process of casting, yearned for answers to a slew of questions:

Where's the best place to train?
What is the industry standard for picture and résumé format?
How do you compose a mailing?
How do you get attention without appearing foolish?
What should you wear to auditions?
What's considered proper audition/interview behavior?
How do you find an agent?
How do you work with an agent?
How do you win a callback?
How do you respond to repeated rejection?
How do you negotiate a contract?
Where do you find new avenues of work?

After years of actors contributing so much to the success of my work as a director and casting director, I want to give back something more than a "thank you for coming in today." The time has come for me to share with actors what they cannot see for themselves—to offer industry insight gleaned from both sides of the audition table. I first began to give back by teaching seminars, visiting universities, and accepting invitations from actors for counseling-over-soda sessions. I reached a broader audience of actors through the Internet with my past column "Ask a Casting Director" at ActorsLife.com.

Writing this book has become an opportunity for me to express thoughts and advice long repressed—blunt commentary I've withheld, in part, because my mother taught me to be careful of the things I say. Her advice maybe worked too well, as there were times that, when speaking to actors directly, I've withheld sorely needed commentary regarding their poor choices in behavior because I'm mindful that many actors possess a unique sensitivity.

I'm stopping that practice here. At times portions of this book may come across as aggressive, or perhaps potentially offensive, or even beyond acceptable FCC standards. Bear in mind that it's my passion to help actors grow and create more fulfilling careers that sparks my occasionally fiery tone.

Within the following pages, you will find interviews with working actors and agents voicing their perspectives, each participant boasting a varying level of visibility. Many of the chapters are designed to answer questions that have been asked of and by me during my twenty-five plus years in the entertainment industry as an actor, casting director, and director. Some questions are based on letters from my column, while others I've encountered near daily from actors in auditions and on the street. My replies, advice, and commentary are generated by a career shared with many exceptional people who added insight, magic, and lasting memories to my ongoing journey in the arts—a journey prompted by an insightful teacher, Mr. DeMaio, to whom I owe many thanks. And maybe some thanks should go to those talent-free cows outside the chorus room windows.

CHAPTER ONE

WORKING ACTORS SPEAK OUT

Candor and the Business

"What makes you a New York actor is not talent. Surviving the streets of New York and surviving the door slamming in your face and surviving the competition and the bar after the show, that's *what makes a New York actor."*

Robert LuPone

Actor-Producer

Dean, New School for Drama

As you read this book, occasionally you will find candid insight from respected, working actors giving their viewpoints, advice, and criticism on a number of subjects, including the business of acting, training, auditions, rejection, and career survival.

When I began this project and decided to include the voices of working actors, I never thought that I would, in a way, be casting for my book. Upon reflection, that's exactly what I did. I didn't want celebrities. I wanted the voices of working actors who I knew to be successful at having on-going careers. I wanted actors of varying visibility; not everyone included had to be a household name. Most of the working actors included are industry names; they are known among part or most of the industry but not necessarily recognizable to all civilians.

THE GROUP OF EIGHT

I assembled my cast aiming to include actors who had diverse and successful professional journeys. Some found themselves working predominantly in TV and film, while others ventured primarily into theater either in New York or the regionals; still others gained employment in all three mediums. Whatever the journey, the reality of being an actor is that you may plan for your destination, be it film, TV, theater, or all three, but you have little to no control over where the road will eventually lead you.

Of the actors whose ideas and impressions we'll explore, some will be recognizable beyond our industry borders, such as twice-Emmy-nominated Charlotte Rae (widely known for her role as Mrs. Garrett on television's *The Facts of Life*) and James Rebhorn (a principal in over forty films, including *The Game* and *Independence Day*). Other actors we'll meet include Robert LuPone, Michael Mastro, Mark Price, and Phyllis Somerville, all New York thespians widely regarded for their performances on and off Broadway, as well as on regional stages, while also crossing over into film and TV. Then there are the journeyman actors, Darrie Lawrence and Bonnie Black, who both boast career longevity but who perhaps enjoy less name recognition within the industry. However, their thriving careers are nonetheless impressive in the regional and Off-Broadway theater scenes, national tours, and/or in supporting roles on Broadway. Black and Lawrence's careers reflect those of the largest percentile of working actors.

No matter what level of visibility, all the actors included have one common denominator: They work. Their professionalism and grounded vision of the business have earned them each respect from their peers and their audience. In this chapter, we meet the Group of Eight.

Robert LuPone

Yes, the last name is the same as his sister Patti LuPone, Broadway diva and vocalist extraordinaire, a woman sometimes referred to as "La LuPone" and for whom I admit I have great admiration. Prior to my meeting with La brother LuPone (referred to as Bobby by friends and industry), his agent repeatedly advised me to not bring up his sister in our conversation. But it's difficult to ignore the 800-pound gorilla in the room that is their tenuous relationship. The social dynamic between the siblings is not what you would call *Brady Bunch* bright. While they share the same last name and profession, there's little else that is harmonious. "We don't get along," LuPone openly confessed. "We're not fighting; we have had a history of feuding."

The son of an elementary school principal, LuPone grew up in Northport on Long Island, a bedroom community on New York's sandy extension into the Atlantic. Ironically, it was his sister who, in an odd fashion, inspired LuPone's desire for the stage.

"I was in the sixth grade and my sister was in the fifth or fourth grade and we had this PTA recital that my father ran in elementary school," LuPone recalled. "My sister was doing a hula dance at the recital and she was wearing one of those plastic hula skirts, and the skirt changed color. I was *fascinated* by that. I couldn't believe that was a possibility in the sixth grade. I said to my mother, 'I want to wear that skirt.' And she said, 'The only way you can wear that skirt is if you go to dance class,' and that's how I started. The whole drive was to try to wear that skirt because it was blue, then it turned to red, then it turned to green, then it turned to yellow, and went back to blue. I just thought that was magic." LuPone paused, then added, "I didn't know what a color wheel was at that time." He laughed at the memory of not recognizing that his sister's skirt was magically changed by a simple Christmas tree color wheel.

ROBERT LUPONE

LuPone moved to New York City at age seventeen and studied dance under Antony Tudor, José Limón, and Martha Graham. After graduating from Juilliard, LuPone began his career as a gypsy, hoofing in numerous choruses of Broadway musicals. But LuPone knew he wasn't going to remain a dancer because, as he stated, "that was a life of poverty."

Combating poverty and social injustice were prevalent themes in conversation with LuPone. He is very conscious of the disenfranchised and disadvantaged. While LuPone has ambition for applying his philosophies on a global scale for the betterment of the less fortunate, he has been able to effect change within the entertainment industry. LuPone was the dean of the New School for Drama in New York at the time of our one-on-one conversation, and he had previously been the board president for ART/NY and the co-founder/artistic director of one of New York's most socially progressive and issue-reflective theatrical companies, MCC Theater (formerly Manhattan Class Company). All of his endeavors are fueled by a passion to enlighten and present storytelling through acting; he deeply desires that acting be seen as a respected profession and as a means for holding a mirror to society at large.

"I believe after forty-one years of being a dancer, an actor, being in musicals, being in plays, TV, and theater and being a producer for twenty-one years and now being an educator for the New School for Drama—I believe that being an actor is a very noble and dignified profession," LuPone asserted. "I think that it's desperately needed in today's world. I think playwrights and directors are needed desperately in today's world, but I think particularly actors are needed."

Earlier in his career, prior to leading artistic institutions, LuPone transitioned from Broadway gypsy to actor. One of his first accomplishments was winning a Joseph Jefferson Award for his role as Crow in *The Tooth of Crime* at the Goodman Theater. He has graced the stages of many regional theaters, including Yale Rep, Hartford Stage, Arena Stage, Berkshire Theater Festival, and the Williamstown Theater Festival. On the boards in New York, LuPone received a Tony nomination for his performance as the demanding director Zach in the original production of *A Chorus Line*, a role mirroring the musical's legendary creator, Michael Bennett. LuPone's other Broadway credits include *A View from the Bridge*, *True West*, *Zoya's Apartment*, and *A Thousand Clowns*. LuPone has appeared on television in *The Sopranos* (the recurring role of Dr. Cusamano), *Law & Order*, *Crossing Jordan*, *Sex and the City*, Comedy Central's *Stella*, and *All My Children*, for which he received an Emmy nomination playing Zach Grayson. His film credits include: *Nick of Time*, *Dead Presidents*, *Jesus Christ Superstar*, *The Door in the Floor*, and *Indocumentos*. The man keeps busy. His crowded résumé accounts for some of his very pointed views on acting and his philosophy for those who wish to follow in his footsteps.

"You're entering a fiercely competitive field and a field that has mostly, I would venture to say, profoundly evolved people in it," LuPone mused. "I'm not saying we're scientists. I'm not saying we're going to save the world, but actors are profoundly involved and evolved people who care a great deal, I think, about an aspiration for humanity that they express through art." His eyes lit up as he admitted that "for all of us, no matter how bitter and cynical we become, there is that 'ah-ha' moment, that feeling of 'I'm home' when the lights go down and the curtain comes up. It's what we live for. It's who we are. If you're *lucky* enough to get a great scene onstage and you're satisfied or you're *lucky* enough to hear the high C that is sung as brilliantly as Audra McDonald or my sister can sing it, how fantastic is that?! *That's* life!"

PAUL RUSSELL: What do you like most about the process and the business?

ROBERT LuPONE: What I like best about the process is rehearsal. I really get bored with performing now. Once we get to opening night ... and within six months, I'm bored because I can't do anything more with the character. If I'm so lucky to have a run of six months, I've really got to get out of it. Because what I like most, what turns me on, is working with actors, the director, the conversations on the play, in a rehearsal studio. There's nothing better, for me. I don't really care about performing. I really like the rehearsal process because of the conversations, and the aspirations in those conversations are really wonderful. Actor to actor, actor to director, actor to playwright ... you're all in this caldron of creativity, trying to create something out of nothing. It's fantastic.

As to the business? I don't know that we have a business anymore. I don't know if we sold it to the corporations. . . . We lost the design, and I think that's true of the theater. I think that's true in film. It's certainly true on TV. There's a whole world of artists who are on corporate mentality. . . . You can't forget that it's a business that's personal. It's a business of people. It's an art of humanity. It's not a corporate-driven, profit-or-loss field. I'm troubled by that. The value system has changed.

RUSSELL: What do you hate most about the process and the business?

LuPONE: In regard to the process, incompetent people and neurosis, of which of course there is a plethora. I also hate the cynical actor; the cynical and embittered actor who does not aspire to what the promise of acting should and could be.

And in the business, what I hate most is the agents, the managers, and the casting directors interfering with the casting process, interfering between the creatives. And they made that relationship a business! Some casting directors have gotten too big for their britches as far as I'm concerned. Casting directors decide whether the creative meets the creative. I don't like that in the business. Now, I've never been successful with that relationship because I'm an arrogant son of a bitch, so that's my particular problem. Had casting directors and agents fawned all over me like if you graduated from Juilliard, and they do today, there might be a different relationship. But I still think theoretically there's interference [created by administrators] between the creatives in the business, making it a business. Call me Pollyanna or idealistic but there's nothing better than when . . . [LuPone begins to pound the table with his hand to accentuate his words] . . . *when a director and an actor talk about a play,* if they're really having an artistic conversation. You'll notice a star has that conversation with a director, but the bit player doesn't! Or a day player doesn't or a job-in doesn't. Can you imagine being a director and having a conversation with Helen Mirren? Fantastic! Or with Judi Dench? Fantastic! Most actors are prevented from that . . . I'm one of a hundred; told to do it louder, faster, funnier, 'Let's try it again.' That's not the conversation. The conversation should be much more about, "Well, what do you think? What's important to you? What do you need? What's the most valuable asset in terms of this character and this moment?"

RUSSELL: When working with other actors in an audition, onstage, or on a set, what are some bad work habits that have annoyed you?

LuPONE: I've been onstage where the star has truly *sucked* the oxygen out of the stage because of the *"I."* The scene was all about the *"I."* I did a sword fight in a Shakespearean play with an actor who couldn't do the same fight every night. I never knew where his sword was coming from. He actually slashed me.

RUSSELL: What do you think actors should do to better themselves?

LuPONE: Learn. If you're going to be an artist, as opposed to an opportunist, then the idea is that every experience contributes to becoming an artist. You learn from everything; to add up to becoming an artist . . . there's going to be mistakes. You're a human being. You're going to fail. That *is* good. You gotta learn from it and grow from it.

Bonnie Black

Bonnie Black is not only a wonderful working actress, primarily displaying her talents on the regional stage, but she's also a close friend and at times my casting assistant and audition reader. I first met her when she served as a reader, by director's choice, for a regional project I was casting. I immediately loved the talent and humanity she brought to the audition room. Since then Black has often been by my side in auditions. Bonnie is a very emotionally giving actress, and that skill makes her not only a great performer but also a wonderful audition reader. It enables her to bring out the best in the actors who audition. Readers who can connect with auditioning actors are a hard find. I'm not thrilled when Black is unavailable, working out of town, which is what has been the foundation of her career as a regularly employed regional theater actress. A rare breed of actor, that, as of late, is sadly disappearing from the business. Most actors today want to pursue a TV pilot that is delivered to them via their cell phone.

BONNIE BLACK

Photo by John Quilty

Black has appeared on many regional theater stages, in both the classical language plays of Shakespeare (*King Lear* [Cordelia] and *Hamlet* [Ophelia]) and Wilde (*The Importance of Being Earnest* [Gwendolin]) and contemporary works, including Brian Friel's *Dancing at Lughnasa*, Kenneth Lonergan's *The Waverly Gallery*, and David Ives's *All in the Timing*. She has done challenging work at the Great Lakes Shakespeare Festival, Folger Theatre, Alley Theatre, Cincinnati Playhouse, and Trinity Square Repertory Company, where she began her professional career.

"Larry Eric saw me do *A View from the Bridge*," Black recalled of the play she did in New London, Connecticut. "Larry was a director who worked quite a lot regionally and in New York . . . decades ago. Larry was a player in the industry, and he said to me, 'Do you know anything about Trinity Square Repertory Company?' and I said no. And he said, 'Well you should audition for them.' Trinity Rep was a renowned regional theater in Providence, Rhode Island. Larry made a call and I went to Adrian Hall's [the artistic director] apartment in Providence for the audition. I sang "Dance Ten, Looks Three" from *A Chorus Line*. I also did another piece . . . they were all sexually volatile," Black chuckled at the memory. "I was very young. I had been doing theater forever at that point but never professionally. The last thing Adrian said to me, in his apartment was . . ." Black then began improvising a stuttering, croaky, southern accent, "'. . . I, I, I, don't see why this shouldn't work out.' And there began the beginnings of my career, happily, extraordinarily, and thankfully. The experience was remarkable, and I became a member of that company for five years."

Getting started as an actress wasn't a journey encouraged by family or peers. "My parents thought that my going into the theater was akin to my becoming a prostitute," Black laughed. "They were horrified, terrified, and did very little at that time to encourage or support my decision. They wanted me to become an English teacher, which was the last thing on my mind and something I would never even remotely consider. So when it became time for me to go to college, because of my parents' perspective and because of their financial situation, and because even my high school guidance counselors dismissed me, going in [for a theater education] wasn't on the table. The idea couldn't be considered. I had no help. I didn't know what was out there, other than I had had dancing lessons, took chorus, had piano lessons, and did school shows. To pursue this professionally, I had to fight. Battle on my own."

In some ways, Black's fierce battle for a career in the arts was always startlingly clear. "There was never anything else I wanted to do," Black declared. "It was never a choice. I knew I was going to do this, since somewhere around three years old. Always, always I knew, this is what I want to do. It's not that there aren't other things in life I find lovely, but as a profession, no, this is it." And with dogged perseverance, Black succeeded.

PAUL RUSSELL: What do you like most about the process and the business?

BONNIE BLACK: I adore rehearsal. I love it, the exploration, the knowledge, learning about a time and place, fully immersing oneself into becoming another person—her habits, her clothes, where she lived, how she walked, how she talked. To me, it's delicious. You're creating. It's just gorgeous. My passion for the art has never diminished one iota.

RUSSELL: What do you hate most about the process and the business?

BLACK: We are one of the few professions where we are asked to work so hard, for no money, so often. I don't mean like lousy contracts. I mean like showcases—SPTs [Small Performance Theater], LOAs [Letters of Agreement]—where we're not working for a living wage. It shouldn't be that way. Even for an audition, the amount of work that is sometimes asked of an actor is close to unconscionable, and we're not paid for all that time.

I find it curiously odd that when I am asked to audition, I am sometimes given massive amounts of material with not a commensurate amount of time to prepare. I don't understand that. I don't think it serves me; I don't think it serves them [the casting people]. I've had over thirty pages given to me with a couple of days notice."

RUSSELL: How do you deal with that?

BLACK: First, I try to start laughing and maintain a sense of humor about it because I recognize there's just no way to do this material [properly]. All I can do is give them a peripheral skim of this; whereas, if they had chosen just a few pages and allowed me to give them a much denser reaction to the material, they would probably get a better idea of what I was capable of. If they're going to give me massive amounts of work, basically what they're going to get is my personality, and they can see I can *read*! I don't understand the logic. But I try to go in with a sense of humor as opposed to going in and feeling angry at them.

RUSSELL: When working with other actors in an audition, onstage, or on a set, what are some bad work habits that have annoyed you?

BLACK: When another actor gives you a note [about what you're doing]. That is completely unconscionable. It should *never, ever*, under any circumstances, happen! It's thoughtless, rude, and shows inexperience and self-involvement.

Also, when another actor steps on your laugh. *Big* mistake, makes me crazy. It shows a lack of skill and technique. Anything another actor might do that shows lack of respect for you as a performer. I think not only as actors, but as human beings, in a collaborative process like this, one wants to be free and open and do what we do in terms of our artistic and creative process, but we also have to realize that we're working with other people. The operative word is that this business is *collaborative*.

RUSSELL: What do you think actors should do to better themselves?

BLACK: For my money, keep informing yourself. I continue to take class and keep my skills honed in ways that I can afford. Cost is a big problem because classes can be expensive. Also I try to keep myself physically and mentally in decent shape. Your mental health is a huge asset as an actor, because it's constantly, *constantly* being challenged. There are very few vocations where you are being told "no" more than you are being told "yes." We have to stay mentally healthy to absorb the rejection.

Michael Mastro

To describe Michael Mastro, a prolific Broadway and regional theater actor, as passionate would be an understatement of character. Michael is a driven artist with a great love for the craft and his fellow artisans. The intensity with which he speaks is impressive. When discussing his journey in the arts or the journeys of others, Mastro nearly tripped over his own words in a rushed fluidity; so much so that it seemed his words couldn't keep up with his rapid thoughts. It's not that Mastro himself is impatient; it's that his desire for helping other actors is as important to him as it is for Mastro to be an actor. His eyes are bright. His words are empowered: "The theater is my church," Mastro professed. "It's my business, too, but it's also a place that I go to celebrate the truth of what it means to be a human being."

MICHAEL MASTRO

Photo by Blanche Mackey

Mastro has more than a half dozen Broadway credits to his name, including *Side Man* (originating the role of Ziggy), *Twelve Angry Men*, *Mamma Mia!*, *Judgment at Nuremberg*, and *Love! Valour! Compassion!* As a regional theater actor, Mastro has appeared on the boards at some of

America's most respected stages, including George Street Playhouse, Papermill Playhouse, Old Globe Theater, and that of the Williamstown Theater Festival. But his career as a thespian is not limited to the stage; Mastro has appeared on TV in *Alias*, *Cosby*, and numerous episodes of the *Law & Order* franchises. He's also done film for large studios such as 20th Century Fox (*Kissing Jessica Stein*), Disney, and Miramax.

Friends tease and mark Mastro as being the "Mayor of Broadway" because of his impassioned devotion to the theater. When not onstage, he can often be found at Joe Allen's, *the* New York entertainment industry magnet—a brownstone, basement bar, and bistro. The moniker "Mayor of Broadway" doesn't bother Mastro. By his own admission he's theater-obsessed and doesn't make apologies for being so. Broadway is his community. Mastro remarked that he is often touted for "knowing everybody," and he unabashedly confessed, "I like to know everybody."

Mastro grew up in the scenic, upstate New York Hudson Valley village of Castleton-on-Hudson. A son of Italian American parents, Mastro knew that he wanted to be an actor after the footlights focused on him in the third grade.

"In third grade we were doing a major production of *A Partridge in a Pear Tree*, which was a pantomime, and they needed one student to do the narration," Mastro recalled. "They were having tryouts in the classroom and I was sitting there watching the other kids try out and I just knew how it needed to be done. So I got up, did it, left, and then the teacher followed me out of the room and said, 'We want you to do this.' Which of course is how, then, I thought the rest of my career would go. Alas, no."

Mastro's career may not have flourished as quickly as his third-grade self may have dreamed, but his desire for a career in acting was further fueled by his father's participation in the arts, and a coincidental school field trip.

"During middle school my father was doing a lot of community theater, and there was a teacher, who I'm still very much in touch with, who set up a bus trip for the drama club to go and see this community theater production of *The Music Man* in which my father played the guy who says, 'Whatya-talk, whata-ya talk, whata-ya talk' in 'Rock Island' at the beginning. Watching that show is when the bug bit."

The acting "bug" may have bitten Mastro on the field trip, but it was later that the infection took full hold of him. "I definitely knew by ninth grade when I was playing Finian in *Finian's Rainbow* that *this* is what I had to do," Mastro asserted. But his love of creating brought attention both desired and unwanted. "I was one of those kids that did a lot of chorus and drama club and got picked on," Mastro told me. "It wasn't pretty in middle school. I remember we rehearsed four months to do two nights of performing in the "gymnatorium." I had the last curtain call, and people were standing up when they were applauding at the end. When I came out they sort of got on their chairs and started screaming. That was Friday and Saturday night. Monday morning I was treated totally differently by the same people who had made my life totally miserable. I was suddenly someone and the resident expert on anything that had to do with acting, movies, or theater. I remember when the high school quarterback came up to me and asked, 'So what is Broadway, is that a building?'"

Obviously, some athletically inclined youths of Castleton-on-Hudson didn't travel beyond their town line. Mastro did though, during and after his high school education.

"I did a lot of stuff in high school, including two summers at the Mac-Hayden Theater in Chatham, New York. It was a wild time, summer of '78, summer of '79. And then in the fall of '79, I was a senior in high school and I took a half a year sabbatical. I worked with what is now called the New York State Theater Institute, doing a semester with them as a company intern. And then I came into New York and entered NYU."

PAUL RUSSELL: What do you like most about the process and the business?

MICHAEL MASTRO: I enjoy the community. I enjoy the fact that I have a community that's big and exciting. I have many hundreds of people whom I consider my community, whom I'm happy to run into on the street: casting directors, agents, actors, writers, directors. *I love it.* I love being with my friends who come in from out of town and in ten minutes walking around the Village, where I live, I'll run into three people I know and my out-of-town friend is like, "My God, do you know everybody?" and I go, "Well, yes I do." I like *that!* I like community. I *like* people.

RUSSELL: What do you hate most about the process and the business?

MASTRO: It's not fair. It's not fair. If you're coming into show business 'cause you think it's fair, check out, babe! You're in the wrong business. It's not fair, and I'll always be angry about that. But life's not fair. But *definitely, show business* is not fair.

It's not fair that a brilliant actor will do a role brilliantly on Broadway and win a Tony Award for it and then when the movie gets made, some movie star will get the part. Does that mean the movie star is not really good in it? No. It's just not fair. It's not fair that a wonderful actor will work on a play in three workshop productions and then at a regional theater out of town and then when the play comes into New York, the producers have to get a TV star or someone with a higher Q rating to sell tickets. Do I understand that? As a business person, of course I do. Do most grown-up actors? Yeah. Is it fair? It's not fucking fair. It's *infuriating* and awful.

RUSSELL: When working with other actors, either in an audition, onstage, or on a set, what are some bad work habits that have annoyed you?

MASTRO: A lack of awareness that everybody in the collaborative effort has work to do. Everybody needs the director's ear for a little bit. People unaware of the needs of somebody else—only of their own needs—who gobble up the director's time or who gobble up time in rehearsal . . . that bugs me.

RUSSELL: What do you think actors should do to better themselves?

MASTRO: Everything you can do to become a better person is everything you can do to become a better actor.

Darrie Lawrence

Darrie Lawrence loves hotel rooms. "Everything gets cleaned and you didn't have to do it," Lawrence quipped during our follow-up telephone interview. That love for being away from home at a hotel and not having to worry about the responsibilities of housekeeping has been fulfilled quite often for Lawrence. She is a rare commodity to casting directors. She wants to work, in and out of town. Which is fortunate for her, as most of the stage work available takes place in regional theaters or on tour.

DARRIE LAWRENCE

Photo by Ariel Jones

When I first interviewed Lawrence, it was in New York, a few weeks before her departure to understudy Cherry Jones in the national tour of *Doubt*. A year later I caught up with Lawrence and she was still on tour in John Patrick Shanley's play, in Washington DC. That's a rare abundance of continual theatrical work for, as Lawrence politely refers to herself, "an actress of a certain age." Lawrence didn't formally audition for the tour. She got the job because of her work as the audition reader for the production.

Lawrence described herself as "southern by heritage." The daughter of a Marine, she was born in Norfolk, Virginia, grew up in the northern reaches of the Old Dominion State, and went to school in the South. "My sensibilities are a combination of southern and Yankee," Lawrence said of herself.

Many regional theaters have employed Lawrence, including Cleveland Playhouse, St.

Louis Repertory, and Denver Center Theatre Company (four seasons). Lawrence is a repeat working offender, meaning, as she proudly asserted, "I worked at a lot places more than once, which is a compliment to the actor, and it's very nice to return." Aside from the rarity of being an actress who is deeply desired out of town, Lawrence has another uncommon gift to offer casting directors, directors, and audiences: She's a quality understudy. "I've understudied divas," Lawrence proclaimed with pride. "Lois Smith in *Buried Child*. Frannie [Frances] Sternhagen and Marsha Mason in *Steel Magnolias*, Rosemary Harris in *The Other Side*, and Cherry Jones in *Doubt*. As someone once said to me, 'You may be an understudy, but you're understudying some pretty classy ladies!'" Lawrence laughed.

Lawrence is pretty classy herself. She's grounded and exceptionally charming. Lawrence has a sterling reputation as being a quality understudy—an honor and rare commodity in our business. An actress hired to step in for a star must possess equal or greater talent than the star and be egoless and affordable. Lawrence meets all these demands. She has also led many fine productions in New York and around the country. The business and Lawrence have had a good relationship during her forty-plus-year career.

PAUL RUSSELL: What do you like most about the process and the business?

DARRIE LAWRENCE: Interaction with people and learning. New experiences. Also I learn a lot of history because of what I've done with plays. You have to do research, you have to read. I now know a lot more about Ireland because I've done *The Hostage* and *Dancing at Lughnasa*. I know a lot about the Salem witch trials because I've done *The Crucible* three times. I know a lot about the Dust Bowl and the Depression because I've done *The Grapes of Wrath*. I know a lot about beauty parlors because I've done *Steel Magnolias* four times! [Lawrence laughed.] I think that's thrilling. It's all grist for the mill for the next thing you do and for life. The more well-read you are the better an actor you are.

RUSSELL: What do you hate most about the process and the business?

LAWRENCE: The insecurity. Literally, the financial lifestyle insecurity. You never know where your money's coming from. Thank God for unemployment. Thank God I'm looking at a pension down the road. Not a great one but there's a pension. Also you can't plan ahead, I can't say now that I'll take a trip in August because I might get a job. And I need all the work I can get. I'm not in a position to turn down work or turn down auditions.

RUSSELL: When working with other actors, either in an audition, onstage, or on a set, what are some bad work habits that have annoyed you?

LAWRENCE: One thing, when you're in a scene and the other actor says either to you directly or to the director, in your presence, "Well if *that* person does such-and-such, *then* I can do *this*." They're, in effect, directing their fellow actors. Young actors do that sometimes, and it drives me nuts. I've actually spoken to stage managers and told them to tell the other actor not to do that. I'm not a diva, I won't get mad, I won't get mad publicly, but other people will.

Also, actors complaining! Complaining about the direction. Complaining about the play, complaining about the job. Just whining all the time. Some of these are just personality deficits, such as actors who don't look at you on stage. I was working in Florida doing *The Perfect Party* and the person who played my husband, who didn't want to do the play, wore reflective sunglasses and a baseball hat in rehearsal! There was no contact with the other actor. It's *very* rude! I worked with another actor who did that. He was a brilliant actor, he didn't like the play, he didn't like the director, he didn't like the process, and he wore reflective sunglasses. So, you never saw his eyes! What good is that? And nobody called him on it!

RUSSELL: What do you think actors should do to better themselves?

LAWRENCE: Live life to the fullest and most lawfully that you can. Also study and read! It *astonishing* to me that I work sometimes with young actors and they say, "Oh, I never read the paper," or "I never do any research," or "I never go to a museum." Everything we can do to enrich ourselves, our personal and intellectual lives, as well as our artistic lives, is important. Go to movies, go to plays, go to museums.

Mark Price

Mark Price is a charming, Puck-like, Broadway musical-comedy actor, who brings lively personas to the stage that contrast his sheepish, humble nature offstage. Price is always cheerful and a tad shy. But one gets the sense that, underneath that charming shyness, there's a bit of elfin mischief that he will release once he gets comfortable.

The first time that I can recall seeing Price charm an audience was when he played Tobias in *Sweeney Todd: The Demon Barber of Fleet Street,* featuring Christine Baranski, at the Kennedy Center in Washington DC. As Price crooned "Nothing's gonna harm you. . . ." to Ms. Baranski, he won over the audience and me with his heartfelt and gentle, gamine bravado. His tender delivery was riveting. Since then I have been to many of Price's opening nights, most of those tux-donning evenings being on Broadway.

Price is part of a small, elite collective of Broadway performers whose names are instantly recognized by anyone connected to casting within the New York theater community. Occasionally, Price *is* recognized by the civilian world. I witnessed this when Julie Andrews directed him in a production of *The Boyfriend* at the Bay Street Theatre in Sag Harbor. Along with his agent, I went to visit Price and the production. Prior to the summer Sunday matinee, we all sat at a picnic table on the Hamptons hideaway's small, ritzy harbor beach, eating ice cream before Price had to report to the theater. As we left the beach, a young girl in her mid-teens, along with her parents, approached Price and asked for his autograph. The pleasant fawning fan in flip-flops had blurted anxiously that she and her family had seen Price multiple times in *DOTV*. Her father chimed in and explained that they had traveled more than two hours from Connecticut to Sag Harbor to see him in *The Boyfriend*!

MARK PRICE

Photo by Deborah Lopez

Whoa! I was floored. Price was developing a loyal fan base beyond the Hudson River. I suddenly realized I was failing Casting 101, for I had no idea that Price had done a TV series or was becoming better known beyond our cozy entertainment family in New York. With polite, genuine humility, Price fulfilled the autograph request and thanked the journeying family of fans for the kind compliments. I then turned to him and asked, "What was *DOTV*?" Price sheepishly looked down at the ground, kicked at the dirt, and mumbled, "*Dance of the Vampires.*" Oh, *that* thing. *DOTV*, as its cult followers tagged it, wasn't a TV series at all. It was an infamous, fangless, vampire-musical, Broadway bomb starring Michael Crawford. One of the production's less embarrassing highlights was a dancing clove of garlic. Price, as Boris, Crawford's demonic onstage assistant, brilliantly rose above the problems that plagued the show . . . and the dancing clove of garlic.

Price has many lines to be proud of on his résumé, including his participation in the successful Broadway productions of Disney's *Mary Poppins*; Disney's *Beauty and the Beast*; *Mamma Mia!*; *All Shook Up*; *Wonderful Town*; *The Rocky Horror Show* (2000 revival); *Chicago*; Paul Simon's less–than–well–received *Capeman*; the Encores' presentation of *70, Girls, 70*; and *You're a Good Man, Charlie Brown*. Not a bad beginning for a youthful actor.

Price grew up in Texas, which he reflected upon as "something I was proud of until George Bush came into office." When I asked which Bush, junior or senior, Price replied, "Well, we can go back that far, too."

Price made the choice to pursue acting because of his growing awareness of self along with an understanding of his home environment. "For me, it was my dysfunctional family. I had a brother and sister growing up, and they were hell-raisers. They were always getting into trouble. I was sort of like the art-fart of the family who didn't really know it yet. Acting was the only place I could go to where I felt safe, a place where I realized that I had something to contribute. I also happened to realize that I had talent. Theater was a place . . . I felt like I had a place. A place where I had an identity, something to contribute. I think that a lot of people, if they're brave enough to answer the question honestly"—Price laughed and become sheepishly self-aware—"honestly can say that a lot of the reason for going into acting, at that young age, is that theater, if you have talent, it's also a way to be affirmed that you're special or have value. So I realized that I had something to contribute and then all of a sudden I had an outlet to do that with."

Fortunately Price didn't need to rely on family or self for recognition of his abilities. "I was also very lucky to come across amazing mentors when I was young. In junior high I had a drama teacher who was this real eccentric woman named Beverly Bubenik. She really took me under her wing, particularly as a young crazy teenager, when I was all over the place. She saw that I had some sort of creativity and found a way to harvest it."

Price's journey into the arts began, like most, early in school. "The very first show that I can remember is a junior high production of *Alice in Wonderland* where I played the Mad Hatter, which was very appropriate. I remember I had to sing, and I remember that I was terrified about that."

But the thought of singing and acting as a career didn't occur to Price over tea with Alice. That desire would come later, but there would be an early challenge. "It wasn't until I auditioned for the High School for Visual & Performing Arts in Houston. There were two of us at the auditions, me and another guy. The other guy got in and I didn't. That was such a setback for me. Such a blow, because I thought, 'Oh, for sure, I'm going to get in.' I was like, 'I have all these trophies [for speech and drama]; don't they know who I think I am?'" Price chuckled at the memory. "The experience made me reevaluate what I was going to do."

The setback made Price even more determined. With the help of mentors, Price sought to be trained, early on, as an actor. "The school zoning where I lived meant I would have been zoned to go to this country-like high school, and here I was this art-fart. I told my dad that if I go to this particular high school, I'll probably get killed." Price laughed but then turned uncharacteristically somber in reflection. "Because at the time, I was also just coming to terms with issues of sexuality, too. As a teenager I was becoming aware of sexuality but not really knowing what that was and feeling terrified to be public like that. So my drama teacher hooked me up to another drama teacher in a neighboring school district and introduced me to my next mentor, Tim Driscoll. Tim used to be a performer and dancer in New York. He ended up making a career change and wound up teaching high school in Houston, Texas. Tim had been notorious for making his high school theater program on the caliber of a professional level. He got the rights to do the first high school version of *A Chorus Line*. His school, Stratford High, was sort of a magnet school for the arts, and I remember thinking, 'That's where I need to be.'

"I didn't live in Stratford's district, but I had a friend who did. My dad and I actually *forged* an apartment lease, using my friend's address, to prove that I lived within the school district so that I could go to this arts magnet high school. I was about to turn sixteen or eighteen, whatever the legal age is for when you can live wherever you want and you don't have to be under the supervision of a parent, when the school found out that I wasn't living within their district. As a result we had to actually rent an apartment for a semester so that I could stay at Stratford. My father realized that I had more potential at this high school and understood the bond I had formed with my teacher, Tim, who had taken me under his wing. My father took that risk for me."

After graduating from Ithaca College, Price came to New York. One of his first jobs was in summer stock at the Hangar Theater in upstate New York. "Oh my God, it was a dream come true!" Price joyfully exclaimed. "I worked there for three summers in a row. My first professional production was *Lost in Yonkers*. I played Jay, the littler of the two boys in the show. And also I did *Sweeney Todd* . . . that was the first time I played Toby. For me the experience wasn't like summer stock can be, where you learn a show in a week and then do it. Then, while you're doing that first show for a week run, you're learning another show that same week to perform for the following week. My summer stock experience wasn't as intense as other people have encountered. It was like summer camp. I loved it. The pay was really, really low, and I was really, really happy to be making it."

PAUL RUSSELL: What do you hate most about the process and the business?

MARK PRICE: I hate the business. Period. [Price laughed.] In fact, I don't like having anything to do with the business end of the arts. I just like to do what I do best and let the business worry about itself. It's very daunting to me. I'm not a very good schmoozer. I'm not a good people person. I just know how to do what I do. A lot of times that can be frustrating because I wish I was better at being a people person. But that's why I have an agent. [Price guffawed.] I'll let him deal with that.

RUSSELL: When working with other actors, either in an audition, onstage, or on a set, what are some bad work habits that have annoyed you?

PRICE: Actors trying to be liked. A lot of times when people just "turn it on," when they become less about the work and more about being liked in a rehearsal. That's dangerous territory. For me, the people who I most respect, who I've worked with in the past, are the ones who take the time to be friends *after* the show opens; who during the rehearsal process are there to work! Sure you can be friendly, and sure you can be nice, but *it is* a *job*. When people treat it as a job others respect that.

RUSSELL: What do you think actors should do to better themselves?

PRICE: Focus on their life. I know a lot of people will disagree with me, but for me, I can't have a career unless I have a life. If it's all about having a career, if it's all about being accepted by other people, then you kind of cease to live. Your life informs your work and vice versa. Your life and work are all connected.

Charlotte Rae

Born Charlotte Rae Lubotsky in Milwaukee, Charlotte Rae is most recognized, by modern audiences, for her iconic television role of the motherly Mrs. Garrett on the long-running sitcom *The Facts of Life*. But Rae has other impressive credentials that few couch potatoes are aware of. The lack of awareness of Rae's other credentials is not due to Rae's talent or management of her career; rather, industry and society should be faulted. We pigeonhole an actor into a stereotype as the result of a single role repeatedly played out in our living rooms on TV. We then brand the actor to the role for quick reference. Like tissues commonly referenced as Kleenex, or cotton ear swabs commonly tagged as Q-tips, we brand television actors with the title (role) with which we're most familiar. It's a practice that is very shortsighted. There's more to Jason Alexander than George Costanza, greater depth to Carol O'Connor than Archie Bunker, more subtlety to Steve Carrell than Michael (*The Office*), and there's more to Charlotte Rae Lubotsky than Mrs. Garrett.

In addition to her Emmy nominations, Rae is also a two-time Tony-nominated Broadway actress (for Best Actress in a Drama in *Morning, Noon and Night* and Best Supporting Actress in a Musical in the Dickens-based musical *Pickwick*). She was in the original 1954 company of *The Threepenny Opera* as Mrs. Peachum (also featuring Bea Arthur and Lotte Lenya). Her other New York theater credits include originating the role of Mammy Yokum in *Lil' Abner*, starring as Jack's mother in Sondheim's *Into the Woods*, dancing and singing in Encores' *70, Girls, 70*, and playing classic and contemporary pieces for Joseph Papp. She also played Mistress Quickly in *Henry VI, Parts 1 and 2* opposite Stacey Keach and Sam Waterston and performed in *The Boom Boom Room* with Charles Durning and Madeline Kahn at Lincoln Center. Among Rae's other Broadway and Off-Broadway credentials is *Whiskey* by Terrance McNally, for which Rae received an Obie nomination.

CHARLOTTE RAE

Photo by JerryDay.com

Aside from eight seasons as Mrs. Garrett on *The Facts of Life*, a role she first played on *Diff'rent Strokes* for several seasons, Rae made guest appearances or starred in over seventy television series, including *The King of Queens*, *Diagnosis Murder*, *Sisters*, *Murder, She Wrote*, *St. Elsewhere*, numerous episodes of *The Love Boat*, the TV broadcast of Thornton Wilder's *Our Town*, *Barney Miller*, *All in the Family*, and *The Partridge Family*. She was also Sylvia Schnauser in the original *Car 54, Where Are You?* series and made multiple appearances as herself on nonstory television programming, including *Night of 100 Stars*, *E! Hollywood True Story*, *Broadway Plays Washington on Kennedy Center Tonight*, and *The New Hollywood Squares*.

Rae recalled why acting became her interest early on. "I knew that I had talent. This was for me, and I really didn't feel I was handy at anything else!" Rae laughed. "I said to myself, it was either this or nothing. This is it."

But acting and Rae didn't come together through happenstance or from lack of civilian skills. Rae firmly believed that her talent was a gift given to her. "It was a gift from God," Rae explained. "The talent, you see, is a gift. You work on the craft and all that stuff. I felt that this was my calling. This was where I was being led. Because of the God-given talent, although at the time I didn't know that the talent was a gift to get from . . . you know, from some higher power."

PAUL RUSSELL: What do you like most about the process and the business?

CHARLOTTE RAE: Aside from the work, which I love, I think it's the camaraderie that comes along with it. It's a community. I have been at calls for commercials with Eileen Heckart and Rosemary Harris and all these brilliant actresses. We all laughed. It would be so funny when we'd ALL get called in for a commercial. Whoever got it, what the hell . . . we all had a good time. The camaraderie was fun while we were waiting for the audition!

It's a real community of people who love drama, who love comedy, and who are very loving toward each other. It's a wonderful family. Especially in New York, I *love* the whole community there. In California it's all spread out. It's not that easy to have that kind of feeling of community that you have in New York.

RUSSELL: When working with other actors, either in an audition, onstage, or on a set, what are some bad work habits that have annoyed you?

RAE: This one actor, it was in *Lil' Abner*, he made fun of my stance. I don't know what his problem was, but he made fun of me. And, it really was hurtful. I had developed a certain way of standing, and because I'm so short and I was supposed to be the leader of the town, I developed a very, very powerful, strong stance and didn't move much. I only moved when it was important for me to move 'cause that gave me the strength that I needed because the stage was filled with all these tall people. He was very big and he made fun of me. Sometimes he would do it onstage, but mostly it was offstage. It really was hurtful. After a year I left the show and I said to him, "You're a very good actor but I hope that I never have to work with you again."

RUSSELL: What do you think actors should do to better themselves?

RAE: The most important thing is generosity. And that we all know that the most important thing is the play. That we will, all of us, be there for each other; we're in a lifeboat together. We are there serving each other and serving the play. People who are generous onstage and give and listen and are there doing the proper focus, on whoever and whatever. *These* are the kind of people you want to work with. These are the kind of people where things really happen onstage . . . when people give like that to each other, wonderful things happen. If everyone is just for themselves, being selfish and pushy, they may do well but the play suffers and wonderful things don't happen between other actors. You can be selfish and self-centered or you can serve the play.

James Rebhorn

James Rebhorn, Jim or Jimmie, to those who've worked closely with him, is the paradigm of a career actor. Rebhorn has worked in film, television, and theater with barely an interruption since he graduated from drama school. Rebhorn is part of a small percentile of continuously employed actors who audiences will often witness giving consistent, fine performances but will rarely know the name behind the familiar faces. Or as Rebhorn described himself, he's "that guy in the suit."

JAMES REBHORN

Photo by Timothy Lampson

The industry, and some keenly aware audiences, know Rebhorn's work very well. His extensive credits span over forty films, enough for several acting careers. He has appeared in *The Talented Mr. Ripley*, *Independence Day*, *The Game*, *8 Seconds*, *My Cousin Vinny*, *Basic Instinct*, *Scent of a Woman*, *How to Make an American Quilt*, *Snow Falling on Cedars*, and *Meet the Parents*. On TV, Rebhorn has had recurring or guest-starring roles in over twenty-eight popular series including CBS's *Hack* and *Waterfront*; several *Law & Order* episodes; the two-part *Seinfeld* finale on NBC; the ABC mini-series *J.F.K.: Reckless Youth*; and HBO's *From Earth to the Moon*, produced by Tom Hanks. Rebhorn has also been a contract player on daytime serials including *Guiding Light*. Onstage in New York, Rebhorn has appeared on Broadway in *Twelve Angry Men*, *Prelude to a Kiss*, *Dinner at Eight*, *I'm Not Rappaport*, and *Far East*.

Apart from a stellar Broadway career, Rebhorn has worked at many high-profile New York theater companies, including Lincoln Center, Manhattan Theatre Club, Playwrights Horizons, Second Stage, and Ensemble Studio Theater, of which Rebhorn is a member. I first met Rebhorn when I was working on HBO's *Mistrial*, starring Blair Underwood, in which Rebhorn was cast. I later caught up with him when I was the casting director for an Ensemble Studio Theater Marathon in which Rebhorn was also cast.

The start to Rebhorn's career as an actor was inauspicious, compared to his current visibility, but the low-profile experience brought him great joy. "Right out of drama school, I went and did the leads in all four shows at a summer theater company called the Viking Theater, in Atlantic City, New Jersey, which was in what is now Resorts International Casino. It was then called the Chalfont Haddon Hotel," Rebhorn recalled. "We were given a room with no bathroom. We had a sink in it, but we had to share a bath. We got three meals a day and thirty-five dollars a week. And I thought, 'I could do this forever.' It was great. It was terrific. It was my first paying job on stage as an actor."

But being an actor wasn't Rebhorn's first desire. "When I went to college my intention was to actually become a Lutheran minister. That was what I was gonna do. I'm still very involved with the church, but it didn't turn out to be what I thought I was ultimately called to do." When Rebhorn turned to acting, his gentle humanity, social awareness, and grounded nature became a fortunate gift for us, the audience. But his turn to acting wasn't an obvious choice for him.

"I don't think there was any clear event," Rebhorn remembered. "When I was a senior in college I didn't have a clear vision of where my life was going. I had had a tentative job lined up with the YMCA in Chicago because I had done a lot of work for the YMCA. My intent was to go up there and work as a social worker; that was my ambition. I had enjoyed the theater, and by the time I had graduated college I had two majors: one in political science and one in theater arts. I thought I might as well see what happens, and I applied to drama schools, all of which were accredited institutions, thinking I would likely teach. I applied to Minnesota, SMU, and Columbia, got accepted at all of them, and I didn't know anything about any of them. I didn't know about Yale or Juilliard so I went to the one I knew in New York. I went to Columbia. There was a teacher there by the name of Ted Cassanov, head of the acting program, and it wasn't so much his encouragement but his approach to the craft of acting that I had found so impressive and something to be emulated and a worthy kind of career to pursue. So, out of that I decided to give it a try. And I got lucky. Most of my first jobs, as are most first jobs for everybody, were through friends that you worked with at graduate school: directors or writers, friends of friends who would recommend you. I was nonunion then and I'd done a couple of nonunion public service films and ads. And a producer of an ad directed me to a couple of commercial agents, Ann Wright and Marge Fields. Marge Fields ultimately became my commercial agent. So that was sort of how it all started. Then I just kind of kept at it, through friends and contacts. That's how I got started."

PAUL RUSSELL: What do you like most about the process and the business?

JAMES REBHORN: The exploration of human behavior. I love thinking about other people. Given a play or a script, to be able to get more clues or the insight into what human lives are like.

RUSSELL: What do you hate most about the process and the business?

REBHORN: The film industry, I don't like the way it's headed with the decisions that are all made by MBAs far away in some kind of office building. It's not made by movie people anymore. Movies are increasingly made by market surveys, screenings, and focus groups and all that. The director's vision has been compromised. I think that's really unfortunate.

RUSSELL: When working with other actors, either in an audition, onstage, or on a set, what are some bad work habits that have annoyed you?

REBHORN: There are selfish actors, but in my experience, generally the tone that the director sets establishes the tone in the rehearsal hall. Occasionally in film there are some stars who are not interested in acting; they're interested in directing their own feature. But that is very, very rare. In my experience most stars are good actors. They are stars because the camera loves them, but they don't get that opportunity to be loved unless they're—first—good actors. Most stars are terrific to work with. They may stretch the limits of their lunch hour and they may insist on going home before we do, but most stars and actors I've worked with want to be there for your close-up, they want to be on the other side of the camera for you.

RUSSELL: What do you think actors should do to better themselves?

REBHORN: Get engaged in the world. John Huston was asked what he thought the key to success in life was, and he said, "To stay interested." That's very important. Stay interested.

Phyllis Somerville

Phyllis Somerville, the daughter of a rural Iowa Methodist minister, has a boisterous laugh that is so hearty, it's as if her laughter proclaims, "Life is good and I love it! Isn't life great?!" Life has been great to Somerville. Her acclaimed work in the film *Little Children* (with Kate Winslet) brought awareness to a larger audience of what many in the industry had known for years: that Somerville is a class act. And it's not that Somerville had been hiding. She's been featured in more than a dozen films, including *Lucky You*, *Better Living*, *Bringing Out the Dead*, *Above Freezing*, and *Arthur*. Somerville is a frequent presence on TV, having appeared in a recurring role on *NYPD Blue* and featured in many of the *Law & Order* franchises. She has also worked on *Third Watch*, *The Sopranos*, *Homicide: Life on the Streets*, and *Sex and the City*. She also had recurring roles on three daytime serials, including *All My Children* and *One Life to Live*.

While having a prolific career on the screen, theater is where Somerville's love for acting originated. "I was asked," Somerville began, "'When you thought about being an actress, did you think about being onstage or in movies?' I thought about being onstage. That person asked me why, and I said, 'That's a good question,' because I had only seen films . . . other than the class plays, and that's not professional stuff."

Somerville explained when the desire for acting struck. "I knew from the time I was that tall [she holds her hand out, indicating a child's height]. I always looked forward to going to the junior class plays and the senior class plays . . . I always looked forward to that from the time I was in kindergarten. My dad would take me as a little girl to college productions, since he loved theater so much. I saw *Pygmalion* and *Romeo and Juliet*. He'd take me to various colleges in the area because that was the only place to see good theater. But being an actor is still not something, one would think, one could earn a living at. I don't know why or where it [a desire for a career] came from, maybe doing pieces in the Christmas pageant? I don't know," Somerville laughed heartily. "That could have been it!"

PHYLLIS SOMERVILLE

Photo by Joe Henson/www.JoeHenson.com

As Somerville's career flourished it would have been very unlikely that you would have found her onstage in a Christmas pageant, sporting a pipe cleaner halo and cardboard cutout wings glued with feathers. She graduated from dollar-store theatricals to starring on the stages of the New York theater. Among her accomplishments, Somerville originated the role of Hannah in the musical adaptation of *The Spitfire Grill*. "I just *loved* that show!" Somerville exclaimed. "I could have done that forever." In New York she also appeared in *The Sum of Us*, *The Night Hank Williams Died*, *Marisol*, and the original Broadway companies of *Over Here* with the Andrew Sisters and *Once in a Lifetime*. But New York theater had not been Somerville's only creative theatrical playground. She'd happily go out of town for projects that excited her creativity, and it would seem that her creativity had been often enticed. With a lengthy list of credentials, an impressive near impossibility for a single career, some of the regional venues she visited include Paper Mill Playhouse, Hartford Stage, Yale Rep, Long Wharf Theatre, Arena Stage, Humanafest, and Baltimore Center Stage. Whether the productions are classical (*Othello*, *Twelfth Night*) or musical (*My Fair Lady*, *The Robber Bridegroom*, *The Threepenny Opera*), Somerville is a versatile and accomplished artist.

Somerville's early desire to perform was something that she kept quiet. "I used to pretend that I wanted to be something else when teachers would go around and ask students in the class. 'Cause I was sensitive about being laughed at," Somerville recalled. "If you lived in a town of 1,600 to 3,000 and said you were going to be an actress you would have been hooted at." Somerville laughed loudly, the cackle echoing throughout the audition room in which we were speaking. "So I just kept very quiet about that."

When I asked her what she would tell her teachers she wanted to be when she grew up, she said, "Oh, I would tell them that when everybody wanted to be a nurse, I wanted to be a nurse and then actually for a while, since I was such a sports fan (my dad lived and died with the Iowa Hawkeyes—and we didn't just go to football and basketball games, he took me to track meets and baseball games), for a while I said I wanted to be a sportscaster. Because I already knew that I was a little odd. But [being a sportscaster] was still in the realm of something that would be possible. Then I realized I didn't have *that* gift. It was just something to say, but all the time I *knew* I was going to be an actor."

Somerville's start was, like for most actors, far from high profile. "My first professional job was doing gunfights in melodramas in Buckskin Joe, Colorado," Somerville recalled with amusement. "I did melodrama at night—*Poor New York* and *The Drunkard*—and then I sang in the bar after the show. I played the saloon girl with the opera hose and a feather in my hair. And I did gunfights. I did *Gunfight at the O.K. Corral* and *Killing of the Dalton Gang*." Twirling a Colt .45 and dancing on bar tops wasn't Somerville's only means for a paycheck that summer. "I played organ at the Episcopal church on Sunday mornings. It was a fun summer. It was the first time I ever got paid. On a job that was paying me twenty-five bucks a week plus room and board, with the tips I got from singing in the bar, and playing the organ in church, I actually paid for college tuition and room and board for a semester. Of course it was a state school, but I was doing well with the tips."

PAUL RUSSELL: What do you like most about the process and the business?

PHYLLIS SOMERVILLE: I *love* the community! I think it's one of the best small towns in the world.

RUSSELL: What do you hate most about the process and the business?

SOMERVILLE: As far as doing stage work, I don't like the fact that I'm actually more frightened now being out onstage than when I was a kid. I thought I could do anything back then. I don't know, now, if my being more frightened is because I know all the things that can go wrong or whether maybe I know too much [about the business].

RUSSELL: When working with other actors, either in an audition, onstage, or on a set, what are some bad work habits that have annoyed you?

SOMERVILLE: I think it annoys me when it is indeed all about you [the actor]. Of course you're the one out there, so it *is* about you. But when any scene becomes about the other actor thinking, "Well, what do I do here?" [and not about the story], I get annoyed. I've probably done it myself, but I try not to.

Another thing is taking up time during the middle of rehearsal with questions that could have been done outside of rehearsal. I'm the type of person who would prefer to rehearse a scene twelve times rather than talk about it for a half hour. That's what works for me. So consequently it annoys me to hear all that talk. But some people come up with questions before I do. When I'm ready for questions it's usually the middle of the first dress rehearsal, and by then nobody wants to hear an actor with questions [Somerville laughed].

RUSSELL: What do you think actors should do to better themselves?

SOMERVILLE: Just keep your eyes and ears open. Watch others. Go to all kinds of films and all kinds of theater and all kinds of ballgames and concerts. Enjoy life.

During my conversations with the Group of Eight, one theme that was repeated throughout was "community." It would seem that as artists we not only have an intense desire to present story through performance but also we have an equally strong need to belong. While we're busy craving acceptance, we're also standing back a bit from the world around us, watching. Watching so that we can reflect in our art all that we observe and sometimes join. It's as if we're standing behind a two-way mirror, observing but not fully participating. And when we do participate, it's in disguise. Disguised as the character(s) telling a story. Or as a temporary civilian worker at a job we know is not our true calling. Maybe it's because we're disenfranchised observers and part-time participants that we as actors, directors, playwrights, composers, and designers feel the strong need to turn to one another and become family. For who else better understands us? We know that, regardless of our time spent (begrudgingly or not) in the civilian world, there's another place for us to return to—a community, a home—which will welcome and value our hopes, desires, fears, and laughter.

To succeed in this neurotic yet wonderful community, one must learn the basics about how to become—and remain—a professional working actor.

CHAPTER TWO

BEING AN ACTOR

A Tough Love

"Acting is a worthy, noble profession and deserves the attention of people who have talent and want to express themselves that way. And there's no support for it. None. Your parents aren't going to like ya. Your parents are going to be upset about it. Society says, 'Thank you very much.' They're only going to like you when you're royalty and you make a million or twenty million dollars a film. The rest of the time it's, 'Oh, you're an actor. Where do you work in the restaurant?'"

Robert LuPone

Actor-Producer-Educator

When I began my column "Ask a Casting Director," I was idealistically expecting the bulk of the inquiries to be about an actor's daily struggle for survival. Or at least about making mistakes. As new recruits and veterans alike falter from time to time, I anticipated questions from actors who wondered how they could avoid repeating past foibles. Questions similar to those I had when I was acting. I was woefully wrong in my assumptions. As a therapist once wisely told me: "Paul, not everyone is you." Thank God. If everyone were this highly critical Virgo, the planet's population would be seeking perfection in every miniscule chore. Little would be accomplished without anxiety.

So what were actors asking? "How do I become an actor?" Young hopefuls who want to embark on a career in the talent trade throw this inquiry at me without relent. I could easily say, "Study, study, study the performing arts." Many talent academics and working entertainment professionals have been saying it since before I was born and many more will repeat that tired but on-the-mark phrase long after these pages have browned with age.

My initial gut reply to "How do I become an actor?" is "Forget acting." Harsh, I know. But I have reason. One does not *become* an actor; actors are born. The aptitude for performing is inherent within the genes. Just like hair color, acting is part of an actor's DNA. Just as hair develops tone, texture, and shade over time, so too will acting develop at different stages in a person's life. Some people discover the acting-able gene early in life, while others stumble across the gift for performance storytelling later in their journeys. But it's not just having the ability alone that makes an actor. Many people possess the acting-able gene to some degree, including lawyers, politicians, and car salesmen, but they're deficient in what is most vital to *being* an actor: honest love for our craft. To be an actor, you must pursue your career for that reason alone.

The pull of the arts must be a fundamental force that gives an actor daily reason for living. Acting and continual study of performing must be the oxygen on which you thrive and survive. Except perhaps relationships, personal well-being, and enjoyment of life, little else matters other than focusing on the craft. The competition is too fierce for one to regularly lose sight of the responsibilities of being an actor. The work and continued training to repeatedly obtain employment must often come first. The amenities of one's personal life fall lower on a dedicated actor's priority list. Forget dinner-and-flower romances; because of your lack of amorous attention and cash, the bloom of your admirer's lust wilts. Forget romance. Forget wealth. Forget eating lavishly. Going into the arts means prioritizing focus and funds for training. What little cash starving artists do have, for most are poor, is sacrificed unto the training gods. Training gods being experienced teachers of the arts.

For me the question "How do I become an actor?" never echoed in my head. After Mr. DeMaio tossed a shy and reluctant me into the chorus of *Brigadoon*, instinct took hold, the gift was discovered, and I knew I was going to be an actor. I soon forgot my childhood desires to be an architect or veterinarian. When I realized that creating was my lifeblood, the question that oft rattled my psyche was "How do I become a *better* actor?"

"How do I become a better actor?" seems an obvious question for both veterans and novices, but there are some who aspire to be actors for the wrong reasons. When I began writing my column "Ask a Casting Director," one of the first e-mails I received was a misguided query from a hopeful who appeared to wish more for obtaining celebrity than skill. The question seemed arrogant, but this was probably a reflection of its author's ignorance.

[From "Ask a Casting Director:"]

This Week's Mailbag: Fame . . . and remembrance.

Dear Casting Director,

How do I become a famous actor?

Sweethands5@***********.com

Oh, good God. Next!

When I received this e-mail my initial reaction was to reach for the delete button on my laptop. My inner alarms went off. Red flags. Here was someone who was missing the mark of what it means to be an actor. Here was someone whose priority was the bling-bling of fame. And that pissed me off. Whatever happened to the basic desire of being a working actor? When was the passion, unexplainable, for creating replaced by a sense of entitlement to a star on the Hollywood Walk of Fame?

So you want to be famous? Fame is a byproduct, not a career. If the goal is talk shows, paparazzi, lack of privacy, agents who are lawyers, sycophant associates, and monthly Botox injections, then by all means go seek a venture in which you'll be the darling of the tabloid press, as the lowest common denominator Google your name for a millisecond. Best wishes. But please, do something new and unique. Keep away from the run-of-the-mill, Fast Passes to fame that flood the 24/7 news cycle with faces we forget by the time the next male-enhancement commercial flails before our eyes. The reality TV option is wearing thin. Who cares that you were on *Survivor 37: Crawford, Texas?*

And what is fame? Fame is ... oh God ... must this tired cliché be repeated? Fleeting. OK, I said it, Mea culpa. Fame is fleeting. Also ... there's fame vs. celebrity.

There's a recognizable actress I know, a friend, who was a lead in a long-running 1970s top-ten sitcom. From the sitcom came several movies, and more series, followed by variety shows. Then her activity swirled down to mixing drinks with Richard Dawson on the set of *Match Game.*

I met her in the 1990s. She was working as a talent agent's assistant. She was now calling out audition appointments to actors and stapling their headshots to their résumés. Her headshot and résumé had long been retired. Later she became a talent manager. The days of trading vodka recipes with Dawson and Charles Nelson Reilly were now videotaped history. One day as we were talking about her past career as an actress, she interrupted me and said, "Honey, I was no actress. I was a celebrity."

She is well aware of her place in the industry and how it had utilized her presence. She has no delusions of grandeur or amazing craft. She knew that she had been lucky, for she had never focused on the art and skills required for longevity. But don't think for one second that with all the successes she had as a celebrity, her life was happiness and sunshine. It was difficult then and even more so now.

True, honest fame is longevity. Longevity is rooted in talent, craft, and the continued exploration of pushing beyond boundaries. Very often those who have successful, ongoing careers are/were famous because they focused on the craft first: Robin Williams, Michael Caine, Jack Lemmon, Susan Sarandon, Glenn Close, John Spencer, James Earl Jones, Anthony Hopkins, Albert Finney, to name a few. ...

Versus those who have been passed over for talent shiny and new (the performing arts are a bitch that way):

Ron Palillo (Horshack, *Welcome Back Kotter*), Lindsay Wagner (Jaime Sommers, *Bionic Woman*, now pushing mattresses on late-night TV), Robert Blake (well, yes he's been in the public eye, but let's not to go there ...), Burt Reynolds (once rated #1 box office star), Barry Williams (Greg Brady of *The Brady Bunch* who appeared in a nonunion tour of *The Sound of Music* as Capt. Von Trapp and was fined by AEA for doing so) ...

Versus ... WHY!?:

William Hung (*American Idol* exploitation ... must our suffering continue?)

What kind of "fame" and/or career do you want? Casting, talent reps, directors, and producers highly respect the actors and actresses who live by the credo "I want to work and I will. I want to learn both as I continue working and when I'm not employed. I push myself beyond insecurities and doubt. I honestly and objectively know who I am. I will accept projects that interest and excite me, and those that I must accept to help pay the health insurance, rent, and grocery bills. Wherever my talents, luck, experience, life, and the bonds I make guide me, that is my career. A lasting career. Fame would be a fun fringe benefit, not a requirement."

Give me that actor instead of the shortsighted "Where's my pilot?"/"How do I become famous?" self-centered, narcissistic, paparazzi whore. Work, discovery, and growth come before the possibility of fame.

Besos,
Paul

P.S.: As I was proofreading the previous rant I received a phone call, which brought sad news. I was told that my friend, the actress I spoke of—the "celebrity"— had passed suddenly. Her name was Debralee Scott. A classy broad, and I am honored to have known her.

Debralee played Hotsie-Totsie on *Welcome Back Kotter*, and later was a series lead on *Mary Hartman, Mary Hartman* and *Angie*. I smiled every time I saw her on TV in her films, one of which was *Earthquake* (Debralee was the neurotic newlywed on the airplane). She also was in the *Police Academy* films. After seeing one of her repeats on TV, the next time we had spoken I chided her and asked if she had gotten the residual check. The chiding was much more fun when she gave an outrageous answer on *Match Game*. She'd blame it on her youth and/or the effects from the on-set bootleg.

I look forward to the next time I see her on a rerun of *Match Game*. I'll hear that distinctive, gravelly, lispy voice, see the smile, and enjoy the promise in her youthful eyes. Debralee, not knowing what's to come. I'll know that she was having a ball, because in that cup, on the counter, next to her name was part of the fun, a secret, she and the cast enjoyed.

In 2000, Debralee called me with great excitement. She had finally met the man of her dreams and they were engaged. She told me that her life was finally going to be set and that she couldn't be happier.

September 11th, 2001, took away that happiness. Her fiancé was a Port Authority officer working at the World Trade Center. His body was never recovered. They never had the opportunity to wed.

Debralee was a wonderful, loving spirit. How odd I learn of her passing as I post this column.

WHAT IS AN ACTOR?

What are the predominant traits of people who are actors? Well, a few talent reps, casting directors, producers, and directors who have been around for a while will quickly offer a kneejerk response that includes a litany of derogatory descriptions, any of which will include:

Vain

Insecure

Egotistical

Self-serving

Self-absorbed

Unpredictable

Opportunistic

A fucking pain in the ass

Now if you're an actor, actor-hopeful, or a relative or pet of an actor, don't get out the poison pen just yet (save your lethal letters for critics). Just as many who agree with the descriptives above might also dissent and refer to actors as the following:

Intelligent

Hard-working

Dedicated

Community-minded

Hopeful

Visionary

Why the flip-flop of responses? Working with an actor is not always simple or easy. Being an actor is not simple or easy. The life of an actor is an emotional roller coaster. The jarring twists and turns on a journey in the arts often outnumber the airtime thrills. Being an actor brings a life that challenges with surprises both positive and negative. But before taking this journey, the rider must assess his or her reasons for the venture.

BEING AN ACTOR FOR THE RIGHT REASON

Storytelling through performance is at the foundation of your nature.

BEING AN ACTOR FOR THE WRONG REASONS

If your motivations for acting are mostly driven by the thrill derived from applause, the promise of great rewards, houses on both coasts while owning a vacation ranch in the nouveau, Hollywood-star refuge that is Montana—to you glamour-seekers I say find another field of employ. Now. You're not actors. You're Paris Hilton or Kato Kaelin wannabes. Celebrity fodder. The performing arts are not for you. Try the medical arts if you're after luxuries and cash. Unfortunately on that path you'll have to forgo red carpets and paparazzi. Every journey requires some sacrifice.

Lately I find more and more actor-hopefuls and working-actors demand fame and dismiss the basics of how to become a better actor, which is actually the path to success. Only you can determine for yourself what qualifies as success. For some it's cash and household name recognition or getting to eat a cow's rectum on a reality show; for others, it's earning a living and honing their craft. Being an actor does not equal being famous. In every profession, people toil at their jobs with varying degrees of visibility. Not every waiter can work at Le

Cirque. Not every actor can star in a network series. Working well within your chosen career should be the primary goal, not your level of visibility. But sadly, many actors assume that to be validated professionally, they must achieve global celebrity.

I partially blame reality TV for the rise in "fame in under sixty seconds" pursuers. I also blame us, both the audience and the industry. We've come to a point where we settle for mediocrity because few enlightened alternatives are being offered. And in talent, there is a lot of mediocrity getting paid for being substandard (i.e., people focused on the rewards of fame masquerading as actors). It's shameful. Sit in on an audition session with me and your eyes will widen upon seeing performers with great credits who are not deserving or representative of what is on their résumé. Am I being cranky and jaded? No. I'm being honest.

BEING AN ACTOR MEANS KNOWING WHO YOU ARE

Actors, to succeed, need to be aware of what roles they can play believably as opposed to the type of inappropriate roles they yearn to perform. For instance, I'd love to play Sweeney Todd, but I ain't no Sweeney Todd.

As an actor, be realistic as to who you are and what your range is. If you need help figuring this out, ask colleagues who have objectivity. Don't ask family. Family may mislead you because they're blind with love. You don't want to hear "Oh you can play anything." If every actor could play every role, we wouldn't need auditions, would we?

BEING AN ACTOR MEANS HAVING PASSION

An actor needs a passion for the craft, a passion for the fight to survive, a passion to continually better himself, and a passion for shamelessly promoting himself without end. If you lack *any one* of those passions, then enter another field. Try Burger King. An actor has to nurture, promote, advance, and maintain a career with 24/7 vigilance. Workers in the civilian world don't have that pressure. I highly doubt that waste collectors or cashiers encounter the constant career politics that one does in the performing arts. Also a cashier doesn't have to look for a job day-to-day. Being an actor is being a professional job-seeker. The hunt for work never ends. Even when employed as an actor, the job will come to an end soon enough. The civilian world enjoys the luxury of only having to be on the prowl for work a dozen or so times within a lifetime. An actor does the job prowl of several dozen lifetimes—seeking employment both as an actor and as a civilian.

BEING AN ACTOR MEANS LIVING IN TWO WORLDS AT ONCE

There's the world of entertainment and then there's the civilian world (those people who were sane enough to avoid a career in the arts). For an actor, these two worlds often blur together, most commonly when attempting to earn money for basic survival. It's the price a working actor pays to remain a working actor.

Here's one of many bitch-slaps for the aspirant: You're not going to be acting all the time; in order to survive—i.e., eat—you're going to be doing shit civilian work that no one else wants to do. Few waiters on both coasts of this expansive country are just that, a waiter. Same holds true for freelance fragrance technicians. If you're wondering what the hell a freelance fragrance technician is, he/she/it is the retail soldier in that menacing army of perfume spritzers who block the cosmetics aisle at Macy's, dousing customers with an offending spritz of a celeb-du-jour fragrance.

Many actors who hold civilian service jobs consider the positions to be temporary while living in a hyphenated existence. They're actor-waiters and actor–fragrance technicians, straddling both worlds at once. By day the hyphenates diligently go about the "real world" earning meager wages for survival. Later as the clock ticks into evening the hyphenates abandon the civilian world and perform in their career of choice. The actor an audience member recognizes in *Mamma Mia!* may have been that nice, cute, single boy who served her lunch. Broadway doesn't pay the big bucks that civilians fantasize about.

In my career I've crawled into and cleaned dumpsters at Burger King, served burgers and hot chocolate to obnoxious New York tourists at a Pocono ski resort, tediously sorted thousands of envelopes for mass-mail marketing, managed a movie theater, been a front desk clerk, cleaned toilets at a gay resort, marketed cars, written ad copy for beer, folded T-shirts at One Shubert Alley, and, worst of all, I've done the cliché actor temp jobs: singing telegrams and children's birthday party entertainment. Yes, I've been a dancing, singing California Raisin, Big Bird, Ernie *and* Bert, a Teenage Mutant Ninja Turtle, Power Ranger, Stork, Spiderman, and a nearly pornographic singing gorilla.

None of my civilian jobs were assignments that I wanted to do. They were jobs that I *had* to take to survive. This Big Bird wasn't thrilled at getting punched and kicked by unparented, hyperactive, five-year-olds. But you do what you must to pursue your love for creating live story through character.

The Group of Eight on Civilian Jobs

The Group of Eight has had their share of crappy civilian jobs. Robert LuPone probably had the worst job of all among these talented thespians.

"I was a petroleum transfer engineer for four weeks," LuPone began. "And I couldn't do it any more because . . ." I interrupted LuPone, suddenly realizing the occupation behind the euphemism "petroleum transfer engineer."

"You mean gas station attendant?" I asked.

"Yes," LuPone admitted. "I was a New Jersey gas station attendant. I was broke. I couldn't do it because the public is just ridiculous. I would say, 'Fuck you, I'm not pumping your gas!' and walk away. So I was really a tempestuous petroleum transfer technician."

Darrie Lawrence looked upon her civilian work with optimism. "I think it's important psychologically for us to have things to do." Lawrence advised. "If you have a day job, it's great to have a place where you go and they like you, they need you, and they will *pay you*. You have a place to be. One of the most debilitating things for many of us is to have empty days. Unless you're auditioning all the time, you *are* going to have empty days. I need the structure of a place to go and be wanted. I'm much happier."

But that doesn't mean Lawrence had a love for the civilian work that came her way. "I worked in a copy shop," Lawrence said, "making copies on old equipment, with crotchety clientele. That was hard." Then there was the job Lawrence toiled at that definitely blurred the line between the entertainment and civilian worlds. "I worked in my agent's office," Lawrence stated. It wasn't that Lawrence was being philanthropic or cheap. Working in her agent's office meant that she didn't have the money to pay off commissions from her previous acting work. Just because an actor earns money from acting doesn't necessarily mean an actor has money to spend on anything beyond food and shelter. It should be noted that Lawrence's agent didn't force her to work in the office. The unconventional idea was Lawrence's and one that is not condoned by unions and talent reps.

Lawrence has paid her dues. Actors who do not encounter similar hardships often have an unappealing work ethic. Those who get acting jobs right after graduating from a performing arts school are sometimes less than gracious about their luck. Lawrence and I have come across this attitude far too frequently. She harbors a justified resentment: "I've had young actors complain about getting a job right out of school and I think, 'Oh, man . . . you're so lucky. You just left school and now you have a good Equity job. You are *sooo* lucky.'" Some of the more common complaints vented by a number of fresh-from-school spoiled actors include having to work out of town in regional theater (they'd rather be on Broadway right away). But even some Broadway debuters, just beginning their journey in the arts, complain because they've been placed in the ensemble or saddled with a walk-on role instead of a principal part. These whiners do not understand, or more often than not refuse to accept, that building a career requires a foundation beyond training. Practical experience through work where networking connections are made, earning the trust of directors, casting directors, and other creatives are crucial in the structuring of a career. A TV pilot, major studio film, or Broadway lead does not land in an actor's lap merely because the actor just graduated from an arts institution (unless he's extremely lucky, the child of a celebrity, or a celeb beyond his own imagination).

Of the Group of Eight, some ventured into the actor cliché job of waiting tables. Charlotte Rae recalled one of her ventures into the waitron workforce: "I had a job in a place called the Sawdust Trail on Forty-sixth between Broadway and Sixth. It was a place where the waiters were singers and there was sawdust on the floor. We'd get up on a platform and sing. That was my first job in New York! My father wanted to take me home, because one waitress was hustling him. And I said, 'Don't worry, Daddy, I don't do anything upstairs in my dressing room, don't worry.' The customers would come in and sometimes they'd hand you a quarter for a tip. It was a wonderful experience."

Mark Price's venture into waiterdom wasn't as wonderful. "I'm an awful waiter," Price asserted. "I'll never do that again. I really suck as a waiter. I like babysitting 'cause you're around kids. They kind of remind you what's real and what's not real."

Michael Mastro recalled, "The only person I know who waited on tables longer than I did was Edie Falco," his friend and star of *The Sopranos*. "I waited on tables for thirteen years. She did it fourteen." But running between kitchen and table for hungry, sometimes demanding diners, wasn't Mastro's only means of income from the civilian world. "I have done office work, hung wallpaper, I've cleaned toilets as a janitor in a nursing home. I have been a personal assistant for rich people. I've decorated people's apartments for Christmas. I've been a personal shopper," Mastro admitted freely. "You really don't have to have a 'B job' that you hate. Don't do what I did. I knew that after the first year, I hated waitering. Really look to find B jobs that you can enjoy. Think of the other things you love doing as well that you can turn into money."

Money. There it is. Look at the word. Possess the word, because most actors, when working as a civilian or in the entertainment world, have very little of it. Having money is not about wealth. Having money is about being able to eat, live, and remain healthy.

BEING AN ACTOR MEANS FLIRTING WITH POVERTY

I'm surprised by how many people want to be actors. In a society that is obsessed with wealth, there is little of it in the arts. Only the privileged and lucky few in the arts maintain a lavish, debt-free life and appear on the cover of *People* magazine. Many actors can't even afford to buy *People* magazine. They read the issues in bookstores while nursing, for hours, a single small latte. The high unemployment rate for an actor is as scary as a proctologist with abnormally large hands. Upon encountering either of these horrors, I would think many people would flee screaming. Sadly, like mosquitoes to a bug lantern, many talented (and talent-free) actor-hopefuls zoom toward the footlights and get zapped.

There are many more actors than there are jobs. No surprise there. That long-established trend will not soon change. But unemployment in the arts consumes more than just long periods of time without a paycheck. Unemployment has a direct effect on an actor's health. I'm not talking about the mental anguish and depression associated with unemployment. That's a side dish. I'm talking about the main entrée vital to one's health maintenance: health insurance, or the lack thereof.

Three words of advice for the nonunion actor: Don't. Get. Sick. Health insurance for the nonunion actor doesn't exist unless the actor is self-insured. Before being welcomed into a performing artist's union, you're out on your own when it comes to coverage. For the union actor, health insurance is tenuous, but the unions do offer a safety net should an actor's health fall into peril. Flimsy though that net may be, with large holes, there is some hope for rescue from mounting medical costs. But the safety net is not guaranteed. Coverage depends on the number of weeks worked within a fiscal year.

Reread that last sentence and you'll realize the added importance of winning every audition. Each year an actor must work a required number of weeks, under a union contract, to receive some form of health insurance coverage. Each performing artist's union is different as to their healthcare eligibility requirements. One union requires more than twenty weeks of work per year for minimal coverage. Plus, with this particular union, the actor must now pay into the plan, along with their employer(s), after the actor has booked the minimum workweeks.

The number of weeks required to be eligible for health insurance can change year to year. Actors cannot carry over work weeks from one year to the next. Each year, the actor begins anew at zero.

BEING AN ACTOR MEANS A LIFELONG COMMITMENT

Many beginners venturing into a career in the arts don't think long term. This surprises the hell out of me. If you're going into the arts, prepare to go in for the long haul: forty to fifty years. No half-assed, tentative commitment such as "I'll try acting for a while and if it doesn't work out, I'll try something else." If that thought is tucked away somewhere within the gray matter upstairs, put this book down now, sell it online, or give it to a friend. You're not an actor. The arts are not for the tentative who want to stick their toes into the water, testing the temperature. You have to jump fully committed into the cold reality of entertainment.

When planning a career in the arts one must be mindful of long-term monetary considerations. Put simply, what happens to the bank account when retirement rolls around? Actors, unless uber-wealthy, struggle during retirement. An actor needs to store money away early—the sooner, the better. If you haven't already begun planning a nest egg, begin an individual retirement account (IRA) now. Put down this book, go to your bank, and put away whatever money you can. I'm not kidding. The book will wait; retirement doesn't.

BEING AN ACTOR MEANS KNOWING WORK IS NOT CONSTANT

Work is either feast or famine. Were you expecting an all-you-can-eat buffet? No actor gorges continually on work for his or her entire career. Work comes plentifully in spurts and then disappears, causing long droughts. An actor's cycle is usually unemployment to employment back to unemployment. That's one of the few constants in being an actor. If you want continuous, secure employment, I suggest enrolling in an embalming class.

There are four fundamentals in the search for employment in the performing arts:

1. There are more performers than there are performer job openings.
2. Rejection comes before an offer.
3. An artist spends a lifetime justifying his or her value to others.
4. Past achievements are exactly that, past achievements. Live with an eye toward tomorrow. Move forward.

Moving forward is an actor's best defense *and* offense against having the emotional effects of job search anxiety and/or rejection wash over you like a tsunami. Optimism, proactive thought, and engaging yourself constantly in seeking new opportunities are the best weapons an actor can have against job search anxiety.

The Three Ps to Pushing Past Job Search Anxiety

Be Positive

Don't play Eeyore. The longer you wallow in "*Woe is me,*" the further away you'll drift from your goals. Negativity consumes lust, ambition, and hope. The more positive thoughts, actions, and energy generated by you and put forth into the world, the more likely that positive energy will be returned upon you. Now, I'm not saying you need to rush to the nearest musk-drenched New Age store, load up on crystals and white candles, and max out the credit card on incantations. You needn't reach for the bloodstone just yet. Your success in generating affirmative feedback to your desires lies within the positive thoughts inhabiting your gray cells. If your gray cells are bereft of such thoughts, quickly host an open house and invite some in. Think negative, you receive negative. What you give is what you get.

Be Patient

Not every actor can be continually employed. Even if every producing entity worldwide simultaneously staged, taped, and filmed Dickens's epic *Nicholas Nickleby*, there would still be actors bitching about being out of work. Reality check: too many actors, too few jobs.

As I've said before, employment in the arts is feast or famine. Sometimes, job opportunities flood an actor's voicemail and inbox. Other times . . . crickets. The availability of work for a performer is akin to the saying for the shifting weather patterns of New England: "Just wait ten minutes and it'll change." And your situation *will* change.

Know and understand that auditions perennially slow down. There are predictable high and low tides of activity. During slow stretches, a breakdown with a wage that offers scale, allowing an actor to eat two meals a day, becomes a talent rep's treasure.

Take note: Here is the audition slowdown schedule:

Late March–Early April

The industry is catching a *brief* second wind from the first wave of pilot season. Summer stock, pilot season clean-up, and the late casting of features shooting over the summer are kicking with auditions.

Late May–Early August

The industry on both coasts is OOT (Out Of Town) during this period. If you're not booked for these months, enjoy the summer. Put the cell phone on vibrate, place it in your pants pocket, lay back, and treasure the infrequent vibrations. Better yet, study and grow as an actor.

Mid December–First Week of January

Be merry and gay no matter what your faith or sexual identity (if any).

Be Proactive

Continue marketing yourself through mailings, networking, paid auditions, and the Web. Blitz the industry with news of you. Granted, being noticed above the overwhelming competition is like screaming into the wind. The scream is carried back, away, lost on the currents. As an artist you must push through the wind, determined not to let yourself be blown adrift. Create opportunities.

Proactive Guideline #1: Network

Call past employers, work associates, friends, schoolmates, and teachers and ask them about future and present job openings. Remind those with whom you've had great relationships that you exist. Even contact those with whom you had fair to middling relationships. Attitudes and people change as memories fade. Let people know of your availability and desire. Don't be passive and hope for the work come to you, because it won't. Charge after opportunities. As an actor you must always be on the offensive when fighting for work in the entertainment market. Never stop. Never yield. Be optimistic in voice, prose, and spirit when contacting your network. Don't appear desperate, mournful, bitter, rambling, or, worse, Disney-esque ecstatic. Spin positive your availability without going overboard on the faux sugar and schmaltz.

Proactive Guideline #2: Find a Home

This doesn't mean contacting your local realtor. "Finding a home" is a euphemism for locating an artistic base or outlet where you will feel most supported and welcomed. Volunteer at a performing arts organization, become involved with theater companies that develop new works, join a theater's literary wing, be a production assistant on a film, or gofer for an arts council. Find a backdoor into a performing arts organization in a non-acting-related position and eventually you may find yourself being called upon to apply your craft as an actor. You'll meet lots of new people, and the more people you know the larger your network will grow.

Proactive Guideline #3: Work at a Casting Office

Working at a casting office offers actors an opportunity to learn the proper dos and don'ts of auditioning and actor marketing. It also affords you the chance to meet, if not in person then on the phone, agents, managers, directors, artistic directors, writers, and producers. Your network will grow. There are many casting office duties, including being a reader during auditions, that can be eye-opening for an actor.

Working in a casting office is fairly transparent, and casting directors know that the actor is not being altruistic and will not be going about his work thinking, "Gosh, I want to solve thespian world hunger in the arts by helping other thespians get work." SLAP! We're aware actors are helping us to advance their own agendas. But if you choose to follow this path, make sure you display an excellent work ethic. Don't be lazy. The better you can multitask, be an organizational skills wizard, and have a pleasant, charming demeanor and can-do attitude, the better you'll be looked upon. Even though at heart we know you're a career-advancing whore, we will still love you.

BEING AN ACTOR MEANS KNOWING THERE IS NO JOB SECURITY

There's no job security. Even when employed, an actor should be auditioning, looking for the next two to three jobs. Even actors presently in Broadway shows are out looking for work. Actors can be dismissed on short notice. The stage manager, producer, and/or director may feel that the actor no longer fits the requirements originally sought, and gone is the actor. Also, very often, when a Broadway show's receipts begin to falter, a celebrity will be brought in to take over a role previously performed by a lesser-known actor. The change brings a boost to the box office and pushes the lesser-known actor onto the unemployment line. Also, the closing notice is always a quiet, looming menace. Television actors are not safe from similar dismissal scenarios either.

A new television series is generally optioned for several episodes. If ratings aren't immediately stellar, gone is the show. Actors on long-running hits are equally as vulnerable. At any point an actor's contract can be bought out. Depending on how much money a studio or network is willing to throw away and toss to an actor, the actor's role can simply be written off. Ciao. No matter how successful a project or actor, audiences and/or producers have been known to suddenly lose interest and move onto the next hot hit or actor.

When I was an actor, I was jolted into this reality of employed performers looking for other work. I had just attended the Broadway opening night of *Ain't Broadway Grand*, a summer-stock-type musical not well received by the press. The next day I was at an audition and there waiting for another audition was one of the leading ladies from *Ain't Broadway Grand*. I was floored. At that time, the show's future had not yet been determined. I approached her and congratulated the talented actress on her performance of twelve hours prior. She was gracious but seemed a bit embarrassed. Abashed or not, she was smart enough to know that being in a Broadway show, hit or miss, did not guarantee job security. *Ain't Broadway Grand* limbered on life support for little over a month before going dark.

BEING AN ACTOR MEANS TAKING LESS-THAN-DESIRABLE ACTING GIGS

Unless you're wealthy and debt-free, you cannot be choosy about the acting work offered or available. While your heart may desire to beat in passionate sync with the Bard's meter or your tongue trill with Bernstein, or your wit summon laughter on a sitcom or your brawn fly fighters in an action adventure film, there are times an actor *must* accept less-desirable roles or projects. The average actor's bank account cannot hold out for the art that nourishes the heart and soul, while creditors demand cash.

I have taken on creative jobs as an actor, casting director, and director that I *hated*, sometimes even compounding the offense by revisiting the despised gigs because, simply put, I needed the money. Members of the Group of Eight have also had to do projects that they disliked in order to pay the rent and buy groceries. One of the Group of Eight, after a year originating a role in a new Broadway musical, knew he had to sign on for another year even though he didn't care for the role or the production. He understood that if he didn't renew the contract he would be back trudging from one audition studio to another looking for work. As to when and *if* that work would come, who knew?

To be a working actor you have to accept the work offered, not wait for the work desired. So if you're a picky person who will only perform for nourishment of the soul and enlightenment of the mind be ready to join the ranks of the homeless on the streets or leave the business altogether. As an actor you take the acting work you get. If you want to be an actor, you have to act whether that means wielding a scrub brush in a toilet cleanser commercial or dancing like a hyperactive animal in a cartoon-turned-stage spectacle.

BEING AN ACTOR MEANS BEING CONSTANTLY REJECTED

Rejection occurs daily. Hourly. Rejection sweeps faster through an actor's life than does the second hand of the clock. Whether working or not, rejection is unavoidable. Not getting an audition? Rejection. Not getting a callback? Rejection. Not getting the job? Rejection. A control-freak director doesn't allow an actor to make choices during rehearsal? Rejection. Your love interest runs into the arms of anyone who is not in the arts? Rejection. Big-time rejection. Almost all rejection, which is covered later in these pages, is not personal (unless it's the lover thing—then yeah, it's personal; way personal). If there is anything comforting to say about rejection it's this: In an unpredictable business like the arts where nearly nothing is constant, there does remain one constant that can be relied on, and that is . . . rejection.

BEING AN ACTOR MEANS ACCEPTING CRITICISM DAILY

Criticism comes at an actor without end. Criticism is given in auditions, in rehearsal, from the audience, from friends, from family, and from the press. All the chatter and font are just opinions. Good or negative, the chorus of adjectives for *fault* or *brilliance* is only the collective opinion of individuals. Opinions about what is being offered. None of it (good or negative) should be taken personally, even if the criticism is about physical features. Auditors and others passing judgment are commenting on product. What you're offering is the product. Don't confuse your product (talent and body) with who you are as a person (your soul and personality). Learn to separate the two and you'll survive better.

Opinions about what an actor has to offer (product), are thrown at thespians like darts. Some hit the target with accuracy while others are carelessly hurled, miss the mark, and do damage. The actor must differentiate between criticism that helps and criticism that destroys. And here's the surprise: Both positive and negative criticism have the potential to help or destroy. Differentiating between the two is not always an easy task. Actors must walk a tightrope of self-awareness.

An actor will need to resist diving into an emotional abyss when criticized, and instead spend his energy looking for ways to improve and grow. Sometimes negative criticism, when accurate, can be a good resource for the actor who is trying to boost his product. This happened to me. Early in my career, as an actor, I received scathing criticism for a performance. The unfavorable opinions came not only from the press but also from the audience and my colleagues onstage. And you know what? They were all correct, including the rude cast member who posted one of the brutal reviews on the backstage callboard and scribbled on it in pen, "The reviewer is right, you suck!" My approach to my roles had been foolish. I imitated the performances of actors I had seen previously in the roles. Big mistake. I didn't make the parts relevant to who I was. I didn't invest myself. I manufactured plastic imitations of someone else's finer portrayals. I took the criticism, made alterations, and moved forward. Lesson learned.

Favorable criticism can also be beneficial or dangerously damaging. When the actor keeps in mind for the future what initiates a positive response, it can be a resource for improvement. Simple enough. But sometimes an actor can become lazy by doing the same tricks over and over again, in different projects, hoping to trigger the same accolades. There's no growth, just an "on hold" mentality at a desired comfort level. That's not acting, that's reproduction. Then there is the "false positive" criticism. This usually comes from supportive family and friends who love the actor dearly. They speak with the best of intentions but may mislead a performer into a false sense of ability. If you watched *American Idol*, you've seen this type of positive affirmation brought about by love. A singer painfully screeches through a Whitney Houston song, and you reach for the mute button on the remote just as Simon Cowell puts an end to the horror. Rejected, the tone-deaf singer arrogantly and defiantly returns in tears to her family. The family and friends give false positive encouragement: "*You're a super star! What do they know! You'll have your record in a year, baby.*" Someone just shoot me, please.

Carefully evaluate all critiques. Criticisms, positive or negative, should be used as a tool for improvement, not as a barometer for brilliance or personal dysfunction.

BEING AN ACTOR MEANS BEING SENSITIVE TO THE WORLD

Actors must be keenly aware of the world around them, for how else can one accurately portray the best and worst of humanity without falsehood? Look beyond the scripts, trade publications, how-to books, and entertainment community for participating in and observing life. Explore various cultures and communities, reach out to those whose views differ from yours, listen when advice is offered, and learn new pursuits in addition to performing or that can be utilized within your career. An actor who cannot see beyond himself or herself is an actor who is a failure.

BEING AN ACTOR MEANS BEING STRONG

For anyone who is involved in entertainment, the journey demands an emotional fortitude of iron. It is a life and livelihood that requires a hardened soul that must repeatedly face rejection and failure. But the soul must still be capable of moving forward with hope. The actor needs to be confident in his or her beliefs and abilities while not being arrogant. Have faith in yourself, for doubt will undermine your pursuit in obtaining your goals.

BEING AN ACTOR MEANS BEING RELENTLESS

"I give up" or "I can't" are not part of a successful actor's vocabulary. Whether it's attacking a role or audition, hunting for work, or pursuing a talent rep, the bedrock of an actor's vocabulary is "How can I? What's a better solution? What are my options?" Defeatism is not an option.

BEING AN ACTOR IS TO ENJOY LIFE

Have fun. Invest yourself in the world outside of entertainment for pleasure, study, and enrichment. Being an actor is not an entitlement to being stressed about your level of achievement 24/7 or continually obsessed with all things related to acting. I've made mention previously that pursuit of goals and knowledge within an actor's career are paramount, but that doesn't mean an actor is to be obsessive-compulsive about acting. Maintain your sanity and humor through hobbies and non-entertainment pursuits. Relax. Our industry is for the recreation of others, not a vital component for global day-to-day living. It's only entertainment. It's not brain surgery.

BEING AN ACTOR MEANS ASKING QUESTIONS AND BEING OPEN TO ANSWERS

Let's get started . . .

CHAPTER THREE

TRAINING FOR THE ACTOR

Tend Your Dreams

"Training is key to all skills. How you get trained is even more important. In today's world . . . the actor conservatory training has really increased the level of expertise. I've seen better actors come out of schools lately than I did twenty years ago. The competition is so fierce, your personality and looks are not going to get you anywhere, and if they do it's a very narrow bandwidth. Your looks go, baby."

Robert LuPone
Actor-Producer-Educator

Does an actor need training? Does a working actor need continued training? If you answered "no" to either question, step aside, please; there are people far more realistic about being an actor than you.

If you don't have formal acting training, get some. *Now!* If you're an actor who has had training, good for you, but do you continue learning? Training for an actor, like auditions, never ends. Oh sure, some people are guilty of the "I've had my training, I've spent all the money and time required, I know what I'm doing. I don't need to learn anything more" sentiment. WRONG! To those misguided training-phobes, here's a bitch-slap for you: Get off your asses and learn more. Unless you're ash or six feet under there's plenty more for you to learn and improve upon. No one is above improvement. Broaden your abilities and opportunities for work by reaching beyond what you already know. Training—whether it be by book or, the better option, by active class participation and work in your chosen field—is an ongoing practice for continually bettering yourself. One-time training is just a start.

I'm astounded by artists who arrogantly refuse to continue learning. The old TV ad about "the more you know, the more you grow" is not idle Madison Avenue marketing fodder. It's true and applies to everyone in any occupation and lifestyle. Actors who are not constantly improving their craft or learning new skills are actors who sit at home, watching TV talk show feuds or hanging out online, private messaging in multiple Internet chat rooms, all the while moaning that they're not getting jobs. To those sad souls who blame anyone but themselves for their lack of activity, guess what? You're lazy! By refusing to study more in a learning environment with fellow actors, you not only let your talent stagnate and diminish, but you miss wonderful opportunities to network! People you meet while learning may be people who connect you to employment after the program has concluded.

BFA VS. MFA VS. NO FA

Here's the sad but emerging reality of modern performing arts education. Having a BFA alone is like pushing a Honda Civic into a luxury car show for display: It's practical, durable, cost-efficient, but not terribly impressive. The Honda (the equivalent of a BFA) is overlooked in comparison to what's just down the aisle: a classy, sporty Cadillac STS (the equivalent of an MFA). Having no initials after your training—i.e., no FA—well . . . you're not even inside the auto show; you're pedaling past the convention center, uphill, on a Schwinn. While the Schwinn might get you somewhere, pushing ahead requires more effort than riding comfortably in a Civic or Caddy.

There was a time when an actor didn't need three initials after his or her name. Zounds, no! There was a time when talent and skill (and yes, looks) propelled a young actor into a career. The old-fashioned, pre-1970s training ground was the workplace. You developed skill and craft by working alongside greater actors, almost like an apprenticeship. This experience led to more work.

Those days are near prehistoric. Today many of us on my side of the table look at an unknown actor's picture we may like in a submission, then, not trusting our instincts, we quickly flip to the résumé, bypass the credits, and go straight for the education line at the bottom. We want verification of credible schooling to justify our interest. If we're satisfied, then we look at the credits above. There are exceptions. Solid credits can overrule training, but an actor's education history sways many auditors *prior* to seeing his work. *If* we actually see the work and it's fantastic, then there's little care as to what degree the actor carries. But for an unknown commodity *to be seen*, actors with MFAs, BFAs, and/or solid credits get priority.

Another reason for taking on the bank-busting price of an MFA is that the industry is serious about attending MFA showcases. We know that the participants (who have spent lots of cha-ching) approach their careers with great sincerity. OK, now you might be thinking to yourself, "I'm serious about my career." And that might be completely true. But when an individual lays out upward of fifty to a hundred grand for an education in the arts, the appearance to others is that he or she is *damned* serious. That's a lot of debt and time invested for what eventually is an opportunity to have five to ten minutes in front of an audience of agents, managers, and casting directors at the graduating showcase. Industry heavies attend the "Industry Approved" MFA showcases. Assistants are sent to the BFA showcases.

Is going for the diploma accompanied by initials worth the cost and time? Yes. Will a BFA or MFA guarantee work? No. Will a BFA or MFA make a better actor? Sometimes yes and sometimes . . . there's no hope. The results depend on the individual and/or the program. Some programs are wonderful. Some programs teach students to ignore their instincts and follow a long-taught, manufactured acting procedure. Some programs maintain a racial or gender quota. Most programs are generally very stringent as to who gets in, except occasionally the talent bar is lowered to create a racially- and gender-diverse graduating class. This is *not* always the case but, when it is, it's very obvious, come showcase time, who slipped under the talent bar for the program to achieve its desired diversity ratio. Creating a diverse class doesn't necessarily mean adding women or a particular ethnicity. Programs also seek white males to round out ratios. A school is selling product (actors) to industry. The industry wants diversity. It's like shopping at a supermarket. Would you shop for food staples at a grocery store stocked only with kumquats?

"INDUSTRY-APPROVED" SCHOOLS, A.K.A. THE IVY LEAGUE FOR THESPIANS

It's no secret, at least not among agents, casting directors, directors, and some actors, that there is a "list" of "industry-approved" schools. What is an industry-approved school and how does it become acknowledged as such? Industry-approved schools are predominantly colleges and universities whose programs and graduates are generally well-received by agents, casting directors, and others within the industry. The list is short and can change year to year. The better the program and talent over a period of consecutive years, the better that school's standing in the collective judgment of the industry. If the program's results (trained actors) weaken, that school falls off the industry's radar and fails to make the industry-approved list. There is no formal, written list that we surreptitiously pass around to each other. A school's ascendance to industry-approved status is unofficial, existing as an informal, common consensus of those who push and hire talent. The stamp of "industry approved" is not like that of "kosher" offered by a rabbi standing over a pretzel factory's conveyer belt. Ask me in private and I'll gladly tell you which schools have received the latest blessing of the industry.

HOW TO RESEARCH "INDUSTRY-APPROVED" SCHOOLS

Other than pulling me aside for a one-on-one conversation (or via e-mail at my website, www.PaulRussell.net), how do you learn which schools are industry approved? There's no Zagat's guide for "Industry-Approved Programs," but there is a similar source given out nightly to thousands in New York and around the globe: playbills. If you've attended a number of shows (mandatory curriculum for an actor) either on, Off-, or Off-Off Broadway, at national tour presentations nearest to you, or at a highly visible regional theater, read the actor bios within the playbill and look for their training. Most actors note the schools or programs they attended. After a while, you'll begin to notice a pattern. Certain schools will be routinely found in numerous bios. When this happens, you've discovered one or two of the industry-approved schools.

Don't have playbills? Go to the Internet. The search engine is your friend in sleuthing out who went where. Type in an actor's name, followed by the keywords *bio, training,* and/or *education.* You'll soon discover where these people studied. If the search engine sleuthing is too much work for your fingers (God forbid), skip the search engine and go to IMBD.com and enter the name of an actor you admire.

IMDB.com is the Internet Movie Database, which contains bios for nearly anyone who has appeared in film or on television. Training credentials are sometimes included within these bios, which are posted by actors, their agents or publicists, or the site itself. You can also check out www.IBDB.com, the Internet Broadway Database. Here you won't find actor bios, but you will find credit listings for actors who have worked in numerous Broadway shows. Once you begin discovering names that repeat in multiple Broadway shows, TV series, and films, go back to a search engine using the school sleuthing technique mentioned above. Don't just look for the star names; look for the industry names, names found repeatedly in numerous productions, that are lesser known to the general audience. The industry names work more on stage and screen than do expensive stars. Also, being a star doesn't necessarily equal quality theatrical training. Some of Broadway's headliners are on the boards because their offstage exploits effectively sell tabloid magazines and commercial time slots on tabloid TV programming.

Another way to research industry-approved schools is to solicit the opinions of highly regarded directors, artistic directors, talent reps, and casting directors. Ask which schools they believe are respected by the industry and have been known to produce high-caliber, continuously working actors, with an emphasis on the "continuously working." Don't take one person's list or recommendation. Ask at a minimum two dozen industry professionals. Make note of the schools that are recommended repeatedly.

THE LEAGUES: FIVE MINUTES @ $10,000+ PER MINUTE

The investment made for the four- or two-year training program is basically the price tag for your five minutes in front of an invited audience of industry professionals upon your graduation. That costly five minutes is part of an industry spring ritual known as the "Leagues."

The Leagues are where graduating theater arts students are brought to New York, L.A., or both coasts by their school and presented as a class, performing scenes, monologues, and/or songs for an invited assembly of agents, managers, and casting directors. Schools that are considered industry-approved attract a larger attendance of industry professionals: an audience of senior agents and high-profile casting offices. Schools with less-than-stellar programs or community colleges attract, at best, agency assistants and crickets.

The Leagues was once a large conglomerate of schools that grouped together to present their graduates in a showcase. The original grouping of schools that made the Leagues disbanded for a time but the term "Leagues" remained as a general term of reference for these spring showcases. In recent years a small group of schools have banded back together to revive the Leagues, now known as the "New Leagues." Some within the New Leagues are industry-approved, with the industry filling all available seats and overflowing into the aisles, while some of the participating schools provide a welcome excuse for a lunch break.

There is a disturbing growth sprawl of accredited and nonaccredited actor training programs presenting graduating showcases. Casting offices and talent agencies now receive invitations from tiny community colleges in rural America! Academia's drive to put their students in front of industry creates ridiculous congestion. This sprawl is not beneficial to newly trained actors because the buyers (industry) have very little time. Many of the schools, to which the students pay tons of money, get overlooked because there are just too many showcases to attend. The better the school, the larger the industry attendance. The lesser known the school . . . you get the idea.

The outcome of your five-minute showcase performance will determine the difficulty or ease at which you'll be paying off your student loan(s). The school showcase is a new actor's make-or-break moment in a first attempt at finding representation *and* to be seen by multiple casting directors. This opportunity will *never* happen again. So choose wisely the school you attend and, more important, choose wisely what you present in the showcase.

Choosing Appropriate Material for Your Industry Showcase

Choose material that is you. Do not choose material that you'd like to do because you find it to be fun, despite your being completely wrong in type for the character. *That* would be a costly mistake. Your graduating showcase is a time for you to show us *who you are*, not who you want to be! Stay away from excessive profanity or vulgarity. You're not showing us your edge; you're showing us that you're disturbing (we then collectively pray for the next scene/actor to arrive). The more defined the choices you make to accurately represent your type and skill, the easier it is for the agents, managers, and casting directors in attendance to quickly understand how they can exploit your product.

If you've got a good voice, ask your program director that you be allowed to sing. If you can tap circles around Savion Glover, get an opportunity to go into your dance. If you can play an instrument well, demand of your program director or professor that you be able to show us your musical ability. The more marketable you are, the more we'll likely want you as an actor. Think of yourself as a car on a showroom floor: The more perks and accessories you display, the more likely the buyer (us) will pick you up.

In some cases, a school's program director or a particular professor chooses the material their student actors will present. If this is your situation and the choices fit you, then great! If the choices make you uncomfortable, don't display who you are, or limit your abilities, then fight for material that is you! It's your future career on the line during those valuable five minutes before the industry. A professor who unilaterally chooses inappropriate material for you goes back to the comfort of tenure, but where does that leave you?

CAN YOU BECOME A WORKING ACTOR IF YOU DON'T GO TO AN "INDUSTRY-APPROVED" SCHOOL?

Yes. Non-industry-approved schools may not make "the list" because the programs are overlooked by industry through ignorance. We don't know every training program and there are many outlets for learning in the arts. There are many fine teachers teaching at lesser-known schools. If you can't afford or are not accepted into one of the tonier industry-approved schools, go back to researching playbills and talking to industry professionals to discover where great, overlooked teachers or programs are creating wonderful students. You needn't let the wealthy, who can afford the pricey schools, be the only well-educated performers.

Then there are those lucky few who get by on raw talent or raw talent and looks . . . or, oh hell, let's just be honest, faux-actors getting by on looks alone. When it comes to those looks-alone sensations, well, we know who you celebrities are. Casting pros in film and television take into account the following attributes (in order) when considering non–box office names:

1. Looks
2. Youth
3. Talent

If that hiring prioritization process angers you, then look within and at your peers. We're all to blame for creating the beauty-over-talent demand.

CAN AN ACTOR BE AN ACTOR WITH AN NFA?

Yes. I'm a holder of an NFA (No F-ing Arts degree). I graduated from my self-proclaimed school, the Nike School of Acting, following the company's tag line: "Just Do It!" As I wrote earlier, I fumbled at having a proper secondary education after high school. Because of limited financial resources and other factors (ignorance being one), I never received a college degree despite my eagerness to attend Carnegie Mellon.

My lack of an accredited education has come back to haunt me many times, both professionally and personally. One such time was when I was directing *The Scarlet Pimpernel* for the Barter Theatre (the State Theater of Virginia, boasting its own Tony Award). One night, sitting on the porch of the company residence, I was talking to a young company intern and asked her why she was working the long, hard hours for weekly pay that equaled the cost of a full tank of gas? Her response was that she wanted to have the Barter, a nationally recognized and respected theater, on her résumé for when she applied to an MFA program. She felt the experience of the internship and what she learned at the Barter would make her a stronger candidate for an MFA program and further her career down the road. It will.

There I sat, thinking of the irony. I had no college education and there I was directing a large-scale musical at a well-respected theatrical institution. The respect both she and the company granted me was more than I thought I deserved because I wasn't formally schooled; I just had practical experience, raw talent, instincts, courage, and luck (emphasis on luck). I was too embarrassed to tell her my truth. I just muttered . . . "Good for you. You're damned smart." And she is. Separate journeys. Shared crossroads.

I'm no longer ashamed to admit to my lack of a college education. In fact, when I'm asked about where I got my degree, I kind of enjoy seeing the shock on people's faces when they learn my story. Occasionally that surprise is accompanied by resistance, as potential employers and peers balk at accepting me on my merits. These people, favoring a formal schooling similar to their own, ignore practical experience. I *do not* recommend other artists follow my path. It was far too difficult and many times limiting. But know that if you can't afford the luxury of an accredited arts education, you can still make the journey. But don't expect expedience or a detour-free trek toward your goal.

CONTINUED TRAINING: TEACHING OLD ACTORS NEW TRICKS

Going to an accredited program for a degree in the arts is not just for the young aspiring actor. Often, actors who have agents and have worked on Broadway and appeared in films and on TV have wisely gone back to school to receive additional training and a degree in the arts. These returning-to-school actors may not have had the tuition money at the start of their careers, but now, years later, after having established themselves, they find that their funds are plentiful. Not only are they learning anew and refining their craft but also they're earning a degree that will allow them to teach at colleges and universities. Teaching the art of storytelling through performance is where actors, no longer marketable, work the remainder of their careers.

Degree = A Secondary Arts-Related Career

More actors teach than work as actors. And to teach at a university or college, a master's degree is often, if not always, mandatory. So heed these words: Get the arts degree at some point in your career. There may be times in your life when you'll want health insurance and a steady income. Teaching facilities offer their staff such civilian benefits. How wonderful would it be to stay within your craft, share your knowledge with others, and get a weekly paycheck with the possibility of tenure? Ooooh, what next, a mortgage? How nice.

THE GROUP OF EIGHT ON ACTOR TRAINING

When I asked the Group of Eight, "Which do you believe is better for an actor's training: having a formal degree in the arts or attending independent classes while pursuing work?" I got some surprising answers, particularly from actor-producer-educator Robert LuPone.

"However an actor gets there is however you get there," LuPone firmly asserted. "Start at Yale and work down. Or start at the highest schools that you can afford and work down. Start with a master's degree program like at NYU. The minute those students graduate, they have a career." LuPone chuckles at this modern day, career-on-a-plate reality. "Start wherever and work your way down. I was a dancer and I couldn't get into Yale. I just graduated from Juilliard. I didn't want to go back to college, so I started on the streets. I worked every acting class that I could find for five years."

Michael Mastro voiced a similar response but with a real-life solution to the high cost of grad school. "It completely depends on the actor. I didn't go to grad school. I went out and continued to make my *own* grad school. I have other friends who are the same way. I have one friend who came to New York when he was seventeen with five hundred dollars in his pocket and literally slept on a bench in Central Park for the first few nights. He learned to act by doing it. He took a class by an actor teaching one night a week. I know other actors who you would have never thought had anything to offer, and then they went to a four-year program with some really good teachers and some amazing blossoming happened."

Mastro, though, is aware of the growing reality and importance of a grad school education for an actor's career. "What I'm hearing now from casting directors and actors . . . is that the casting directors are looking to the grad schools to do the screening for them. Yes, it does matter if you came out of NYU. Yes it does matter if you went to Juilliard, Yale, Rutgers, or Old Globe [San Diego]. And there is this *fierce* trend happening because I coach actors for grad school auditions. When I came to New York, there were not a million theater programs and universities to choose from. Now it seems that every college or community college has a theater program, and there are more and more and more grad programs *everywhere*, all the time, competing for the best students."

James Rebhorn was more philosophical on his reply to the question of what route of training he thought best for an actor. "A lot of actors make it without any training at all," Rebhorn says without bitterness. "They just show up in New York City one day and they're on a soap opera the next day. It does happen. I think increasingly, though, in a world that gets more and more complex and more specialized and where we look to e-mail or Starbucks as opposed to looking for a real coffee shop, we look for shortcuts. I think likewise the industry looks for shortcuts and they generally go and look for actors at Yale, NYU, or Juilliard; which is not to say the training there is going to be any better than at the Neighborhood Playhouse, the American Academy of Drama, or through some teachers at HB Studios. In my experience most young actors who are cast in shows and movies that I work in have come from Yale, Juilliard, or NYU, sometimes Temple, sometimes Rutgers Mason Gross School of the Arts. Generally [the graduate program] is a shortcut; it doesn't mean that they're any better an actor, but it's a shortcut to an actor getting their foot in the door."

What's Vital to an Actor's Training?

I asked the Group of Eight this question: "Beyond choosing the kind of schooling, what is vital to an actor's training?" Most agreed that what is vital is something to which we all have free access. As explained by Mark Price: "Life experience. There's a difference between watching a performance that's technically perfect and hits all the right notes and then watching a performance that comes from a deeper place that's connected to something very, very real. And I think that comes from life experience. I think, that is, getting older . . . maturity, and *that* you can't really teach. It's just something that happens over time. Even if you graduate with the most sharpened skills as an actor, say you graduate from Juilliard or one of the top conservatory programs, [what you've learned] may not really settle in until you have a little more experience with life. It sounds kinda lofty, but I think it has to do with confidence in yourself as a person and knowing what you can bring to the table. A lot of times when you graduate you have the drive, you have the ambition, but sometimes it's making sure you have the goods to bring to the table . . . that just comes from confidence in what you're doing and confidence as a person."

Michael Mastro also commented on confidence as it applies to training: "You better feel more confident when you come out than you did when you went in. I have no patience for teachers who are cruel to actors. I think there are a lot of acting teachers who think that their job is to break the actors down and then rebuild them. Some of my teachers had that attitude."

While confidence is one training issue for Mastro, self-awareness is also key. "I think that it's important to grow an awareness of what your habits, tensions, and tricks are. Tricks that you hold onto that you know work. I think it's important to be aware of what those things are so that you can make the decision to set those things aside and see what else is there. That can make you a very exciting actor.

"On the other hand, sometimes what you're being hired for is your tricks. An actor has to be aware of those things. I have certain kinds of characters that are in my back pocket, things that my friends look at and say, 'Oh, Michael's doing his thing again.' And I say, 'Well, yes, I am doing my thing again, but *Law & Order* is paying me six grand a week to do my thing.' So I'm going to do my 'thing' because I need to pay the rent this month."

James Rebhorn, in response to the question "What do you think is vital to an actor's training?" took a more technical approach. "I advise actors to get training that in some ways traces its roots back to the Group Theater (a theater collective, formed in New York in 1931 by Harold Clurman, Cheryl Crawford, and Lee Strasberg). When you think of acting in America, almost all the acting teachers came out of the Group. There was Sandy Meisner, Stella Adler, Bobby Lewis, Lee Strasburg, and Paul Mann. All the great acting traditions in this country come out of the Group Theater. They all had different takes on it. They all had different approaches to it. . . . The disciples of those teachers are the people who are teaching today. . . . [It's that way of working that] I respect the most."

Darrie Lawrence dryly quipped that what is most important to an actor's training is something that our "me-driven" industry could bear more of: "flexibility and openness . . . openness to direction. Openness to what is going on with the other actors, so that you're open to what's coming in. Civility."

Vital Tools an Actor Should Retain from Training

An institution for arts training can lead the actor, but what each actor takes or discards from that training is what will greatly influence his or her future. When the Group of Eight was asked the question "What should an actor take from training as vital tools for being a better actor?", most talked about technique. Jim Rebhorn's advice reflected the general sentiment: "I think actors should have a system, a way of working," Rebhorn replied. "From Paul Mann I carried away a whole system, a way I work. And that is basically that I look at each scene for the action that I'm pursuing and an object that I hope to achieve. In other words, I'm doing something in a scene in order to achieve something of great importance for the character. That's basically the core of my work and the core of my system. There are other things, too. Relating to objects, relating to environment, talking and listening. I think basically an actor should have some kind of system so that when they look at the scene, when they look at the play, they have some way of breaking it down and understanding how they're going to approach working on it. That's what they have to get from any education."

Bonnie Black took Rebhorn's commentary even further: "Technique is a very personal thing," she said. "If there were one way to do this, somebody would be a millionaire, because they would write a book to 'do it like this' and everybody would be a brilliant actor." I interrupted Black, reminding her that Uta Hagen made a nice bit of change with her book. Black replied, "Yes, but not everybody uses Uta's technique. You have to take what works for you. Use that and throw away what doesn't. There are all kinds of teachers out there, spouting all kinds of rules and regulations for what one does and some of it is . . . well, doesn't work for a particular individual. Almost any teacher will always say the same things—'Who am I? What do I want? How do I get there?' Everybody does that. I would replace 'What do you want?' with 'What do you need?' so that the stakes are the highest."

Charlotte Rae felt one vital tool to take away from learning is to keep learning: "I really admire people who continue to study," Rae complimented her peers. "People who are in the business and still work out with a teacher and do scenes." But Rae confessed, "I'm a naughty girl. I don't do it."

Robert LuPone stressed that from training an actor should enable his or her imagination. "Engage your [emotional] triggers so that you're able to release the imagination." LuPone further stressed other vital tools for the actor: "A sense of confidence. The voice, an expressive voice, and a supple body. Those are things that you have to have."

LuPone pulled no punches when placing blame on some who are responsible for what their actor-students take from training after graduating. Just like a recipe, the end result lies more with the chef (the institution) than the ingredients (the actors). "Now that I'm traveling the country looking at people who want to get into this school [New School for Drama], the BFA training is unbelievably bad," LuPone freely criticized. "There are exceptions, of course. But in the South, for example, I've seen people who come to me with BFA degrees and it's incomprehensible what they think they're doing." LuPone then referenced the quality of the BFA students that he spoke of. "I'm talking about summer stock. The worst of summer stock. What you take away from training is how good your training is."

What Should an Actor Discard from Training?

Not everything one learns need be retained. As I wrote at the beginning of this book, "Everything I say is right. Everything I say is wrong. . . . Take what works best for you." There may be techniques garnered in training or actual work experience you may wish to dump. They work well for others, but for you, it's a no-go. Bonnie Black had once such experience.

"A fellow actor, during training at Trinity, told me that I should only have the theater be my life. I didn't agree with that," Black began. "Throw out anything that doesn't help you to move forward—as an artist or as a human being, anything that doesn't work for you. If somebody says to you, 'You must always do this!' and you find yourself knocking your head against a wall, and it makes no sense to you, then you have to rethink your approach and find another way to go. You never want to do anything that diminishes you."

Michael Mastro was in strong agreement. "Be very careful of anybody who says, 'This is the way, this is the only way.' There is no only one way. There is every different actor; every different actor has his own instrument, his own imagination, his own way of being."

The responses from the Group of Eight as to what an actor should discard from training were passionate. Robert LuPone was vehement in advising actors to rid themselves of ineffective tools given to them by "sadistic teachers." LuPone spat with contempt, "They're not helpful, even under the guise of art and inspiration and creation. The destruction of the ego or the psyche for the sake of art, for the sake of technique. Bullshit!" LuPone laughed and then shot out, "Cult." I asked him to explain.

"Any teacher who has a cult around him. Get rid of that sensibility. What you should discard is a loyalty to any given technique. What you should discard is a loyalty to any given process. What you should invest in is the moment-to-moment reality and your own creativity and imagination and *your* personal point of view. Like most of the great actors, you have a really individual point of view about the work you do. You work with that. You don't give it up because you're in a production or give it up because you're working with a director or give it up because you want a job. That comes with confidence, that comes with vision, that comes with commitment. It comes with teachers who understand that and support that as opposed to breaking it down! Break it down because you're living this technique and you walk away with it but you forgot yourself. And you forgot your point of view."

Darrie Lawrence shared similar thoughts. "[Discard] all those things your instructors said you couldn't do." Lawrence recalled a time in her early training. "I remember one of my teachers saying, 'We're here to fix what you don't do well and then when you get out in the world you're going to be hired and paid for what you do well. But you'll do it better because we've been working on the deficits.'" I saw regret on Lawrence's face. Like a gossamer, it passed over her countenance, a haunting of teachers from long ago who continued to spook her. "I think the following is true for all of us. When I was first working I had been worried about the things that I had been told that were my weaknesses. So I had a lack of confidence in my abilities or decisions. I still feel, a lot, that I've got my teachers on my shoulders, whispering into my ear."

While LuPone and Lawrence spoke of sadistic and omnipotent teachers, who, in training, break the actor down and remain as inner critics, James Rebhorn offered advice on overly supportive instructors: "Praise is one thing an actor should discard," Rebhorn countered. "If somebody praises you, that's a trap. The actors who are young who get that kind of stroking, that kind of false feedback . . . they begin to believe their publicity. And that is a huge trap for actors at any level at any age. If you start to believe the good reviews, you are in trouble, especially if you're not willing to believe the bad reviews. Praise is something you should discard and ignore. Encouragement is one thing and you should seek that out for work that is done well and is honestly earned. But praise, get rid of that."

Bonnie Black didn't see eye to eye with Rebhorn on the tossing out of praise in training. "I don't agree with Jimmy Rebhorn." Bonnie laughed (they know each other). "Why would

I throw out a teacher giving me praise? If a teacher praised me, why would I not pay attention to that? [As an actor] you have to develop a healthy ego. You're going to be a disaster if you try to enter this business as a sniveling, frightened person. And if your teacher made you feel utterly worthless, how does that help you? If your teacher made you think you were the greatest thing since toast, I'd hope you would temper that with an understanding of what you could and couldn't do. But some of the most successful people I know came from being completely single-minded and had huge, huge egos and were only focused on their achievements. And that served them."

Mark Price furthered the debate on praise, but his advice was not about the effects of praise but the desire for it: "The need for approval. That's the killer, right there," Price believed. "I think in any sort of creative juncture, the minute you start wanting to be liked, the minute you start wanting to be the most popular, the minute you start wanting to be the most commercial, the one with the most jobs, that's when you completely fuck yourself."

CHOOSING YOUR EDUCATION

When making choices for training, investigate a school's program thoroughly. If you're looking at a single class, audit it. Ask questions. Who came out of that program/class? Who attends the showcases (if there is one)? Are working, industry professionals participants of the faculty or guest faculty? What do industry professionals think of the program, graduating talent, or class? If a school, does the program have an affiliation with an established regional theater? This is a definitive plus to an actor's education. Regional theaters (members of the League of Regional Theaters, a.k.a. LORT) that have an affiliation with a university or college use the school's theater program students to round out the professional company. It's an opportunity to work and learn with the pros and to begin networking while learning.

Be wary of acting classes taught by actors or industry professionals who have little credible work history within the industry. Be wary of strip mall acting academies, nonaccredited acting schools, and training studios. There are some academies and training studios in New York and L.A. that are valuable, but some are the fast food education outlets of acting: cheap, quick, and of little substance. Some of these studios and academies once enjoyed success and favor within the industry long ago. If the place where you wish to train no longer has the respect of the industry, why are you paying them money for a less-than-credible arts education? If you want to attend a long-revered academy for the performing arts that has a stellar reputation, I recommend that you later expand your training with an accredited program that offers more than just acting. Also, find a program that teaches the business of the business. Once you graduate, you'll have to know how to market yourself. Even when you have representation, you'll still have to be effective at finding work on your own. Much of your career's success will depend not only on your talent but also on how well you sell your "product."

Successful marketing begins with learning how to put together an actor's business card effectively—i.e., the picture and résumé. Are you getting the most out of your picture and résumé? Are you sure? Read the next chapter and learn.

CHAPTER FOUR

THE PICTURE AND RÉSUMÉ

An Actor's Business Card

"I like a résumé to match a picture. If I'm looking at a face on a headshot I really like a résumé that reflects roles that I think the actor would play, in reality. I think it's really weird sometimes when I get these really strange photos of people wearing weird things and they have roles that are completely unrepresentative of who they are."

Jack Menashe

Agency Owner/Agent

Independent Artists Agency

Apart from training and the actor's instrument (the body), the P&R (picture and résumé) is the most important marketing weapon in the battle for employment opportunities. Before casting directors or agents are willing to see you for the first time, the only criterion they have to judge you by (besides other printed materials, personal recommendations, or knowing you) is your business card: your picture and résumé. That's it. Nothing else. Your face, along with your career history placed onto paper, stapled together (or together in electronic form), is what gets you into an audition room. Or keeps the audition room door shut, barring your entrance. You're in control of that business card, on which audition appointment decisions are made. Format and present your business card wisely; the competition is fierce and plentiful.

Casting, whether it's an independent casting office, studio, regional theater, or struggling showcase company in New York, receives thousands upon thousands of headshots in one year. Most of those P&Rs go immediately into the trash. P&Rs are discarded to the burn pile for one or both of the following two reasons. First, the actor is not appropriate for what is presently being sought. *Toss the P&R.* What, you thought we kept everyone for our files? Hell no! Do you know how many warehouses for hardcopy P&Rs or hard drive memory for electronic P&Rs the onslaught in one year would require? We're talking an obscene amount, folks. And it's not just a size issue. It's also the precious time and labor that would be lost to filing each P&R and creating and managing a database for P&Rs received. There's just no way we would have the tick-tock and energy for saving every P&R you send us.

Second reason (and the most common) for a P&R being discarded is that it is poorly formatted. The picture is hideous and/or the résumé is a cluttered mess. Or the P&R is an eye-rolling, sideshow attraction. Often we receive P&Rs that are burdened with misguided gimmicks and "attention grabbing" graphics, styled in an in-your-face font, finished off with a "going for the shock value" headshot. These go straight to the Freak File—a file every casting office secretly keeps for amusement when the day is long and a laugh is needed. But it's not laughs we desire when receiving an actor's P&R. We want the actor to be exactly what we're seeking. Our job is to help you get jobs. Far too many actors hinder us from helping them achieve employment opportunities by submitting ineffective P&Rs.

I'm not alone in complaining about haphazardly formatted résumés attached to head-shots less flattering than high school yearbook photos. Casting and talent reps are bombarded daily with P&Rs that are in no way professional. And that's the key here folks: Acting is a profession. To be successful in a profession the participants must respect both the profession and their role within it! Got that? It's simple.

An actor's level of respect for the field is first displayed by the hardcopy or electronic version of his P&R. Your past, your puss, and, more important, how you present both as a unit are just as significant as the talent you present in person. Give great care and thought to making your P&R unified. Staples and glue alone do not unite a picture and résumé. The picture must reflect the personality of the roles on the résumé and vice versa (this does not mean costuming in the picture). The overall design of the résumé and the accompanying photo must be attractive, professional, free of clutter, and cleanly constructed. By cleanly constructed, I mean no fuss, nothing fancy, no gimmicks, just functional and straightforward, similar to that of Scandinavian design. If you're not familiar with Scandinavian design, make a quick trip to Ikea to view the lowbrow interpretation.

THE PICTURE

The Headshot: Initial Considerations

The headshot must look *exactly* like the actor when the actor enters the audition room each and every time, for the life expectancy (three to four years) of that headshot. One would think that this point wouldn't trigger so much hand-wringing and sleepless nights for an actor. It's simple. The image we see on paper is what we should see in person. Every time. Repeat. *Every time.* Those behind the table expect—no, demand—to see in corporeal form, standing before us, the person presented to us on paper. This does not mean that an actor has to be wearing the same clothing in the audition setting as in the picture, although I do know of one actress who used to do that. I haven't seen her in a while. I don't know if she still reflects that picture and wears the dress to auditions, but if so that blue velvet dress must be thin shreds by now.

Keeping the Headshot Current

Of the many poor headshot examples kept in my Freak File, there is one in which an actress drew a horizontal line across her neck and wrote next it, "My hair is now this long." Hello?! Wake-up call analogy: You're buying a six-foot-long sofa online for your tiny, studio-shoebox of an apartment. The website picture is exactly what you want. When the sofa arrives it measures nine feet in length. The sofa won't fit into your cramped quarters. It's not what you wanted or saw in the online catalog picture! Upon complaining to the retailer, you get a reply, "Oh, well, now it's this long." Hair takes a long time to grow. An updated headshot could have been taken during that period of lock lengthening. As your physical features change (due to, for example, plastic surgery, extreme hair growth, or thinning) your headshot must reflect the present you.

Actors should have their headshots taken every five years, even if they believe they haven't changed. Older actors are the biggest offenders when it comes to holding onto out-of-date headshots like life preservers. Ten, fifteen, twenty years go by and the aging thespian refuses to get new pictures taken. Is it vanity or cheapness? I say a bit of both. In this book, there are prime examples of this behavior. Some within the Group of Eight (I won't embarrass them by naming names) have let their headshot renewal lapse ten to twenty years! One of the Group of Eight had his last headshot taken so long ago that he could not recall the photographer!

The second biggest offenders in this category are continuously working actors. They falsely believe that since they're known and regularly employed they don't need to have an accurate photographic representation of themselves on paper. Wrong! Old headshot-hugging actors (like too many in the Group of Eight) need to stop being cheap and lazy. Just remember, casting directors, directors, and talent reps all get really pissed off when they find an actor is using an outdated headshot. So keep your headshot current!

Cheap Headshots for $99, Aisle Five!

WARNING: Don't go cheap. If the photographer's price is Wal-Mart low, more than likely the quality of his or her photography will reflect the big-box store price. Comparison shop as you would for a car. Ask agents and casting directors which photographer(s) they prefer. Ask other actors. Look at multiple headshot examples by photographers. Shop around. A headshot is an investment.

Joseph and His Amazing Technicolor Headshot

Color headshots became an unstoppable trend starting around 2001. It began with a dangerous combination: models and cheap color photography reproduction. Like a virus, the infection for having color headshots raced through the acting community from L.A. to New York. Actors pressured by photographers and peers pushing a "keeping up with the Jones's" mentality rapidly became a giant color collective, eradicating the standard black-and-white headshot. The quality at first was uneven. Often the prints resembled high school graduation portraits or, worse, air-brushed porn pinups. Sadly, some photographers continue to produce color headshots that barely rise above the expertise of DMV photography. Shot well or not, color is the new black and white.

What Makes an Auditor Respond to a Headshot?

You'll never know. No, I'm not being catty. Finding the answer to this question can be as frustrating as trying to solve a Rubik's Cube. Like others in casting, when I view a headshot, what I respond to depends on what I'm seeking at the moment. Talent reps look for marketability—i.e. youth, and/or look— that generates a kneejerk response of "This actor is a winner!" Creative personnel who hire talent, such as directors, producers, and casting directors, are much more specific in their demands. We want your headshot to match our mental image of the role.

Image = Role

Auditors want the headshot to reflect what they see in their mind's eye for the role they're casting. If casting is seeking a one-legged, Hispanic-Himalayan who sings, dances, and plays the saw, they don't need to see in the headshot a Costa Rican Mummer strutting with a Craftsman blade. What they need to see is a picture of an actor who matches the ethnicity sought, accompanied by a résumé that lists the skills required. A headshot does not need to be a depiction of any one character, nor should it be. Your headshot must represent you and what you offer in personality and appearance. If I'm seeking sophistication, then I'm looking for that same sophistication in the actor's headshot. If I'm looking for a sense of humor, I'm searching the eyes of the actor to see if there is wit and intelligence within. This will clue me in to the actor's ha-ha potential (intelligent actors tend to be funny). Gimmicky headshots in which people dress as characters are simply not proper. Let your face and eyes, by their natural beauty, show that you are appropriate for the role.

Your Eyes in the Headshot

Eyes project an actor's intelligence, self-esteem, and talent. I've had great success in matching my assumptions about an actor by viewing his eyes in his headshot and then meeting him in person. As my casting colleagues and I view headshots, we make quick assessments based on the eyes alone. Have lifeless eyes without soul? Ciao, baby; into the trash you go. Have an expression within the eyes that pulls in the viewer? You've got me interested. Be false in the headshot and seem like a cartoon? Then, "Ipitee-ipitee-ipitee … that's all folks!" Eyes are great indicators to personality, as are facial expression and wardrobe. My casting colleagues and I use these indicators to evaluate if the person we're staring at has what we or our client(s) need. Those needs can include any or all of the following:

- ✓ Character/type appropriateness
- ✓ For a role requiring comic wit, a natural sense of humor, not humor that is forced, contrived, gimmicky, or aided by props

- ✓ For a dramatic role, a strong or commanding presence, which is not forced or contrived
- ✓ Ability to play well with others: Actor appears to be low maintenance and will get along with all involved in the project (this is often a crucial criterion for choosing actors)
- ✓ Appearance of having one's shit together: The person in the picture looks sane

Your Face and Your Attitude

On the checklist you may have wondered how auditors can discern if an actor is going to play well with others. Experienced auditors have seen thousands upon thousands of headshots. We pick up quickly on how to read a person's potential attitude from the headshot alone. A headshot can be a billboard for personality disorders. Or it can be an advertisement for medication-free happiness. The camera rarely hides attitude, good or bad. Some actors can mask being high maintenance, but many cannot. A high-maintenance actor constantly brings unnecessary drama to a project and to those around them, whereas someone who is low maintenance is easy to work with. The way an actor gets along with others offstage/off screen is just as important as the actor's talent. Just like a mechanic evaluates a disabled car on the shoulder of a road, we scrutinize your headshot to ascertain whether you'll need a gentle nudge or a diesel tow truck in order to survive.

Obvious Headshot Indicators of a High-Maintenance Actor

- ⊘ Heavy makeup (screams insecurity)
- ⊘ Staged poses that attempt to indicate intelligence, such as the chin resting on a fist
- ⊘ Arms folded (uninviting body language indicates a tendency for being defensive or arrogant)
- ⊘ Props in the headshot such as a book, mug, wineglass, or gun (another indicator of insecurity)
- ⊘ Brooding expressions that scare away little children and furry animals (no further commentary required)

Bad Headshots

Some actors send out headshots that are better suited for the "wanted" bulletin board at the post office. Daily, I'm confronted by bad headshots of actors with sneers, crossed or bulging eyes, and hideous frowns. Then there are the headshots in which the actor is gaping at the camera with his mouth hung half open and a face void of expression, so much so that the viewer wonders if the actor is submitting himself for the role of a Neanderthal. And it's not just embarrassing photography that makes for a bad headshot; it's also how the headshot is presented. Those on my side of the table often receive photocopies of a photocopied, candied image submitted as a headshot. These "headshots" and many like them end up in one of two places upon receipt: the trash or the Freak File. The more notorious, bad headshots inducted into my Freak File include:

An actor stands naked in profile, in front of foliage. A fedora his only article of "clothing." His muscled left forearm, blocking the viewer from seeing his groin, is the only obstacle keeping the soft porn picture from graduating to a DVD cover for Falcon Studios.

An actor faces the camera, with a headshot of himself placed in front of his face. The headshot he holds, blocking his face, is a headshot of him holding a headshot blocking his face, which features a headshot of him holding a headshot that blocks . . . oh, man . . . this guy has way too much time on his hands.

A fifty-something woman dressed in black, sporting uneven bangs, stands in New York's Central Park. Her arms outstretched while holding aloft a glass of wine in one hand and open sheet music in the other. Outdoor drunken funeral singer anyone?

In a postcard, there's a brick wall. Standing before the brick wall, an actor. Unfortunately the viewer cannot see the face of the actor for the actor is facing the brick wall!

A mature actress, with an 8 x 10 composite, displays her versatility by hiding her face in photos behind multiple objects. In one size-reduced photo, a white lace handkerchief curtains her features. The top of the handkerchief runs across the bridge of her nose just below her eyes. Those eyes peer mischievously at the camera. Those eyes—my God, those eyes! They're staring at me! Next photo quick! In another, a violin covers her face. The bow ready in hand at an angle. But wait! There are those eyes again. Stop staring at me, woman! In the third image . . . is that . . . YES . . . it is! I see a face! Glory Hallelujiah! A face! But . . . uhmm . . . where's her hair? It's hiding under a tall, flowering, feather plumage sprouting from the top center of her head. She desperately reaches with one arm outstretched to the camera. Her fingers taunting the lens. Her eyes ablaze. Oh my God. It's Norma Desmond!

A lanky-legged, blonde actress, straddling a Harley-Davidson in a sexually provocative pose from which no Baptist could recover, has her lips apart, tongue taunting, and her cleavage provocatively thrust to the camera lens. Black fishnets, a leather brassiere, and the crotch rocket she straddles comprise her wardrobe. On her résumé under "Theater" she lists her credits as "Over 20 plays and musicals." Actress?? She looks less like a hoofer and more like a fluffer.

What's sad is that these actors (dare I risk calling them actors?) and many others with similar inappropriate headshots believe that what they send is flattering and acceptable. I wish that I could display the images here, to better persuade others from making similar career-stopping blunders, but these people who willingly send out their visual assault to industry are surprisingly shy about having their business card viewed by a broader audience. To be seen by many, isn't that one of the appeals to being an actor? Guess not.

None of the headshot mishaps that I receive are appealing. They are so far removed from what is normal that they are almost unbelievable. When I first see an outrageous visual assault I don't even bother to turn it over to look at the résumé. Nine times out of ten the résumé will be just as uninviting as the headshot. Intelligent, self-assured, and self-aware actors have great pictures and résumés. Actors who don't know who they are reflect their lack of self-knowledge in their pictures and résumés.

Makeup and Headshots

Hire a professional makeup artist and hair stylist, preferably excellent professionals with vast experience in headshot cosmetology and highly recommended by other actors and industry.

Max Factor Missive for Women

While many are proficient in stage and day-to-day makeup, most actresses don't have the knowledge of how to properly apply makeup and style hair for the still camera. When makeup, in a headshot, is poorly applied, the result is beyond a fright-fest. Get professional help.

WARNING: The makeup and hairstyling should not glamorize you beyond how you will appear in the audition room. No county-fair beauty-queen blowouts. No heavy pancake and rouge that adds five pounds to your weight. No globs of eye shadow glitter that would rob even a Hooter's waitress of her dignity. Keep the makeup and photo shoot hair simple, both of which are true to you and how you will appear before auditors.

Max Factor Missive for Men

Don't. Men, don't mess with makeup unless at the time of photography your skin is extremely pale or you have an unfortunate outbreak of acne. Resist temptation to falsely tint and tone the skin yourself. If absolutely necessary, get a professional makeup artist and hair stylist, highly recommended and with vast experience in headshot cosmetology. A man's headshot in which a self-application of Max Factor or Revlon can be detected will elicit the unwanted auditor inquiry, "Is he wearing makeup or is he just a tranny?" The focus of the people viewing your headshot should not be their lingering doubts about that abnormally healthy pink glow from your cheeks or their perception of you as a drag queen. Unless of course you are a drag queen. Then by all means, you go, girl! (Just don't expect masculine roles to come your way.)

Masking Nature's Mischief

With the advances of cost-effective, digital enhancement technologies, actors no longer need worry about skin blemishes or temporary imperfections as they did in the past. With the click of a mouse acne can be cleared, skin tone can be enhanced, and eyes brightened. The danger of this technology is that an actor will be tempted to have himself pixilated and Photoshopped beyond what is reality. Resist the temptation to have plastic surgery done to your headshot via computer. Only remove or mask what is temporary. Don't go Michael

Jackson via digital retouching.

A semi-low-tech method to enhance skin tone for the pale is a trip to the tanning salon. Get a bit of base color, either by safer ultraviolet light or full-body spray. Wait several days until *after* the faux tan has peaked, and then have your headshots taken. CAUTION: You don't want to have your headshots taken while deeply tanned, unless that is you 365 days a year, which is not recommended. Perpetual tanning rapidly ages your skin. So unless you want a short-lived career as a character actor weathered with premature wrinkles, lines, leathered skin, and prone to melanoma, approach self-tanning in moderation.

Choosing Your Photographer

A photographer with a portfolio that wows, possibly one who has star clientele, is not necessarily the person you want capturing your headshot. Why? To have a successful headshot you want a photographer who wows you both with his work *and* with his personality. The manner in which a photographer treats you upon your inquiry will indicate how he will treat you during your photo shoot.

Being met (either by phone, e-mail, or in person) with respect upon first encountering the photographer will later translate into a relaxed and comfortable photo shoot. Brusque behavior and inefficiency in responding to your inquiries in a timely manner will later translate into a miserable photo shoot. A photo shoot gone bad because of the photographer's behavior will not provide the actor with a business card that will later open casting doors.

A photo shoot is a collaborative process. For the collaboration to be a success, two objectives must be achieved. The first objective is compatibility: Find a photographer you like as a person. You must be comfortable and relaxed during your photo shoot and trust the person behind the lens. You must believe that the photographer will capture the best images of you while making the experience enjoyable and effortless for all involved. Photographers should not make you feel that you're fortunate to be in their presence or that they're doing you a favor. You're the customer, and the photographer is serving you. Remember that.

The second objective is that you freely communicate to the photographer how you intend to use the captured image. You need to explain how you market yourself (explored in Chapter 6). Inform the photographer what age- and type-appropriate roles you've previously been cast as and roles/types that you will be believably cast as in the near future. The photographer should then strive to capture the traits in your personality—your natural state—that will best reflect these roles.

Headshot Do's & Don'ts: Quick Reference

✓ Recommended	vs.	⊘ AT YOUR OWN RISK ⊘
✓ G-rated.	vs.	Nudity, unless you're a triple-X wannabe. Keep your privates private (or for personal ⊘ exchanges online).
✓ Your name accompanying and printed on the image (preferably below the photo).	vs.	No name on the headshot. ⊘
✓ Engaging expression that is relaxed, states your personality and is not forced or staged.	vs.	Gimmick headshots. They're not funny. They're side show disturbing. ⊘
✓ Blurred or solid background.	vs.	Busy patterned backgrounds, other people ⊘ in the background.
✓ As much natural light as is possible.	vs.	Shadows and/or harsh artificial lighting ⊘ which obscures/washes out your features.
✓ Comfortable clothing, be it formal or casual. Wear solid colors that complement skin tone.	vs.	Clothing with distracting patterns or clothing that is unflattering to your figure or ⊘ reveals too much of your figure.
✓ A hairstyle that matches your everyday look.	vs.	Wigs, extensions, and blow outs. Any hair or hairstyle that you've selected exclusively for the headshot session ⊘ that does not reflect how you appear on the street or in auditions.
✓ A makeup artist/hair stylist who understands headshot photography, if your budget allows.	vs.	Drag. Excessive makeup (if the makeup crinkles when you smile, you've put on too ⊘ much).
✓ Varying headshots to match the different aspects of your personality.	vs.	Homemade composites comprised of candid photos taken by you, family, or friends. ⊘ (Professional composites are to be used for modeling, print, and extra work only. **Don't** send composites for principal auditions.)
✓ Headshots that accurately reflect your age and significant changes in your appearance. Always update. No one can be twenty-one forever.	vs.	Photocopies. Don't even think about sending out photocopies because you can't afford the cost of hardcopy reproductions. ⊘ The message a photocopy headshot sends to industry is "this actor is not serious about his/her profession."

Recommended Headshot Examples

What follows are preferred examples of actor headshots. Each is an accurate representation of how the actor appears in person. The photography is complimentary and doesn't distract from the subject. The expression and form captured in each photograph is not forced; the actors appear relaxed and the image captured truly indicates their personas.

By including these headshots in this book, I am not endorsing any photographers. I actually did not seek photographers. I burrowed through my files and those of talent agencies for engaging, accurate images of actors. If any photography in this book intrigues you, I strongly suggest that you view the photographer's portfolio, have a dialogue with him or her, and, most important, speak to actors who have previously engaged the photographer's services. As I stated previously, you need to educate yourself about the photographer's personality and work ethic before you release your valuable money. You'll need to discover for yourself which photographer's personality works best for you. It's like dating, without the romance.

Important note regarding headshot images within this book: While color is now king in the casting world, the headshots within this book appear here in black and white, although most of the originals are in color.

SARAH SCHREIBER

Photo by Peter Hurley

WILL PAILEN

Photo by Chia Messina

TINA CHILIP

Photo by Laura Rose

SANDRA PROSPER

Photo by Theo Fridlizius/theoandjuliet.com

JAY NIXON

Photo by Jack David Menashe

HOPE CHERNOV

Photo by Jack David Menashe

KAILI VERNOFF

Photo by Tracy Toler

SAMANTHA IVERS

Photo by Peter Sweyer

TJ LINNARD

Photo by Chris Macke

NATALIE KNEPP

Photo by Peter Sweyer

And then there's this headshot below: For several years, once a month, many of my colleagues in casting and representation and I would receive a copy of this questionable headshot. It's a true example of an extreme risky actor photo, a marketing ploy that I don't condone. It could limit the actor's broader chances for work, but a limited number of casting people might respond differently.

PETE TRAINA

Photo by Frank Fontana

THE RÉSUMÉ

How Much Information Should Be Included?

First and foremost, less is more on a résumé.

On my side of the audition table, we scan. We don't read. Reading takes time. Less than seven seconds is initially given to a résumé. *Seven seconds.* If our interest is piqued within those seven seconds, then we give full attention to the résumé—full attention being a generous thirty seconds. We skim the résumé looking for indicators relevant to our scrutiny. What kind of indicators? If casting for a specific project, we look for credits that match the project. We then move on to education indicators. MFA, BFA? Graduate of an "industry-approved" school? We then scan the credits to see what directors the actor has worked with, as well as the stature of the performance venue(s).

Directors on a Résumé

A note of caution about advertising the directors with whom you worked on your résumé: Don't single out one or two directors from your past—give equal billing to all. Indicate who directed each project you list. You'll never know in whose hands your résumé will land. It could be the one director of the one project you list that excludes a director credit. Ouch! That director will feel slighted and more than likely will not want to see you again in one of his or her projects. When exploiting your past and those with whom you've worked, be an equal-opportunity exploiter. And make sure to spell the exploited's name properly.

Paper Strength: How to Make a Résumé Read More Powerfully

Paper strength is the potency of your résumé as determined by your credits on paper and the order in which those credits appear. In simpler terms, paper strength is categorizing on paper "You did what where, with whom?" and putting the more prestigious or recognizable credits first. Under each performance category you should always begin with your most-impressive credits. No brainer, right? Wrong. Many actors believe in listing credits chronologically, starting with the most recent. My argument to that is that if your most recent credit was a walk-on role, it will not intrigue the résumé reader to look further down if a principal role is now being cast. You may have done a great principal role years ago, but if that credit is farther down on the list, it's likely it'll be overlooked because a first glance indicates that you're a day-player or background actor. Remember, we scan résumés; we don't read and digest all the information that is on the page. Grab us with the first credit.

Quality, Not Size, Matters

You should consider more than a role's prominence when determining the order in which you list your credits. Industry regard for the director, venue/studio/producer, or the level of recognition attached to the credit may trump the role's size. Base your decision on what you want auditors to know about you immediately. Begin with the strongest credits and then follow up in order of descending importance.

A snob factor comes into play when I examine a résumé, I must admit. My clients expect a certain level of quality and history from the talent I bring in. This attitude is nearly universal among casting directors. For a language play we give stronger consideration to an actor who has worked at the Guthrie or Yale Rep than someone who has only done musicals at the Song-n-Skillet Show Palace. Mea culpa.

Actors often will submit themselves for projects for which they have no prior related experience or training. This is a waste of the actor's money and time. But hope remains for those with lesser-known or irrelevant credits. If we're casting for the screen or a language play, and a dinner theater credit is the only one the actor lists, something else on the résumé (or the picture) might push us into meeting the actor. Every casting director makes the decision to offer an audition subjectively, but an actor should be realistic as to what he or she has to offer, on paper, and how that will fare against the competition, before spending money on a submission.

Sloppy Résumé = Sloppy Actor

Casting personnel avoid calling in actors with sloppy résumés. What's presented on paper is the first impression an actor presents to an auditor. The formatting and presentation of the résumé gives us insight into the work ethic and personality of the actor. A sloppy résumé screams, "I'm a mess and don't know how to get my life in order!" A clean, organized, well-formatted, three-columned résumé, void of clutter, tells us that the actor will likely be punctual and organized, has pride and good self-esteem, and is relatively sane. That's the type of actor my clients and I want. Make a good first impression on paper and your résumé may be spared from the trash.

Résumé Relevance

Keep only relevant information on the résumé. If you're a twenty-five-year-old actor still listing adolescent achievements, take note: Your high school highlights have long passed the statute of limitation for being a barometer of your brilliance. Same holds true for actors in mid-life who on their résumé continue to cling to younger leading roles from early in their careers. Your résumé should reflect the fact that time moves forward.

I know that parting with favored past credits is like saying farewell to a cherished pair of socks. But when those socks are worn thin, peppered with holes, and it's been years since they've seen life beyond the dresser drawer, what purpose do they fulfill? None. Keeping useless items, such as inappropriate age/type roles on the résumé (or frayed socks never to be worn again), displays that you're either too lazy or too insecure to toss away what is no longer of use and value. Get rid of the worn sock credits. If I'm casting a forty-year-old rabbi for a film, I don't need to know that in your adolescence you played Tevye at an all-girls high school. I only need to know roles you've performed relevant to your current type, ability, and age, thank you.

Résumé Font and Paper

The font used on your résumé should be one that is simple, easy to read (not a distraction), and is universally found on most computers. Your résumé will be viewed more often electronically either via e-mail or online than it will be read as a hard copy. Arial, Courier, Helvetica, Times New Roman, and Verdana are considered the most universal of fonts for Macs and PCs. Specialized fonts (of which there are hundreds upon hundreds) such as: **BUDMO JIGGLER**, **DIRTYBAKERSDOZEN**, Buttzilla, or **COPPERPLATE GOTHIC HEAVY** are not commonly found on computers. While the intriguingly titled fonts appear attention-grabbing, and you may believe Buttzilla will make your résumé unique, specialized fonts are distracting and difficult to decipher by human or artificial intelligence. Remember, a computer that is not programmed with your font will translate it into one it can read. As a result, your lovely formatting will more than likely be disfigured in the translation.

If you're thinking of having two résumés—an electronic one formatted with a universal font, and a separate, hardcopy résumé formatted with specialized font—banish that misguided creativity. Don't be tempted by specialized fonts. Budmo Jiggler and its ilk impart an immature and unprofessional appearance that negatively reflects upon the résumé's subject: you. Your appearance as an actor, on paper, whether via Hammermill paper, a Mac or a PC, must be unified and professional. Having two font-contrasting résumés or a single specialized-font résumé, because you fancy specialized fonts, sends the message that font is more important to you than your professional history.

Choice of paper on which the font is set is equally important. White paper, please—*white*. The eye adores white paper. Many trees are killed for white paper. Put good use to the timber slaughter. No pastels. No fluorescents that blind and send casting personnel to the ER. Use of "creative" paper that you believe will gain attention only gains you less money in the wallet and the immediate attention of an environmental services manager—i.e., the trash collector. What is put on the paper—the credits and training—is what is important. Not needed is Budmo Jiggler on paper imbedded with a bucolic, floral watermark. Save that for a Mother's Day greeting.

Electronic Résumé Formatting

Documents, like a résumé, created on one computer can appear vastly different on another computer when opened, unless you create or transfer your résumé into a PDF document (Adobe). Adobe PDF or similar document format preservation software is your best bet for making sure that everyone sees your résumé, as you intended, in its original appearance. Otherwise the format, size of tables, font, margins, and more will often be altered by whatever document program the recipients of your résumé use on their computers.

Contact Information

Include contact information on the résumé. Obvious, right? No! Hard to believe, but I've received far too many résumés *without* contact information. When this happens it's as if the actor is playing hide-and-seek. Those in casting do not play that game. To the growing number of actors who send me contact-barren résumés: *I'm a casting director, damn it, not a psychic!* Contact information should always be at the top of the résumé.

Contact Information That Should Be on a Résumé

- ✓ Talent representation (if represented)
- ✓ Cell phone number (or primary phone number)
- ✓ Service phone number (or a secondary phone with voicemail)
- ✓ Business e-mail address (have a separate e-mail account designated for your acting correspondence; one that is business-like such as JoeSmith@***.com instead of potentially embarrassing, GhettoGirlSnaps@***.com)
- ✓ Website address (every actor should have a website)

Contact/Personal Information That Should NEVER Be on a Résumé

- ⊘ Home address
- ⊘ Social Security Number

Personal Statistics

Personal statistics on a résumé greatly aid the casting process. On occasion we need to know an actor's physical measurements prior to giving that actor an appointment. When my client wants men who are 5'11" and over, that's what we're seeking—that's who we must bring into the audition room. If the actor does not meet physical expectations, I can't waste my client's or the actor's time. Sometimes an actor has to fit into a premade costume, match the height of others already cast, or be of certain proportions for historical requirements. On occasion the actor hired is the actor who fits the costume and not the actor whose talents fit the role.

Many talent reps remove personal statistics such as height and weight from client résumés. Why? An agent selling an actor is like a car dealer selling a ride; just as the dealer wants to get the buyer on the lot and into a car for a pitch, the agent wants to create a one-on-one situation with the buyer (casting), via phone or e-mail. The seller will try convincing the buyer in conversation that the product (the actor) is appropriate, even if the product does not match what the buyer demands. No matter how hard the talent rep pushes, if the actor doesn't physically match the casting needs, there's little hope for an offer. To prevent all involved from wasting time, include your physical stats on the résumé.

NOTE: Now that color headshots are industry-standard, there is little need for including eye and hair color, unless your headshot is old-school black and white.

Personal Statistics That Should Be on a Résumé

- ✓ Height
- ✓ Weight (current truth, not your wish weight)

Personal Statistics That Should NEVER Be on a Résumé

- ⊘ Age range (we'll make that call, thank you)
- ⊘ Gender (your name and/or picture hopefully indicate one of the two available gender options)

Union Affiliations

If you belong to any of the performing artists unions, indicate your membership at the top of the résumé, under your name. Don't make us guess if you're union or not. Many union actors are instigators of this guessing game. We don't have the patience or time. What follows are the applicable union delineations and their monograms as they should be indicated on a résumé.

> SAG (Screen Actors Guild)
>
> SAG-Eligible (indicates the actor has previously worked on SAG-governed projects as a nonunion actor, but in order to work on a SAG-governed project again, SAG requires the actor to join the union upon hire.)
>
> AEA (Actors Equity Association)
>
> EMC (Equity Membership Candidate; signifies the actor is earning points toward taking a test to receive membership within the union. EMCs *are not* members of AEA.)
>
> AFTRA (American Federation of Television and Radio Artists)
>
> AGVA (American Guild of Variety Artists)

Categorizing Legit Credits

Outlets for entertainment rise and fall in popularity as tastes and technology move forward. Live theater once ruled. Now it's the screen: movies, TV, Internet, and the personal miniature video playback device. As mentioned earlier, when categorizing your credits, give priority to high-profile project(s) in which you had a principal role. These are the credits you want the reader to see first, thereby quickly validating your worth as an actor (at least on paper). Continue listing credits in descending order of greatest exposure for you as an actor (principal roles) plus greatest audience/industry exposure (based on the producing organization's level of respect and visibility). Then categorize genre in descending order of importance.

Here are the appropriate genre titles to be used on a résumé.

Film

Includes studio, independent, and student film credits. As an actor accumulates experience in commercial film projects, student film credits should be dropped.

TV

Includes series, half-hours, MOWs (movies of the week), daytime serials, on-camera hosting, and pilots (aired and unaired).

New York Theater

That's the city, not the state. This category includes Broadway, Off-Broadway, showcases, and workshops. An actor doesn't have to subcategorize, as auditors are generally smart enough to figure out the level of production from the production's venue. We can differentiate *Godspell* at the Booth Theater (Broadway) from *Godspell* at the Temple for Wayward Actors (showcase).

The Great Off-White Lie: Upgrading New York Credits

Listing credits honestly would seem simple, but many actors become inventive. And nowhere more than in New York do actors, on paper, white-lie their way into Off-Broadway via a showcase or reading credit. The practice has got to stop!

Many green actors in New York will list any appearance below Broadway stature that involves an audience of one or more as "Off-Broadway." Performing in a self-written showcase, such as the fictitiously titled *Naked Shakespeare Sings!*, at the Producers Club or at the Sanford Meisner is *not* Off-Broadway unless the production is covered by an AEA, Off-Broadway contract! If it's a limited production performed in a space that seats fewer than one hundred people and AEA requires only one of its members in the cast, then it's a *showcase* . . .

This practice of falsely upgrading lesser New York credits to Off-Broadway stature has spread to narcissistic solo nights in cabaret and singing waiters warbling Webber while serving shakes and waffle fries to tourists. No one is fooled by deceitful actors bundling showcases, workshops, readings, and singing waiter gigs as Off-Broadway. Don't do it! Not only do you look foolish but also you're tagged a liar. And a fool can be forgiven more readily than a liar.

Tours

Include productions on tour under AEA contracts and professional nonunion tours.

Regional Theater

The mindset in New York is that theater outside of New York City, within America's borders, under an AEA contract or a professional (i.e., paid), nonunion production is "regional theater." For actors based and working onstage in the United States outside of New York City, theater credits fall under the category of "Theater." This would include those who receive pay for theatrical work in major cities such as Chicago, Boston, L.A., Philadelphia, and elsewhere within the country. When the regional actor, based and working outside of the metro New York area, having never worked in New York, moves to the world capital for theater, the theater credits previously listed under the all-encompassing genre title of Theater should then be listed under the category of Regional Theater.

Webcasts

Studios and networks have begun to develop online programming. Internet series are being produced in the same manner as broadcast television programming. Having a homemade video posted on YouTube or other Internet multiple-user video outlets does not merit a credit on your résumé. The webcast must be a project that is professionally produced for entertainment content similar to what can be viewed by audiences at a movie theater or on a televised program.

Educational Theater

Educational Theater is a temporary category for recent conservatory and/or college-trained actors. When listing your educational roles, retain those you would be believably cast as in the professional world. Dump roles that are not relevant to your age or type. Often in educational theater young students are cast in roles twice, sometimes three times, the student actor's age. That's not likely to happen in the professional world. While you may be proud of playing, at twenty-one, old King Duncan in the Scottish tragedy, announcing that academic credit on your professional résumé at twenty-five tells auditors that student age-appropriate role(s) went to others; this could prove detrimental. At best, keeping roles beyond your age range on your résumé, roles you could not possibly play in the professional arena, informs casting personnel that you're adept at wielding gray stick.

Working actors should dump educational credits when their professional accomplishments outweigh their academic achievements. Sadly, some with long-standing, professional careers keep worn, outdated educational credits as unnecessary filler. Are they exercising the vain, fruitless hope that youth will return vis-à-vis their résumé? Hmmm.

Community Theater

This category is for the actor who is either beginning to cross over into the professional world and has done community theater or is strictly contented to be a weekend thespian. Unless the roles performed by an actor in community theater befit him or her with respect to type or talent, or if the community theater is of high regard (e.g., the Players Guild in Ohio), community theater holds little relevance to the professional world. Why? The quality varies greatly, and most creative professionals are not familiar with community theater beyond the stereotypes of stiff acting and poor production values achieved on a dollar-store budget.

If as a professional actor you wish to list community theater credits, do so under their own category, but know they will likely generate little respect. You may have been beloved as Will Parker in a community production of *Oklahoma*, but that doesn't translate into your being cast as Ado Annie's pursuer in a professional production. Some community theater actors, aware of the casting world's dismissive attitude toward their genre, upgrade their credits from community to regional theater status. Don't do it. Eventually you will encounter an auditor who knows the difference between Haddonfield Plays & Players and the People's Light and Theatre Company. Be honest about and proud of the work accomplished, be it gratis or paid.

International Theatrical Credits

If you're an actor with a residence in the United States and have theater credits abroad, list them under a category heading that includes the foreign city, country, or continent where the performances took place (e.g., "Toronto," "London," "England," "Europe," "Asia"). Tours in Europe and Asia are often categorized similarly as "European Tours" or "Asian Tours." Those two continental markets have proven profitable for the touring producer and nonunion actor.

NOTE: For a Legit résumé (film, TV and theater), if your credits are in film and TV only, categorize film credits first, followed by TV (and/or webcasts). If your experience is only upon the stage, begin listing your credits in order of venue prominence. The one similarity between résumés of both screen and stage actors is that training history should be included at the bottom of the résumé, after your categorized employment history and before your special skills.

Categorizing Commercial Credits

Omit commercials from Legit (film, TV, and theater) résumés. The actor who has worked in commercials while working Legit needs two résumés: one for Legit credits and one for commercial credits. The commercial credits are of little value to Legit casting. The commercial résumé *can* have Legit credits on it. This additional information provides commercial casting directors insight that the actor has more to offer than just a marketable face and/or great voice.

On-Camera

On-Camera is basically what it sounds like: commercial work done on-camera whether it is an ad for a local car dealership or a national televised campaign for prescription medication.

Print

Print includes still photography modeling in catalogs and print ads in periodicals.

Voiceover

Voiceovers are not limited to commercials, radio, TV, and webcasts. Voiceovers also include the vocal personalities used for corporate training/information presentations, public service announcements (PSAs), and in public venues. When I travel on the New Jersey Transit train between my home in New Jersey and work in New York, my fellow commuters and I hear the recorded voice of an actress who announces the train stops and train safety procedures. She's the voice of New Jersey Transit. If you have a marketable voice, there's a lot of work out there for you in places that you'd least expect.

A Thin Résumé

What does a new actor put on a résumé? Simple: the truth, even if the truth adds up to few or no credits. Everyone begins with a blank sheet of paper. Sir Laurence Olivier did not pop out of his mother's womb with an Oscar.

If you're just beginning your career and all you have to list is training, put that down. If you've only been in productions in school or community theater, that's the résumé. Don't fake it! Making up credits is an industry sin. You'll be caught. I've confronted résumé liars and have witnessed other auditors do the same. The result: great humiliation for the actor and disgust from the person who caught the actor's lie. It's not pretty. Better to have nothing at all than fill a résumé with falsehoods. Be proud of what you have. There's no shame in being a beginner, as long as you're an honest beginner.

Special Skills

The "Special Skills" portion of a résumé is not a landfill for useless information. At the bottom of the résumé, include only relevant, practical, special skills, which are generally required of actors. List only what you can do with great proficiency, and be prepared to show off any one of your special skills with little notice.

Keep the Special Skills section brief. Recall that in the hectic pace of casting, a casting director's eyes quickly scan a résumé. Don't approach this section the way you might an essay contest. It's a sound bite. The Special Skills section of a résumé is for informing directors, casting directors, and agents as to how they can further exploit your talents.

Avoid the obvious: Dancing and singing *are not* to be placed under Special Skills. These talents belong in the education/training area of the résumé.

The Five Categories of Relevant Special Skills

Musical Instruments Played

Indicate the type of instrument(s), proficiency, and the number of years played. If you own any of the instruments you play, make note of this as well.

Stage Combat

Indicate certification including the weapons and type(s) of combat for which you have been certified. Also include the number of years certified, plus the stage combat teachers who have trained you, as well as your proficiency.

Dialects and Languages

List which dialects and/or languages you can speak, your fluency, and the number of years of fluency.

Gymnastics and/or Acrobatic Skills

List the type of skills, proficiency, and number of years of training and practical use.

Circus/Side Show Tricks

Juggling, fire eating, sword swallowing, etc. Physical deformities and extremes in weight or height *do not* count as tricks or skills.

Résumé Cookies

What's a résumé cookie? It's an enticement on the actor's résumé for auditors to bite at and that hopefully provides a basis for conversation. The best résumé cookie is a *useful in performance* but off-the-wall special skill. With caution, allow for one, *and only one,* truly wacky skill (if you have any) that can be done in an audition room setting. Be prepared to perform this skill at all auditions when asked. If I see a cookie on an actor's résumé, I reach for and exploit it as a stepping-stone toward dialogue. This allows me to begin to learn how an actor interacts as a person. I've seen other casting directors and directors use this ploy as well.

No-No Skills

"No-No Skills" are useless items that should never—repeat, *never*—be listed as skills on an actor's résumé. Regardless, some performers blindly charge forward and add to their résumés "skills" that bear no practical use. As I cast Shakespeare or Sondheim, the special skill I once found on a résumé, "Defending Needle Exchange Programs in Middle America," I can say with assurance, is not one I need to see in an audition. I'm frightened of needles. I'll pass on the syringe soliloquy.

What follows is a true sampling of No-No Skills that should never have been put into font but, alas, have sadly found their way onto actor résumés:

Truant officer

Works well with animals and children

Janitorial work (Is this person waiting for the musical *Disney's Mr. Clean—LIVE!*?)

Palm reader

Flower-arranging

Perfect teeth (Good for you; how much did they cost?)

Common-law chef (Huh?)

Can drive a horse (Standard or automatic?)

Perceptive people person (Does that mean this person is perceptive, relates well to perceptive people, or are perceptive people attracted to her?)

There's more . . .

Use of power tools (No comment)

Married to a professional acrobat (Definitely no comment)

Licensed driver (Far too many of these on résumés)

Willing to travel

Flight attendant (More peanuts, please!)

Owns tuxedo

Smoky voice

Jedi mind tricks

Levitation

Walking

Can sit at a computer and type fast (So can I; just ignore the typos)

And . . .

Can make the sound of an angry badger (I've heard the angry badger actress, and that's one damn angry badger)

I have a personal favorite not on the list. But my sensitive sense of smell does not permit me to take breath of his unique . . . special skill, which he boasts as: "Can fart on cue." No pun intended but . . . I'll pass. But wait, the on-cue flatulent is outdone by another performer who has a special skill that causes my eyes to roll. There is an actor out there (probably not the only one) who wants to drive home the message that, yes, he is indeed an actor. Under Special Skills he adds:

Acting

The aptitude for the skill may be in question. Of the overkill of sixteen special skills listed on his résumé, acting ranked last behind "extreme cat lover." Now, yes, I'll admit that acting is a skill, but listing it as such on an acting résumé is repetitive redundancy.

If your résumé has anything remotely related to these true No-No Skills examples, go to your computer this instant and delete from your hard drive the irrelevant and foolish offenders. Versatility is wonderful but only when practical.

No-No Skills vs. Résumé Cookies

There is a distinction between the two. A No-No Skill similar to those listed has little to no practical application in performance, is not a skill, or can be done by nearly anyone with a pulse. Whereas a résumé cookie, an off-the-wall skill, such as fire-eating, requires training, is theatrical, and dare I say . . . is an actual skill.

Résumé Examples

There is no cookie-cutter formatting to résumés. Not everyone's résumé will look exactly alike, but an actor, to be taken seriously as a professional, needs to adhere to the industry standards previously outlined.

What follows are résumés of working actors of varying career accomplishments. Aside from being actors, what they also have in common is that their résumés contain content that is well-organized and can be readily scanned by the reader's eye.

Note on examples: Two of the four résumé examples that follow are based on those of real-life actors John Hedges and Michael Mastro. Personal contact information on the résumés has been omitted/altered by the author to protect their privacy. Content may not reflect the actor's current, updated résumé. The other two actor résumé examples (Sandra Kay's and Kevin Kemperer's) are fictional.

Recommended Résumé Format Example

SANDRA KAY

SAG ❖ AFTRA ❖ AEA

917-555-1212 (Cell)
212-555-1212 (Service)

SKay@____.___
www.SandraKay.___

Height: 5'9"
Weight: 125 lbs.

FILM

ACE THE DAY	Rhonda	Universal/Jim Gibson, Dir.
ALIENS WITH ALTOIDS	Nicky Biggscrueh	Warner/Jack David, Dir.
HARDWARE	Bette	Sony/Thom Ryan, Dir.
CAMPFIRE STORIES	Ashely	Fine Line/Harry Gerald, Dir.

TELEVISION

JUSTICE & JAIL	Suzanne/Guest Star	NBC/Nicole Neyenesch, Dir.
SHOE PAINT	Snuggles/Lead	BBC/Jack Russell, Dir.
MISS ALLIANCE	Ann/Guest Star	NBC (Pilot)/Holly Barkdoll, Dir.
EDUCATION OF THE BEAVER	Debra/Guest Star	CBS/Miles Lott, Dir.
ONE COOKIE	Tammy/Recurring	CBS/Quentin Beaver, Dir.
ALIENS WITH ALTOIDS	Nicky Biggscrueh	Comedy Central/Jack David, Dir.

THEATER

END GAME	Maria	Variety Arts/Charles Graver, Dir.
PERSONAL BAGGAGE	Silvana	Variety Arts & Hartford Stage/ Richard G. Ney, Dir.
THE BED STAGE LEFT	Carmela	Bay Street Theatre/ Michael Osman, Dir.
AH URBANITY!	Muriel	Guthrie/Bob Elderkin, Dir.
A MONTH IN THE SUBWAY	Trudy	Guthrie/Misha Angelovskiy, Dir.

EDUCATIONAL THEATER

The Juilliard School

THE THREE SISTERS	Irina	Dennis O'Connell, Dir.
TARTUFFE	Flipote	George Pappas, Dir.
RICHARD III	Lady Anne	Vikki Lucas, Dir.

SPECIAL SKILLS

Instruments: Guitar (*10 yrs.*), piano (*20 yrs.*) & accordion (*18 yrs.*). Dialects: Central London, Cockney, Welsh, Irish, Southern Appalachian. Stage Combat: SAFD Certified, broadsword, hand-to-hand, dagger, and rapier

MICHAEL MASTRO
SAG – AFTRA – AEA

917.555.5555
212.555.5555

WWW.MICHAELMASTRO.COM

HEIGHT: 5′ 11″
WEIGHT: 170

FILM

KISSING JESSICA STEIN	Supporting Lead	Fox Searchlight/Charles Herman-Wurmfeld
2B PERFECTLY HONEST	Supporting Lead	2B Pictures/Randle Cole
BOROUGH OF KINGS	Supporting Lead	Ind. Feature/Elise Lewin
JUNGLE 2 JUNGLE	Featured	Disney/John Pasquin
THE NIGHT WE NEVER MET	Featured	Miramax/Warren Leight
DEAD FUNNY	Supporting Lead	Avondale/John Feldman

TELEVISION

ALIAS	Guest	ABC/Ken Olin
HACK	Guest	CBS/Kristoffer Tabori
LAW & ORDER/CI (2 *Episodes*)	Guest	NBC/Gus Makris
LAW & ORDER/SVU	Guest	NBC/Rick Rosenthal
LAW & ORDER (2 *Episodes*)	Guest	NBC/Don Scardino-Martha Mitchell
DEADLINE	Guest	NBC/Alex Cassini
COSBY	Guest	NBC/Don Scardino
ON SEVENTH AVENUE (*MOW/Pilot*)	Featured	20th Century Fox TV/Jeff Bleckner

BROADWAY/NEW YORK THEATER

TWELVE ANGRY MEN	Juror #5	Roundabout/Scott Ellis
CAT ON A HOT TIN ROOF	Gooper	Music Box/Anthony Page
JUDGMENT AT NUREMBERG	Rudolph Peterson	Longacre/NAT/John Tillinger
SIDE MAN* (*also in London & Kennedy Center*)	Ziggy	Golden & Roundabout/Michael Mayer
BARRYMORE (*with Christopher Plummer*)	Frank	Music Box/Gene Saks
LOVE! VALOUR! COMPASSION!	Buzz/Perry/Arthur	Walter Kerr/Joe Mantello
BEST FOOT FORWARD	Chester	York Theatre & Mufti/Jay Binder
THE WATER CHILDREN	Roger, Jim, et al	Playwrights Horizons/David Petrarca
ALONE BUT NOT LONELY (*by Warren Leight*)	Tom	Naked Angels/Gary Winick
ESCAPE FROM HAPPINESS	Stevie	Naked Angels/Joe Brancato
HOT KEYS	Link Rosado	Naked Angels/Jeff Weiss

REGIONAL THEATER

THE PILLOWMAN	Michael	George Street Playhouse/Will Frears
GUYS AND DOLLS	Nathan Detroit	Papermill Playhouse/Stafford Arima
TAMING OF THE SHREW	Hortensio	Old Globe Theatre/John Rando
PICASSO AT THE LAPIN AGILE	Freddy	Chautauqua Theatre Co./Mark Nelson
INSPECTING CAROL	Phil	George Street Playhouse/David Saint
THE DINNER PARTY (*remount of B'way prod.*)	Albert	Coconut Grove & Papermill/John Rando
BUFFALO GAL (*World Premiere by A.R. Gurney*)	Roy	Williamstown Thtr. Fest./John Tillinger
A TUNA CHRISTMAS	Arles, et al	Capitol Rep/Michael Scheman
THE SUBSTANCE OF FIRE	Martin	Coconut Grove/Tony Giorano

Helen Hayes Award Nominee
Member of **Naked Angels** and **Circle East**

EDUCATION

NYU | Tisch School of the Arts

Kevin Kemperer

Age Range 20 – 40++
Type: Leading Man
Vocal: Baritone
Hair: Brown
Teeth: Removable

Actor/Singer/Dancer/
Comedian/Poet/Athlete

Height: 5' 11 1/2"
Weight: 250
Shoe: 12
Eyes: Luscious
Brown
SS: 144-278-1809

H: 973-555-1212 / C: 201-555-1212
84 Essex Street, # 405-D, Montclair, NJ 07042

Experience:

WROTE, PRODUCED, DIRECTED AND PLAYED A ROLE IN "PATH PLOTTER"
WROTE, PRODUCED, DIRECTED AND STARRED IN "MY LIFE SUCKS"
WROTE, PRODUCED AND DIRECTED "THE SOBBING SIBBLINGS"

PLAYS:

PLAY	ROLE(S)	THEATRE
PATH PLOTTER	JUDAS ISCARIOT	STUDIO SCENES, INC.
MY LIFE SUCKS	MYSELF	THEATER 12
"	"	PARK PLAYERS
DEATH OF A SALESMAN	WILLY (THE SALESMAN)	GENISUS PRODS.
ROMEO & JULIET	ROMEO (LEAD)	PS SHAKESPEARE
OUR TOWN		GENISUS PRODS.
THE FOREIGNER	ELLARD (THE DUMB ONE)	PARK PLAYERS
CAT ON A HOT TIN ROOF	BIG DADDY	THEATRE 12

MUSICALS:

MUSCIAL	ROLE(S)	THEATRE
FIDDLER ON THE ROOF	MOTEL (THE TAILOR)	LUNCH BOX D.T
THE SOUND OF MUSIC	ROLF (THE CUTE NAZI)	LUNCH BOX D.T
PHANTOM!	THE PHANTOM (LEAD)	LUNCH BOX D.T
PIRATES OF PENZANCE	FEATURED PIRATE W/PARROT	Beaver Playhouse
FOOTLOOSE	STUDENT /PRINCIPAL	Beaver Playhouse
VARIOUS CHILDREN'S MUSICALS	FEATURED ROLES	OHIO PLAYHOUSE

FILM/TELEVISION:

TITLE	ROLE(S)	DIRECTOR
SEX & CIGARS	FEATURED AS A SUBWAY STREET PERSON PASSERBY AS A OFFICE WORKER ON THE WAY TO WORK.	DIRK BERMANN
SEX IN THE CITY	PLAYED A CHURCH CASUAL PASSERBY AND GOER	HBO
STOMACH	CROWDED BAR PATRON	LINA LAMONT
STARTERS	A BIKER (LEAD)	RUSSELL NEY

SPECIAL SKILLS:
Driver's license, Reading, Odd noises, Tarot cards, Bartend, Penn State Fanatic, Able to sing hanging upside down, Can sing underwater, Naturally curly hair, Drag Queen outfit available, Great wardrobe, Chess, Explosive Film Noir Dangerous, Avid moviegoer, Life of the party.

Ⓢ Age range and physical statistics other than height, weight, and vocal range.

Ⓢ Include home address and social security number. Resumes have been discarded in public places and the actor's personal information exploited.

Ⓢ Multiple, mixed-matched fonts.

Ⓢ Color paper.

Ⓢ Paper with theatrical clip art. (You're an actor. We got the message by your having a résumé.)

Ⓢ Include fictitious credits to bolster a thin résumé. Lies are easily detected.

Ⓢ Make us guess what you did on a project by listing the project but not what you did. Contrary to popular belief, casting directors are not omnipresent.

Ⓢ Inflate extra work by assigning character names and descriptions.

Ⓢ List special skills that are not relevant to skills asked of actors.

Résumé Salvage Yard

Poorly formatted résumés can be salvaged. Prune objectively. Discard outdated credits, questionable skills, and extraneous education achievements so that résumé content is orderly and can be easily read. Every résumé has the potential to attract the attention of the reader if it is well-formatted to meet industry standards.

Bad résumés happen to good actors. While writing this book, I came across the résumé of John Hedges, an actor I've known for many years and have directed. John is an extraordinary chameleon of character, a phenomenal storyteller on- and offstage. His communication skills are exquisite. Knowing that John was once a theater administrator and possessed organizational skills that make my Virgo anal-retentiveness appear amateur, I asked him if I could use his acting résumé as a well-formatted, detailed, free-of-clutter example. John promptly sent it to me via e-mail. When I received it, my first reaction was, "What the fuck?! You've got to be kidding me! This is a mess!" Did this curriculum vitae travesty come from the same man who in rehearsals carries a note pad and paper and fastidiously scribbles down of all given direction? This résumé had to be a joke.

When I called John, I was cautious. No, I was more like a stuttering fool because I respect him tremendously. I wanted to be tactful. I couldn't tell him that his résumé was . . . well . . . "It looks like shit, John," I blurted out. So much for tact. To his credit, John was very professional and in his customary calm tone, similar to a priest reciting prayer during communion, he softly replied, "Oh. Well how can it be fixed? Do you have any suggestions?" John's a class act. I asked him if he wouldn't mind my taking a weed wacker to his résumé. I cut out the clutter and made important information, lost within the thicket of tight type, more prominent. And would he mind it being displayed, in public, as an example of what not to do? John immediately replied, "Absolutely." He stated that if his résumé blunder could assist other actors, he would be delighted to be publicly humiliated. That's just how John is: ready to assist others even if it means sacrificing pride. This industry needs more John Hedges.

Before . . .

JOHN HEDGES
AEA

(555) 555-1212
jhedges@ ****.***

5' 11" 167 lbs
brown hair/eyes

NEW YORK

Out on Hooks, Chris (world premiere)	Theatre Row Theatre
The Tempest, Alonso	New York Theatre Ensemble
Caffeine, Mr. K (new musical)	Stewart Lane Workshop
Judy Garland Live!, Guest Star	Don t Tell Mama
Peer Gynt, Ensemble	Open Gate Theatre
The Changeling, Jasperino	The Manhattan Ensemble
Freedom Train, Overseer	Town Hall/Promenade Theatre
Wheelchair Willie, Joseph (world premiere)	Actors Outlet Theatre Center
The Homecoming, Adam Brant	South Street Theatre Company

LORT/REGIONAL

The Scarlet Pimpernel, Chauvelin (directed by Paul Russell)	Barter Theatre*	
1776, John Adams (directed by Evalyn Baron)	Barter Theatre	
Macbeth, Title Role (directed by Richard Rose)	Barter Theatre	
The Importance of Being Earnest, Jack Worthing	Barter Theatre	
A Christmas Carol, Ebenezer Scrooge	Barter Theatre	
Sleuth, Andrew Wyke (directed by John Hardy)	Barter Theatre	
Miracle on 34th Street, Kris Kringle	Barter Theatre	*Member
Oklahoma, Jud Fry (directed by Evalyn Baron)	Barter Theatre	RESIDENT
To Kill a Mockingbird, Heck Tate	Barter Theatre	ACTING
Falsettos, Marvin (directed by Richard Rose)	Barter Theatre	COMPANY
The Second Mrs. Wilson, Henry Cabot Lodge (world premiere)	Barter Theatre	10 Seasons
A Midsummer Night's Dream, Oberon	Barter Theatre	(Selected Credits)
The Grapes of Wrath, Jim Casy	Barter Theatre	
Dracula, Mr. Renfield (directed by Richard Rose)	Barter Theatre	
The Foreigner, Charlie Baker (directed John Hardy)	Barter Theatre	
Eleanor: An American Love Story, Teddy Roosevelt	Barter Theatre	
My Fair Lady, Alfred P. Doolittle	Barter Theatre	
Perfect Wedding, Bill (directed by Tom Celli)	Barter Theatre	
Big Love, Nikos (reading/directed by Jon Jory)	Actors Theatre of Louisville	
An Interview, Attendant (workshop)	Actors Theatre of Louisville	
The Failure to Zigzag, Reporter (world premiere)	Indiana Repertory Theatre	
Oedipus at the Holy Place, Guard (directed by Tom Haas)	Indiana Repertory Theatre	
The Cherry Orchard, Stranger (with Olympia Dukakis)	American Stage Festival	
Room Service, Simon Jenkins	American Stage Festival	
Working, Ensemble (with Michael Rupert)	American Stage Festival	
The Little Prince, Businessman (with NH Symphony Orchestra)	American Stage Festival	
The Music Man, Harold Hill	Music Theater of Louisville	
The Crucible, John Proctor (directed by David Silberman)	Indiana State University	
Lend Me a Tenor, Max	Indiana State University	
The Snow Queen, King (directed by John Dillon)	Stage One/Louisville	
Romeo & Juliet, Capulet (directed by Moses Goldberg)	Stage One/Louisville	
Henry V, Chorus (directed by Drew Fracher)	Kentucky Shakespeare Festival	
The Two Gentlemen of Verona, Valentine	Kentucky Shakespeare Festival	

TRAINING

Acting:	Sanford Robbins, Robert Taylor, Leslie Reidel (PTTP, University of Delaware) Stephen Strimpell (HB Studio/NYC) Mario Siletti (National Shakespeare Conservatory) Edward Stern (Indiana Repertory Theatre) Gary Stewart (Indiana State University)
Movement:	Jewel Walker (PTTP, University of Delaware) Peter Lobdell, Steve Tague (Suzuki), Nancy Hauser Dance Company (Modern Dance) Claude Kipnis (Mime)
Voice:	Susan Sweeney (PTTP, University of Delaware) Robert Perillo (National Shakespeare) Charlotte Anderson (Alexander Technique) Roy Hart Theatre (PTTP, University of DE)
Singing:	Dominic Guastaferro, Richard Carsey, Winston Clark, Harry Garland, Mark Davis

Certified Actor/Combatant: unarmed, rapier & dagger, broadsword
Special Skills: guitar, juggling, mime, dialects, sports, own hairpieces
Degrees: M.F.A., Stafford University, England

And after.

- ✓ Enlarge the name, thereby giving it more weight and importance.
- ✓ Place the contact information top center.
- ✓ Less is more. Highlight the roles that best define you.
- ✓ Isolate the director names.
- ✓ Isolate roles in a column.
- ✓ Remove roles for which you are no longer age-/type-appropriate.
- ✓ Basic rule of print marketing: Let the eye enjoy white space. Place spacers between each credit.
- ✓ In the training area, place degree(s) first.
- ✓ Single out the teachers whose names and skills are known within the industry.

STATS REMINDER: A résumé attached to a color headshot doesn't require including eye and hair color. A résumé attached to a black-and-white headshot does require hair and eye color in the stats.

Now, if all of what I've laid out for proper formatting of your picture and résumé seems nit-picking and obsessive, well, yes, it is. You'll find no apology from this veteran casting director. In the daily explosion of pusses and production credits I encounter, it's the actors with the well-formatted, attractive, professional, organized, and clean P&Rs, actors who know who they are and whose P&Rs reflect this knowledge, who receive my attention and that of my industry colleagues. Actors who represent themselves well with their business cards are the actors who move forward. What does your business card say about you?

CHAPTER FIVE

COVER LETTERS

Covering Your Assets

"I do try to write a casting director and often the director and/or the artistic director, after an audition, even if I don't get the job. I worked with a director and he had cast a young woman and he was happy he had cast her. And he said, 'You know the thing that surprises me is that she never called and thanked me or wrote and thanked me for that.'"

Darrie Lawrence

Actress

Does an actor need a cover letter when sending a headshot via snail mail? Is New Jersey a toxic nightmare? The answer to the requirement of a cover letter is as obvious as the stench from Chemical Mile along the Jersey Turnpike.

Yes, of course an actor needs a cover letter no matter what type of mail, be it electronic or USPS! The basic protocol for finding work in the entertainment industry is really no different from that followed in the civilian world. Acting is a profession. Treat it as such. The less professional in appearance an actor is, the less likely he or she will be taken seriously. As a reminder, this business is about image, image, and image. If an actor sends out submissions that are less than professional and poor in appearance, then our perception of the image projected by that actor is that he is not serious about his craft. He's perceived as a potential flake. A cover letter is as important as the picture and résumé it accompanies. An actor submission without a cover letter leaves an auditor to ask the following questions:

1. Is this actor submitting for a present project?
2. Is the submission for the files?
3. What is this actor's present and future availability?
4. Is this person lazy? Illiterate? Font phobic? All of the above?

Often my colleagues and I receive only a headshot in a hardcopy mailing, nothing else. No résumé. No cover letter. Just a picture indicating "Hi, I have a picture!" (*Mazel tov for you!*) The trend for submitting a picture with no letter of introduction extends to actor Internet submissions. An actor will send an e-mail with an attached headshot but within the body of the e-mail there's nothing, nada, zip, just an empty white field where there should be some introductory content. Then there is the forwarded electronic submission scenario in which actors forward multiple, previously sent submissions in a single e-mail that, when opened, reveals to its recipient a lengthy history of dates and prior addressees. All that unnecessary information cannot mask the one thing that's missing: a cover letter!

The laziness (or ignorance) goes even further. Marketing-inept actors have initiated a new trend for postal submissions: They hand-scrawl the casting or talent rep's office address on the back of the headshot, attach a stamp, and drop the 8 x 10 in the mail without a résumé or envelope!

To those guilty readers who utilize any of these inappropriate submission tactics as standard form, I say STOP!!!! By sending only a picture without a cover letter, no envelope (in the case of snail mail), or forwards (in the case of electronic submissions), the recipient (remember me?) has no idea what you want, as I place the misguided mailing where it belongs—in the trash. Why so coldhearted? Simple answer. My clients (producers and directors) desire actors with a strong work ethic and healthy sense of self-worth. A weak mailing (hardcopy or electronic) indicates neither of those qualities. Creating a cover letter does not require a PhD in English. What you do need are the following elements: common sense, an understanding of your objective, and access to a computer, spell check, and, in the case of hardcopy submissions, a printer and quality paper. A successful cover letter is professional in appearance, content, and tone. Follow the guidelines listed on pages 90–91 and you will see the response percentage increase; ignore them or avoid cover letters altogether and your submission will have greater potential for going unnoticed.

On the next page is one of many 8 x 10 headshot submissions with no résumé, no cover letter, and no envelope!

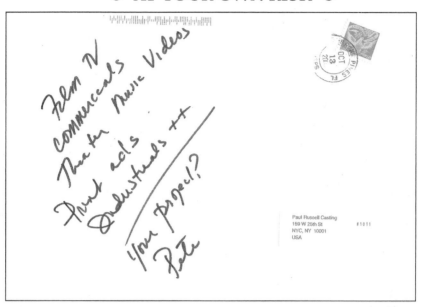

Film TV
commercials
Theater Music Videos
Print ads
Industrials ++

your project?

Pete

Paul Russell Casting
159 W 25th St   #1011
NYC, NY 10001
USA

Pete Traina
S.A.G. / A.F.T.R.A.
6'2"   235 lbs

"Cocked, Locked & Ready To Rock"
"I Am Always Ready For Action"
"Have Passport Will Travel"

COVER LETTER BASICS: HARDCOPY SUBMISSIONS

✓ Print on quality, white or ivory, heavy-bond paper; paper quality reflects an actor's self-image. If you think well of yourself, you'll use quality tools to market yourself well. Think poorly of yourself (or be clueless), and your mailings will then reflect the same.

✓ Follow business format (see the example).

✓ Use clean, easy-to-read letterhead containing your name, contact information, and unions.

✓ Present content that is brief and precise. Limit the letter to one or two short paragraphs, three to four sentences per paragraph.

NAME-DROPPING: "KEVIN SPACEY SUGGESTED . . . "

Another basic to a cover letter, hardcopy or electronic, that gains attention of the reader . . . what is it? Name-dropping: the insertion of named references to people or producing entities that you and the reader know on a personal and/or professional level. Name-dropping is also the inclusion of a *well-known* person (actor, director, writer, teacher) or producing entity with whom you have closely worked.

Why name-drop? It's not to impress alone; it's also an instant recommendation reference for the reader. There's a myth/joke in entertainment that there are only six people working within the industry. Of course the field is more populated than that, but it *is* very insular. Your network of work associates and industry friends will continually cross into those of others within the industry. Exploit this insularity by name-dropping.

When to Name-Drop

✓ Name-drop within the first sentence, preferably the first two words after the salutation. Example: "Kevin Spacey, who produced *Cobb*, in which I appeared, suggested I contact you in regard to . . . "

✓ When the name-drop is associated with the project of interest *and* you have an established, healthy working relationship or personal acquaintance with the name-drop.

✓ When the name-drop knows you well and the person to whom you're writing.

✓ When the name-drop is a household or industry name, reachable for a reference.

When Not to Name-Drop

⊘ When the name-drop's reputation and/or professional and/or personal behavior is questionable.

⊘ When the name-drop is not recognizable to the reader(s) of your cover letter.

⊘ When the name-drop doesn't know you exist.

Matching the Name-Drop to Your Readership and Career Level

When name-dropping, you needn't refer to a celebrity like Paris Hilton (*God, help us*) or a famous producing entity. Name-drops can be used at any level of a career. If your work is primarily summer stock, and you want to broaden your summer stock/regional theater experience, send cover letters to other summer stock and regional theaters using recognizable name-drops you and your target reader know and worked with in the summer stock/regional circuit. If your work has led you into studio and independent feature film and you want to expand your film résumé, send cover letters with recognizable film name-drops to film casting decision makers. These guidelines for matching your reader to a name-drop can be used for every entertainment career medium and level.

Name-Drop Alienation

Cover letter name-drops from a higher level of visibility (e.g., Disney, Sam Mendes, Tom Hanks) presented to a lower level (summer stock, student film) can alienate and turn off the recipient. This happens for two reasons. The first is when the recipient assumes that since you're associated with a highly visible name-drop, you're going to cost more (salary) and demand quality perks (better accommodations and travel). The best way to counter that scenario is to make clear in your cover letter that your priority is to be a working actor, not an actor of luxury.

The second scenario and less common reason for alienation is insecurity—the recipient's not yours. Some producers, directors, and casting decision-makers let their insecurities prejudice them into hiring an artist associated with name-drops of a higher visibility. I've witnessed this happen. The best way to deal with it is to move on and seek out confident people who are open to working with talent, not status.

COVER LETTER EXAMPLES: HARDCOPY

We all have our own style of writing, expressing ourselves in font. Creativity is wonderful as long as it doesn't get in the way of the message. Yes, we are in a creative business, but remember that when writing an introductory letter as an actor to creative decision-makers within our business, business trumps creativity.

What follows are examples of hardcopy cover letters for an individual; specific recipient; mass-mailing examples; and salvageable cover letters. In Chapter 6 we'll examine electronic cover letters. The first hardcopy example (fictitious) is a direct, to-the-point, proper, one-on-one cover letter. The second cover letter (also fictitious) resembles the many rambling missives we in casting and talent representation receive. It's not an example one should follow.

Recommended Cover Letter Example for Hardcopy Mailings

✓ Always, **ALWAYS** include a typed cover letter. Entertainment is a business; treat it as such.
 	
✓ Use professional-grade stationery.
 	
✓ Create a clean, crisp, professional-looking letterhead that includes your full address, phone contact, e-mail, website, and union affiliation(s). Contact information can be used in the footer or to the left side to avoid clutter and a top-heavy letterhead.
 	
✓ Name-drop within the first sentence.
 	
✓ Keep content brief, to the point, and professional. Casting directors (and agents) receive up to 75 pieces of mail per day. *We scan.* We don't read. With content, think sound bites, not *War and Peace.* Think laser-guided missiles, not carpet-bombing. Quick, to the point, with impact.
 	
✓ List projects, training, and/or background that are relevant to the project for which you want an audition appointment. (Including your high school rowing team record would not be relevant if seeking an audition for the musical *Titanic.*)
	John Carter Paulson
	AEA - SAG - AFTRA
	
	49 Oak Street
	             January 1, 2008
	Nyack, NY 10960
	
	845-555-1212 Mr. Paul Russell
	                      Paul Russell Casting
	JohnCPaulson.com 38 West 38th Street
	JCP@mymail.com Second Floor
	                      New York, NY 10018
	
	RE: Nebraska Shakespeare Festival
	
	Dear Paul,
	
	      Rick Rose, Artistic Director of the Barter Theatre, suggested I contact you in regard to the upcoming casting for the Nebraska Shakespeare Festival. I am currently playing the young lover, Florizel, in *The Winter's Tale* at the Barter Theatre and would love the opportunity to audition for you in February. I thank you for your time and hope to hear from you soon.
	
	Sincerely,
	
	John Carter Paulson
	
	John Carter Paulson
	
	Enclosure

DALE F. JONES

Dear Sir / Madame:

New York City! The hustle and bustle of the world's greatest city. Dreamers dream. Manhattan skyscrapers and penthouses. Brownstones and coffeehouses. Hello 42nd Street! How I dream of this city! The pie in the sky! Maybe slicing off a piece for myself, or maybe just part of the crust, or maybe just a crumb or maybe… whew! I've been caught up in my own personal hurricane! Returning from a trip to Los Angeles one Sunday night, I picked up * 82 * e-mails on one of my several Internet accounts.

That Tuesday a playwright/director friend of mine called me at 5:00 p.m. He had an emergency. His show was opening in TWO DAYS and an actress needed to be replaced. His adolescent son was seriously ill. There was a rehearsal at 7:00 p.m. that night, and could I step in immediately? I attended two rehearsals and held a book for the first weekend of the run. By the next weekend, I had my lines <u>memorized</u>. Yeah!! Fortunately the play takes place on a sex phone line, so it didn't matter what type I was! Enclosed is a flyer for the show even though the show is over and was in LA but the cast was very sweet.

Oh and did I mention that while I was learning my lines, my cat, Boo-Boo got a cold and I had to not only learn my lines but deal with the veterinarian and Boo-Boo at the same time?

Ooops! I don't have time to tell you about all the fun I had appearing as an Elf in the MACY*S Thanksgiving Day Parade. If you were watching, I was the Elf with the red nose, green ears and stripped shoes. I danced a hoe down, down Broadway! (I have this on my reel). Hope you're staying busy! I am!

Regards.

⊘ No cover letter.

⊘ Dear Sir/Madame form letters.

⊘ Clip art.

⊘ Any kind of paper that is not standard business letter paper, such as stationary from your civilian job, pastel paper, or picture paper with a sunrise / sunset ("on slow days, I spend hours guessing which way the sun is going").

⊘ Long, rambling autobiographies that inflict such tedious pain upon the reader that suicide seems a promising alternative.

⊘ Personal stories about pets, exes, or highlighting the acting achievements accrued at summer camp.

MAKING MASS MAILINGS PERSONAL WITH A SINGLE COVER LETTER

Ok, so you want to announce your latest endeavors to several hundred producers, casting directors, talent reps, and other artistic power players who can assist you in pushing your career forward. How do you do that without writing a stale, impersonal "Dear Sir/Madam" dispatch? Type and print hundreds of individual, personally addressed letters? God, no! Your computer holds the solution.

Technology is your personal assistant. Within every computer, no matter if it's a PC or Mac, there is factory-installed software for creating hundreds of personal letters with just one click of the print icon. What's the miracle program? A database. For the technologically challenged, a database is a program in which the user (you) compiles data (names, addresses) and then later inserts the stored information into any document, such as a cover letter. Use of a database for cover letters may seem oh-so obvious, but I'm still amazed by the overwhelming number of photocopied "Dear Sir/Madam" missives I receive.

So how does a database help an actor create hundreds of multiple "personal" letters at once? With each database program there are "fields." In these fields the user enters the information to be printed for each individual letter. You can have as many fields as your creative wordsmith heart desires. What follows are the primary category fields you'll want to create for your personal mass mailings. You can title the fields however you wish for your own purposes. The titles I give in the examples are what I use when creating a database for my mass mailings:

- **Field One, "Name"**: Recipient's full name, including the Mr., Ms. (for addressing women in entertainment, Ms. is the standard address)
- **Field Two, "Title"**: Recipient's job title, such as Artistic Director, Executive Producer, and Casting Director. When sending to agents, no need to put the job title "agent" after their name—it reads silly.
- **Field Three, "Company"**: Full name of recipient's company or producing entity.
- **Field Four, "Address 1"**: Street address, such as "10086 Sunset Boulevard."
- **Field Five, "Address 2"**: Secondary address, such as office or suite number. This fifth field is handy for when the address is at a studio lot, includes a building number, or is a college. Colleges (many have professional theaters) and studios have addresses that are near novella in length. In case you come across a casting contact with an address with more than four lines, add an "Address 2a" field to your database.
- **Field Six, "Address 3"**: Town, city, state, and zip code. To make your mail move faster, always include the recipient's full zip code plus four (e.g., 07042-0011).
- **Field Seven, "Salutation"**: First name of the recipient.
- **Field Eight, "Company Abbreviated"**: Shortened, informal name of recipient's company or producing entity. For example, reduce "Guthrie Theatre" to "Guthrie." As you'll see in the following personal mass-mailing example, this further helps to disguise your mass-mail marketing as individually addressed letters.

Putting Information in the Fields

Once you have created all the necessary fields, the next step is to enter the relevant information into each field. So if you have 150 people you wish to write to, time to start placing their information into the fields. It's time-consuming, but once you have the information in a database, you can use it again and again for future mailings.

Multiple Cover Letter Topics and Targets

A single database can be used for different letters. Actors must have cover letters/mailings for announcements of activity, film projects, theatrical projects, and general "keeping in touch for your files." All of these specific cover letters can be attached to various target audience databases (film, television, theatrical, and talent rep readerships). As someone who works as a director, casting director, and instructor, I have multiple mass-mailing "personal form letters" for my job search that relate to each of my vocations within my career. My snail-mail marketing attack to potential employers is similar to the direct mail marketing assaults we all receive from credit card companies that address us personally. An actor must do the same to be competitive.

Creating the "Personal" Form Letter with a Database

Next step is the letter. Time to get down to business and tell the entertainment world what you desire with a one-on-one approach conveyed in a mass announcement masked by sleight-of-keystroke trickery. Your cover letter to the masses should contain the basics as outlined earlier in this chapter but with one major difference. In the content of the letter, you'll be inserting the fields from your database. For your fields to print with each letter, make sure that you have the preferred database attached to the document. If you don't know how to do this, click on the Help button of your word-processing program and enter "Document with database" or "Setting up a database" into the search box. You'll get a step-by-step guide to creating a document with database fields.

To simplify the explanation of field insertion, what follows is a past cover letter once used as part of my outreach for seeking new clients.

Mass-Mailing Cover Letter with Fields

Prior to printing . . .

PAUL RUSSELL CASTING
FILM ◆ TELEVISION ◆ THEATER

38 · W. 38th Street · Second Floor · NYC 10018

www.PaulRussell.net
212-555-1212

January 1, 2008

«Name»
«Title»
«Company»
«Address 1»
«Address 2»
«Address2a»
«Address3»

Dear **«Salutation»**:

I've had the fortune of working alongside award-winning stage and film directors including Josephine Abady, Michael Mayer, Ed Zwick, and Glenn Gordon Caron plus serving the Ensemble Studio Theatre, Asolo Theatre Conservatory, Barter Theater, 20th Century Fox, and Kevin Spacey's presentation of *COBB*, for which my contribution was recognized by a Special Drama Desk Award. I would be flattered to be considered to serve **«Company Abbreviated»** casting needs in the near future.

Enclosed is an updated resume. Supportive information can be accessed via my website: PaulRussell.net.

I look forward to your thoughts on my potential to serve **«Company Abbreviated»**.

My Best,

✓ In many document page set-ups, you'll have the option to check an instruction similar to "don't print empty address fields." If your program has this feature, mark it. There may be some recipients for which all fields are not used (e.g., the additional address fields). When set up properly, your printer will not print these fields.

If your program does not include this option, print a test document in which a field is not to be printed.

✓ Postdate your letter to a date one or two days prior to expected delivery. This will give the appearance that your letter was written for the individual, not the masses.

✓ Have additional address fields for addresses that include building numbers and/or departments.

✓ Place the salutation field (the first name of the recipient) after your greeting.

✓ In the body of the letter, reference at least once the name of the company, studio, or theater. This will make the letter appear as if you wrote it specifically for the recipient. (The more personal in approach, the better.)

✓ Leave an area for signing your name.

Mass-Mailing Cover Letter with Printed Fields

. . . and print!

PAUL RUSSELL CASTING
FILM ◆ TELEVISION ◆ THEATER

38 W. 38th Street · Second Floor · NYC 10018
www.PaulRussell.net
212-555-1212

January 1, 2008

Ms. Abigail Adams
Artistic Director
The People's Light and Theatre Company
39 Conestoga Road
Malvern, PA 19355-1798

Dear Abigail:

I've had the fortune of working alongside award-winning stage and film directors including Josephine Abady, Michael Mayer, Ed Zwick, and Glenn Gordon Caron plus serving the Ensemble Studio Theatre, Asolo Theatre Conservatory, Barter Theater, 20th Century Fox, and Kevin Spacey's presentation of *COBB*, for which my contribution was recognized by a Special Drama Desk Award. I would be flattered to be considered to serve People's Light and Theatre's casting needs in the near future.

Enclosed is an updated resume. Supportive information can be accessed via my website: PaulRussell.net.

I look forward to your thoughts on my potential to serve People's Light and Theatre.

My Best,

✓ In entertainment, formality with informality is the rule. The recipient, in the address. is due all respect that comes with his/her position. So don't forget to use the Mr. or Ms. But the greeting is informal, using the recipient's first name. There was a time when this was considered a major social faux pas, but societal manners have tilted toward the informal, especially in entertainment.

✓ Have informality carry over in the signature by signing your first name only. This makes you appear approachable and friendly. I prefer to sign my letters with a blue felt-tip pen that matches my letterhead color. The felt-tip pen is thicker than a regular pen and adds weight (i.e., importance) to the signature.

COVER LETTER SALVAGE YARD

Not every cover letter is destined to be beyond redemption. Some gaffes can be corrected with a bit of focus and common sense. In the cover letter salvage yard we look at two fictitious cover letters, both representative of cover letters I've received. With before and after perspectives, see how each writer could have been better at presenting his message to the reader.

Before . . .

Dominick Romerio
888 West 43rd St., #34
New York, New York 10036
212-555-5555

Dear
Sir/Madam
(not at all
personal).

Dear Sir or Madam;

Hard to read
font.

I am a born-and-raised Hell's Kitchener who is 21 years of age. I am Irish and Italian but look more like a Westie.

I am writing to you with hopes that one day, you will consider me for an interview. I am sure I would get work.

Humor that
may, in
person, be
light-hearted,
but in fact
reads as
extreme
negativity

My training consists of HB Studios (which everyone and their mothers went to), Acteen, (which was a big mistake) And the world renowned American Academy of Dramatic Arts ("World Renowned" my ass!!!)

But seriously, I am a dedicated actor who just needs to work. And please do consider me for a job.

Need a pen or
just too lazy to
include a
signature?

Thank you...

DOMINICK ROMERIO

888 West 43rd Street • Apt. No. 34 • New York, NY 10036
212.555.1212

January 1, 2008

Mr. Paul Russell
Paul Russell Casting
38 West 38th Street
Second Floor
New York, NY 10018

RE: General Submission - Actor

Dear Paul:

My considerable training includes the American Academy of Dramatic Arts, HB Studios, and Acteen. As a dedicated working actor always wishing to expand my abilities I look forward to new professional opportunities that your office offers. An Irish Italian, born-and-raised "Hell's Kitchener," I am in close proximity of your office and look forward to our meeting at your earliest convenience.

Thanking you in advance,

Dominick Romerio

Enclosure.

✓ Simple, clean letterhead created with a basic graphic or document program.

✓ Standard business format. Gone is the lazy and impersonal, "Dear Sir or Madam" address.

✓ Easy-to-read font.

✓ Name-drop (three) within the first sentence.

✓ Positive content.

✓ Spacing between the lines (sentences) makes for easier reading by the recipient.

✓ Signature.

✓ Enclosure included.

Before . . .

TYLER NEY
AEA / SAG

September 17, 2008

Paul Russell
Paul Russell Casting
38 West 38th Street
Second Floor
New York, NY 10018

Dear Paul,

It's been a good summer (I returned from the Old Vic in London, where I performed in *Hamlet*—in time to do a workshop of *The Seagull* with the Sparrow Theater here in New York, which will lead to a full production to be mounted in 2003, at a space TBA), and the coming months are looking even busier. Next week I'm heading off to New Stages in Washington, D.C., for a three-week run in September of *The Man in the Glass Bottle*, the one-man show I won the OBIE for in 2001. Then, in November, the show will move on to another three-week run at the Actor's Repertory Theater in Chicago.

In between the two runs of *Glass Bottle*, I will be appearing in the East Coast premiere of *Urn*—a new play by Alberta Smythe, which I'm very excited about. It's a farce with a great cast. *Urn* will perform at IRT (where *Purple Squirrel* just vacated) and promises to be a great event—stay tuned for further updates.

On top of all of this, Beach Four Films is planning to release *Shames*—a feature film that I star in, produced by Simon Geddes—nationwide. Needless to say, I'm looking forward to a hectic fall.

I've enclosed an updated résumé, for your files. I hope the summer treated you well and that the coming autumn will be fruitful

Sincerely,

164 WEST 25th STREET #8 • NEW YORK, NY 10018
PHONE: 917-555-1212

Important information is lost within the clutter.

Dates???

Industry Comps. available?

How can I see your work if I don't know when the performances are? Plus no indication if I, as industry, must pay out of pocket or be offered customary industry comps to see your work.

TYLER NEY

AEA/SAG

September 17, 2008

Mr. Paul Russell
Paul Russell Casting
38 West 38th Street
Second Floor
New York, NY 10018

RE: Beach Four Film Release & *The Man in the Glass Bottle*

Dear Paul,

In 2001 I won an **OBIE** for my one-man show, *The Man in the Glass Bottle*. **New Stages** in Washington, D.C., and the **Actor's Repertory Theater** in Chicago have invited me to perform *The Man in the Glass Bottle* during the early fall. Also this fall, **Beach Four Films** is releasing, nationwide, *Shames*--a feature film that I star in--produced by **Simon Geddes**.

In between my appearances at New Stages and A.R.T., Chicago, I return to New York as part of the East Coast premiere of *Urn* by **Alberta Smythe**. *Urn* will be presented at the **Sparrow Theater** August 10–21. Industry comps to attend *Urn* are available for you and a guest by calling the number below. I look forward to meeting you in the near future and wish you success on your upcoming projects this fall.

Sincerely,

Tyler Ney

Enclosure.

164 WEST 25th STREET • #8 • NEW YORK, NY 10018
PHONE: 917-555-1212

The picture, résumé, and cover letter are several of the tools necessary to an actor's marketing campaign. Having these instruments of self-promotion organized, well-formatted, and professional in tone is only the beginning. How the actor utilizes these tools is equally important. The next step to being a better, professional working actor is to brand and market yourself effectively using technology old and new in union with your photo, credits, and creative introductory copy. Do you as an actor have an effective marketing campaign or strategy? Are you an efficient, aggressive promoter of yourself? Move on to the next chapter on actor marketing and discover the answer.

CHAPTER SIX

ACTOR MARKETING

Set Yourself Apart from the Crowd

*"Marketing yourself never stops. That's the thing about this business—
it's a hustler's paradise. Promoting yourself never stops."*

Mark Price

Actor

Truth: Actors are merchandise, product. Actors are no different than boxes of macaroni and cheese on grocery store shelves, sitting alongside other mac and cheese brands, except actors have respiratory systems and ... OK ... feelings, and all that other human emotional baggage. What will set one actor apart from another actor in their employment search? Brand. Image. Marketing. Talent alone will not propel a career forward unless the actor is very, very lucky.

Take the "show" out of show business and what are you left with? Business. Business is about making money. In business, successful craftsmanship of image, branding, and marketing strategies are rewarded by excellent commerce. To succeed, actors must, like a business, create a brand, build a strong image, and market and package themselves well to the consumer—i.e., the industry.

When you as an actor send out marketing materials, the tone of your written voice in the cover letter, the look of both your letterhead and résumé, and the design of your website should all be unified in appearance. They should accurately represent you and the roles that, within your present age range and physical type, you can play believably. That look and tone is your brand. That brand instantly gives us insight into who you are and how you view yourself.

Your brand defines who you are as an actor. It grows out of your self-awareness and an objective vision of what your talents offer to those who buy—the buyers being both audience and casting decision-makers. Not only must your brand reflect the roles for which you are suited but also it must express those characteristics that are inherent in your personality. To stand out among the competition you must define who you are and what you can offer. You must define your brand. When you as an actor market yourself well, and properly, notice by casting personnel and opportunities for employment are the reward.

THE GROUP OF EIGHT ON SUCCESSFUL MARKETING

I asked each of the Group of Eight the question, "What marketing or outreach worked best for you in getting an audition?" With each journey, the replies for the paths taken were, of course, varied. Changing attitudes and technologies have greatly affected the forms of outreach. James Rebhorn spoke of a time when access to the decision-makers in casting was more open:

"When I started you could make cold calls, you could slip your picture under the door, knock on the door, and follow up with a phone call, and you might have even gotten a response. That doesn't happen nearly as much now," Rebhorn recalled, with a touch of melancholy. "Also back then there was a considerably more vibrant Off-Off Broadway community. There were a lot of shows going on, and there still are, but now it's become more 'professionalized.' Now submissions are taken for Off-Off Broadway. Back then you could get the jobs through *Back Stage*. If you wanted to, you could audition for something bizarre every day and people would occasionally see these shows, and it was a way to build a résumé that was professional as opposed to community theater and college credits. I think in a way there were more opportunities to get exposed based upon your own initiative back then than there are now. You need a lot more help, I think, now, to get going."

I understood the change Rebhorn spoke of and made mention to him that today there were many more gatekeepers between actors and those who made final decisions in casting. He agreed. Robert LuPone suggested that to counter this trend, the actor should get closer to the people making decisions, through personal contact.

"This is a people business," LuPone emphatically stated. "Go to where the young directors are hanging out. Where are they? Go to readings. Go to the nonprofits, intern in theaters." LuPone also suggested targeting the gatekeepers themselves by joining them. "Intern in casting directors' offices. Know casting people."

But LuPone cautioned actors to be open and honest on intent as to why they're getting closer to the casting decision-makers. "You can tell when an actor is really genuine and when an actor is bullshit," LuPone candidly offered. "I had a benefit recently and an actor came up to me and I said, 'You're an actor?' and he said, 'Yeah and you're an actor, too?'" LuPone then described how the actor didn't see LuPone as a person but sought LuPone as an opportunity for career advancement. LuPone dismissed the encounter as an instant "turnoff." He went on: "We're professionals. The people who are aspiring to be a part of the business have to get that the people they're going to be a part of are very smart if they're still surviving."

Darrie Lawrence advocates one-on-one, sincere contact as a successful marketing tool. "For me it was more about meeting people than doing concentrated mailings of a picture and résumé to every casting office around," Lawrence recalled of her journey. She does, on occasion, use pen, paper, and stamp as part of her post-audition marketing campaign. "I have been good about following up with people I have met at auditions; writing a thank-you note, or sending a postcard and telling them I'm doing something. At one audition I wrote back a thank you right away and then eventually I was hired to do the job. When the job came they said, 'Well, we thought it was really neat that you wrote to us and we thought about you again and decided we wanted you to join us.'" Sometimes the pen is mightier than the audition.

Michael Mastro is a firm believer of fronting himself through font. "I will write letters—" Mastro then admitted to pushing himself beyond letter writing "—and phone casting directors." Many in casting abhor when an actor calls them. It's a verboten practice unless you, the actor, know the casting person beyond the audition room or together you two have a solid professional relationship history.

Mastro doesn't limit his push pursuit with calls to casting directors. He's got larger cojones than most actors when it comes to selling himself to the industry. "I will call producers' offices to get information about what I need to know. If I don't know when an audition is happening I will do whatever I have to do to find out. I will contact directors. I will contact producers. I ask myself, 'What's the worst thing that can happen?' I've grown some hair on my balls; I've gotten a little more courage because I've dared to practice putting myself in the arena with those people simply by contacting them."

Mastro also believes that for actors to be effective as businesspeople, they must create their own actor business offices. "I think it's really important for an actor to have a place in their apartment that is their office," Mastro instructed. "It's really important to have office hours. Whether it's two hours in the morning or whatever . . . sit down for two hours and do something to promote your career . . . researching for new avenues of work."

Networking: Marketing Through Those You Know

The best form of marketing is the oldest: networking—i.e., getting work by word of mouth through friends and associates. Networking is the strongest tool for an actor. Actors get most of their jobs not through formal auditions before strangers and passing acquaintances but through friends and past work associates. An actor must always be building sincere relationships with those with whom they work and train. Relationships formed from their earliest days in training to the low-rent jobs of summer stock, readings, workshops, and student and independent films to the high-profile projects of Broadway, major studio releases, ad campaigns, and broadcast programming.

James Rebhorn and Mark Price of the Group of Eight offered their insights into how networking has greatly benefited their careers. Long before Rebhorn and Price both had agents, their outreach for employment wasn't a blitz of headshots sent to strangers. Their opportunities for work were founded upon the forging of relationships with people they knew from training and past work experience and from friends who also were in entertainment.

I asked both Rebhorn and Price how they got jobs prior to their having an agent. Reborn unabashedly responded, "Mostly through friends and through friends of friends. I can trace the beginning of my career through friends. I don't think that's uncommon. People you have met in class and later bump into, those are the ones who are going to give you your very first opportunities."

For Price, the beginning of his career can be traced back, like Rebhorn's journey, to getting job and audition opportunities through contacts he had made earlier in his life. "My first audition experience [in New York] had come from a connection I made as a teenager," Price wistfully recalled. "I had gone to a theater camp started by Ann Reinking. When I first moved to the city she knew that I had just graduated from college and she actually brought me in for an audition for a swing for the Broadway company of *Chicago*, which then led me to my audition for the first national tour of *Chicago*. That was one of my first professional jobs after I moved to the city."

Bonnie Black gave insight into how she exploits her network to her advantage. "If I know someone attached to the project or if they know my work I would try to send them a picture and résumé with a note and tell them I heard about the project and was interested. I would say a huge percentage of the time, people I sent to would call me in. Contact people you know," Black advised. "Or contact people who know your work and are amenable to have you come in for an audition."

Michael Mastro is a strong supporter of networking. "Finding new avenues of work may come from going to cocktail parties with friends or hanging out at Joe Allen's," he advised. "Meeting people, keeping your ear to the ground and finding out what the hell is going on out there." Mastro just doesn't go places, see individuals within his network, and hope happenstance will deliver an opportunity for work. He plots, like a general going to war, finding ways to breach barriers. Mastro explained how he utilizes his network as part of his plan of attack for being seen for a project that interests him. "There are three questions I always ask," he began. Mastro then stressed with deliberate cadence, "'Who do I know? Who else do I know? Who do I know who knows someone who knows?' When I was in L.A., several of the auditions I got, like when I got an episode of *Alias*, I got because I knew someone who knew the casting director."

And it's not just knowing people and forming a network of industry friends and contacts. Mastro also ardently asserts that an actor must ask that network (and strangers as well) for help in obtaining his or her desires. "You have to ask for favors," Mastro believes. "You're a good and generous person, too, and someday you'll return the favor. You'll get nowhere if you don't ask for things. You have to ask for things."

TECHNOLOGY PAST AND PRESENT: CHANGING THE WAY ACTORS DO THE BUSINESS OF FINDING WORK

Technology for communication is rapidly changing. Today's new technology becomes outmoded and ancient within days. The breakneck-speed advancements continually change how actors do the business of selling themselves. E-mail, actor websites, and online video are quickly superseding the old methods actors have used to market themselves—e.g., headshot mailings, flyers, postcards, and sending reels on DVD. Our lives are hyperpaced and our present communication systems, with instant text messaging and telephone contact anywhere, anytime, reflect a need for sending and receiving information instantaneously. To be competitive the actor must exploit the marketing opportunities of the recent past while continually engaging in new forms of technology of the near tomorrow (beta-form media) to sell themselves.

For decades the standard marketing for getting an actor's face in front of casting personnel had been through the mail with a headshot, résumé, and cover letter in a stamped envelope. Yawn. Today sending and receiving information via the two-legged mail carrier is parallel to communicating long distance via smoke signal. Grand letters of introduction on paper have been replaced by abbreviated, broken phrases of font on computer monitors. But the old marketing must not be forgotten as technology pushes actors into new forms of communication.

Despite the increased usage of electronic headshot submissions by actors and their talent representatives to casting offices, hardcopies of pictures and résumés remain a must. Casting directors, directors, and producers insist upon hardcopy pictures and résumés of auditioning actors. Snail mail and messengers remain the delivery systems for hardcopies to the casting offices. Before addressing advancements for actor outreach to casting personnel via electronic transfer, let's take a look at old outreach methods assisted by new technological twists. These should not be overlooked if you wish to remain competitive in the search for work.

New Ways to Break out of the Envelope

There are several "tricks"—with the assist of a computer—to having your headshot snail-mailing opened. I can't ensure your envelope will be opened every time it's sent out, but I can offer basic marketing techniques on how to make your envelope stand out above all others.

Branding Your Name

Branding involves the use of logos and/or monograms on mailing labels and letterhead. Talent agencies often use the agency's initials or last name as their brand—i.e., a logo. When an agency sends submissions via mail or messenger to a casting office, it's in an envelope affixed with an address label, and on the label is the agency brand. Branded mail is given priority and opened first.

Casting directors often give strict instructions to their mail sorters (interns and assistants) as to the rules of engagement for the large volume of incoming mail that daily bombards the casting office. The mail sorters are instructed to first open mail that looks as if it is coming from an agency, studio, or an entertainment-related business or arts organization. This type of mail is often branded. The mail sorters have a desire to please their employer but are often intimidated by the person they want to please. This intimidation leads to doubt and confusion while inspecting envelopes. A confused, intimidated mail filterer is a vulnerability ripe for your marketing-by-mail exploitation.

Using your monogram or last name as a graphic in your return address will assist in making your unsolicited submission look professional while giving the subtle implication that it may be coming from a business, such as a talent rep or a performing arts organization. Creating your own brand can be done simply with a basic graphic or document program. The brand should look crisp, define your personality, and appear professional. Most important is that the brand you create must be created *without deceit*. DO NOT be deceptive by adding "Inc.," "Artists," "Talent Management," or "School," to your brand. Outright fraud and misrepresentation is never tolerated or forgotten. You want to create ambiguity with your brand so that whoever receives your envelope, whether a busy casting director or flustered intern, becomes curious, leading them to open the envelope to discover who it is from.

Branded Return Address Mailing Label Examples

49 Oak Street • Nyack, NY 10960

TO: Paul Russell Casting
Paul Russell
38 West 38th Street
Second Floor
New York, NY 10018

Re: "A Very Brady Musical"

159 West 25th Street
New York, NY 10001

To: Paul Russell Casting
Mr. Paul Russell
38 West 38th Street
Second Floor
New York, NY 10018

RE: Nebraska Shakespeare 2009

Attn: Paul Russell Casting
Paul Russell
38 West 38th Street
Second Floor
New York, NY 10018

Re: "Following Bliss" – Submission

303 Shady Lane • Marlton, NJ 08053

TO: Paul Russell Casting
Paul Russell
38 West 38th Street
Second Floor
New York, NY 10018

RE: "Buzzards"

It's not just creating a brand for your mailing labels and letterhead that will make your mailing stand out from the bland office-supply-store manila envelopes used by the masses. How the label is addressed and the envelope to which it is affixed are of great importance as well. What follows are recommended guidelines to increase the likelihood of your snail-mail submission being opened quicker than the other hundreds of actor headshots.

Envelope and Mailing Label Guidelines

✓ Recommended	VS.	🚫 AT YOUR OWN RISK 🚫
✓ Use a professional-grade white, cream, or gray 9 x 11 envelope. These colors and the size are similar to the envelopes used by talent agencies.	VS.	Use standard manila, pastel, or blinding neon color envelopes. Use envelopes as a canvas to promote your doodle skills (I've seen many a doodled envelope but rarely the contents within). Use envelopes from your civilian job (tacky, tacky, tacky, and it's also thievery). 🚫
✓ Create a professional-looking address/ return label for use in the center of the envelope with the recipient's information typed.	VS.	Freehand, physician-scrawled address and return address. A handwritten address immediately announces your mailing to be an unsolicited headshot. 🚫
✓ ALWAYS put "RE:" (regarding) and the project's name or reference	VS.	Misspell the recipient's name or send a submission to the wrong recipient. (I often get mail addressed to other casting directors but with my street address on the envelope.) 🚫
✓ Seal the envelope ONCE! No additional tape, glue, or staples. Refrain from "pad-locking" your submission with excessive sealant or fasteners. (Life is short, time is valuable, and spending fifteen minutes to open an envelope in lockdown mode annoys the recipient.)	VS.	Secure your envelope like Fort Knox. Use fiber envelopes. (Try opening one with a letter opener and you'll lose an hour of your life.) Use a bubble-wrap envelope for a headshot (it's a headshot, not Waterford crystal). 🚫
✓ Use a single stamp.	VS.	Blanket the envelope with a stamp collection. Have stamped on the envelope "Fragile," "Do Not Bend," or "Handle With Care." Agencies send submissions without those warnings. Even with the warnings, the submission arrives bent and folded. The less crap on the envelope, the more professional it appears. 🚫

The Envelope As a Résumé

I'm revealing my most valued secret for marketing by mail: using the envelope as a "résumé." It's a tool I created for teasing the recipient's interest. Whether it's business-size or large enough for headshots, an envelope has valuable space on the back that goes wasted; but with a bit of creativity that wasted space can be exploited to your advantage.

By using the envelope as space for a résumé, I'm not advising you to print a traditional résumé on it. That's too obvious. You want to generate curiosity, not sell your wares completely before you get the reader inside the envelope. Again, aided by a computer, with a simple graphic program you artistically place your credits in an arrangement on the back of the envelope, creating a background graphic. What follows is an example of this technique for the back of a standard No. 10, business envelope.

```
. 20th Century Fox... COBB... HBO... PER
eatre...    The Rocky Horror Show...   Melting Pot The
hakespeare Festival... Carsey - Werner TV...
AS... Ensemble Studio Theatre... The Lark Theatre
    The Barter Theatre... San Jose Rep. ..
The Sunshine Boys... Asolo Theatre Festival...
```

See-Through and Window Envelopes

Don't use them. A trend began in the late 1990s with actors sending headshots in envelopes that were either all clear or had a large window on the back side so that the picture of the actor could be seen. While the actors using cellophane envelopes might think these would get them immediately seen, they unwittingly provide the recipient with an immediate opportunity to quickly view and dispose of the headshot without investigating further who the actor is! All curiosity is lost and a fast judgment is made based on look alone. With see-through and window envelopes there's no mystery, nothing to discover. With a picture and résumé in an envelope that completely masks the contents, the recipient has to make the investment of opening the envelope and then read the cover letter and résumé—which is exactly what you as a marketer are after.

"Blind Mailings" via Snail Mail

As to the effectiveness of blind mailings, it's a crapshoot. An actor is gambling that:

1. The address of the recipient is current (casting directors, agents, and managers are nomadic).
2. The mailing will be opened.
3. The mailing is viewed by a person of authority and not an intern (interns are often assigned the task of opening actor mailings).
4. The headshot and résumé survive scrutiny and are filed or held for a current or upcoming project.
5. If the headshot is filed, it will be recalled when needed.

If you can afford the cost of blind mailings, mail away. It's proactive. But be warned. Not every casting director or agent handles his or her mail in the same manner. Your mailing may be opened or it may not. There are no entertainment guidelines or guarantees as to how, why, or *if* actor mail is opened or tossed directly into the trash.

Some casting directors open all their mail, while others let the mail pile up and then after three or four months toss it all into the trash. There was one New York casting office that was very guilty of this practice. I should know—I once was the casting intern who was routinely ordered to heave-ho mountains of unopened actor mailings into the dumpster. I doubt this office has changed practice.

Having my own office, I will not toss out blind mailings for several reasons. First, I never know if what is in the envelope may match a project I'm currently working on or may soon be working on. Second, I appreciate the time and cost an actor has spent to send the mailing. Third, Karma. I'm sending out mail to market myself as well, and I would want someone to open my envelope.

Snail-Mail Headshot and Résumé Frequency

Send a headshot only when you're relevant to a project or if you've got something new to say. One of each, please. I often get mailings from actors who send five to seven of the same headshot in one mailing! It happens daily! Why? I have my suspicions, but I'll refrain from commenting about insecure actors. This kind of buckshot, multiple-headshot explosion in a single mailing drives me nuts. Am I to paper my walls or wrap holiday gifts with the extras? When I receive more than one headshot, if I save one, the rest go into the trash. That's a hefty amount of money spent by the actor gone to waste. Be conservative with how much you send out to one person.

Snail-Mail Postcard Frequency

How often should you snail-mail a postcard to a casting director? Rarely, unless you have important news that is of use to the casting director and will assist you in getting a future audition. Postcards sent to remind a casting director of your existence do little to help either of you. If after the first sentence there is nothing of significance being announced, those postcards go into the trash.

Also a postcard with no room for a résumé offers a casting director very little history on an actor he doesn't know. Most Legit casting directors prefer to receive a full headshot and résumé, not a 3 x 5 index card with "Hi, I'm available and so is my cat!" scrawled upon on it. Postcards are best-suited for commercial and extras casting, where look counts more than content in the decision process. Match your marketing materials to the appropriate entertainment-professional demographic.

Mailing Disfiguration via the Post Office

Send a postcard to yourself. Why? Because you need to see how the postcard's appearance has been changed by the time it's delivered to the recipient. The post office places a bar code sticker on postcards. This sticker often covers important material like your name and contact information. When the sticker is removed, it peels that information off the card. The post office also has a machine that imprints barcodes and other markings on a postcard. These markings will often obscure your message or your face if the postcard contains a miniature of your headshot. Before sending out hundreds of postcards, mail a few testers to yourself and confirm that all the information you want to be visible remains visible after the postal system has had it's time with your mailing.

Snail Mail vs. E-Mail

An actor must adapt to new methods of communication to be an effective businessperson. I continue to recommend that an actor send snail-mail headshot mailings with a cover letter but also that that mailing should be accompanied by an electronic submission. Not too long ago, an actor e-mailing a casting decision-maker was considered taboo. No longer is that true. Until the next communication evolution, electronic transfer of information is the strongest weapon in the war to get your message out.

Do actors sending a headshot and résumé to casting personnel via the Internet better their chances of being seen for a project? Yes and no. On the affirmative, electronic submission speeds up the process. Audition slots fill up quickly. The *appropriate* talent who first enters the mind of the casting director wins the first available audition slot. In this respect, winning the race to get your headshot and résumé in first, with the help of the Internet, could give you a leg up over actors who rely solely on snail mail.

On the negative, your electronic submission is one of hundreds, possibly thousands, of actor e-mail inquiries that will bloat the receiver's e-mail inbox. Just because you're one of the first three hundred actors to inquire electronically about an audition doesn't mean that you're guaranteed an appointment (that would make for many unbearable audition sessions). Your electronic submission must stand out above the others.

The same concern for professional appearance given to the packaging of a hardcopy submission applies as well to how you package your electronic submission. You need a professional, well-written electronic cover letter, an easily assessable electronic résumé, and, most important, an Internet presence (actor's website) to complement and support the electronic submission.

E-MAIL: THE BASICS FOR AN EFFECTIVE ELECTRONIC COVER LETTER

E-mail is a powerful, cost-effective tool for speedily and simultaneously getting a single message to multiple recipients. The guidelines for an electronic submission vary little from those for a hardcopy submission cover letter:

- ✓ Keep the content brief and precise.
- ✓ Be quick to the point as to why you're submitting your headshot and résumé.
- ✓ Limit the letter to one or two short paragraphs.
- ✓ Only use three to four sentences per paragraph.
- ✓ Include hyperlinks in your text to projects that have an Internet presence.
- ✓ Include in your signature your e-mail and telephone contacts.
- ✓ Include in your signature a link to your website.

With an Internet submission, the actor has two format options. First is the typical tired, text-based, lackluster e-mail with a short paragraph stating "Blah, blah, blah . . . see me, blah, blah . . . attached is my picture and résumé." Snore-fest, boring! The second, better option is an HTML e-mail submission that contains colorful graphics, a thumbnail of your headshot, and clickable links within the "blah, blah, blah."

HTML (Hypertext Markup Language) E-Mail

HTML e-mail has surpassed text-based e-mail in popularity, for both senders and recipients. It's now the most common form of communication businesses use to reach consumers. Retailers announce sales and specials in "personalized" e-mails with stunning graphics. The entertainment industry successfully exploits HTML e-mail as a marketing tool for attracting new and old audiences to their projects. Theatrical producers regularly send out colorful production announcements to herald their latest hits. Studios announce new films and broadcast programming via HTML e-mail. Actors, to remain competitive, must utilize HTML e-mail for electronic correspondence when seeking or announcing new work.

HTML e-mail is sophisticated in appearance *and* requires less work on the part of the recipient. By "work" I mean the amount of mouse clicks required to fully view the e-mail's contents. On average, a traditional text-based e-mail with a headshot and résumé attachment requires that the recipient's index finger click more on his or her mouse to retrieve all of the actor's information. With an HTML e-mail, in which all actor information is viewed immediately, far less finger action is required. Text-based e-mail requires of the user the following finger workout:

> Click on the mail program to retrieve mail . . .
> Click on the e-mail to open . . .
> Click on the attachment(s) for download . . .
> Click on virus safety warnings about attachments . . .
> Click on "open file" to download . . .
> Click on the file to decompress it, then, *finally* . . .
> Click on the file to open and view.

That's *seven* mouse clicks! Seven mouse clicks required of the recipient to view your electronic business card. Seven mouse clicks versus two clicks for an HTML e-mail. A reluctance to require the recipient to press and depress a mouse button multiple times might seem absurd and overly cautious, but remember . . . the recipient, a busy casting person, has many more important things to do with his or her limited time than participate in a day-long click-fest. We're reading scripts, negotiating with agents, assuring clients, attending auditions, etc. Your text-based e-mail is one of hundreds of e-mails with an attachment received in a day. Opening a hundred e-mails with attachments would be seven hundred mouse clicks!

Also, a text-based e-mail with an attachment from an unknown source is a potential technological threat infested with hidden electronic viruses. In this age of hacker hoodlums, we are continuously cautioned against opening e-mails with attachments from unknown senders. The recipient, whose paranoia mixes with the barrage of warnings he receives, will often delete without viewing e-mails sent by unknown sources. Or, in another scenario, the e-mail with an attachment may automatically land in the recipient's e-mail spam folder, where it is likely to be deleted without being viewed.

How to Create a Simple HTML E-Mail

Option one: Hire a professional HTML e-mail designer.

Option two: Hire yourself. There are many tutorials for creating HTML e-mail, which can be found online or at a bookstore. Creating an HTML e-mail does not require the sender to be technologically talented. With patience and basic understanding for designing web pages and a website, creating HTML e-mail on your own is cost-effective, simple, and gives you complete content control.

Guidelines for Effective HTML E-Mail

- ✓ Keep the design simple and limit your use of graphics so that your recipients will not endure a lengthy download of your document in their e-mail software.
- ✓ Include your brand within the design.
- ✓ Replace time-consuming download graphics with colored cells within your table (this book is published in black and white; the gray-shaded areas in the second HTML example that follows represent where vibrant color was used in the original artwork).
- ✓ Avoid JavaScript, Flash, style sheets, framesets, rollovers, or nested tables. Your recipients may not have the software or programs in which to view your techno-savvy e-mail.
- ✓ Scan your handwritten signature into a graphic file that can be inserted into the HTML e-mail as your signature.
- ✓ Send a test of the e-mail to yourself prior to sending it out to your marketing targets.
- ✓ Test-send the HTML e-mail to several of your friends who have different e-mail programs/servers and computer operating systems (PCs vs. Macs) to verify that your targets will be able to view the HTML e-mail on their computers properly.

HTML E-Mail Marketing Example with Graphics

John Carter Paulson
AEA – SAG – AFTRA

*"**John Paulson** is **wonderfully witty** as Sir Darryl, the self anointed leader of day laborer knights, The Knights of Around the Table…"*

Charles Gaskin
Times-New Leader

Pavilion Arts Center
presents

Help Wanted: Princess

A New Mad Madrigal Musical

Book by Marc Oneida

Music Adapted by B. Schade

May 1 - June 30, 2008

"Pavilion Arts Center's latest production, Help Wanted: Princess, is a musical comedy that manages to hit all the right marks of a farce thanks to an uproarious comic menagerie of talented actors, an inspired design, and clever writing."

Dorrie David
Herald Press

Performances:
Tues – Sat @ 8 PM
Weds. & Sun. Mat. @ 2 PM
Industry Comps. Avail!

Good Day:

As my guest, I invite you to a hysterical evening of madcap misadventures in the new musical *Help Wanted: Princess*. Performances are Tuesday thru Sunday at the Pavilion Arts Center.

Prior to *Help Wanted: Princess* I was at the Barter Theater as Florizel in *A Winter's Tale*. My next project is the new comedy *Confessions of the Conch* by Kevin Kemperer at Manhattan Stage.

Below are links to my website, JohnCPaulson.com, which has my full résumé, headshot gallery, photos of past productions, and letters of recommendation.

Contact me for complimentary tickets for you and a guest to *Help Wanted: Princess*.

Warm regards,

John Carter Paulson

E-mail: JCPaulson@JohnCPaulson.com
Internet Presence: www.JohnCPaulson.com
Phone: 917.555.1212 (complimentary tickets & contact)

John Carter Paulson

AEA - SAG – AFTRA

*"**John Paulson is wonderfully witty** as Sir Darryl, the self-anointed leader of day laborer knights, The Knights of Around the Table…"*

Charles Gaskin
Times-New Leader

John Carter Paulson

in

Help Wanted: Princess

The NEW Mad, Madrigal Musical

Pavilion Arts Center

May 1 thru June 30th 2008

"Pavilion Arts Center's latest production, *Help Wanted: Princess*, is a musical comedy that manages to hit all the right marks of a farce thanks to an uproarious comic menagerie of talented actors, an inspired design, and clever writing."

Dorrie David
Herald Press

Performances:
Tues – Sat @ 8 PM
Weds. & Sun. Mat. @ 2 PM
Industry Comps. Avail!

Good Day:

As my guest, I invite you to a hysterical evening of madcap misadventures in the new musical *Help Wanted: Princess*. Performances are Tuesday thru Sunday at the Pavilion Arts Center.

Prior to *Help Wanted: Princess* I was at the Barter Theater as Florizel in *A Winter's Tale*. My next project is the new comedy *Confessions of the Conch* by Kevin Kemperer at Manhattan Stage.

Below are links to my web site JohnCPaulson.com, which has my full resume, headshot gallery, photos of past productions, and letters of recommendation.

Contact me for complimentary tickets for you and a guest to *Help Wanted: Princess*.

Warm regards,
John Carter Paulson

E-mail: JCPaulson@JohnCPaulson.com
Internet Presence: www.JohnCPaulson.com
Phone: 917.555.1212 (complimentary tickets & contact)

WEBSITE: EVERY ACTOR SHOULD HAVE ONE

Every actor needs a website. As the casting industry has become more tech savvy, we search the Internet for talent. When an actor I don't know is suggested to me and I don't have a hardcopy of his or her picture and résumé, the first place I turn to is an Internet search engine. I type in the actor's name and fully expect that the actor has a website. When the actor has a website, fantastic—my job is easier. When an actor doesn't have a website I disregard him or her and move on to the next referred actor. Time is precious in the casting process, and actors who can be readily accessed with ease are the ones whom we reach out to first with audition appointments. If you're an actor and don't have a website, get one immediately or get out of the business because you'll go nowhere fast if casting people cannot locate you online.

The website should be yours and yours alone with a domain name that reflects your professional name. If your professional name were Mike Ostroski, then your domain name would be MikeOstroski.com or .net. The most important part of the web address is what comes before the dot: your name. What comes after the dot (such as com or net) is not as important as it once was unless you're a dot org (nonprofit organization) or dot gov (government). Just make sure that your name is in the title of the domain to aid users in finding your website. Domain names are inexpensive, and you can own them for as long as you desire.

If you're new to the domain name obtaining game, don't fret. The registration process is simple. Enter into a search engine the key words "domain name registration" and you'll get a plethora of companies that will gladly take your money to register a domain name for you. If you'd rather not do the search engine work, try Register.com, a popular domain name registry.

Collective Websites

A MySpace page or a similar cyber web-page collective junkyard does not a personal website make. The message of marketing yourself online solely with a single page or several pages on a multiple-user domain (that is often plastered with banner advertising) will imply that you are cheap and unprofessional. Have a website of your own, with a domain name that is yours alone.

Website Building Guidelines for Actors

There are two ways to go about building a website. The first is to build your own, which gives you complete control over content and design, and the freedom to update when necessary. Wonderful, simple tutorials and user-friendly software can assist the technologically disinclined or naïvely ambitious (as was I when I built my first websites) in creating a website. Building a website yourself can be fun, challenging, and, in the end, very rewarding.

The second option is to hire a professional designer experienced in creating websites for actors. This option will be more costly than building a site on your own, but if you're technologically challenged, having a professional designer will make the debut of your website less frustrating and painful. Also, if you've never ventured into HTML, Flash, or similar programming, more than likely the overall design will be better in appearance and navigation than if you keyboarded the creation by yourself.

Presentation guidelines for an actor website mirror those I've discussed previously with respect to picture, résumé, and cover letter. The resulting design and content on the website should be straightforward, attractive, user-friendly, and easy to navigate. Resist excessive biographical information, adding animations that distract, background music, or implementing page transitions found in amateur PowerPoint presentations.

Apart from the Index Page (the first page that your visitors see) an actor's website should include the following pages:

Résumé Page

Think you know the content for this page, right? OK, yes, it's your résumé. But the résumé should be updated constantly with each new project. Also, the résumé should be available to the user in a downloadable, one-page, printer-friendly format such as PDF or DOC.

A thumbnail picture of you in the upper left- or right-hand corner of the résumé should be on the printer-friendly résumé page *and* the website résumé page. Having this thumbnail image of you will help the viewer put a face to the credits after printing. Also, having a thumbnail picture on your résumé is user-friendly, saving the recipient paper upon printing.

Reel Page

If you have a reel, transfer it to an electronic file for streaming Internet video. The reel should not be more than three minutes in length. Remember, our time in casting is limited, and just like a résumé, we scan the reel, fast-forwarding our way through it. Include your strongest clips, where you are the primary focus.

ONLINE REEL WARNINGS: Do not post your reel for industry viewing on YouTube or other multiple-user, Internet video outlets. Leave those video posting/viewing sites to the amateurs and exhibitionists. Also, do not post video clips of trailers, films, broadcast media, or commercials unless you have been given written permission by the producing entity to do so. Studios, networks, and advertising agencies are very protective of their material in which you happen to appear. Just because you're in a video or film does not mean that you own the rights to your image.

Headshot Page

As stated earlier, graphics take up a lot of digital storage space, which means that the larger the graphics (headshots) and the more of them on a page, the longer the page takes to load for the site visitor. Keep your headshot display to a manageable size that doesn't take more than seven to ten seconds to access. If you have multiple headshots you'd like to offer, place these in thumbnail selections, which are then linked to a larger, digitally manageable version.

Recommendation Page

Let the world know that others think highly of you. Place recommendations you've received over the years on your website. Don't have any? Don't be shy! You should always ask for letters of recommendation from directors, producers, and teachers with whom you have had great working relationships. Always get the recommendations on the letterhead of the person or organization supplying you with the prose of praise.

To place a recommendation on your website, scan the letter into a PDF file. Then, on the recommendation page, quote a small section from the letter and place a link to its full (printable) PDF version. After each quote place a link to the full letter of recommendation.

Highlight (put in bold letters) key phrases. Remember reading takes time, and in our busy casting lives we scan. The highlighted commentary gives the viewer immediate points of reference. Beyond the highlights the reader can then choose to read the quote fully and/or click on the link to the full recommendation.

Press Page

The press page would follow the same guidelines as the recommendation page. Scan print press into PDF format and place a link to the full press document within or after the quote pulled from each review. Within the quotes on the press page, highlight (in bold) short quips that immediately deliver and encompass the tenor of the full press clip.

Past Projects Page

The past projects page features links to individual pages for each of your past productions (film, TV, and theater) that you wish to highlight. On this directory page highlighting past achievements, you place a single still shot (or title) to represent each project. From the still shot and the production's title under it, provide a link to a designated page for that individual production. On each designated page, place commentary about the project (from press and peers) along with additional production photos. You need not post every project in which you have appeared, only those that meet the following requisites:

- ✓ High production values (sets, costuming), which make for impressive photos.
- ✓ Project received great recognition from industry and audience.
- ✓ Producing entity is held in high regard within the industry and by the audience.
- ✓ Your participation in the project was as a principal role.

WARNING: Only post images that you own or images for which you have been given written permission to post publicly. Do not post still photography from a production unless you have been given written permission by both the photographer and the producing entity to do so.

Upcoming Projects Page

An upcoming projects page is a must for every actor website. The page broadcasts to friends and industry that you're busy, proactive, and optimistic. Even if you haven't got a paying industry job on the horizon, always post truthful, new news: listing recent callbacks (no narcotic narrative details, just the project and creatives involved), readings, workshops, showcases, training, potential productions . . . anything within your career field in which you are actively involved. People who are busy (or look busy) attract the busy people who hire. It's best to give the honest impression that you're wanted and active than to openly acknowledge that paying work may not be coming as readily as you would like. As I've mentioned before, this feast or famine business is all about image. Let the industry think that your feast is bountiful (even if you're feasting on nonpaying, sporadic readings in roach-infested basements).

Contact Page

How much contact information you want to display is best left to your discretion. I strongly recommend listing a phone number and e-mail contact, but know that if you place either on a web page, you create the potential for hundreds of thousands of people viewing your personal information and reaching out to you in ways you won't like. Also, if you post your e-mail, keep in mind that spammers have robot programs that search the Internet for e-mail addresses posted online. The programs pick up these e-mails and then you will automatically begin to receive sex ad e-mails, spammed to you without relent. There is a solution. Instead of posting your e-mail address, place on the contact page a form for users to fill out in order to contact you.

A website form program takes information supplied by the visitor and sends it to you in an e-mail. A website form contains those little boxes we've all filled out when buying a product online, finding a great hotel for cheap, or submitting our mating requirements. To properly set up a form you will either need to read a tutorial or have a website design professional assist you. A form program is effective in protecting your privacy and reducing spam while allowing others to contact you.

CRASHING AUDITIONS: ACTOR GORILLA MARKETING 101

"Crashing auditions" is when an actor without an appointment forces his or her way into an audition session that is by appointment only. Crashing an audition is the actor's equivalent to gorilla marketing, an aggressive tactic through which marketers force their way into events to promote a product. Crashing auditions is no different a tactic for assertively presenting the brand (the actor) to the consumer (casting). Crashing auditions is also a controversial subject between casting personnel and actors.

Some in casting abhor audition crashers, mostly because the casting process's control and order wind up getting interrupted. Casting personnel who are emotionally and professionally secure welcome the opportunity to see additional people who may have been overlooked. I'm one for accepting an audition crasher, *but* I'll only see the crasher on my terms. Those terms being: if I have the time, if I can review the crashing actor's headshot and résumé prior to allowing him or her into the room, if I feel the actor is truly appropriate for what is being sought, and if the audition monitor gives me a favorable report on the actor's personality and appearance. If *all* of the proceeding terms are met and the other creatives in the room are amenable to seeing the crasher, then more often than not I will allow the audition crasher into the room.

Habitual audition crashing is *not* a tactic that I recommend. There's little tolerance for repeat offenders. But if, on occasion, you as an actor know without a doubt that you're absolutely perfect, that "no one else on this planet can play the role better" than you, and you *objectively* know that you're what the creatives are seeking, then by all means, judiciously try crashing the audition for which you could not get an appointment. BUT! You had better be damned well-prepared with the audition material requested and be damned impressive! Crash and be talent-free, wrong for the role, make an ass of yourself, talk excessively about how brilliant you would be for the role, and then audition for the role sans brilliance . . . well, then, wave goodbye forever to the people whose audition you just crashed. Crashing an audition is like leaping off a cliff. Before taking that step into the abyss of the audition room, be sure—be very, very sure—that you'll land without injury.

Michael Mastro has crashed auditions. He explained his view on the aggressive-actor action and how he participates in this industry taboo. "There are a lot of casting directors who say, 'Don't crash auditions! Don't do it!' There may be casting directors who truly hate it. What they hate is an actor showing up to the audition, ill-prepared, and lying that they signed in on the sign-in sheet as if they have an appointment." Mastro cautions those who crash and lie. "You think the casting director is stupid? You think casting directors don't know who they called in for the project?"

For Mastro, crashing an audition means being prepared and overtly polite. "I showed up at auditions [for which I didn't have an appointment]," Mastro explained. "I had all the information. I got the sides. I worked on them for days. I showed up ready with a picture, résumé, and a letter to submit myself. I approach the audition monitor with charm and say, 'I'm sure you're very busy, but I've got the next three hours [free], I've got the sides, I'm ready. I'm ready to kick ass. I'll sit in a corner and read a book. If you have five minutes and you can possibly see me, it would mean so much to me. If you can't, I totally understand. Here's a letter for the director and maybe you can see me another time. Thank you so much for considering.' And I've gotten in. I've done this even when I've had an agent who couldn't get me into projects." Okay, so Mastro's address to the audition monitor *may* sound like saccharine bullshit to cynical skeptics, but his earnestness has served him well. If Mastro can master crashing, maybe you can as well.

Crashing an audition is always a gamble for the actor. Mastro understands that risk but thinks it's one worth taking. "There are probably some casting directors who you should never, ever, *ever* crash an audition with, but how will you find out who those people are unless you take the risk? I have friends who are casting directors, and I don't know a casting director who would tell you, 'I have a shit list, and if an actor ever comes to me and tries to crash an audition, even if they're nice and funny and charming, I don't care, I will never see them again and I'm going to call everyone and tell them about this actor.' I've never met that casting director. I've met a casting director who said "don't do it," but over martinis I have said to that casting director, 'So you say don't crash but have you ever completely lost respect for an actor who had the balls to do it? Have you never called in [that] actor again?' And they hawed. The only time a casting director has not called in an actor again is when the actor has done something incredibly rude and inappropriate—if they had bad manners or displayed rage or poor work habits."

RESPONSIVE MARKETING: ANSWERING THE TRADES

The trades: *Back Stage*, *Show Business*, *Variety*, *American Theater* magazine, *Theatrical Index*, plus many regional and major city arts publications. These sources of actor employment information have been the starting point and often backbone for millions of careers in entertainment. *Back Stage* is the leading trade for employment information. *Variety*, *American Theater Magazine* and *Theatrical Index* are resources not for auditions but for news on upcoming projects, including who is involved. Often actors overlook this latter form of trade information, which is valuable for its insight into yet-to-be-announced auditions.

Michael Mastro, in spite of his success and having a dedicated agent, continues to use the trades as a valuable tool for finding work. "There are plenty of publications out there to find out what's coming down the pike," Mastro explained. "I'm shocked at how many actors don't know what the *Theatrical Index* is! Then there's the *Season Overview* put out by Drama Book Shop. It has every regional theater and what's going on for the next year at regional theaters: when those projects are happening, who's directing them, and whose writing them, if they're new plays. *American Theater* magazine is indispensable for anybody who wants to grow their résumé in terms of regional theater, which every young actor should want to be doing."

Nearly all of the Group of Eight have turned the pages of *Back Stage*, searching for opportunities. But even though this essential trade publication offers contacts for employment, many of the Group of Eight who used *Back Stage* felt that it alone was not going to propel their careers as quickly as desired. Robert LuPone recalled how he first found jobs.

"The classic way. Read *Back Stage*, send a picture and résumé, go to an open call, *phft!*" LuPone dismissed. "Who has come out of open calls? OK, that's not true. I'm being harsh, because actually Bernie Telsey has found a lot of people through open calls, but they usually end up in ensemble roles or in small roles in plays. It's a way to go; it's a waste of effort as far as I'm concerned."

Darrie Lawrence also used *Back Stage* early on in her career. "I got my jobs through *Back Stage*," Lawrence said, looking back on her start as an actress. "I would go to open calls. I had a very slow start to my career. It was tough and I think it's tougher now. I began in New York when there weren't as many casting directors. I was in New York for almost four and a half years before I got my first Equity contract . . . I got that through an ad in *Back Stage*."

Electronic Trades and Audition Information Online

Today the paper trades are being supplemented or replaced by Internet publications. Just as trade publications, like *Back Stage*, augment their message with an online presence, actors must widen their employment searches online via the Internet. Online audition sites multiply daily and thrive. Most popular are Playbill.com, BackStage.com, and Craigslist.org. Other online audition sites can be found easily by entering "audition posting," "audition site," or just simply "auditions" into a search engine. There are also many regional and city-specific online audition information sites. Once again, use a search engine as a tool for information by adding the name of the city or region to the suggested audition keywords.

Additional Online Audition Resources

✓ Regional theaters, theatrical producers, and some casting offices will post upcoming audition information on their websites.

✓ Most performing artists unions offer online audition information boards for their members.

✓ Audition mail groups. Offered for free or at a small fee, an actor can subscribe to one of these groups and receive daily audition opportunity information via e-mail. These can be found through Yahoo!, Google, and other major e-mail providers as well as actor information websites and forums.

✓ Minority or ethnic heritage actor organizations with an online presence often have audition information boards. Some of these online information outlets include HelloHola.org (HOLA: Hispanic Organization of Latin Actors), HollywoodMasala.com (a website with audition information for Indian actors), and BlackTalentNews.com (a site with focus on information for the African American actor). Search engines with the keyword "audition" matched with the formal name of an ethnicity or classification will often produce leads to audition information sites that are specific to a certain ethnic heritage or minority.

Exploit the resources that can be mined by exploring the Internet for treasured jobs. Since the electronic revolution, seeking opportunities for work has never been easier. But because more people can readily access the Internet, more actors are responding to opportunities. To stay ahead of the other actors looking for work you must be constantly active in your online search. Set up a routine for looking for work posted online:

✓ Have a favorites list for all the audition sites you access. Three times a day (morning, midday, and evening) check all sites on your list for audition information updates. This constant checking may read as obsessive, but in the age of instant online communication, information changes rapidly. Don't fall behind; if a new audition posting has been online for only a few hours, hundreds of actors will have already applied before you have become aware of it. You have to be quick.

✓ Once a month, do search engine sleuthing for new audition sites and forums.

✓ Subscribe to multiple e-mail audition announcement services.

✓ Read online trades daily (including periodicals that feature information on the industry, such as iCOMMAG.com (film and video production news), StudioDaily.com, Variety.com, and the online versions of the *New York Times* arts section or your local/regional arts publications).

✓ Once weekly (or biweekly), check for audition and season updates on the websites of regional theaters and theaters in major cities that you're targeting.

THE GROUP OF EIGHT ON MARKETING FAILURE

Because I'm a hypercritical Virgo, always looking to the flaw that needs improvement, I asked the Group of Eight, "What marketing didn't succeed in getting work?" Most of the

Group of Eight answered with an "I don't know." At first this casual, nearly unified reply seemed uninformative. But then I realized that if they don't know what marketing is not working then they're not going to know what marketing does work!

One of the Group of Eight asked how could she know what didn't work if she hadn't heard back from the targets? My reply to both her and other "I don't know" actors is, if you're not aware of what's not working, or if you're not hearing back from any of your targets, then whatever attempts at marketing you're making are failing. Lack of response indicates one of two things: First, you're either inappropriate in type and/or talent for the role. This reflects your own failure to understand who you are as an actor; you don't know your brand. Second, your marketing materials and how you present yourself on paper are inappropriate.

Receiving replies in response to your marketing outreach, whether that reply is "Yes we want to see you" or "No, thank you, no opportunities at this time," means you're onto marketing that *is* getting attention! Zero responses from your targets (where the silence is deafening) means your marketing is failing and it's time to ask your peers for feedback. Whether getting responses or silence from your targets, you should always allow peers in the business to review your headshot, résumé, cover letter(s), envelope packaging, e-mail outreach, and Internet presence. Ask them to be objective in their evaluation of your materials. Be open to the criticism and implement changes for the better.

Some actors fail Actor Marketing 101 completely by doing little to no marketing at all. Darrie Lawrence admitted that she "didn't do enough of marketing." Lawrence was very lucky that her lack of promotion didn't keep her from working. But her example is one that should *not* be followed.

Lawrence once had a valuable opportunity to sit on the other side of the casting table and see the marketing mishaps in which actors regularly, and with great ignorance, engage. "I actually did work at one of my agent's offices. I did see what people were sending in, and some of it was pretty lame," Lawrence remarked, bemused. "Sometimes I would sit there and open the envelopes of actor mailings and I would think, 'Why are these people even bothering?' because they had *nothing* to sell about themselves. You've got to wonder about the people who send you a bad picture and then you turn it over and there's nothing on the résumé."

For Lawrence, working at her agent's office and seeing firsthand how others market themselves was a great learning experience. If you truly want to learn how to market yourself, the best way is to witness what others are doing. Take an internship in a casting or talent rep's office, open the mail, and study the mistakes and successes. Copy the actor marketing formulas that work. Ignore the ones that are abysmal failures. You'll know immediately upon opening actor mailings which succeed and which ones are destined for the trash. Actor marketing that is no-nonsense and professional in appearance gets a response. What fails are the gimmicks by actors sending food, candies, gift certificates, clothing, and other "bribes" to accompany their headshots—all of which go directly into the trash or onto an intern's desk (interns need the food and clothing).

I'm continually amazed by the multitude who call themselves "actors" and send me marketing materials that are not any better than a failed "How I spent my summer vacation" grade school report. Lawrence commented that actors, assisted by computers, "are much smarter now, and also they have much better tools to do a handsome package." I wish that were 100 percent true, but sadly only about 25 percent of actors sending me materials are acing Actor Marketing 101. Many actors remain just as inept in marketing as they did prior to the advent of desktop publishing and the Internet. The younger ones seem to approach promotion in a more savvy manner, but overall the packaging by most actors doesn't look any better than before desktop publishing.

Worse off are the actors who don't sell themselves at all and wait for auditions to come via the trades. By holding off until then, the actor falls behind the competition. If you want to push ahead of the herd, beyond your peers, talent alone or waiting for jobs to come your way will not a career make. To be competitive, actors must sell, sell, sell themselves without relent. Effective marketing creates the work. The work itself showcases your talent.

CHAPTER SEVEN

AUDITIONS ACTORS ENCOUNTER

Are Your Auditions Safe?

"My early auditioning was about getting someone to like me. Auditioning now is about personal achievement. Auditioning now is about pushing beyond my comfort level. It's also about doing the best that I can without having to depend on the auditors liking me. If I approach an audition with that in thought and do the best that I can, then when I leave, I don't care what the auditors think 'cause I know I've done the best job that I can. It's about me; it's not about them."

Mark Price

Actor

"Are your auditions safe?" was one of the more bizarre questions I, as a casting director, have received from an actor. It came at me in an e-mail. I was dumbfounded. Was the actor inquiring as to whether I carry weapons with me to the audition room? Um, no, it's been the other way around. On two separate occasions, I've had a knife and a gun pulled on me during auditions. Actors used them as props to make the experience more real. Reality check: Using a weapon in an audition does not guarantee a callback.

The question "Are your auditions safe?" should have been one that was rhetorical for this woman. It's a question that should be asked by all actors of their own audition abilities. Eighty-five percent of actors remain "safe" in their auditions, not daring to take chances. In safe auditions, actors hold back, staying within their comfort zone, not daring to push beyond their potential. A safe audition by an actor will prompt the auditor to dryly quip, "Thank you very much for coming in today . . . NEXT!"

Actors receive many audition opportunities to push beyond their potential. Auditions are a near daily requisite in every actor's life, even for some of the famous-at-the-moment actor-personalities. No one is beyond escaping some form of an audition. If you have been a working actor for some time, you've encountered varied audition procedures that have tried your patience. For you new actors, the audition scenarios that await you will make your past academic and community theater auditions seem like a Disney vacation.

In an upcoming chapter we'll look at techniques to prepare for an audition. Within the pages of this chapter we look at nonacting technique tips for surviving the multiple auditions actors will encounter throughout their careers. Each scenario has its own personality and procedures; each requires a specific plan of attack. There is no blanket "all auditions are the same" and "one audition fits all" technique. What follows is a mini-directory of the more common types of auditions encountered throughout a performer's journey, along with tips on how to approach each and go beyond being "safe."

OPEN CALL

Ah ... open calls, the most humbling and humiliating experience within an actor's life. If you've been around the block (literally) as an actor, you've endured the hell that is standing on the street, in either unbearable heat or frost, waiting among hundreds of other actors, for a chance to sign in, which possibly will allow you a generous twenty to thirty seconds in front of casting. Open calls are often referred to as "cattle calls." Like cattle, actors are herded together simultaneously, and out of the hundreds who trample by, a few chosen pieces of meat are selected. The major difference between an actual bovine cattle call and an actor cattle call is that in the final cut the blood loss among cows is slightly more profuse than from the actors herded to the slaughter.

Open calls can be for any type of project, be it film, TV, theater, webcast, theme park, or cruise ship. Actors' Equity Association dismisses the term "open call" (the AEA's politically correct titles for their open calls are discussed a bit later). If you've watched *American Idol*, you've witnessed the mother of all open calls.

Many open calls will advertise that they're seeking a specific gender, physical type, or ability. If an open call is advertising for female dancers, five-foot-ten and above, who can sing, tap dance, and play an instrument, *that's exactly what the auditors want!* If you're a female who "kinda dances" and doesn't play an instrument, *don't attend the open call!* By attending an open call even though inappropriate in talent and/or type, you waste your time, the auditors' time, and most important, the time of your fellow actors who are actually right for the role.

Now, I know that my reprimand might seem condescending and obvious, but performers who do not match what is being advertised will always show up. This bad behavior can be traced back to teachers and peers who relentlessly preach to inexperienced and ignorant actors that "you should audition for everything and anything even if you're not right for it. The more you're seen, the better." Here's some truth: Take that misguided academic propaganda and toss it into the trash where it belongs, because you're pissing off a lot of people on both sides of the audition table! Attend open calls for which you match exactly what is advertised as needed by the casting personnel. Got that? Good, let's all take a breath and move on and discover appropriate ways talent can make the best of an open call.

Open Call Survival Tips

The lengthiest and most grueling part of an open call is the wait. Actors waiting in a long, serpentine line at an open call are moved forward slower than road kill is pushed aside to the shoulder. The period of waiting during an open call can be anywhere from several hours to several days. The wait will depend on the efficiency of the casting personnel and the popularity of the project. The more popular the endeavor (as recognized by either the industry or audience), the higher the response of eager actors to the open call, and thus the longer the waaaaaait.

Waiting in line for an open call can be about as exciting and productive as watching dead grass grow. But that wait can provide you with a great opportunity to be enterprising. As you're stationary, push your career forward with trade-related tasks such as studying, marketing, and seeking out other audition opportunities for which you can stand in line and repeat this whole process again. It's a cycle of a circle within a circle, within a cir ... OK, enough. Here's some productive practices to pursue:

- ✓ Your laptop computer is your actor office on the go. Bring your laptop with a wireless connection to seek additional audition opportunities while you're waiting for your current opportunity to happen. You can also catch up on your employment correspondence, update your actor website, or design a new mailer that announces your latest endeavors.
- ✓ Be a social slut (sexual activity not required). Network with those sitting/standing near you. They may know of other auditions/job opportunities for which you could be suitable. You might also make new friends.
- ✓ Read the trades, seek other audition opportunities, and be informed on what's next in your industry.
- ✓ Learn while you wait. Bring a book on the arts (if you're reading this book now while waiting at an open call you get a gold star for the day).
- ✓ Have patience. Be polite, gracious, and courteous to all you meet. You never know who, standing near or talking to you, may be one of the decision-makers.

If attending an open call that requires singing, have prepared both a sixteen-measure and an eight-measure cutting of the music requested or music that best displays your vocal talents; at open calls you rarely get an opportunity to sing beyond sixteen measures when first seen.

The organizational skills of the auditors at open calls will often appear chaotic and their personalities cold; know that the auditors are deeply focused on finding solutions (actors) for their casting puzzle. While I don't condone discourteous behavior on either side of the table, any animosity you may perceive from open call auditors is not directed toward you personally. That frost you feel is just a byproduct of the auditors wishing, like you, that there were a more civil way to match talent to opportunity.

Be thick-skinned emotionally and ever-pleasant; sincere, positive personalities always rise above those that are sour and negative.

Typing Out

Casting in an open call is a numbers game; too many people, too little time for all to be seen. While the phrase "typing out" may be new to you, it's a necessary evil of casting you'll encounter often. It refers to when a large number of actors at an open call are taken into the audition room for the creative team to quickly scan the line. Creatives then choose those who match the physical type sought. Those who match stay to later display their talent. Those who don't are thanked for coming in while encouraged to return for future auditions for which they are better suited.

"We're typing out!" shouted by an audition staff member over the heads of job-hungry, waiting actors is one of the most dreaded announcements at an open call. The actor's inner voice screams an expletive. Internal monologues of anguish abound. Open discussions of frustration soon race up and down the line. All the time, money, and line-lingering invested, and most may not even get a shot to display their talent because they might be typed out. So again, I strongly advise, if an open call advertises for specific physical qualities or abilities, make sure you possess them before calling out sick from work (losing a day's pay) to attend an open call for which you may not be seen at all.

Typing Out Survival Tips

There are no tips to get past typing. Other than a quick hair dye or rinse, you have zero control over being typed out if your physical features are not what are being sought. If you're typed out the best thing to do is to move on and look forward to the next opportunity. Best advice I can offer: Being pulled out of one audition because your height, hair, or nose doesn't suit the director is not the end of your career. One casting decision-maker will love you for what another found to be a fault.

ECC and EPA

The Equity Chorus Call (ECC) is the stage actor's union version of an open call. The audition is primarily for actors who are fully paid-up members of the Actors' Equity Association (AEA). Non-AEA actors can try to attend, but first-see priority is given to union membership. The decision to audition non-AEA actors after the union actors have been seen is at the discretion of the auditors.

With an ECC, there is a regulated attendance policy put forth by AEA. The policy is referred to as Chorus Call Procedure. Generally, for an ECC, the published audition notice will contain the phrase "Chorus Call procedures in effect." Check AEA's website, www.actorsequity.org, for present Chorus Call Procedures or contact your closest AEA regional office (Contacts in the Appendix of this book).

Then there is the other AEA version of what civilians would consider an open call. This is referred to as Equity Principal Auditions (EPA) and Equity Principal Interviews (EPI). These calls are for principal roles within a stage production or principal roles in productions within a theater's season. For present regulations, again visit AEA's website or contact your closest AEA regional office.

The AEA audition codes for ECCs and EPAs consist of a lot of language. If you get a copy and read the rules, you might think that ECC and EPA auditions are very militaristic. However, the tone of the actual audition process will depend on the personality of the official audition monitor assigned by AEA to the call and the auditors.

When AEA membership actors arrive at an ECC, they are given a 3 x 5 index card. On the card's front, at the top, AEA provides printed information lines (blank) for their members to place their name, the audition, their phone number, and the date of the audition. Beneath that is an open area, titled "Experience." The actor has two options. First option: Scribble in pen or pencil your résumé (not a good option). The second and better option is to have your résumé typed on a self-adhesive label, as shown in the following example:

FOR USE AT EQUITY CHORUS AUDITIONS

NAME: _Scott Breitbart_

AUDITION: _Barter Theatre_

PHONE NUMBER: _____   DATE: _3/14_

EXPERIENCE:

Broadway

ABE LINCOLN IN ILLINOIS with Sam Waterston	Soldier	VIVIAN BEAUMONT THEATER, NY Dir. Gerald Gutierrez

Regional

FIORELLO	Ensemble	GOODSPEED OPERA HOUSE Dir. Gerald Gutierrez • Chor. Peter Gennaro
GUYS & DOLLS	Rusty Charlie	INDIANA REPERTORY THEATER Dir. Tom Haas • Chor. Karen Azenberg

Stock

SINGIN' IN THE RAIN	Diction Coach (Roscoe Dexter/R.F. Simpson U/S)	BIRMINGHAM THEATER, MI Dir. Ted Pappas • Chor. D.J. Giagni
SWEET CHARITY with Georgia Engel	Ensemble	BIRMINGHAM THEATER, MI Dir. Jack Allison • Chor. Susan Stroman
ANNIE GUYS & DOLLS	Drake/Ensemble Harry the Horse	CLUB BENE DT, NJ Dir. Mary Mickelheim • Chor. Bob Rizzo
PIPPIN NO, NO, NANETTE	Ensemble (Lewis Understudy) Ensemble	EAST CAROLINA SUMMER THEATRE, NC Dir. Jay Fox • Chor. Mavis Ray
HOW TO SUCCEED IN BUSINESS	Bud Frump	WESTSIDE THEATER, CA
THE SECRET AFFAIRS OF MILDRED WILD	Roy Wild	HORSESHOE THEATER, CA Dir. Martin Sokup

Equity Index Card

Tips for Attending an ECC and/or EPA

✓ Be prompt.
✓ Be courteous.
✓ Be patient.
✓ Have a legible, reduced résumé.

AEA Required Calls (ECCs & EPAs)

ECCs and EPAs are divided into two categories: required and nonrequired. What does each mean?

Required calls occur when a theatrical producer has a contractual agreement with AEA in which the producer must hold a specific number of auditions for the union's membership within a prescribed time period. "Required call" also implies that a casting director (or theater) is casting a production that has a chorus and principal roles; and in addition to their scheduled auditions in which they bring in talent from outreach through talent reps, files, the Internet, trade publications, and mail, they *must* also have a set number of EPA and/or ECC calls that are run by the union. The standing rule is that these required calls must happen prior to all other auditions for the project. Officially, unless there is an agreement between AEA and the producer, no role is to be cast prior to holding a required AEA call.

The rule is often broken. The audition hallway gossip that roles are cast prior to the AEA required calls is not whispered actor paranoia; it's a fact of casting. My first exposure as an auditor attending a required call in which no roles were available occurred after the casting of a new Off-Broadway play written by a long-ago Broadway-bound sunshine boy, good doctor, and playwright of laughter on any floor (guess who yet?). The play, set in a hotel suite across the pond, had been cast and was several weeks away from first rehearsal. Despite that, a required Equity Principal Audition was mandated by the union. I was then a lowly casting assistant, but that perfectly positioned me for attending the required call because none of the casting directors in the office wanted to go. I was thrilled and nervous to be the representative behind the table. I was also *very* naïve. As I left the casting office for the audition, the headmaster of casting growled, "Take a newspaper with you so you don't get bored." He further stated that if I saw anyone who might have potential to be an audition reader/monitor for prescreens that I should hold onto to his or her résumé. I was instructed to toss all other headshots and résumés. Beyond that, my purpose and instruction for the required call was to be a warm body, representing the casting office, reading a newspaper—hi-ho, the glamorous life.

A similar scenario actors knowingly or unknowingly encounter (depending on how astute they are) is the required union call in New York City for regional theaters. These AEA membership calls in New York are to occur before the theater's scheduled season ends. Often these calls are held *after* the theater has cast its season or its scheduled season is nearly complete. I've attended, as a theater's casting director, regional theater required union-call scenarios when there was no work to offer. On one occasion my casting office had to hold a required Equity Chorus Call for a musical for which I was also the director. Months before, the show had been fully cast from within the theater's resident acting company, something of which the union was aware. A week before the start of rehearsals, I sat through eight hours of auditioning musical theater performers who truly believed they were chasing after an actual employment opportunity. It was a painful experience because I couldn't tell the job-hungry actors that the show had long ago been cast. Any transparency on my part would have put the theater, my client, in jeopardy with the union, even though the union was aware of the resident AEA acting company and that there were no contracts being offered.

More absurd is when the union decides that a two- to five-character musical requires an Equity Chorus Call but there is no chorus! This has happened to my office many times. Despite my heated questioning of the Equity representative demanding a chorus call for a two-character musical—"Have you read the script?!"—I have had to sit through chorus auditions for productions that had fewer people onstage than there are openly gay-black-Jewish Republicans!

While the intention of AEA required calls is to give the union's membership additional opportunity to be seen and heard, it's often a waste of time for both actor and auditor. If I find myself with an AEA required call when no job for the actor exists (which is often), I try to take advantage of the opportunity by referring actors who interest me to talent reps. I'm not going to read a newspaper. Before you make the decision to attend an EPA or ECC, investigate if it's a required call (code for "There are no jobs available, we're forced to hold these auditions") or if it is a nonrequired call. The latter often means there's work to be had! Yes!

AEA Non-Required Calls (EPAs & ECCs)

If "non-required call" appears in the casting notice, this means that employment is available. If type-appropriate, go to the audition! Auditions are like a lottery: You have to play to win. Sometimes actors hit the jackpot!

When I was working with the casting office for the original Broadway company of *Disney's Beauty and the Beast*, many non-required calls were held. And from those calls came success stories such as that of one young actress, fresh from school and new to New York. It was her first audition in the city. From that first audition, an open call in the theater mecca that is New York, the recently graduated actress got cast in the original company of a Broadway smash hit. Dreams do come true. Magic can happen.

AUDITIONS BY APPOINTMENT

For some auditions, casting personnel schedule individual appointments for actors. Generally, the actors seen in this scenario come from talent rep submissions, casting files, references, and creative team requests or from actor self-submission.

Standard practice for appointment assignment is that an actor, either directly or through a talent rep, receives a slot from the casting office. When an appointment is given, *that* is your appointment, and changing it is tantamount to pushing yourself through the closing doors of a subway. The train has to move forward, but it can't do so with you stuck in the car entry. The sliding doors are often opened, slightly, to allow you in and for the train to proceed with its job. Sometimes a casting office will slightly open their restrictive scheduling procedures (because it's their job to solve casting puzzles) and consider an audition appointment change for actor conflicts such as work, a doctor's appointment, or another audition. Because the casting office wants to see you, they'll make an effort to do so. Just don't make a career of changing your appointment time for nearly every audition to suit your timetable tastes or sleeping habits. Only do it when absolutely necessary. You don't want to cause conflict before going into the room (or once in the room).

Tips for Auditions by Appointment

✓ Arrive fifteen minutes before your given appointment ("freshen up" and fix your hair in the restroom; more important, arriving early gives you time to focus on the work about to be asked of you).

✓ Have and KNOW your audition material.

✓ Have TWO hardcopies of your picture and résumé (most submissions now are electronic, but casting and directors prefer to have hardcopies of pictures and résumés).

✓ Don't listen to the competition before you as they audition (hearing others audition will just play havoc on the psyche). If you can, move yourself away from hearing what is going on behind the audition room doors (but stay near enough to hear when your name is called).

✓ Be polite and courteous to all you encounter.

PRESCREEN

A prescreen, sometimes referred to as a "work session," is what the title suggests: An actor is screened (auditioned) by the casting director alone before a decision is made about whether to bring him or her in to be seen by other members of the creative team. prescreens generally are for actors new or relatively new to the casting director. A work session is not so much an audition as it is time in an audition room between casting director and actor to improve the actor's audition prior to being seen by the final decision-makers. Serving two purposes, a prescreen gives the casting director an opportunity to audition more actors he or she is unfamiliar with and to provide the actor with a "dress rehearsal" audition. The latter is an advantage for the prescreened actor over those who will be coming in cold, directly for the creative team.

Some actors shun prescreens. They shouldn't. A prescreen is a wonderful opportunity for having more than one random shot at the job being offered. It also provides the actor an opportunity to develop a one-on-one professional relationship with the casting person.

In prescreens, many of my colleagues and I exploit the relaxed atmosphere, sans a table banked by multiple auditors, for getting to know an actor better. Personally, I don't use the valuable time to puff up my ego and become the director. I'm there to help the actor succeed, which in turn makes the actor a promising prospect when presented to the final decision-makers. If in a prescreen I discover that an actor has potential to be brought back for the producer and creative team, I work with the actor, giving him or her feedback and direction as to what the director is seeking. That's a huge advantage over the actors who come in directly without a prescreen.

The desire to coach an actor or a lack of familiarity with him or her are not the only reasons to hold a prescreen. The availability of the final decision-makers ordinarily determines our audition schedule. Prescreens allow us to extend the audition process so that we can see as many people as possible. If casting directors only called in talent for the final decision-makers, not as many actors would be seen for each project. Prescreen sessions open the door of opportunity for more actors.

Often, the final decision-makers don't know who was prescreened. Call it a casting director's "don't ask, don't tell" policy. Our silence makes the returning prescreened actor's audition more impressive to the final decision-makers if they believe that the actor is coming in cold without the aid of coaching. During my career as a casting director I've noticed that on projects that had prescreens, a higher percentage of the hires came from the pool of actors who had prescreens versus those who came in directly without one.

Some actors abhor prescreens and consider them an insult, believing the casting director has little or no confidence in his or her ability. This may be accurate for some casting directors but I doubt it is for the majority. If we didn't have confidence in an actor's ability to match what is desired, we wouldn't be calling in the actor at all. The time that casting directors are allotted to see actors is valuable, and we can't afford to waste it on people we assume will fail. Every moment in the audition room must be used as effectively as possible. When called in to be seen, be it prescreen or direct, an actor can be rest assured that casting has a presumptive confidence in his or her ability for matching what is sought.

An important note for those actors who have been prescreened and then called back for the creatives: Make your callback appear as if it were your first time being auditioned for the project. Don't make any statements about your having been seen previously. An innocent comment such as, "Should I do what I did before?" will raise the decision-makers' expectations of you, and you'll have to meet those elevated beliefs because they know you've been given a "stamp of approval" by the casting director. This will not be an advantage for you; rather, it will be a challenge. Put yourself on an even expectation playing field with the other actors who are coming in for the first time.

MEET AND GREET

A meet and greet is an actor interview process used primarily by talent reps, casting directors, and directors. This is an opportunity for you, the actor, to shake hands, sit down, talk, and present yourself for who you are, without an audition (almost). When the meet and greet is strictly with creative personnel like a director, writer, producer, or casting, the creatives are engaging you in conversation to discover how your work ethic and personality will benefit the character that they might want you to portray. To ace a meet and greet, be polite and gracious and do whatever is asked of you, particularly if you greatly desire the role being dangled before you.

Meet and greets occur higher up in the food chain of audition scenarios. High-profile projects in film and television, along with some New York theater, utilize meet and greets. Once an actor's work has become widely known and respected, the meet and greets begin to replace reading for roles, although that actor may still be required to audition for certain roles.

After or during a meet and greet, the creatives will decide whether the talent is someone they wish to pursue. It's not unusual for a script to "magically" appear near one of the creatives during a meet and greet, and the actor will be asked, "Hey, would you mind, ya know, maybe, just for the heck of it, reading a bit?" Usually this is followed by a lame follow-up of courtesy, as in, "Just to see if the material is something that you're comfortable with and the words marry with your integrity." Oh puh-leze. Everyone in the room knows that the script was going to come out sooner or later, but when dealing with high-profile projects and high-profile people, bullshit is a requisite.

THE COMBINES: SETCS, NDTAS, NETCS, UPTAS, AND OTHER ABBREVIATIONS

The challenge: Present two contrasting songs and a monologue in ninety seconds or less. *Ready. Set. Go!!!!*

Welcome to the world of "the combines." Combined auditions, held in many regions of the United States throughout the year, are great opportunities for hundreds upon hundreds of actors to present the full range of their talent to multiple theatrical producers. The drawback is that a stopwatch limits your chance to show off your abilities—you can expect to be granted two minutes or less. Some regionals (a term commonly used for the combines) only allow sixty seconds per auditionee. It's the speed dating of auditions.

The number of producers attending varies with each combined audition site. At the larger combined auditions there can be over two hundred entertainment venues represented. Smaller regional combined auditions that restrict participation to producers from within in a single state or city may have as few as twenty entertainment venues represented.

The stressful audition-as-fast-as-you-can scenario of the combines is usually held in a large hotel ballroom or sometimes on the stage of the audition host (if the host is a theatrical producer). The combines are where most of the nonunion theater and theme park venues procure their actors for a season. Some union theaters will be present as well, looking for both union and nonunion talent. The combines are a great place for nonunion actors to gain entry into a union theater. But don't expect your Equity card. Union theaters need nonunion actors to fill out their season's requirements. The hiring of nonunion talent at a union house, with approval from the Actors' Equity Association, puts less of a strain on a union theater's bottom line.

Nonunion tour producers (or their casting directors) also mine the combines for talent. Nowadays, a nonunion tour is substantial money in the bank for the non-Equity actor. Producers for cruise lines and theme parks commonly participate in the combines as well. Actors may not look upon these players as grand creators of art, but Celebrity Cruises, Disney, Busch Gardens, Six Flags Entertainment, Cedar Fair Parks, and similar venues can offer checks that far exceed most abysmal summer stock, regional, and dinner theater remunerative offerings. Contact information for some combined auditions that regularly attract a decent number of producers appears in the Appendix.

Let's take a look at how combines operate and how best to present your skills and land a job.

To participate in a combined audition such as the one held by the Southeastern Theater Conference (SETC), New England Theater Conference (NETC), or any of the regional organizations, an actor must first obtain an application from the combined audition host or organization. A fee is required, and the application tariff varies from organization to organization. Students are generally required to submit recommendations from their academic advisors with their applications. With each application, the actor submits a résumé and picture. For nonstudents, admittance into the audition is dependent on the professional credits on the résumé. The fee and application are then mailed to the audition-producing organization and the actor waits for the nod of approval. If you've worked at least one recognizable venue that attends the combines you're focusing on, more than likely you'll be given a thumbs up.

For the attending producers, the combined audition process is a long, fanny-fatiguing test of endurance. Over a two- to five-day, ten-hour-a-day stretch, the producers will sit through an assembly-line parade of auditioning actors. On most applications for combined auditions, the actor is given three choices for when they'd like to be seen. Having attended many of the combines myself as both an auditor and actor, I know of three times when the producers are at their freshest and most attentive. On the application, if the auditions are to be held over several days, list your priority of choices to be seen as follows:

Choosing Your Combine Audition Time Slot

✓ Recommended	vs.	🚫 AT YOUR OWN RISK 🚫
✓ **1st Choice:** First day, early afternoon session after lunch (if there was a previous morning session).	**VS.**	Ask for the first slot of auditions. There will always be producers absent for various reasons, including running behind schedule. 🚫
✓ **2nd Choice:** Second day, morning session (request a time between the first and last groups of the morning).	**VS.**	Choose a time that is within the half-hour before or after a producer meal break. For the forty-five minutes prior to a meal break, producers experience a collective catatonic state attributable to low blood sugar levels. For the forty-five minutes after a meal break, some producers will be returning late to the audition site because of slow food service, heavy traffic, or catching up on their administrative duties via the phone. 🚫
✓ **3rd Choice:** Second day, after the producer lunch break (request the second or third group after lunch).	**VS.**	Choose the last day of auditions. Not all producers stay for the full conference. Their leaving early does not come from poor manners but from the constant attention their job requires of them back at the office. 🚫

You've Been Accepted to the Combines . . . Now What?

You've applied for and received one of the coveted slots to speed-audition in front of numerous producers. Now what? Operation Target! Time to investigate, target, and prepare.

To better your odds of receiving callbacks from several producers, you should target several producers. Investigate what is being produced by each venue that plans to attend. Some simple Internet search-engine sleuthing will help. Enter a theater's name in quotation marks (e.g., "Barter Theatre") in the search box. Within the top search returns, you'll find a link to the theater's website. Aim your talent, type, and audition to center on seasons that best match you.

If you discover from your detective work that there are one or two specific roles in a season that you know you are absolutely, dead-on correct for, then by all means, go for those roles! If it's a musical theater role, sing an emotionally powerful sixteen-bar selection from one of the songs that the character sings in the show. The sixteen bars chosen must also demonstrate great musicianship. And by great musicianship, I don't mean sing loud and belt the money note (by "money note," I mean the climax of a song). Good musicianship in sixteen bars or fewer shows that you can properly phrase a lyric, breathe when appropriate, and keep in tune while telling a story with conviction. Draw in your audience with your heart instead of alienating them with flashy, presentational gimmicks such as mannered blocking or screeching the final note until all dogs within earshot howl in agony.

If your search yields nonmusical theater roles for which you have potential, pull a monologue or two from the characters within the plays. If you discover a musical theater role and a nonmusical theater role within the upcoming seasons for which you consider yourself perfect, and you're an actor who can sing, do pieces from both. Cover your bases. The more versatile you are in ninety seconds or less, the higher your initial curb appeal to the auditors.

No upcoming season listed? OK, then investigate what the producers have presented in the past. You'll find clues as to what type of shows they regularly present to their audience. Target your audition to this. If it's mostly big, brash musicals from the likes of Jerry Herman, Frank Wildhorn, or Andrew Lloyd Webber, then this style/aesthetic should resonate in your song choices. If you're not a musical theater actor, concentrate your search on the nonmusical theater venues and make sure your monologues reflect what has been presented or what is planned to be produced.

Don't choose songs or monologues from shows that your targeted auditors have presented within the past several years. Why? Upon hearing your rendition the producer (or director) who presented this show will recall the actor who played the role at their venue. The focus will not immediately be on you, and when it is, you'll have to meet or exceed the performance buried within the auditor's memory.

Make sure that your selections are PG- to G-rated. Offensive material is a major turnoff at the combines. Many of the producers there have venues that are in traditionally conservative regions of the country. As soon as expletives are uttered in monologue or song the chill felt in the room is not from an overactive air-conditioner; that arctic blast comes from the producers. It's vital that actors also avoid potentially offensive subject matter, like sex. Avoid sexual topics unless discussion of it is truly benign, innocent, and can be told to your grand-mother without her slapping you.

When I was an auditor at a combined audition, one girl was doing a fairly innocuous monologue that involved her speaking about her invisible friend. She and her friend went everywhere together. At first, the monologue was light and playful and the producers were responding well to her. Until she got to the end. She revealed that her friend was living within her. The girl slipped her hand down the front of her skirt into her groin region, and uttered the line "I'm feeding him now." Not one of the several hundred producers in attendance was amused. No one called her back. She was never allowed to return to the conference again.

Tips for Getting Callbacks at the Combines

✓ Recommended	VS.	🚫 AT YOUR OWN RISK 🚫
✓ If you're an ace at comedy, emphasize comedy. The producers, who have been sitting for hours watching auditions, yearn for wit and humor. It's a welcome relief.	VS.	Scream drama at the producers. It happens often at combines, and the producers instantly tune out. Use profanity or sexually suggestive material. A big turnoff for producers at the combines. 🚫
✓ Have a monologue that coherently tells a story in forty-five seconds or less.	VS.	Use a monologue that, out of context, is confusing and requires explanation. 🚫
✓ If you play an instrument well, such as guitar or banjo, and can accompany yourself while singing, producers will want to call you back to learn more about you.	VS.	Sing a capella. 🚫
✓ Performers who can't sing benefit from displaying their stronger abilities. If you're a dancer who sings, first display movement that best demonstrates your skills. Sing second.	VS.	If you're weak in the singing department, struggle through a song that does nothing better than show us you can struggle through a song. 🚫
✓ Routinely practice your audition to be under the time limit. The timekeepers at combines are very strict with the stopwatch and cut people off once the stopwatch reaches the end of allotted time.	VS.	Try to go beyond your time limit. A number of actors at the combines will always try it, but doing so results in resentment from the audition staff and auditing producers. 🚫

GOING ON TAPE, A.K.A. BEING PUT ON TAPE

Even though we're now in the digital age, the outmoded phrase "going on tape" remains the term for when actors are placed in front of a camera to audition for a film or a broadcast project without the project's auditors present. If an auditor is present it's generally the casting director and/or their assistant. If it's not the project's casting personnel, it may be your talent rep, his or her assistant, your friend, or someone you hired to capture you on camera. Often, whoever is behind the camera is also the person reading as your scene partner. Once your audition has been captured on video, it's then reviewed by casting and often edited. If your reading makes this cut, your video audition climbs up to the next level of decision-makers.

Going on tape is one of the most nonorganic, unreal audition scenarios actors will encounter. The environment for the audition is usually a cramped office. You sit on either a barstool or chair. If not instructed to sit, you're ordered to stand on a spike mark. Movement is limited in either scenario. The shot is from mid-chest up. Your off-camera scene partner will be as exciting as a dust bunny. Between you and the mumbling mass of breathing lint is the camera capturing your brilliance or lack thereof. You're playing to glass—the lens that is focused on you. If you go into the audition focused on the challenges, particularly the camera lens being an object and not a person within the room, then your audition will be as cold as the glass lens.

Where theater is broad strokes of emotion and movement, screen acting is channeling emotions through speech and the eyes, minimizing gesture and interaction but retaining the strength of the emotion, whether it's joy, sorrow, hate, or enthralled passion. Where internalized motivation on the stage fails to make it past the proscenium, internalized monologues are crucial to successful storytelling on screen.

Later in this book we'll meet agency owner Jack Menashe, founder of Independent Artists Agency. In my talks with him about actors going on camera he spoke of how he instructs his clients to audition for the *Law & Order* franchises. "I tell them, 'Don't act,'" Menashe offers. "Once they begin acting for the camera, they lose the job. The best thing they can do is just go in, read the lines, be the character, but don't act." For the camera, acting is more about truth; truth in emotion, in motivation, and in response. It's not about heightening the emotions; it's about highlighting them.

Tips for Going On Tape

✓ Don't wear white or light-colored clothing; camera lighting, the camera, and white don't play well together. White will also wash out your facial features.

✓ Test your clothing on camera at home (or your talent rep's office) and view the playback prior to wearing that clothing for your on-camera audition. The color you love to wear on the street may be dreadful to wear on camera.

✓ Ask the camera operator how far, and if, you can move and still be seen in the frame; going on tape usually means the audition will be shot with a tight frame.

✓ Normally an audition scene involves you with one other character (sometimes two characters). No matter how many characters on paper are in the scene with you, play the scene with one eye focused to the camera and the other eye just slightly off to the lens edge; this way you don't look as if you're relentlessly staring at the viewer.

GOING TO STUDIO: A TEST DEAL

Imagine that before applying for a job in the civilian world, you had to sign a contract that listed your salary, benefits (or lack thereof), and the length and terms of employment. All of which must be agreed upon by you *before* you fill out the job application. Sound ridiculous? Hah! Welcome to the world of entertainment and studio test deals.

Television and film studios have got a sweet game when it comes to test deals. An actor's contract for employment must be negotiated and agreed upon before he or she steps foot into the audition that will determine whether that actor gets a principal role in a film or television series. Test deals only apply to principal roles in film and principal and recurring principal roles for television. Salary, residuals, percentages of receipts from marketing tie-ins, length of employment, dressing room, housing, transportation, and sometimes even the food served on set—all of these terms are contracted before the final audition.

The studio has the better odds in winning the negotiations. Several to half a dozen actors might test for the same role. Studio business affairs representatives, as instructed by the studio, notoriously lowball the talent in all negotiations. Studios want to pay as little as possible to the talent, knowing that the talent wants and needs the work. It's parallel to casinos throwing open their doors welcoming habitual gamblers. What's the gambling addict to do? Walk away? Same dilemma for the actors. Are they to walk away? They can't. Unless he or she is a mega-star (for whom test deals are ancient history), the process for an actor just to get to the point of going to studio took many arduous auditions. A test deal and going to studio is a rare opportunity that 98 percent of actors never get close to achieving.

Tips for Surviving Going to Studio/Test Deal

✓ Trust that your talent rep will handle the negotiations in your best interest. When given the terms of the contract by your representative, focus on the long-term items that will continue to generate money long after the project has ended. Don't focus on present perks, like the color of your dressing room or demanding a personal trainer.

✓ Have your talent rep or someone you are emotionally close to accompany you on the audition. Your nerves and ego will need familiar comfort.

✓ Get plenty of rest the day before and of your audition for the studio.

✓ View the audition with the same importance as all prior auditions in your career; it's just an audition, not a judgment on you as a person or your career.

Paid Auditions

Sometimes referred to as "seminars," paid auditions are when actors pay to meet talent reps and casting directors at performing arts "schools" and studios like Weist Barron, TVI Studios, One-on-One, and Actor's Connection. Twenty to thirty actors individually meet a casting person or talent rep in a small room and then perform a monologue or scene. There is no project that is being cast or offer of employment. It's a one-on-one form of actor marketing.

Actors and industry both have a mixed reaction to paid auditions. Some feel that by paying the host a small fee to meet industry not readily accessible, the actor gains a great opportunity to be seen. Others simply call this pay to play a form of prostitution, because the industry person you meet receives a stipend from the organization hosting the paid auditions—money that comes from the actors paying the host.

Personally, I prefer the optimism of the first view; paid auditions *are* a great opportunity for an actor to get face time in front of industry. If you can afford the expense, make the investment. For my projects, I have called in many an actor met at paid auditions. I also know of agents who have signed actors they met at paid auditions.

To those who equate paid auditions to actors hustling themselves like whores: Ummm . . . Do you realize the following truths? We in casting receive a fee from our clients when we audition actors for their projects. Talent reps receive money from their clients who they book into paying jobs. Actors *pay* to be seen at the combined auditions like SETC and UPTAs. To attend almost any audition, actors have to pay for transport via bus, train, or cab, or for a tank of gas. Actors have to pay to get training, and the people actors meet during training are the same people who later assist them in getting jobs. Actors have to pay the post office or their Internet providers to have their headshots and résumés delivered to casting or talent reps. For actors to get seen, monies are exchanged, no matter how they put themselves out into the world. So to those actors who say paid auditions are equal to prostitution, I say, get over yourselves and get seen! You're missing opportunities!

Tips for Paid Auditions

Sign up to see people who actually make the decisions in their offices. Many times assistants attend the paid auditions. Don't bother with assistants. Go for the power people.

Sign up for industry people who match your interests. If you want to do strictly film, focus on the film casting directors who attend paid auditions. If you prefer theater, target the casting directors who primarily do theater. If you need an agent, spend your money on agents first. If one likes and signs you, he or she will assist you in getting in front of casting.

Even if you're signed with an agency, sign up at paid auditions for those casting directors you have yet to meet. Also, target those casting directors you haven't seen for a while.

You'll be asked to do a monologue. Do not bring in material that is offensive, requires screaming, or is violent or sexually provocative to the point of obscenity. Avoid material that you couldn't show to clergy.

There's a lot of work out there to be had and many audition scenarios for gaining those opportunities of artistic expression. What will help you succeed in achieving your best for every audition scenario is confidence. That confidence comes partly from believing in your own abilities but also from refining organizational skills for getting and preparing for an audition. This is accompanied by studious follow-through with thorough knowledge of the audition material required for the potential job. You may have balls to believe in yourself because of your stalwart ambition, but that will not be enough to bring success unless backed with proper audition preparation.

Are you always properly prepared for *every* audition? Truly ready? Are your audition skills perfect? If you answered "Yes," then you must be a lifetime employed actor acing every audition and turning down offers left and right. Write a book and tell us how you do it. For the rest of us dealing in reality, continue onward as we seek to further embolden your confidence. No one can be perfect, but improvement is always attainable. And with improvement comes confidence, a self-assuredness based on a foundation of knowledge that there are always ways to strengthen the preparation for nearly every audition scenario encountered.

CHAPTER EIGHT

AUDITION PREPARATION

Be First, First

"I try to get the audition material in my bones, not just in my frontal lobe. Which means it's not just a question of memorizing the material but understanding it and digesting it so that when I work in the room what the casting people are going to see is an actor portraying a human being in that play, in the circumstance prescribed."

Bonnie Black

Actress

The better prepared you are for an audition the better your chances for winning the job. OK, so that's a no-brainer. But often in auditions it's obvious—and shocking—that a large number of actors have been lax in getting ready for what is essentially a job interview. Ill-equipped actors will come into the audition lacking music for musical auditions or appropriate audition material to match the project. Some will not have learned the audition material given to them by the auditors, or they learned it in a rush on the way to the audition.

That last one pisses me off the most—actors learning material at the last minute. Ninety-five percent of the time I give out appointments anywhere from one to two weeks prior to the audition date. I want every actor coming in to hit a home run. That's my job. I'm here to help actors get employment. A week or two of notice is a generous amount of time to prepare and often a rare gift in our frenetically paced industry. Some actors will put off looking at the audition material until the day of the audition call. My reprimand to them begins like this: "If you were interviewing for a *Fortune* 500 company, would you be as careless in preparation with them as you are now with me? Why aren't you prepared?" Applying for work as an actor involves professional preparation as does applying for a job in the civilian world. No excuses.

Sometimes excuses are given, and they're laughable. One of the more popular dog-ate-my-homework excuses from actors is "My agent didn't tell me I had to prepare something."

Ooooohkaaay. So you're an actor, going to an audition … what the hell do you think the auditors want of you!? For you to stand there silently and we'll all be amazed as talent oozes from your pores? Even if there is truth in the pitiful excuse that your talent rep didn't provide you with adequate information, wouldn't it be kind of smart, as an actor, to *ask* your agent or manager, "What am I to prepare?" The person in charge of giving out appointments is not going to call a talent rep and ask for the client to schlep in and stand and do nothing. Although … I am reminded now of an awkward audition where, uhm, we almost did just that.

For the film *The Siege* a crying man was needed. Why the role wasn't the responsibility of extras casting, I have no idea, but we got stuck with auditioning crying men. Older crying men, in their sixties. No lines, no moans, no wails, just silent tears. The men would come into the small cubicle of an office, sit in a chair before a video camera, and cry, silently. Talk about uncomfortable. With each crier I had to turn away and look out the window onto the street twenty floors below. I was both embarrassed and nervously amused at the absurdity of the situation. God, what an actor has to do to get money. But! The actors *knew* what they were to prepare before walking into the audition! They had to cry! The sexagenarians came in with professional grace, and as asked each delivered the saline flow required. After seeing a dozen men wail without sound and emptying a box of tissues, the role was finally handed over to extras. Whether or not "Crying Man" made it into the final cut I don't know. I tried watching the movie on an overseas flight. After ten minutes I turned it off and went to something more entertaining: video hangman.

BEING PREPARED

Auditors generally will not call back an actor who is unprepared. Now when I say "call back," I don't mean a callback for that particular project. No, that would be generous. I mean I will not call back a previously unprepared actor, *ever*, for any other project in the future. The picture and résumé of someone who is not prepared quickly goes into the trash. Why so hard-hearted? There's a lot of competition among actors. I can easily find another actor who is prepared and has his or her shit together. Casting directors don't look fondly upon actors who waste our time. Nor do our clients. Come in unprepared for an audition and more than likely you'll never see those auditors again in relation to employment.

Once, when I was casting a musical for the Asolo Theatre Festival, the director confronted unprepared actors quite bluntly. The audition set-up was typical. The actors were to come in with two songs and prepared sides. A surprise in the audition room for the actors, and to me, was the director asking auditionees, without prior notice, to do a monologue (it was going to be a long and interesting day). Many of the actors fumbled and hemmed and hawed; most were not ready for this curveball. In days gone by when monologues by actors in auditions was standard practice, this would not have been such a challenge. But this director would stop the actor mid-excuse and with a gentle but firm reprimand say, "You don't have your tools. You're asking us to hire you. You're asking us to put you in front of a paying audience, people who can barely afford a ticket, and you're here unprepared for the job interview. Why should we hire you?" Shocked that an auditor called their bluff, the actors would scramble for another excuse, but before two words could be uttered the director would raise his hand to them and advise, "Stop, stop, stop. I don't care what your reasoning is; you have no valid excuse, as an actor, to be unprepared. You can't be an actor without your tools." And he's correct. So correct, that more of us auditors should follow his lead in confronting unprepared actors.

PREPARATION BEGINS WITH OPPORTUNITY

Preparation must begin once you receive the good news that you've gotten an audition. Ask questions. Whether represented or not, ask for detailed information from the person contacting you. Many of the important questions to be asked, below, seem elementary. But I have met actors in auditions who had no clue as to what they were auditioning for.

Audition Appointment Question Checklist

- ✓ Full address of the audition site?
- ✓ Exact appointment time and date?
- ✓ Who is going to be in the room?
- ✓ Who is involved?
- ✓ Commitment dates?
- ✓ Is there a script available?
- ✓ Can I read the script?
- ✓ Are there sides? (often overlooked but obvious question)
- ✓ What else am I to prepare?
- ✓ Title of the project?

OK, OK, I know that last question seems obvious, but sometimes a talent rep will only give his or her client a character name and hope that the actor will know that Prospero is from *As You Like It*. Or is it *Measure for Measure* . . . or *Death of a Salesman*? I wish I were making up the prior example; sadly, I'm not. Similarly, I once invited a lovely young actress to audition for Juliet in *Romeo and Juliet*. Unfortunately she sang "Many a New Day" from *Oklahoma!* Her agent had misinformed her. The young actress believed that she was auditioning for the Rodgers & Hammerstein musical *Me & Juliet*. Oops.

Words of Caution

Be careful of the things you say; auditors will listen. On occasion the people assigned to casting a project go beyond talent reps and call unrepresented talent to offer an audition. If you're receiving an audition directly from the auditor, casting director, or an assistant, don't interrogate them for information, which might seem justifiable to you but in actuality is inappropriate. The following examples are true questions/statements I've received from actors upon my directly offering them an audition:

- ⊘ "How old is the director, and what's his experience?"
- ⊘ "If I get the job, when am I able to leave if I get a better job?"
- ⊘ "I'll audition, but only if my significant other can audition as well."

When I encounter inquiries like these, I do one of two things. The first option is to cancel the appointment and give it to one of the actors I have on my hold list. The second option is to let the actor audition. But . . . if after the person has auditioned the other auditors express an interest, I'll let them know of the disposition the actor displayed when I gave him or her the appointment. Often that information alone dissuades the auditors and they move on to another choice. Why? Because the questioning shows that the actor is not focused on what is primary to his or her career: work. Casting personnel, directors, and producers desire actors who are focused on the work.

BE FIRST, FIRST

Auditions are like a race. Second and third place count for little at the finish line. In the audition race the actor must always maintain first place, even in preparation.

Be First, First Checklist:

- ✓ Ask for an early appointment. Rarely is an actor allowed to choose an audition time. If you are, ask to be seen early. The auditors are at their most alert at the beginning of the audition process.
- ✓ Get the audition material as quickly as possible. The more time with the material, the better prepared you'll be.
- ✓ Get the script whenever possible. Sides and character breakdowns are not enough.
- ✓ Know the character, not just the character's given audition moment.

PERFORMANCE IN AUDITION, A.K.A. THEY WANT IT ALL

At the audition, auditors want a fully realized performance. The creative team looks to the actor to deliver, from whatever audition material was provided, the full, finished product that will eventually appear on stage or screen. This is the actor's challenge. Compress a character's full journey in the story into the abbreviated audition material. For audition purposes only, an actor is required to put the character's entire arc from the play into the scene given for the audition. To begin on this journey of incorporating the character's arc into your audition, some homework must be done. That homework includes reading and research.

Read a Script before an Audition

If available, read the full script—don't skip those scenes that exclude your character. Action in other scenes may directly affect your character's journey. Don't scan the script searching only for your character's lines. Read the script fully and discover the world in which your character lives.

Sometimes a script may not be available. Mostly this will occur for film and TV auditions. When a script cannot be procured, try to get the sides for the other characters that are being cast as well. If you have a talent rep, simply ask him or her for help with this. At least by viewing several pieces of the puzzle that is the script you'll get a better understanding of the story, the writer's voice, and the character's journey in relation to others.

Another ploy for finding a full or partial script that may or may not be openly available is searching the Internet. Often scripts are placed online for private use between the writer and creative personnel. Search engine spiders may have searched those pages. The hunt may take some effort, but the results will be worth the time. In the search box, enter in keywords such as the title, writer's name, character's name, or lines from your sides, and you may hit pay dirt.

Research a Script before an Audition

Many written works for stage and screen are based on historical events, reference a distinct era, explore science, religion, and cultures or are based on the lives of actual individuals. Fictional or not, there will be some aspect of the story—its people, locale, language, or the influence of its period upon the characters—that you can study to better your understanding of the world the author has put on paper. Do your homework. Go online and Google information needed to learn more about the character and the story's time period, plus retrieve information about the writer, the production, and the producing entity. The more informed, the better prepared an actor will be in the audition room.

An Arc Ain't Just a Boat with Horny Animals

It's OK to fess up and admit that you may not be familiar with the term "character arc." It refers to the full emotional journey that a character travels within the story. So let's say you're auditioning for Desdemona or Othello in *Othello*. As an actress/actor you'll need to translate all the emotions and experiences of Desdemona/Othello from the entire play into the one or two pages that have been pulled from the script for your audition. Even if given a monologue, the same rule applies. Put the character's full journey into that one monologue, while keeping within the context of the scene.

Of course this sounds preposterous and difficult. How dare we ask that you present to us the character's entire journey in fewer than fifty words from a scene that has little to do with some aspects of that journey. Well, that's the challenge that is being placed upon you as the actor if you want the job. You're asking us to hire you. We're asking you to bring in an opening-night performance that will convince us you're worthy of the audience's hard-earned money. That ticket revenue goes toward your salary. There are no free rides. You have to work for what you want. Work hard.

Copy That? Seeing a Production Prior to Auditioning

If the casting director instructs you or your representation that you should see a particular current stage production of what you're auditioning for, even though you're auditioning for a tour or regional version of that same play or musical, DO IT! See the production. The instruction indicates that the director wants you to be familiar with the tone of the production and performances, and/or the director wants a near photocopy of what is being presented. Before fearing that you're being asked to photocopy a performance, ask whoever gave you the instruction to attend a performance if that is what the director is seeking. If so, this doesn't mean that you have to imitate, just assimilate. Bring in an imitation and it'll be plastic and false. Assimilate the style of the performance while making the role your own.

Creating the Audition Setting as Part of Preparation

Prepare for your audition as it would occur in the audition setting. If it is a scene in which your character has a dialogue exchange, drag, beg, or Craigslist.org a practice reader for the other role(s). Place the practice reader in front of you where a reader normally is set in an audition room. Where's that?

Readers are set to the left or right of the audition table. Play off the practice reader without touching her or having her getting up from her chair. For auditions put to tape (on camera) the reader is often behind the camera.

To Memory, or Not to Memory?

Ah, the most-asked audition preparation question: Should an actor memorize lines for an audition? Learn the *material*. Memorize the text if you want but not the *performance*. Memorization or semi-memorization of the text boosts your chances greatly. This will free the performance plus demonstrate that you are prepared and serious about the audition. Only 10 percent of actors auditioned take the extra effort to learn the material. It's that 10 percent that get called back and/or hired.

Darrie Lawrence is an advocate for memorization. "I now actually memorize the text," Lawrence admitted. "I used to think that was not important. The memorization process makes you think about the scene and what the other person is saying. You can only figure out what you're going to say if it's really clear what the other person in the scene is going to say. Memorization makes you analyze the script."

But . . . wait!

Memorization or semi-memorization can be an actor's downfall when improperly used. DO NOT memorize text to actions and movement. Avoid being a victim of a manufactured or "learned" performance. Don't make memorization or semi-memorization of the text your primary focus. Treat text memory as an accessory. Keep the script/side in hand. Audition anxiety and nerves play havoc on the memory, so use the script/side for when nerves make the memory falter. *Fumbling for lines is deadly.*

Manufactured by Rote

One of the biggest failures for an actor in an audition (and in performance) is presenting a manufactured, mechanical reading/portrayal/interpretation. In other words, getting trapped into roadmap acting where movement, readings, or singing has a preset course and never ventures into discovery and exploration. Be spontaneous! Don't memorize the performance. Putting text to memory is okay, if you're solid with the lines. But memorizing the performance becomes audition by rote. When that happens, you'll be asked to move on out the door.

When I was a young actor I fell into the manufactured-by-rote trap, a dangerous practice that can happen both in auditions and in production. With one role I got snared twice, first in the rehearsal process then later in an audition for a subsequent production of the same show. My first entrapment was brought to my attention when another actor bluntly acknowledged my failure in rehearsal. I was cast as Mordred in a production of *Camelot*. Eager and woefully ignorant, I wanted to demonstrate to the director that I was prepared for the role by the time we had our first read-through. Prior to that first day of rehearsal I learned my lines, inflections, and motivations. I thought the readings that came out of my mouth were on point. Wrong.

At the first read-through I plowed ahead with my learned performance. After one of my scenes with King Arthur, I heard behind me a heavy sigh followed by a quiet, disapproving male voice. "Manufactured. Plastic," came the critique. The disapproval was in reference to me. It came from Fred Carmichael, who was playing Merlin. Apart from being an actor, Fred was also a prolific playwright and a founder of the Dorset Theatre Festival. I didn't let him know I had heard his criticism. I was crushed. I so desperately wanted to be good that I blinded myself with misguided ambition. I was determined to learn from my error and make immediate repairs. I tossed away the manufactured Mordred and started anew. Fred was a brilliant and mischievous man. Upon reflection I believe that he intended for me to hear his comments.

But did I fully learn my lesson? No.

A year later I was at the AEA audition lounge in New York, auditioning for the malevolent bastard son of King Arthur in another production of *Camelot*. Arrogant that the role would be mine again I re-created my performance of Mordred's "Seven Deadly Virtues" just as I had performed it a year prior. The result was like pulling a comment out of context. I wasn't matching content (material) to form (an audition). I was presenting a fabricated reproduction of a performance that had been appropriate for an audience of several hundred, but my revival wasn't suited for viewing by a single auditor.

"The seven deadly virtues,

Those ghastly little traps (*large hand gesture here*),

Oh, no, Milord, they weren't meant for me" (*sit on floor*).

What the *fuck* was I thinking?! Oh well, we eventually learn and move on.

How to End Manufactured by Rote

Prepare audition material (singing, sides, monologues) while doing mundane chores or activities. Practice the audition piece in settings that have nothing to do with the material. For example, if you're an actress auditioning for Lady Macbeth, rehearse the "out damned spot" scene as you wash dishes, fold laundry, or drive to the mall. If you're an actor auditioning for Sweeney Todd, rehearse his "Epiphany" while planting mums in the backyard or jogging in the park. Focus on the present activity. Don't worry about the hands, movement, and all other baggage. If you're honest in character, any activity will flow naturally if you focus on what you say while concentrating on the chore or task.

This exercise will provide you with several advantages. You'll gain greater flexibility when given direction or adjustments in the audition. Also, it will prepare you for audition distractions (director spilling coffee while you read, reader halitosis, cow-hoofed pianist, etc.).

Rehearsing the audition material outside of its intended environment, as written, will open up discoveries. You'll hear new interpretations. You will be stronger in the audition room when the director begins adjustments. You'll feel secure because, hey, if you can be Maggie from *Cat on a Hot Tin Roof* at your local grocery store, you can be Maggie anywhere in any situation. The point of this exercise is to listen. By listening you discover. Listening is acting, and acting is listening.

Bonnie Black learned an audition preparation technique that would help her listen better. "In terms of learning lines, whoever you're speaking to, take a pencil and underline the operative words and phrases, whatever sentences that are important to hear from the other character. Just doing that helps you further understand the scene," Black explained. "Also when you looked at the page, subliminally what was going into your head was not just, 'bullshit, bullshit, bullshit,' then my line but actually what the people opposite of you were saying that would spur you to your response. It's a good way to look at a scene and understand what is happening."

Black further enhances her listening skills with another technique. "Something else I do is rather than just say my lines out loud, I'll say the other people's lines out loud, doing my line in my head as opposed to doing their line in my head and then my line out loud. I use this reverse process to deepen my understanding and to increase how much I'm hearing the other character. Acting is reacting. It's important to hear what is being said."

AUDITION MONOLOGUES: "OUT BRIEF CANDLE . . . "

Audition monologues are dead. Dead, when it comes to professional auditions.

Academia continues to teach an outdated philosophy that professional auditions utilize monologues. Bzzz! Wrong answer, thanks for playing. Yes, in the bubble of academia, monologues are abused (pardon me, used). Outside the insular world of academia—i.e., the world of entertainment—audition monologues have become near impractical. They're the yard sale equivalent of Donny Osmond 8-track tapes gathering dust atop a turntable in Bum-Fart, Kansas.

Audition sides are used at 99.99 percent of professional auditions. An audition side, for the newly informed, is a section of dialogue, a scene, or a monologue found within the project's script. Prior to auditions, the director and/or casting director decide on the sides that are to be prepared by the auditioning actors.

The progression away from audition monologues to audition sides evolved as TV and film began to dominate the entertainment market. Sitcoms and Shakespeare rarely dance together. When they do, it's an unsightly tango.

Story through soliloquy is a dying craft. Often when I cast language plays (i.e., that Shakespeare stuff) auditioning actors, inexperienced with metered dialogue (even those actors with industry Ivy League credentials), rush through the chosen slice of Bard, grateful just to be over and done with it. After this happens, I'll write on my notes, next to the actor's name, "Jet Ski." Like a Jet Ski skims across water, the actor has skimmed across the text. No depth. No subtleties. No substance. This type of an audition is caused by a fear of the text, a lack of understanding of the language, and, most important, an inability to communicate a story. Doesn't matter if it's Old English or present-day English, storytelling through soliloquy suffers interpretation by the speaker because modern communication skills are faltering. We speak *at* each other, rather than *to* each other.

Advancements in communication technology (and the abuse of it) contribute to the growing inability of people to engage others directly without aid of keystrokes. Communicating themes, ideas, and story with clarity through spoken and written word has deteriorated dramatically as we quickly IM, text message, and e-mail each other with abbreviations masquerading as one-on-one connection. "BRB!," "AFK," and "ROFLMAO" assault communication skills and are by no means personal. Imagine if ole Billy Shakespeare decided to apply similar shorthand texting onto his Prince of Denmark. Hamlet's "To be or to be?" might have been reduced to "2b/not 2b?" Without our knowing Hamlet's mental rifts we'd be under the misimpression that the Dane was seeking a room on the second floor of Elsinore.

Another reason audition monologues are bound for burial is modern society's lazy listening skills. Dialogue and information come hurtling us at lighting speed. Dialogue is reduced to sound bites, quips, and clips. Our ears demand information in short bursts, preferably loud. Before electronic amplification, people engaged in listening. Listening was an active skill. Now it's become a passive activity, where we rely on technology to carry out the work our ears and gray cells once did. Can't hear what's being said on TV? Click on the remote and raise the volume. Can't raise the volume? Is the narrative too long or requires thought? Tune out and switch the channel. The modern ear doesn't want to exert effort on listening. Technology is supposed to do that for us. But technology gives little to no aid in our evaluating the themes, through-lines, and arc of a detailed story. Monologues are detailed short stories but not short enough for our slothful, internal sound systems. Not having a remote to change a live person to someone else more engaging or not being able to raise their volume, we tune out the speaker as our interest wanes.

Audition monologues lumber on to the grave with little purpose except for use in school auditions, nonunion summer stock cattle calls, community theater tryouts, and paid auditions. Those instances and a few Shakespeare festivals are the only venues keeping the coffin for audition monologues from being nailed shut and placed into a hearse. For years I have been trying to wean one of my Shakespeare clients away from asking actors to audition with monologues of the actor's choice. Why? Actors at my level of casting no longer have monologues ready for use. When I call talent reps with a monologues-of-the-actor's-choice audition, I get an earful of complaint. Talent reps balk because their clients charge into anxiety overdrive. Many actors who graduated from school in the last decades of the twentieth century left monologues behind in the black box of college theater. For some of them, monologues are an unpleasant memory best left at school, like the hangovers from all-night keggers.

Having an actor learn a monologue, when sides are offered, is a time-waster. Most auditors and I prefer to go straight to what the actor is auditioning for—the role we want an actor to portray. We're not interested in hearing/seeing another role from a quasi-related monologue. We want the meat. Not a soy and gluten substitute. If the actor is being seen for Hamlet, I have him read Hamlet, so that I can be assured he's capable of playing that role. That's my priority. When there is a role that has monologues, more than likely the casting director or the director will assign to the actor one or two they want to see and hear. I couldn't care less, at that moment, if the actor can do a Chekhov monologue. Save Tolkachov's rant of abused husbandry for when I'm auditioning *Summer in the Country*. But wait . . . !

Don't level your wobbling furniture with monologue books just yet. As mentioned previously, there are instances, especially early in an actor's career, when an actor needs a treasure trove of contrasting monologues. Monologues ready to go at an instant.

Instances for Monologues

✓ Enrollment process for performing arts schools.
✓ Regional combines such as SETCs, NETCs, UPTAs, and NDTAs require audi-

tionees to perform monologues—brief monologues, preferably sixty seconds or less in length.

✓ Community theater and school production auditions rely on monologues as a barometer for an actor being right for a role. (I hope they catch up with the real world. It will better prepare the community theater and/or student actor who later wants to venture onto professional auditions.)

✓ Paid auditions with casting directors and talent reps. It's rare that talent reps would ask prospective clients to do a monologue for the agent in their office. The agent today, in signing talent, prefers to see the actor's work in production on screen or stage. Monologues by actors today in the offices of talent reps is 1940s film lore fantasy.

Alternative Monologue Resources

When I was an actor I was very independent and stayed far away from monologue books. My reasoning was, "Hey, thousands of these books are being sold. Why should I be using the same audition material that is being used by thousands of fellow actors? Screw that! I need to find better resources." And I did. Stay away from the audition monologue books. Find new resources to enrich your monologue treasure chest.

✓ Comedy albums

Bob Newhart was gold for me. When I was a young actor in the mid-1980s I came across one of his comedy albums from the 1960s. I hit a jackpot. I began using several of his comedic monologues including "King Kong & the Night Watchman" and "The U.S.S. Codfish." I was scoring home runs at auditions with both for two reasons. First, the material matched my humor and personality. Second, hardly anyone knew of the material's existence. Auditors loved hearing something unfamiliar. And they loved hearing something funny.

✓ Films

They're a great, untapped resource for monologues. Research older films. Often the writing is skilled, crafted with layers and color.

✓ Classic and modern literature

Jane Austen unknowingly gave actresses many wonderful opportunities for monologues. Michener and Hemingway are wonderful for actors as well. The essay books of Michael Thomas Ford offer great comedic material for the modern day.

✓ Political speeches and addresses by statesmen

✓ Archived radio shows from the 1940s and before

✓ Classic television drama and well-written sitcoms (that don't contain iconic characters, like those on *Seinfeld*)

Monologue Treasure-Chest Elements

Unless specifically asked for, monologues as a barometer of actor talent are dead beyond school, stock, and paid auditions. *But,* once in a while you may be surprised by a director like the one from the Asolo who suddenly, without warning, asks you to do a monologue on the spot (Oh, shit!). That scenario is the *exception* and not typical of the majority of present-day auditions. For those very rare monologue moments and for the common scenarios in which a single voice is called for, every actor should have the following in his or her treasure chest:

- ✓ Two to four comedic, classical monologues
- ✓ Two to four dramatic, classical monologues
- ✓ Two to four comedic, contemporary monologues
- ✓ Two to four dramatic, contemporary monologues

Audition Monologue Essentials

Choose material that fits the project for which you're auditioning. Don't bring in Brecht or Shakespeare for Neil Simon and vice versa. Matching your material to the audition may seem obvious, but far too often other auditors and I have witnessed actors do the opposite.

For the combined regional auditions, investigate the shows being produced in each theater's upcoming season. Match your monologue to the productions in which you'd like to be cast.

For general auditions, be realistic and objective when choosing material that best matches your abilities as an actor. If you're a 5' 4", 130-pound, red-haired, Irish, nineteen-year-old female, there's very little hope that you'll ever be the Marquis de Sade, the genital-flaunting fellow in Doug Wright's *Quills*. Choose material that suits you with characters that match in age and gender.

If appropriate to the audition, go for comedy. Far too often, in general auditions, actors scream out drama with crocodile tears. Give yourself and the auditors a break.

Stay away from topical monologues that involve a personal health crisis. The auditors on the other side of the table may be directly affected by cancer, HIV, etc. When this happens, we focus on our own experience with the health issue and not you. This guideline also applies to avoiding monologues involving disaster, natural or manmade, and terrorism. If a similar event has happened recently in the real world, we will fixate on the tragedy and not you.

Unless you or a friend of yours is a brilliant and accomplished playwright, *avoid material written by you or a friend!*

If you need to give a preamble to explain the monologue and/or scene in great length to the auditor, toss the material and find something else.

Don't explain well-known material. An actor, before his audition, once offered me the following: "I'll be doing a scene from *The Odd Couple*. You may not know it. There's this guy Oscar who is a slob and another guy called Felix. They live together, but not in a homosexual way . . ."

Avoid monologues that involve props, violence, or both. As I mentioned, I once had an actor pull a knife on me during his monologue. He may have thought he was being real. I thought he was fucking crazy.

Audition Monologue Postmortem

Audition monologues (ones not chosen as sides by the auditors) may be dead in most professional auditions, but you never know when a resurrection will occur. Times and trends change quickly. Best to be prepared and have several audition monologues at the ready.

MUSICAL THEATER AUDITION PREPARATION: INTO THE WORDS IT'S TIME TO GO

For musical theater auditions, be more than just a pretty voice with great technique. Approach your audition piece as two separate entities conjoined—i.e., dialogue and music. Many musical performers forget that the lyrics in a musical number are dialogue or soliloquy written to tell a story. Always remember the basic rule: Lyrics are not just random words placed to accentuate the pretty notes. Many of my clients and I want to hear the story in a song. Take the notes away from the lyrics and dive into what is being told. OK, if it's Tim Rice, a lyricist known for the occasional clunker, you may find yourself wondering about the intellectual depth of a lyric that reads "Only goes to sho-wa, greatest man since No-ah . . ." (there are exceptions).

After learning the notes, breathing, and phrasing, approach the text (lyrics) as you would in the exercise to defeat Manufactured by Rote. Separate the lyrics from the music and speak them in conversational form while doing chores and tasks. Listen to what you are saying. Then add the music and do the same exercise, focusing on both the chore/music while in character. Also, sing the song to a live individual as if in a conversation. Use pets as a last resort. Connect.

Prized is the musical theater performer who can connect. Connect themes to within lyric and song. Connect to an audience. Connect to other actors onstage. Often in auditions I am sung at, not sung to. Yes, breaking into song is unnatural and false. Remember *Cop Rock*? And that is part of the problem for musical performers: the perception that breaking into song is false. As a result, the presentation becomes just that—presentation. False, bordering on theme park. Singing doesn't have to be "I stand here, stare forward like a deer in headlights, occasionally give gestures, and go for the money note, baby!" No. That's crap. Singing is storytelling. Musical theater actors would do themselves a great service by performing in and studying language plays such as Shakespeare.

When I direct a musical, in rehearsal I instruct actors to think of their song not as "musical theater" but as a monologue, separating the lyric from the music. I encourage the singer's solo to be more of a soliloquy. I do the same for musical numbers that involve more than one singer. The lyrics are dialogue, an exchange of thought. I focus on that exchange, which is basically communication. Whether that communication is between actors onstage or actors and the audience, communicating with clarity is connecting. Solid, defined connections must be made by an actor to his or her song for the song and actor to connect to the audience.

When I was directing a popular Wildhorn musical at a regional theater, one of my male leads, who is stronger as an actor in plays than as a singer in musicals, had trouble connecting emotion and movement to lyric. After I told him to focus on the song as a soliloquy of lost passion, diminished hope, frustration, and redemption, he improved dramatically, but another step to connecting remained.

The notes are not to be forgotten. I'm not speaking of the melody. I'm speaking of the underscoring. After the actor from the Wildhorn musical scored some success connecting to the lyrics, we then sat at the piano with the musical director. Repeatedly I had the musical director play a section of the song for the actor. It's a great rumbling and churning passage, filled with raw angst. I instructed the actor to listen to the underscoring as it raged with anger. Wildhorn was giving musical clues as to the character's internal fury and angst. Eventually the actor connected. The staging and emotion easily followed.

The next time you listen to a song you want to audition with, forget the melody for a moment. Listen to what the composer and orchestrator have placed under the melody. If either the composer or orchestrator is fairly intelligent (most are), emotional clues and colors abound. I have listened to some scores in my musical theater collection for over twenty years. Every time I listen, I hear new layers. Listen to the layers. Exploit those layers. Layering is a key to success for every actor.

Know What You're Singing about and to Whom

Actors who have no clue as to what purpose a song serves in the musical's story and to whom it is sung commit the biggest errors in musical auditions. When I was casting *Crowns* for the Asolo Theatre Festival two actresses auditioned with "Sister" from *The Color Purple*. Each was stopped barely two measures into the song. The director stopped the first; later, I brought the second to a halt. Why? Neither had a clue as to the context of the song or to whom the character was singing. When both were asked the same question—"Who are you singing this song to?"—both ladies went momentarily blank, then sheepishly replied similarly that they were singing it for themselves, for courage. WRONG! The song is about seduction. To know that is as simple as watching the movie or seeing the musical onstage. When that adjustment was given to the young ladies, my, how the song flourished and came to life, no longer just a melody with pretty notes.

Are There Overused Audition Songs?

Many academic advisors, directors, and other sages will tell musical theater actors to "stay away from overused songs" when auditioning. Personally, I say screw that advice. The unwritten law prohibiting use of "overused songs" in auditions is bull. The b.s. comes from auditors and academics who are lazy listeners. I have no problem hearing countless renditions of "Corner of the Sky" from *Pippin* and "Anthem" from *Chess*. If an "overused song" is presented well, I'm a happy casting director. Reach for that money note beyond your range in "Anthem" with a screech and you're history.

There is a specific audition situation for which, with great reluctance, I will suggest that actor-singers avoid using songs auditors regarded as being "overused." In the world of combined auditions, the people sitting behind the auditor tables resent, with passion, hearing a song more than once. Why? Lazy listening skills. Part of my casting training began as an auditor during combined auditions at Straw Hats in New York. During our breaks, when all the producers and other auditors, eyes heavy with audition glaze, would stretch in the halls outside the audition room, we'd talk about the previous two hundred or so actors we saw. No matter how great a performer, singers would often be bitched and moaned about, and passed on, if they sang a song the auditor felt was overdone. I couldn't believe the shortsighted negativity I was hearing from the "people with power." A person's ability to sing a song well, with great skill, should be the barometer for talent, rather than the number of times the song has been heard.

If you sing and interpret a song well, do it. But don't become hooked on a couple of songs at which you know you kick ass. Having a songbook that covers all genres of music is key to versatility. Variety is welcomed and necessary.

An Actor's Audition Songbook

An actor-singer must have two to four selections from each musical genre included within his or her audition songbook. For each genre in the songbook, you need an up-tempo, a ballad, and a sixteen-bar cutting. Directors, musical directors, and casting directors will want to explore your range, technique, and versatility.

Necessary Genres for the Singer's Songbook

✓ Legit Broadway (Rodgers & Hammerstein, Lerner & Loewe, Gershwin, Styne)
✓ Pop Broadway (Lloyd Webber, Wildhorn, Larson, Lippa, LaChiusa)
✓ Sondheim (a note of warning on Mr. S. later)
✓ Country/Folk (Woody Guthrie, Carter Family, Stanley Brothers)
✓ Gospel/Spiritual
✓ Blues
✓ Rock
✓ Pop (Nonmusical theater pop music)
✓ Jazz

Looking beyond the Familiar

When it comes to filling the musical theater requirements of your songbook, there are many wonderful songs from flops, lesser-known musicals, and older musicals that haven't been beaten into the pavement by "revivalitis." Revivalitis is a plague on Broadway in recent decades. If the show was not a movie first or a Disney-cartoon-turned-musical, it's more than likely a revival. Sometimes the revival is a revival of a revival of a show that closed a mere several seasons prior!

Revivalitis leads me to a pet peeve for many auditors. A revival seems to equal validation to a number of actors that a play or musical, which long ago opened as a hit, ran, closed, then faded from memory is now worthy of the actor's notice because it's been revived. Once a musical revival hits New York, the songs from that show flood the audition circuit for the next five years. Same thing happens with revived plays and their monologues. When Shakespeare is dusted off and brought back to the Broadway stage, actors suddenly discover verse that has been in existence for centuries. To those late bloomers I say, "What the hell took you people so long to learn this material?! Is a $20 million revival required to validate your regard for previously successful and widely known text or song?" When actors come in with songs and monologues from current revivals, the first thought of the auditor is "Lazy actor." Best advice for seeking new material for a songbook is this: Don't follow the misguided herd down the revival road. Find strong material that is obscure, and you'll be looked upon as being resourceful.

Matching a Song to an Audition

Choice of song is important. What you audition with should match what is being sought by the auditors. When I audition a show that requires actors who can sing country or folk music while playing guitar or banjo, my client and I want the same type of music in the audition. Not *Rent*. When I'm auditioning a Lerner & Loewe musical, I want Legit Broadway, prior to 1960. Not *Rent*. When I'm auditioning actors for a gospel musical, I want authentic spirituals. Not *Rent*. Shocking as the following statement may seem, there was music and musical theater before *Rent*. It's an interesting piece of theater, but it's time for Leasers (*Rent* fanatics, as I call them) to look beyond the Lower East Side slum musical. Which they will do as soon as the next cult musical catapults beyond cult status to commercial success (*Spring Awakening*, anyone?). Because a musical is currently popular does not mean that it is to represent, in your auditions, every musical style. You *must* audition with music that is in the style of the musical for which you're auditioning.

Many of my casting colleagues sit at audition tables in frustration as singers present musical material that does not match the project being cast. One of the best examples happened when I was casting a musical for which the singers were asked, in advance, to prepare and present a gospel song or spiritual. One girl, a bit off on genre, brought in Donna Summer's 1970s disco hit "Last Dance." Oh. My. God. Just because a song was originally sung by a black woman, doesn't make it a gospel number! Next!

Singing from the Show

I strongly disagree with another unwritten law for audition song choice. It forbids an actor-singer from singing a song from the show for which they're auditioning. Bullshit. If I'm seeking Laurey in *Oklahoma!*, of course I want to hear her songs, from the potential Laureys I'm auditioning. When I go to Dunkin' Donuts and want a doughnut, I don't ask for a bagel. Same logic should apply to musical theater auditions. If I'm seeking Marius in *Les Miserables*, I want Marius, not Freddy Eysnford-Hill from *My Fair Lady*. I'm always astounded when asked by an agent or actor "Is it OK to sing from the show?" Of course it is!

Singing Sondheim: Everybody Says Don't

You may have heard about this musical theater audition law: Don't sing Sondheim. Why not sing the songs of a genius? Here's why good Sondheim is bad for auditions (personal heavy sigh of disappointment):

Competent audition pianists are rare. Few can adequately play the complexities of Sondheim.

Competent singers of Sondheim are rare. Few can adequately sing the complexities of Sondheim.

I'm a great fan of Stephen Sondheim. I'm not a fawner, yet my hands trembled when I first met the man whose work I greatly admire. I love his work so much that it pains me to advise against using his material in auditions. I do suggest you have at least one or two songs from the Sondheim canon in your audition songbook. You'll never know when you'll be requested to sing Sondheim at an audition.

If, without request, you boldly plan to take on a Sondheim song for an audition, either bring a Sondheim-competent pianist of your own or, if sans personal pianist, be very confident that you can pull off the song no matter what happens with whomever accompanies you.

On a personal note: When an actor succeeds with Sondheim in one of my auditions, my day is brighter. Don't ask me my thoughts about actors who fuck up Sondheim.

THE GROUP OF EIGHT ON HOW THEY PREPARE FOR AUDITIONS

Everyone has his or her own formula for audition preparation. Books, school, and coaching can offer guidelines and tips, but being that we're all unique, no two people will cookie-cutter their process and have identical audition preparation techniques.

I asked the Group of Eight, "How do you prepare for a successful audition?" Some, like Charlotte Rae, find it useful to reach out to fellow actors. Rae spoke fondly of the supportive camaraderie among her peers: "Actors, we all help each other. I'll coach my friend, who is a wonderful actor, and he'll coach me. It's good to have some input."

Mark Price, like Rae, also seeks the input of peers. "I can't just go and do an audition," Price stated. "I always go and do a coaching for the audition or I work on it in a class. One thing I realized, with auditioning: Class never really ends."

Bonnie Black approaches her preparation with questions. "I ask myself, 'What is the event? What do I need?' I always ask myself those questions. Those questions to me are key to success," Black firmly declared. "I have to be playing a verb. I have to need something. That's why I'm there in that audition space. I'm also fond of 'How am I like this person or how am I unlike this person?'"

Black also has an exercise similar to mine for combating Manufactured by Rote. "I try to flop around physically, not just sit in a chair or lie in bed and murmur the words to myself but actually move around and do the audition while I'm washing the dishes or doing the laundry. Sometimes it's pretty amazing how when you're not concentrating on the text . . . you power-phrase your way through the scene. Something new will come to you."

James Rebhorn finds that his most useful preparation for an audition is having as few distractions as possible prior to his appointment. "I try not to have anything going on before an audition. I don't want to have to be rushing around doing taxes or buying groceries. I try to keep the day as free as possible." The time of the audition appointment is equally important to Rebhorn. "I like to have my auditions late in the morning, when I'm still fresh. I try to avoid late in the afternoon because I know the auditors are tired." But Rebhorn stressed that he puts the audition into perspective with his life responsibilities and routine. "I try to think of the audition as nothing more than just part of my day's work," Rebhorn confided. "I don't want to make it too special and invest too much in it either. I want to look at it as, 'Well, and afterward, then I'll do my laundry, then I'll do the grocery shopping . . .' The audition is just one of the events of the day."

Michael Mastro has a more metaphysical approach toward his audition preparation. "I definitely use visualization," Mastro emphatically acknowledged. "I find that incredibly helpful. I believe that what we hold in our mind is what we draw to us. The way I'm using my mind and what I'm choosing to focus on is what I make into my reality. A few years ago I did *Judgment in Nuremberg* on Broadway. I got to play the role of Rudolph Peterson. It's a plum role. It's a role I knew they would try to get a name for. I prepared at least thirty hours for that audition. I worked on the role like it was mine. When you work on an audition for thirty hours, you have really got something incredibly specific in your mind . . . there is a magnetism about that people cannot resist."

Mastro not only utilizes visualization of himself in the role for which he is auditioning but also he visualizes himself at the actual audition. "I find it's very helpful to visualize," Mastro reiterated. "I love to know where my auditions are going to be because I like to sit in [the space] figuratively the day before and the morning of, even on the subway on the way to the audition. I see myself walking into that building. I know that building. I know that elevator's slow so I better get there early. I see myself going up in the elevator, and as I'm getting closer to the audition room the heart starts pounding (this is in my visualization). The nerves start. The little demons start. And if I'm visualizing beforehand I can pause that video in my mind and have a conversation with the demons. I can practice dealing with them in advance. I can practice with the feelings that are going to happen before I walk into that audition room, before that casting director, who maybe I'm a little resentful of because they were rude to me once before and I can talk to myself and that little demon about that. I say things like, 'Look. Let's let go. Forgive that person.' I take myself as specifically as possible through the audition several times to give myself the opportunity to practice."

YOU ARE WHAT YOU WEAR

Just as the preparation of material and technique are important to approaching an audition, so too is the preparation of your appearance. The first thing auditors view when you come into the audition space is your attire. *In those first five to ten seconds of your entrance, 75 percent of an evaluation is made about you!* Carefully choose your attire! This is an interview for employment, not an informal cast party; dress appropriately. The most important rule about attire at an audition is this: Don't let what you're wearing become a distraction or fodder for couture bashing.

Dressing for Interviews

As mentioned in Chapter 7, interviews with talent reps, casting directors, and directors are referred to in the industry as meet and greets. This is an opportunity for you to present, without an audition, the product that is you. What you wear is the packaging for your product. A talent rep or casting person will be looking at your attire and interpreting what it is says about you.

You need to be keenly aware of who you are and how to market yourself properly. If you're youthful and trend-forward, don't dress Connecticut conservative for the interview. If you're often cast as a Donald Trump, corporate persona, don't dress like Willie Nelson for a meet and greet. Dressing opposite of your personality sends confusing signals to the person you're meeting. In general interviews, talent reps and creative personnel want to get to know who you are so that they'll know how they can utilize your look and personality.

CAUTION: If your personality means that you dress in torn, wrinkled, hasn't-seen-the-laundry-since-Pop-Rocks-were-cool rag-wear, don't you dare wear that worn and dirty clothing to an interview. Talent reps will look at you and think, "How can I send this filthy, poorly dressed person out to casting, directors, and producers and expect this actor to make a good first impression?" The only time that it is advisable to dress shabbily for an interview is if the character you're being considered for wears grunge clothing and the casting personnel are expecting that look from the actors.

Dressing for General Auditions

For general auditions (auditions strictly for an auditor's future reference or a theatrical season) actors' personal fashion choices will matter, rather than the way a specific stage or screen character might dress. These will occur as combined regional auditions, performing arts education entry auditions, paid auditions, and general interest auditions, the latter of which are occasionally held by casting offices and some theaters. For general auditions, apply the guidelines of dressing for interviews.

General Auditions/Interviews Dress Guidelines:
Men

✓ Recommended	vs.	⊘ AT YOUR OWN RISK ⊘
✓ Clean clothing that reflects your personality.	vs.	Clothing with holes (intentional or unintentional). Soiled clothing that smells OR looks like it could produce an offensive odor. ⊘
Young or trend-forward male: solid color t-shirt. Casual guy: casual dress shirt with top button opened. ✓ Serious, mature, or corporate male: fully buttoned, pressed, dress shirt.	vs.	Young or trend-forward male: T-shirt with advertising or offensive slogan/image. Casual guy: casual dress shirt from a fashion era long dead. Serious, mature, or corporate male: wrinkled dress shirt with frayed cuffs and/or collar. ⊘
Young, trend-forward, or casual males: high-quality, clean in appearance, denim jeans or khaki pants. ✓ Serious, mature or corporate males: pressed, clean dress slacks.	vs.	Young or trend-forward or casual males: jeans that are torn, appear soiled, or are soiled and wrinkled khakis (young or trend-forward or casual males). Serious, mature or corporate male: dress slacks from a fashion era long dead. ⊘
✓ Minimal jewelry.	vs.	Nose, cheek, lip, brow or tongue piercings, and/or lots of bling. ⊘
✓ Clean shaven or neatly trimmed facial hair.	vs.	Several days of stubble; facial hair that is out of control and for maintenance requires a weed wacker. ⊘
✓ Clean shoes.	vs.	Shoes with holes; laces untied; stains. ⊘

General Auditions/Interviews Dress Guidelines:
Women

✓ Recommended	VS.	🚫 AT YOUR OWN RISK 🚫
✓ Clean clothing that reflects your personality.	VS.	Clothing with holes (intentional or unintentional). Soiled clothing that smells or looks like it could produce an offensive odor. 🚫
✓ Form-fitting or form-flattering dress or two-piece that is current, fashion-forward, and not too revealing.	VS.	Dental floss masquerading as clothing. Clothing that makes a bolder statement than you. Shapeless potato-sack-like dresses. 🚫
✓ Youthful, trend-forward, or casual females: high-quality, clean in appearance denim jeans or khaki pants. Serious, mature, or corporate females: pressed, clean dress slacks or a dress that reflects personality.	VS.	Youthful, trend-forward, or casual females: jeans that are torn, appear or are soiled, and wrinkled khakis. Serious, mature, or corporate females: dress slacks from a fashion era long dead. 🚫
✓ Minimal jewelry.	VS.	Nose, cheek, lip, brow, or tongue piercings, and/or lots of bling. 🚫
✓ Subtle makeup.	VS.	Heavy makeup. 🚫
✓ Clean shoes.	VS.	Shoes with holes or stains. 🚫

Dressing for Character-Specific Auditions/Interviews

Dressing for a stage or screen character does not mean that the actor should be in costume for the audition. It's more like a watermark on paper. You can see the watermark faintly; it doesn't obscure or overpower what is on the page. Same goes for an actor's character audition/interview apparel. The clothing gives a subtle hint of character and is not the focus of the audition.

All within the Group of Eight agreed about being subtle in dressing for character. James Rebhorn put it best: "I think an actor should dress appropriate to the character, but don't go out and rent a military uniform if you're auditioning for an army general. If I'm auditioning for a position in authority, then generally I'm wearing a suit and tie or a sport coat and tie. If I'm auditioning for a farmer, generally I'm wearing a plaid shirt and jeans. I'm not trying to dress *like* the character, but I do dress to try to *suggest* the character. Why put an obstacle in the way by dressing in blue jeans when I'm auditioning for the president of the United States? Also, if I'm auditioning for the president, I take the earring outta my ear," Rebhorn chuckled.

Character Specific Auditions Dress Guidelines

✓ Recommended	VS.	🚫 AT YOUR OWN RISK 🚫
Dress in the style or manner that is similar to the character you are auditioning for, when possible. If not possible, dress as if for a general audition.	VS.	Costumes. Keep your treasured Civil War costume collection in the closet. Along with the pirate shirts and sashes that were worn by too many actors for the *Les Miz* open calls. 🚫
✓ Subtle suggestion. If auditioning for a professional type, wear business-style clothing. If auditioning for a rural character, wear clothing such as jeans with a flannel shirt that gives a subtle suggestion.		Accessorize. If auditioning for a blue-collar type, leave the lunch pail and hardhat at home.

There are occasions, especially on the West Coast and in commercial casting, when actors wearing costumes to auditions is common practice. Darrie Lawrence recalled a commercial audition she attended in which the character was a housewife preparing breakfast. Lawrence arrived in "casual apparel that could be worn to the mall and not seem out of place." To Lawrence's shock the audition hallway was lined with actresses donning bathrobes, hairnets, and fuzzy slippers (this business is truly weird). For commercial casting, heavy accentuating of character dress is customary. Fine; keep it there where it belongs, in commercials.

Don't bring costumes to theatrical and screen auditions unless requested by the casting personnel. Actors are rarely asked to dress like the character for a Legit audition. For a film, Bonnie Black was once asked to dress as close as possible to the character for which she was auditioning: Martha Washington. Imagine the faces of bemused tourists as they encountered several dozen Martha Washingtons in powdered wigs and hoop skirts on the streets and subways of New York City. Only gay pride is more festive.

But that's nothing unusual compared to what Phyllis Somerville once encountered at an audition. "I went into an audition, I think it was *The Departed*," Somerville said. "I don't recall the part, somebody who was ill. An actress auditioned in a nightgown and she had one of those rolling poles with an I.V. with her. I've seen actors auditioning come in as cops, I've seen the waitresses, I've seen the nurses, but I've never seen anybody who came with a gown and I.V. The casting agent actually said to the actress, 'Take that off. Put some clothes on and then come back in.'" Somerville then laughed heartily at the recollection: "It was a little creepy-crawly."

Creepy-crawly. That's how the nerves feel for most involved in the audition process (including those of us about to watch you). We, like you, nervously hope that you're prepared and match what is needed. If you follow the basic audition preparation guidelines I've laid out and combine that homework with your talent and intelligence, you should be more than ready to walk through the audition room door.

But what happens once you enter the room or studio? Are you primed to avoid audition room pitfalls? Are your talent and preparation enough for you to ace the audition? If you answered "yes" then please get into the line of foresight-lacking individuals who rush into war armed but don't carefully think through what happens once the conflict begins or how to peacefully resolve the ruckus. In an audition, you face a talent skirmish of actors. The ones who know how to jockey effectively around the landmines of the audition process are those who win at more auditions than they lose. How many audition landmines have you unknowingly stepped upon? Turn the page and discover how to finesse your audition technique.

CHAPTER NINE

AUDITION STRATEGIES

Leaving a Lasting Impression

"I'm completely arrogant and have always been and therefore for auditions I'm basically unprepared and disinterested. I'm terrible. I'm absolutely terrible because I'm arrogant. I think it's an imposition that I have to audition for a job. I think it's a barbaric process. I've always responded negatively to auditions; not helpful for a career in the business! You pay a cost for that arrogance!"

Robert LuPone

Actor-Producer-Educator

Few people in the performing arts, on either side of the table, enjoy auditions. Despite my opening complaint that "auditions can be hell," I happen to enjoy most auditions. OK, wait . . . I say that now, sitting behind the apparent comfort of an audition table. When I was an actor, I shared with most actors Darrie Lawrence's view: "I hate them!" Lawrence laughed. "I hate being judged. I know that we're supposed to embrace the experience as an opportunity to perform and to not worry about being judged. That really gets in your way and makes you self-conscious and safe."

If it's any comfort to the actors who share Lawrence's disdain for the audition process, know that auditors, who you think are sitting comfortably behind the audition table, are riddled with their own anxieties. While your mind may be muddled with worries about acceptance, pacing, pitch, and the tiny, imperceptible stain on your shirt sleeve that only you notice or the lingering halitosis from the garlic bread at lunch . . . the auditors are obsessing as well. Racing within their heads are questions like "Is it possible to cast this role? What happens if we only have one choice? It's going to be a long day; does the cat have enough food?" You're not the only nervous artist in the room. However, the emotional baggage that actors—both beginning and experienced—bring into an audition can wreak havoc on the process.

Michael Mastro openly acknowledged the "demons" that he must confront when approaching some auditions. "I've been at this for thirty years and I battle still with feelings of resentment," Mastro revealed, "especially now, at having to do what feels like a dog-and-pony show for things I know I'm right for. Now I'm not saying that this is reasonable. It's not at all reasonable. This is what I battle with inside. There's a part of me that feels like, 'Don't these people know who I am? For fuck's sake I've done seven Broadway shows and if they don't know who I am, they should be ashamed of themselves!'" Mastro continued on how his demons intensify. "Why didn't they see me in *this*, or why didn't they see me in *that*. Why isn't it enough for me to give them my reel?! Why don' they just offer it to me? Those are all little monsters inside. They're useless. They're unhealthful."

Mastro further opened his audition-emotion bundled baggage from which more of his "little monsters" escape. "I'm grappling with a lot of demons that have to be tamed. Almost always on my way to an audition, I find myself in a subway or in a cab, or walking there, having a rage fantasy not at the casting director I'm going to see but at some other casting director. Like clockwork . . . in my mind I'm bitching out some casting director. Yes, I have resentment. Do I think that that makes any sense at all? No. Is it reasonable? No. Do I really hate those casting directors? No. It's that part of me that resents auditioning, and I think a lot of actors have it. I'm grateful that I'm aware of it. I'm grateful that I can creatively deal with it." Mastro explained how he tempers his demons: "I literally talk to those demons as if they're monsters and say, 'OK, I hear you and I know you're angry right now, but I'm auditioning. This is the best we have right now. There's no other way for these people to find out who you are. So if you could do me a favor and just go sit in a corner right now, hang out, and chill. We can have a conversation later.'"

You might recognize some of Mastro's demons. Most actors encounter them at some point in their careers. You may not have urges to wallop a casting director, but as Mastro continues to expose his demons, you may recognize destructive psyche critters that have visited you as well. "I have the perfectionist demon who wants to be perfect," Mastro continued to confide. "I have to talk to that demon and say, 'Could you go and sit? We have to do what we can do; we're gonna play today. We're going to bring our best, playful self to this and I . . . thank you for being here . . . because the nerves that are engendered by all you little demons keep me sharp.' When actors tell me they're not nervous, I'm very suspect. Nerves to me means you care."

Being nervous about an audition, as Mastro stated, indicates the actor with sweaty palms, a palpitating heart, sitting, and waiting outside the audition room door has placed great importance on the occasion and truly wants to do well. That's wonderful, and the auditors waiting to see you deeply appreciate that you honor yourself and the moment; just don't have a nervous breakdown while doing both.

What about those actors who appear calm, cool, and collected, corralled in the cramped hallway outside the audition room? The ones who enjoy auditions like Phyllis Somerville? "I rather like them . . . for the most part," Somerville admitted with a playful grin. "There are exceptions to that. Basically, I like 'em." Do Somerville and actors like her place less importance on their auditions than do their nervous peers? Of course not. They just happen to be those rare performers who love auditions, actors with a preference for auditioning that is equal to or beyond performing. They view the audition as an opportunity to perform a role at least once—in the audition. They don't focus on the process as a test of their ability but rather as an invitation to play and explore the possibilities of the role. And maybe, depending on the others being seen, and the personal preferences of the auditors (and their disposition during the audition), a job for the actor will come out of that exercise of play.

Now, if you're an actor who dreads the audition process like I did when I was an actor, your anxiety may call upon you to you slap silly those who are deliriously overjoyed by auditions. I wouldn't recommend assault; it doesn't read well on the résumé. An alternative would be to ask the audition-happy what the hell pills they're taking and please share with the rest of the class. But it's not about meds; it's about having a positive attitude and a specific, winning approach. Performers who are comfortable in auditions know two things to be true. First, they know who they are, and they know what they, as actors, bring to the auditors. Mark Price is a believer of this first truth.

"The audition is my time. It's not about the auditors. It's about me," Price bluntly declared. "When I walk into the room I try to make it, for however many minutes, *The Mark Price Show*. That doesn't mean bullshitting them or buttering them up. It's about, this is the package that I have to offer and I'm going to see how well I can do this package for myself. If they like it, great! If they don't like it . . . great."

The second truth for the audition-comfortable is that they know the audition is not an evaluation of their lives or careers. An audition is not even about them; it's about the product they have to offer and how the people sitting behind the audition table can exploit the product. The creative team and producers are seeking a solution to their own needs and wants. James Rebhorn understands this truth. "I try to look at the audition as if I am there to help solve a problem because you [the auditor] have a problem in casting a role," explains Rebhorn.

An audition is a moment in the formation of a jigsaw puzzle. The performer is presenting what could be the missing piece to the puzzle. It's the job of the auditors to decide which pieces, displayed in auditions, are appropriate. The onus of being right rests on the auditors more so than it does on the actor. But how do they reach this decision?

Bonnie Black, who has sat on both sides of the audition table, knows well how an auditor's subjectivity plays in the decision process. "I've come to realize that how I do or don't do in an audition has little to do with the auditor's final choice," Black said with a bit of disdain. "Having been a reader, being in the room and hearing what is being said or implied by the auditors I sometimes wonder how anyone gets work at all, because it is so freaking subjective! The points of view come from the experience of the auditors. Those experiences are varied, and sometimes if the auditors are young, they haven't done a lot and are coming from a younger perspective. You don't know what they're looking for; you can't outguess them. All you can do is go in and be prepared." Black is correct. The best thing for you as an actor to do at an audition is be yourself. Be the best you can be with the resources and knowledge available at the time. And hit or miss, know when walking out the audition room door that that audition is just one among many to come.

The Group of Eight has been through many an audition individually. Charlotte Rae, an actress for more than six decades, has repeatedly crossed the threshold of the audition room door. "I always feel that I'm a little social worker and I'm there to help them cast," Rae said of her life auditioning. "You want to be of help to them instead of putting it on the other shoe that they're the judge. Don't go into that. You don't have time for that. You don't have time for fear. Wipe the fear out and do your homework and if you have to read cold, try to find some truth in what you're working with. Go with the strength of truth. Be full of something positive. The nervousness and the anxiety take away from your creativity. Then you're not free."

Rae is correct that an actor should be free in the audition, but an actor is never free *from* auditioning. Being an actor requires you to audition until retirement or death, whichever comes first. From their first to their last audition, each of the Group of Eight dutifully pushed themselves to be emotionally naked and vulnerable in front of peers and strangers. As each audition passed, replaced by another audition, attitudes changed and adjusted as the actors became more accustomed to what some in the industry call the necessary evil that is the audition process. I asked each of the Group of Eight, "How has your approach to auditioning changed over the years?" The response I was expecting, of actors becoming more comfortable with themselves as the years and auditions passed, was not what I received.

Bonnie Black offered: "I've gotten a lot harder on myself. I demand more of myself . . . which I regret. I think it's interesting in this industry, and I don't want to sound like a wiseass, you want to hope that you're always open to learning and becoming better than you are. But a little knowledge is a dangerous thing. It's like the more you know the more you realize you don't know. Also your expectation, because of your experience, on yourself, starts to go up. Because it's not like when you're a kid, when you're working innately, you don't have technique, you don't know what you're doing, and you're doing it because you love it."

James Rebhorn, because of his high profile in the industry, also demands more of himself as he walks into an audition. "Now there's sort of an expectation on me," Rebhorn confided. "So I actually am more nervous now than I was when I was starting out, when I was just bold and naïve, because I have my work out there instead of being just a fresh, clean slate to the auditors. Sometimes when they say to me in the audition room, 'I really love your work,' that's the worst thing to [hear]."

Mark Price, the charming, gamine optimist he is, confessed, like Phyllis Somerville, that he's "actually one of those strange people who likes auditioning! But the higher the stakes, the more nerve-racking it is. My early auditioning was about getting someone to like me. Auditioning now is about personal achievement, about pushing beyond my comfort level. It's also about doing the best that I can without having to depend on the auditors liking me. The audition is about getting it right, playing the scene effectively, being comfortable in a scene to where I feel like I'm not pushing. Auditioning has become more about a personal achievement than a public achievement. If I approach an audition with that in mind and do the best that I can, when I leave, I don't care what the auditors think 'cause I know I've done the best job that I can. It's about me; it's not about them."

Price's positive attitude is spot-on correct. His audition attitude is one of enjoyment. Most important for you, the actor, in an audition is . . . to have *fun*! Fun is letting yourself enjoy the opportunity to demonstrate what you can bring to the project. But apart from enjoying the audition, and being prepared, wonderfully talented, and physically right, is there anything else an actor can do to be more successful at an audition? Yes. Be yourself.

The audition is not just about talent but also compatibility on an actor-to-director and actor-to-actor basis. If hired, the creative team will be working long hours with you, not with the character for which you're auditioning. Imagine if actors auditioning for the role of Sweeney Todd came into the room as the razor-wielding, blood-blind, demon barber of Fleet Street. The auditors would protect their own throats with their hands throughout the entire audition process. *Be yourself* while maintaining a pleasant, sincere, and courteous demeanor. This would seem like obvious advice, but often nervousness will counter pleasantry and the actor appears brutish and cold. How you interact socially is just as important as how you act.

BE EARLY TO BE PREPPED

Arrive at your audition at least fifteen to twenty minutes before you are scheduled to be seen (thirty minutes prior for open calls). This will leave you time to prepare yourself (hair, clothing, mental state) and review your audition material. If additional material is being presented at the audition, your being early gives you time to learn it. If you know that you're going to be delayed for an audition-by-appointment, you or your representation *must* call the casting office to advise the auditors of your impending tardiness. Never make a habit of showing up "just in time" or late for your audition. *Never.*

FIRST IMPRESSION

Fact of life: First impression is the most critical moment when meeting new people socially and potential associates in business (remember that entertainment *is* a business). You get just one shot at making a good first impression. In casting interviews or auditions, that single shot happens nearly as quickly as a bullet discharge. Within the first ten seconds upon entering the audition room, the auditors will make 90 percent of their evaluation about you. This evaluation occurs before you speak! How the actor enters the room, walks in, and moves toward the auditors is just as important as how he handles the audition material. Your entrance behavior, stance, stride, where your eyes look, the expression on your face, your clothing (is it appropriate and clean?), your greeting upon entering, and what you bring into the room (backpack, handbag, briefcase) are all bits of information that the auditors consciously and unconsciously accumulate and process. The auditors quickly assess this information and make early assumptions as to your appropriateness for the project based on who they believe you are as both an actor and as a person. All of this happens very quickly. You must be ready for your first impression before you're let into the audition room.

The more genuinely confident and positive the actor's entrance, the more likely the auditors will be open to what the actor is about to present. The obnoxious actor or an actor lacking self-confidence, shuffling in with slumped shoulders, darting eyes, or lacking organization will have a hard time winning over the auditors during the audition. Your body language upon entering the room and during a preliminary conversation with the auditors will determine if, for your audition, you're going to have to meet or exceed the expectations they have immediately set for you. Make the audition easier on yourself and the auditors. Be prepared to make a good first impression before you walk into the room. Once there, know who you are and be comfortable and proud of that knowledge, but don't be arrogant and cocky.

What follows are guidelines for appropriate audition behavior. If you want to increase your odds at winning a callback and the job, follow the recommendations and steer clear of the at-your-own-risk behavioral traits.

Audition Behavior Dos & Don'ts—Quick Reference

✓ Recommended	VS.	⊘ AT YOUR OWN RISK ⊘
Do your best runway walk when entering the room. It's the confident stride used when the personal attention of others is desired (keep it G-rated). ✓ Enter the room with purpose. Bright eyes, a casual, earnest relaxed smile, aided by self-confidence with a touch of humility. Keep the shoulders back and relax the arms. This will demonstrate that you are open, friendly, and confident.	VS.	Darting eyes that scan the room; fear on the face; arms crossed; hesitant, slow walk; shoulders slumped. This type of unconscious behavior does, unfortunately, happen often. The causes are anxiety, nerves, and a lack of self-awareness. ⊘
✓ Keep five to ten feet back and away from the auditor's table. *Make strong eye contact with everyone* in the audition room, even with those not seated at the table. Every person in the audition room is a candidate for being part of the decision-making process. SHAKE HANDS ONLY IF OFFERED. And if you shake hands, please, please, *please* have freshly sanitized hands. (We recall those who made us ill . . . and the recall is not a callback.)	VS.	On your initiative, go to each individual in the room and shake hands, forcing them to get up from their chairs, thereby interrupting their work. (They'll also worry as to whether a cold will be coming their way.) ⊘
✓ Keep the conversation light in topic and brief.	VS.	Bring the outside world in — i.e. announce being late. Auditors may not have even noticed your tardiness until you brought it up. Complain about stalled subways, traffic, and poor mental focus issues. Remind us of the beautiful weather outside while we're trapped inside enduring a twelve-hour audition marathon. ⊘

✓ Recommended	vs.	⊘ AT YOUR OWN RISK ⊘
Before entering the audition room, do whatever preparation you need for your audition. Preferably away from others so as not to annoy or distract the preparation of fellow actors.	vs.	Prepare in front of the auditors as you summon the spirits of creativity to your place of Zen. (I'm reminded of an actress who dressed in front of me, donning a black bed sheet as a poncho and pinning a floppy, plastic-gel, orange lizard to her left breast. The only thing that was moving in her audition was the lizard.) ⊘
ALWAYS introduce yourself to the reader if one is present. Play to the reader and use the reader's presence, unless otherwise instructed.	vs.	Ignore the reader . . . it happens and it's surreal and uncomfortable for all involved. Also, physicality with a reader — kissing, fondling, or grabbing — won't get you bonus points for being "real." It's detrimental because you're abusing someone's personal space. Unless overtly welcomed to do so, refrain from touching the reader. (Good readers are hard to replace.) ⊘

ASKING QUESTIONS

It's OK to ask questions in the audition room. In fact, it should be mandatory of every actor. Asking questions related to the character, scene, and/or script will most likely give you an advantage over the other actors who, before and after you, come in silent, read, and leave. The actors who ask intelligent questions are generally the ones who'll go further in the audition process.

Now, don't go in with a laundry list of questions for the sake of asking questions. It's an audition, not an inquisition. Ask questions that will assist your audition. Here are some examples:

Top Five Audition Questions Actors Should Ask but Rarely Do:

1. "What can I do that no one else has done?"
2. "What would you prefer to see in the character and/or scene?"
3. "Would you prefer that I play to you or choose a focal point? (if there isn't a reader)
4. "May I play off of you?"/"Would you mind standing?" (if there is a reader)
5. "Will there be Krispy Kremes on the craft service table?" (Okay, the last one is a bit off the wall, but if you can find a moment for humor, use it whenever possible as long as you're not obnoxious or an embarrassment to your parents.)

UP-SPEAK AT AUDITIONS

Up-speak is a speech contagion? It spread, like, from the Valley girls of the '80s to, like, modern conversation? And it's annoying?

If you haven't guessed yet, "up-speak" is when the speaker raises his or her inflection at the end of a statement, mistakenly transforming a declarative statement into a question. The result is that the auditor perceives the up-speak as an indication of the actor's lack of confidence. Young and/or nervous actors most often commit this modern linguistic foible.

When an actor enters the room, I'll go through the normal pleasantries of introducing myself and the creative team to him or her. If the audition is for a musical I'll ask the actor, "What did you bring in today to sing?" Often the actor will reply with what sounds like more of a cautious question than a statement of fact, such as, "Um, 'Amazing Grace'?" Spoken in up-speak, I'm left wondering if the actor is or isn't going to sing "Amazing Grace." Or is the grace not that amazing?

Once during an audition I asked a young singer-actress what she was going to sing and she replied with "I'm going to sing 'If I Could?'" I quickly shot back, "If you could what?" With her up-speak, her selection of song sounded more like a request for permission to sing than a statement of the song's title. I get this impression of inquiry often, including monologue announcements ("I'll do Mercutio's Queen Mab speech?"). Actors shouldn't be asking for permission; they should declare what they're about to perform and be confident that what they have chosen is proper for the audition! And that they will perform it well!

Up-speak happens not only when actors introduce a song or monologue but also when engaged in conversation. Often, auditors will look over the résumé of the performer in front of us and try to find a common interest that will trigger a dialogue. This way we can get an idea about who the actor is as a person. Our questions are often met with replies that sound more like questions than statements of fact. For example:

> AUDITOR: So, I see on your résumé we have something in common: You and I both worked at Bucks County Playhouse. Who directed you?
>
> UP-SPEAK ACTOR: Norb Joeder?

Bzzzzt! Wrong choice of inflection in the reply. Two-point penalty.

The statement by the actor should have been a firm declaration. Instead, the up-speak makes the actor sound as if he is either lying, unsure of who the director was, or cautious as to whether the director's name is in good standing and should even be mentioned! Have confidence in your responses when asked questions. Have confidence when speaking at all times. Not only does up-speak display a lack of assurance, but also it's damned annoying.

The following two examples of a single dialogue exchange are typical of an auditor-actor audition conversation. Both have the same content. The first version is declarative, while the second conversation, same dialogue, is up-speak. Notice the difference in sound as you read. Which of the two actors sounds more confident?

Declarative Conversation

> AUDITOR: So tell me a little something about yourself. What was your first job?
>
> DECLARATIVE ACTOR: Oh, God, that was so long ago. I first started doing summer stock at Shawnee Playhouse in Pennsylvania way back in '84. The pay was good. So was the food. We got three meals a day, included. It was one of my better early experiences.
>
> AUDITOR: What shows did you do there?
>
> DECLARATIVE ACTOR: The first show I was in, I was a temporary replacement in *They're Playing Our Song*. Then I was in *Joseph and the Amazing Technicolor Dreamcoat*. *Joseph* was directed by Carmela Guiteras.

OK, the conversation sounds fine—positive, informative, and declarative. But what happens when an up-speak actor puts forth the same content but makes every response seem like a question?

Up-Speak Conversation

> AUDITOR: So tell me a little something about yourself. What was your first job?
>
> UP-SPEAK ACTOR: Oh, God, that was so long ago? I first started doing summer stock at Shawnee Playhouse in Pennsylvania way back in '84? The pay was good. So was the food? We got three meals a day, included? It was one of my better early experiences?
>
> AUDITOR: What shows did you do there?
>
> UP-SPEAK ACTOR: The first show I was in, I was a temporary replacement in *They're Playing Our Song*? Then I was in *Joseph and the Amazing Technicolor Dreamcoat*? *Joseph* was directed by Carmela Guiteras?

Not only does the up-speak actor sound as if he has a bad memory and desperately seeks validation for nearly everything said, but after those questionable responses I'd be suspect as to the quality of the productions and fear eating any food near Shawnee Playhouse! Be firm with all responses. What you say and how you speak during what you believe to be "idle chitchat" can make or break an audition no matter how great your talent.

KNOWING WHEN TO SPEAK,
A.K.A. THE WALLS AND HALLS HAVE EARS

An actor's inflection during conversation is important at auditions. So is the content of what he or she says. And when speaking, you never know who is listening . . . no matter where you are.

During one of my auditions for a regional theater client, the resident choreographer was in the ladies bathroom stall and overheard a conversation involving an actress who was about to dance for us. The actress was telling another actress in the bathroom that she didn't come to her audition for us the day before because she was too tired to get out of bed. Well, that didn't set well with the choreographer. When the choreographer returned to the audition room she told me what she had overheard and stated that she didn't want the "lazy sleep-in actress" in her cast. I told the choreographer, "No, problem, I'll find out who it is as we go through auditions." And I did. How? Ha! I'm not giving up that trade secret. Just know that it's best to keep your mouth shut at an audition about anything that might be considered negative. Don't speak negatively in the hallway outside the audition room, the bathroom down the hall and up the stairs, in the elevator, or in the lobby. Be positive. And be sincere with your optimism. If you must vent, vent at home or to a therapist.

PERSONALITY: IT'S PART OF YOUR AUDITION

Casting directors and their clients want to hire actors who are low-maintenance, friendly, and have a good work ethic. During auditions, we're not only scrutinizing the talent, but we're also scrutinizing personalities. The scrutiny begins with the audition monitor, the casting staff member who first greets the actors as they arrive. This is where positive people shine favorably and actors with personality disorders first reveal the truth about themselves. Generally, the audition monitor is a casting assistant or—surprise!—the casting director. The audition monitor reports directly to the auditors what he or she encounters in the waiting area. The monitor will describe actor attitudes good or poor, their willingness or impatience, and their affable warmth or rude commentary.

When the audition day is over and the creative team is sorting through the possibilities, we go to the person who has had the most contact with the actors: the audition monitor. Call the monitors our spies if you will, but they are invaluable to the audition process. I have seen many an actor for whom the creative team was hot lose a job because of an audition monitor's report of bad behavior. When the audition monitor's feedback on an actor's out-of-the-audition-room behavior is positive, the auditors are all the more thrilled by their choice. When feedback is negative, auditors move on to the next choice. But it's not just what an actor says to the audition monitor, it's also how the actor behaves with others during the entire audition process. Throughout the entire endeavor, actors are constantly being watched as to how they interact with other actors and us.

If I'm holding an open call, where I don't know the actors as well as I know those seen by appointment, I perform a certain personality primer test when typing out occurs.

The soon-to-be-typed actors are standing in the audition room, lined up against a wall, waiting alongside other actors. First, as I walk down the line, I go up to each actor and have a brief introduction with him or her. I'm looking into their eyes seeking a sincere connection. I'm also listening for the tone of voice during their replies to questions. Is the tone warm and inviting (a potential candidate to keep)? Is the tone theme-park ecstatic (careful; this one could be a false optimist)? Is the tone agitated or bored (next!)? A gentle smile, assured answers, and direct eye contact from an actor will do wonders in this part of the test. And the response must be genuine, not put on or Disneyesque. After I have gone down the line, I then go back to the creative team for making the cuts. Unbeknownst to the talent, this is where positive people excel and unsocial actors or people with behavioral problems are first weeded out. I instruct the performers standing in line to talk amongst themselves as we (the creative team) talk about them quietly, in front of their backs . . . or chests. I'll then turn away, backside to actors, and face the other auditors. Before we begin whispering among ourselves about cuts, I wait to hear conversation from the line of actors behind me. Once I know conversation has begun in the line, I know that it's time to turn around and observe how the actors interact with each other.

As the actors chat, the whispered cuts from the auditors begin as we scan the line. We may be looking for certain physical characteristics, but if an auditor or I notice something odd or antisocial about an actor in line, someone who seems a loner or appears self-centered, *he or she is cut.* They're gone. History. The reverse can also happen. Say that someone is not the right physical type but is very sociable and seems like a really fun person to know; we'll keep that person and watch what happens during the rest of the audition process. So next time you're in a line for typing out, remember that it is not only how you look but also how you interact socially with your fellow actors.

Now speaking of typing and poor social behavior, there was once an actress who not only shot herself in the foot, but she built her coffin and drove the hearse.

I was holding an open dance call for nonunion dancers. I had advertised to talent reps, in trade papers, and on the Internet that the female dancers needed to be 5'8" or taller. In the audition waiting room, on a wall mirror, was a line of black electrical tape, five feet, eight inches high, measured from the floor. I instructed my assistant to tell the ladies, prior to checking in, that every actress should first measure herself against the tape. Whoever didn't measure up, in heels, should go home, for she would be cut. Shortly into the check-in process my assistant came to me with a complaint from an actress who was shorter than 5'8". Since she was going to be cut and not seen, she wanted my client or me to pay for her travel to the audition, which Ms. Complaining Actress considered a waste of her time.

The auditions were in New York. I had no idea where Ms. Complaining Actress came from, and she was asking for thirty dollars to be paid then and there in cash! I thought this had to be a joke. When I spoke to Ms. Complaining Actress, whose heated words matched her blowout, flame-red hair, I discovered that she was indeed serious. I told her that this was an open call, very typical of the casting process, and that no one, not even Equity actors, who were cut the day before, received travel money. She was fuming. To cool the situation, I offered advice, letting her know she could deduct the travel expenses from her taxes the following year. This only seemed to anger her more. This girl was completely oblivious to the fact that, from the start, she had two choices. First, go to another audition or home. Second, keep her mouth shut, go through the typing-out process, and maybe, just maybe, if Ms. Complaining Actress displayed a positive attitude while in the line, she may have been kept to dance for us. Instead, she made a stupid, stupid mistake that cost her any hope of my ever wanting to see her again. I wonder if when Ms. C.A. goes out looking for civilian work at, say, McDonald's or Hot Topic, she asks the store manager for travel pay for the interview? As an actor you can be the greatest talent in an audition, but if you speak negatively or behave improperly, don't expect a callback for that audition or an invite for future auditions. This also holds true for high-maintenance (non–box office draw) actors known to have attitude issues. They're not even brought into the audition process.

At any audition, whether it be an open call, prescreen, audition by appointment, callback, or test deal, your personality will be carefully scrutinized through the conversations you have with all you encounter in and out of the audition room. It's important that you're constantly aware of the personality message your conversations deliver. But your words are not our only barometer for measuring your personality. We're also watching your physicality; your body language.

BODY LANGUAGE

Your body can often betray your positive words. As mentioned earlier, the first ten seconds of your entrance are the most important. Your body is advertising to us how you feel about the audition, your attitude toward us, and your attitude toward yourself. Your body language continues to broadcast your feelings during your audition (when not in character) as you interact with the auditors. Often, auditors, if time and their interest allow, will engage the actor in conversation. How your body moves, reacts, and positions itself can be more important than the idle chitchat that you produce. I have witnessed many actors win and lose jobs because of their body language. What your body is saying about your attitude will indicate whether the auditors will want to work with you in the future. Be aware of how your body speaks to the auditors.

Body Language (Nonverbal behavior) and Interpretation

✓ Recommended		
NONVERBAL BEHAVIOR		**INTERPRETATION**
Brisk, erect walk	=	Confidence
Sitting, legs apart	=	Open, relaxed
Hand to cheek	=	Evaluation, thinking
Sitting with hands clasped behind head, legs crossed	=	Confidence, superiority
Open palm	=	Sincerity, openness, innocence
Fingers and palms pressed or clasped together upright	=	Authoritative
Tilted head	=	Interest

⃠ AT YOUR OWN RISK ⃠		
NONVERBAL BEHAVIOR		**INTERPRETATION**
Arms crossed on chest	=	Defensiveness
Sitting with legs crossed, foot kicking slightly	=	Boredom
Walking with hands in pockets, shoulders hunched	=	Dejection
Touching and/or slightly rubbing the nose	=	Rejection, doubt, lying
Rubbing the eye	=	Doubt, disbelief
Hands clasped behind back	=	Anger, frustration, apprehension
Locked ankles	=	Apprehension
Head resting in hand, eyes downcast	=	Boredom
Pinching bridge of nose, eyes closed	=	Negative evaluation
Tapping or drumming fingers	=	Impatience
Patting/fondling hair	=	Lack of self-confidence; insecurity
Looking down, face turned away	=	Disbelief
Biting nails	=	Insecurity, nervousness
Pulling or tugging at ear	=	Indecision

There is one common body language practice everyone does without thought: standing with hands on hips. This stance can be interpreted as either positive or negative. On the plus side, hands on the hips indicate that the person is ready to do or accept what is being asked of him or her. On the negative, hands on the hips can indicate aggression, a "don't fuck with me" warning to others. What is being expressed by the countenance of the person—willingness or defensiveness—will determine the meaning of the hands-on-hips gesture. If you're in an audition and you find yourself, while not in character, with your hands on your hips, be damn sure that your face is lit up with sincere interest and charm.

YOUR FACE AND WHAT IT SIGNALS TO AUDITORS

You're focused on the audition material, attentive to your verbal inflections in the dialogue with auditors, and aware of how your body is broadcasting your personality and attitude . . .

but then there's that mug of yours. You need to be very aware of what your face says to others. Our facial expressions can be our biggest asset or our biggest liability. On the asset side, it's simple. People who have a naturally warm, engaging smile with bright, alert eyes whenever encountered are those who others want to be around. You must strive to be one of those people, always—whenever you audition, are in rehearsals or in your dressing room, or at a social occasion with peers and employers.

If you're not one of those naturally bright people who always shine, get in front of a mirror and learn quickly how to put a natural-looking smile onto your face. People don't want to be around brooders, even if your brooding is unintentional. I'm a perfect example of unintentional brooding. Often people will come up to me and ask, "What's wrong? You look intense." or "Are you okay? You look down." The repeated inquiries over the years annoyed me until I saw a picture of myself, in rehearsal, directing a musical. I saw what the world was seeing, and it was scary and not at all reflective of how I felt emotionally. When I'm in thought or relaxing, my face somehow hides my optimism or concentration. Many experience a similar phenomenon: Their countenance takes a holiday from the polite and socially acceptable while the mind is focused elsewhere. As an actor you need to be aware of what your face is telling others at all times.

USE THE SPACE

During my introduction to an actor at a theatrical audition (not on camera), I suggest that he or she feel free to use the space. For those who may not understand the phrase "use the space," let me put it more simply: Don't be a tree! Move about! Many actors don't. With feet bound to the floor, actors who don't get my obvious clue/direction stand still as a statue. This behavior stems from the Manufactured-by-Rote scenario. At home, or wherever the actor rehearsed his or her audition, he or she stood still and never took into account that there is an environment for the character to live in. With feet rooted to the floor, the actor never envisioned a world beyond that practice area of the apartment or shower stall. Just because it's an audition, and there's no set, doesn't mean that a set designer must be engaged to provide an environment in which to bring a character to life! The writer didn't have a set designer when creating the character via font. The writer had an imagination, and the same is expected of the actor.

OK, now, I'm not saying that using the space means that you have to be a pixie and jump, prance, and flit about the audition room spreading happiness and joy. Please don't. I'm asking, no, begging, that when you come into an audition room for a theatrical audition, use the room! I have seen confident actors creatively tackle a huge empty studio space that offered them only blank walls, floor-to-ceiling mirrors, and a bare floor. These smart, space-user actors exploit all those unassuming elements as support for their audition. When appropriate to character and situation, movement creates interest.

However, movement must have reason beyond the thinking, "Hey, I feel uncomfortable, and I think I need to move just for the heck of it." No. Just as in life, action must be based on motivation within the character, whether that motivation is fear, joy, angst, nervousness, deceit, or whatever. As with physics, for every action (i.e., motivation) there is an equal reaction (i.e., movement). Emotion leads to motion. Utilize movement and motion for the character and the story, not to be a jumping flea to keep our attention. Standing still is fine, if it is appropriate for the character and story. If a scene requires a character to display intestinal fortitude, standing still and holding ground keeps the character strong. Movement can lessen the strength of a character and chip away at building tensions. Every character and audition will present different movement requirements. You must play the room as is appropriate to character.

Place the character into an environment for your audition. Create the world around him or her. And when you create, be ready to do so on the fly because your tiny studio apartment living room, where you rehearsed valiantly, will not be anything like the audition studio. Be ready for adjusting what you prepared to match the space in which you're presenting the audition. This is another good reason to take on the exercise in Chapter 8 that challenges Manufactured by Rote. Combining that exercise along with the following Environment-on-Cue exercise will help you place your character into the surrounding environment of your audition.

Environment-on-Cue

Nearly all audition studios have one thing in common: They're barren and devoid of personality, unless you consider dull and sterile lively. To practice creating an environment from nothing, place yourself in an empty room. Clear all furniture, especially chairs. Discover what you can create with the blank palette that is an empty room. The more you create, the more surprises, the more interest we'll have in you during your audition.

When encountering a typical bare wood floor audition studio with white walls, floor-to-ceiling mirrors, and a door, there are many things to do with that room. Does your character require a dramatic or an angry entrance? Leave the audition room and come back through the door, slamming it shut. Want to sit? Sit on the floor, if appropriate to the character. Is the reader playing your lover and you want to get into an intimate position? Slide up next to the reader. Character a bit aloof? Lean against a wall, back to the wall, knee bent, one foot up, resting against the wall. Look away from the reader, then walk over to him or her when your character reignites with a declarative statement. Want to add a touch of vanity to the character? Use the mirrors! Indulge in self-effacing fun with your character by having him or her admire him- or herself in any reflective surface found! (Just don't overplay it; less is more.) Nervous character? There's plenty of space for pacing, stopping at a wall, rapping fingers against that plaster, then slapping the wall in angst, turning toward the auditors, stepping closer to and abruptly stopping before reaching us. You'll definitely have our attention. Also, don't forget to create physical levels. Levels create interest as well. Kneel, squat, crouch, rock back and forth while crouching, or lay down flat with your back to the floor, eyes to the ceiling. The audition space is your character's environment; bring life and depth to that space relative to your character and the story!

Office Reads

What to do when an audition is in an office? Use the office space and its contents, of course! Books and magazines often litter an office; a character, to mask deceit, can show a moderate to passing interest in a book, pick it up, and casually flip through the pages. Pencils? They're great toys for nervous types. Take one off the auditor's desk and tap it, roll it, chew it, break it (always replace property of others that you break and chew). Is your character holding back some information? Human instinct is to turn away when deceitful, so go look out the office window to hide your character's treachery. Be inventive!

Getting Familiar with an Audition Space

After you have greeted the auditors and staff, just before you read, take a quick look around to view what the room has to offer you as a playground for your audition. That playground becomes your character's environment. Once you've made the assessment, dive into the audition and use the space. After time, you'll begin to know the audition spaces in the city you've chosen to call your base. Soon the audition rooms around town will be like second homes, and you'll know in advance how to exploit them to your best advantage. Bring movement variables to your audition as previously stated (pacing, crouching, rising, etc.). Whatever audition space you encounter, use it! Exploit it!

Chairs Are Your Enemies, a.k.a. Chairorrists

Chairorrists are actors who self-destruct during an audition or in performance by sitting on a chair as a substitute for action. The performance dies, for lack of energy, before leaving the chairorrist's lips. The number of chairorrists is growing as TV and film become more pervasive in our culture, highlighting internal acting over the more expressive and external style of the theater. Actors are taking theatrical auditions and morphing them into small, internalized made-for-the-screen auditions. It's damned annoying during theater auditions to have actor after actor slump in a chair as if in their living room, channel surfing. Wrong choice! That may be fine for the camera, when put on tape, but not for an audition that requires broad-stroke theatricality. To counter this trend, when casting for the theater I will remove all chairs from the audition room except the ones used by the auditors and reader. That ploy often fails as an actor will come into the room, see there is no chair, and then quickly dart back outside to the hallway to bring in one of the waiting area chairs. There's a cold war going on between actors with chairs and me. But I'm not alone on my side of the combat.

In a conversation I had with the Barter Theatre's artistic director, Richard Rose, he also noted that young actors who rely on chairs onstage have become more prevalent in recent years. "A lot of times," Rose began, "in rehearsal, during a scene, when an actor is not speaking, they'll go to the nearest chair onstage and sit down. I'll ask them, 'What the hell are you doing? You're in this scene. You should be listening and reacting!'" Rose is correct. Unless otherwise directed, the actor, not the chair, should always be an active participant in a scene. Now, this doesn't mean that the actor is to be running around the set, or if in an audition, prancing about the audition studio. Good God, no. Just as in our daily lives we offer varying reactions to those around us, so should an actor do with another actor in an audition or performance.

In life, chairs are not attached to our bodies as an appendage or accessory. We stand, walk, pace, shuffle, trip, and fall on our asses daily. When we react, we don't immediately look for the nearest chair as a bum pulpit to make a statement. We stand. Standing equals strength. Why should an actor do what is opposite of what is natural to reality and sit? Many chairless choices can be made, whether it's standing with a slight diversion of the eyes when confronted with uncomfortable information, displaying strength through stillness, or having the character display nervous bad habits such as knuckle cracking, leg crossing, and finger tapping. As I noted before, bold statements can be translated through stillness. There's power in being still. But stillness by sitting in a chair at every possible moment isn't acting. It's called being lazy! It's also rude to fellow performers onstage around you, as if to say, "OK, I've said my lines, your turn. Talk amongst yourselves. I'll just sit down, wait, zone out, until I have to speak again. Then I'll stand and rejoin the action." Oh puh-leeeze! Give the audience, your fellow actors, and auditors a break from such laziness.

Am I a chair bigot? No. Do they serve a purpose beyond being sat upon or abused as temper-tantrum toss toys for divas? Yes. Use of a chair in a scene can provide tension, such as a character who wants to rise and run but is emotionally restrained by her personal demons. Chairs can also be used as an extension of emotion or intent. Chairs, when straddled backward, suggests sexual provocation. Alternatively, the chair in the same position suggests that the sitting person is placing a subconscious barrier of protection between himself and the person to whom he is speaking. "Sit tease" is also an interesting option. "Do I want to sit? Yes . . ." The character begins to sit but then indicates "No, I think I'll move away and stand . . . no, I want to sit. OK, I'll stand." As long as the actions match the character's emotion and story within the scene, use of the chair is justified. But using a chair as a place to sit, slump, and disconnect is death onstage and in an audition. Save the chairs for the camera and channel surfing.

RISK-TAKING

Risk-taking, an often-preached mantra for audition advancement, doesn't necessarily mean be odd or create a gimmick to gain attention. Risk-taking is journeying to emotional themes and levels that are normally uncomfortable for you as a person and artist and therefore are usually unexplored. That's the risk: venturing into uncomfortable or unfamiliar territory.

Examples of Appropriate Risk-Taking

Going Beyond Your Comfort Zone

Say the role you're auditioning for is one that requires heightened theatricality—i.e., emotion, gestures, and inflections that are magnified. But you as an actor are more comfortable with internalized, minimalist performances. You fear being broad. Overcoming that fear and thus going beyond your comfort is the only way you'll succeed. That's risk-taking.

Challenging Yourself with Difficult Material

Sing a song (appropriate to the audition) known to be complicated, one that only the most proficient of singers bravely take on, such as "Meadowlark" (*The Baker's Wife*), "Art Is Calling Me" (*The Enchantress*), or "Being Alive" (*Company*).

If you're auditioning for a Shakespeare festival (or production), be bold and tackle an iconic Bard monologue (if character-appropriate to you and the audition) instead of going for the "easier" or less familiar Elizabethan playwright's prose. Do the same with contemporary iconic monologue material. Don't shy away from something because you doubt you can match the performances of actors previously associated with the well-known writings. Actors are not expected to be identical in performing a role. Color and shading of character may be the same, but each person brings individuality to the role. Celebrate your uniqueness. Challenge your doubts.

When offered opportunities to audition for screen or theatrical roles in which the character has values opposed to yours, don't pass on the chance to be seen because your moral meter is going red. Challenge yourself, audition, and invest in the character. You may gain new insights into yourself, others, *and* . . . you may get a new job.

Beyond getting a callback or landing the job, you will also give yourself the chance to learn new material and garner self-confidence. Plus, when faced with tasks that put into question our self-perception, we often focus harder on the work needed to successfully accomplish the challenge, thereby creating better product. The flip side of this risk coin is that no matter how hard you try to succeed, your work can't overcome given deficiencies in ability. Oh well then, push forward and congratulate yourself for taking a risk.

Pulling Yourself out of Typecasting

If auditioning at an open call or EPA for a language play such as *King Lear* or *Saint Joan*, choose a monologue written for a character for which you would not normally be considered. You can do the same with contemporary plays/characters during open calls and EPAs. Your audition (if executed well) may spur the auditor to reevaluate preconceptions of you, thereby considering you for the role you read or for another character or project. The negative to this risk is that the auditors will think you chose material inappropriate to your type and won't take time to investigate you further for that production.

An Example of Inappropriate Risk-Taking

I have seen many an actor do many a silly thing at auditions. Gimmicks that backfire and acting abuses that actors thought were risk-taking only risked robbing them of dignity. There's one occasion that justly sums up what risk-taking *is not* and *shouldn't be*. I was casting a new play for the respected but now defunct Off-Broadway company UBU Rep. An actor decided to go beyond the script in the audition, unexpectedly giving more of himself to us than was required. Much more.

The project was a relationship play. The soon-to-take-an-inappropriate-risk actor auditioning before us was reading for a role that had a violent edge. The character was a dangerously impassioned person whose physical stature immediately announced, "Keep your distance." This actor in front of us was much shorter than the role required; he was a cuddly, diminutive, dark-haired Latino with a bit of chub around the waist. As we were watching his audition, I realized that I had called him in for the wrong role and thought he would be better suited to play another character in the play—a cuddly, insecure sidekick. In an effort to save face for both the actor and myself, I leaned over to producer Françoise Couriliski to whisper my discovery. The actor continued to read. Barely did I get beyond two words of whisper before the actor turned the audition into a strip show.

Suddenly he loosened his belt buckle and dropped his pants. Down fell his tighty-whities, and he was fully exposed. Oh my God! Imagination certainly went out the window. The actor fondled, thrust, pulled, and twirled his Mr. Happy with glee. All the while continuing his audition, reading with the reader. As if viewing his frontal personals was not risk enough, the brazen bare actor did a 180-degree spin and moon-jiggled his flabby buns in our direction.

I froze. Françoise, a strong-willed woman, went pale and then red. To say that we were stunned would be an understatement. I should have stopped Mr. Bare-All Actor, but the bizarre experience was like watching a pornographic car wreck. I couldn't pull my astonished eyes from the collision of character and cockiness. My shock overpowered my place of authority.

As Mr. Bare-All continued to read, on he went with his wiggle and jiggle. He seemed oblivious to our shock and dismay, for when he completed his audition, Bare-All smiled, dressed without word, then gave thanks to us and left. When the door closed behind him, a cold silence permeated the room. The producer and director were mortified. What had I just allowed to happen? I was fucked. We all sat quietly for several moments, not knowing what to say, until I, with head bowed and embarrassed, muttered to my assistant, "Next."

Why the actor took a naked leap of faith into an abysmal risk, I don't know. Nothing in the material he was reading called for nudity, groping, or a wiggle-waggle of his Willy. Did Mr. Bare-All get a callback? Of course not! Did his agent get a call from me reporting the ribald read? Oooooh, yes.

If you're going to take a risk, use self-restraint, and at the very least, keep your pants on. Use common sense as to what is appropriate to the situation and character. Don't go for shock value for what essentially is a job interview. I've seen many actors folly into foolishness and fail. I've had actors kick and break mirrors, smash furniture, graffiti tag the audition studio, give impassioned tongue drillings to the less-than-welcoming mouths of my readers, and thrust weapons upon me. One actress in her early sixties brought a five-foot-tall ladder with her to the audition. As she climbed, she sang. The song? "Climb Ev'ry Mountain," of course. With every rung she reached and every withered, shrill note she sang, like a church choir matron, I hoped more and more for her to reach the end of either song or ladder. Whichever came first to end the sexagenarian circus act. And how the hell she lugged that ladder, at her age, around NYC, on the subway or in a cab, up and down staircases, navigating streets and halls, I've no idea. That image alone of having her returning through the streets of New York, with her ladder collaborator, determined my decision not to offer her a callback—it would be cruel and unusual punishment for all involved.

Placing yourself unprotected and vulnerable before the judgment of others in an audition is a huge risk in itself. Be true to the material and do the best job that you're capable of without resorting to gimmicks. Actors who engage in gimmicks, bad behavior, and ladder gymnastics confuse such foibles as risk taking. Taking a risk is going beyond your comfort zone.

DON'T SHOOT THE PIANO PLAYER!
AN AUDITION PIANIST SPEAKS OUT

At a required musical Equity Principal Audition that occurred during the writing of this book, actor-singers were coming into the audition either without sheet music or with sheet music that required the pianist to be a contortionist, holding the music with one hand while playing the piano with the other. During one audition when the latter happened, I watched as my audition accompanist struggled to keep ten loose pages of sheet music upright against the piano. Pages were falling from the piano like autumn leaves. The actress kept on singing as the pianist fumbled for the piano keys while simultaneously chasing the diving leaves of paper. It was both comical and distracting. And the person at fault was not the piano player but the young lady singing before us, who brought in the poorly prepared material. She had not been the first singer that day to come in disorganized, and she wasn't going to be the last.

Having been a singer-actor, I know about proper material preparation, but after witnessing the accompanist's juggling act, I wanted to get a pianist's perspective. My accompanist for the day was Mark Baron. Mark is an accomplished composer (*Frankenstein*), musical director, and audition accompanist. I trust him. I have to. I must trust my accompanists and readers more than I trust the abilities of the actors coming into the audition. Auditioning actors need competent, friendly support during an audition. Mark meets the requirement and offers warm reassurance to the performers.

Being that this audition was an AEA required EPA and the show had long ago been cast, there were few actors showing up to audition and plenty of downtime between singers. While waiting, Mark and I spoke about singer-actors and proper music preparation.

> PAUL RUSSELL: What's the best way singers can present their sheet music to an accompanist?
>
> MARK BARON: In a three-ring binder with laminate inserts. The inserts are the ones where you can slide a single sheet of music inside and it's protected behind plastic. For each insert page there should be one page of music on both sides. The

binder in which the music is held makes it easy for the pianist to flip the pages. Plus, binders stay open on upright pianos. Most actors, you'd think, would know that in an audition room the piano is gonna be an upright. The music needs to stand up on its own against the piano.

RUSSELL: What are some of your biggest pet peeves with singing actors at auditions?

BARON: The biggest pet peeve I have is when actors walk in, put the music on the piano, and walk away, thinking the pianist is just a machine and can play whatever is placed before them. With every song and audition the singer must talk to the piano player. It's either a song the player's never heard before or it's a song he's played in a thousand different tempos. So if you don't talk to the piano player, he goes into default. "Default" meaning the pianist plays the music either as written or how he's played it before for another actor.

The other pet peeve is singers who give nasty looks to the piano player when things are not going well. It doesn't do the singer well because the people who hired the pianist have confidence in him, and we know that it's all you [the singer] and not the pianist."

RUSSELL: (*Chuckling*) Unless the piano player fesses up.

BARON: (*Laughing*) Right, unless the pianist fesses up! And if I make a mistake, I'll own up to it, but if the singer starts throwing darts my way, he's on his own.

RUSSELL: What are some of the biggest sheet music errors committed by actors?

BARON: Photocopies. Biggest problem. Singers will forget to copy the whole page including the piano part at the bottom, which is what the pianist needs to read to play the piano. Actors think that all they need to copy are the lyrics and/or the melody . . . Sometimes I've been left with nothing to play!

RUSSELL: Okay, some people are less than brilliant; other mistakes?

BARON: People bringing in songbooks that don't stay open, like the singer anthologies.

RUSSELL: What about marking cuts? Is there something you prefer? Should the singer have the cut typed or printed?

BARON: Use the standard symbol for cuts. When you write or type in "cut to," the piano players will not see it if sight-reading a new piece of music. They're focused on the notes, not lyrics or inserted words.

Example of a cut symbol on sheet music. The first marking, a large "*l*"-like letter with a circle through its center, indicates where the cut begins. The second marking, another large "*l*"-like letter with a circle through its center, indicates where the cut ends. The music is to continue, marking to marking, without interruption. The cut, what's not to be played and sung, is crossed out by a single line that curves from the first marking to the end marking.

"The Coming of the Dawn" from *Frankenstein*

Reprinted here with permission of Mark Baron

BARON: Make all markings in a bright red or green marker, *not black*. A piano player has played a hundred songs before yours. His mind is jelly. He needs to see your markings easily.

RUSSELL: Other mistakes? Any big ones?

BARON: The biggest mistake: Singers think that every print [sheet music] of a song is the same key as the recording. Big mistake. Check the keys and arrangements in the sheet music against the recording. There's one song in particular where people think that what they're singing matches the sheet music. The end of the song "Tomorrow" [from *Annie*], the way the cast recording goes, it doesn't match the sheet music sold in stores or online. You can only get that music, which matches the recording, from the score itself. But people will sing what they hear and not realize that the sheet music for the pianist is different. There have been times when I've ended the song as written but they're still going.

RUSSELL: You would think that would be something the person discovered on previous auditions or at least in conversations with other pianists. What about the conversations you have with the singer prior to their singing. Anything specific?

BARON: Let the pianist know if there is a point for them to hold and then jump back in, in effect following you. Tempo changes and such are information the actor should also give to the pianist. Point out any tempo changes. Many inexperienced singers don't know how to give a tempo. Best way to give a tempo to a piano player is to sing a bit of the song to the pianist as you would sing it in front of the auditors.

Only give the tempo for the beginning of the song. During the roadmap or blueprint, talk with the pianist, point out where the tempo may change, either slower or faster. If there are sections that the pianist needs to follow the singer, *colla voce*, then point those sections out. Then he knows to look for those to follow you. And again, you [the singer] should clearly mark this in a color other than the black. Something that jumps off the page.

RUSSELL: What about transposing?

BARON: Most piano players don't transpose on sight. Some pianists refuse to do it in auditions. For ten to fifteen dollars per page there are people who transpose. They advertise in *Back Stage*. Also there is software that can be bought: one program is Finale, the other is Sibelius. Finale scans the music and then alters or transposes the arrangement. This of course is for people who can read music. If you can't read music, go to one of the many people who do it for thirty to fifty bucks a song. It's money well-spent to have the music in your key.

RUSSELL: What about a song you'd like to sing but can't find the sheet music? At Lincoln Center's Library for the Performing Arts, a singer can find the scores for nearly any show, but what about other songs like pop, country, or folk or music out of print? How does a singer get sheet music that is not readily available?

BARON: Hire a transcriber. Transcribers often advertise in *Back Stage*. Or call the local musician's union [American Federation of Musicians] and ask about transcribers. A transcriber can listen to a song and then make you the sheet music.

RUSSELL: I've noticed today, with a lot of the green singers, that you're helping them out when they go off melody.

BARON: If someone starts to go off pitch, I'll lay into the melody to help them.

RUSSELL: I prefer that. The person is nervous enough coming in here. Any help given to them is greatly appreciated.

BARON: There's a general rule for all pianists: If the singer is pleasant and nice to the piano player, the pianist will help them out as much as possible, because we want to make you [the singer] look good. That's part of my job. That smile and hello from an actor is invaluable to their audition. Be nice to the pianist, and he/she will be nice in return.

The AEA audition monitor interrupted our conversation. It was time for us to get back to work with another audition. When I asked the singer what she was going to sing, she replied with "God Bless the Child?" Up-speak strikes again. Oh well. After Ms. Up-speak departed, Mark and I touched upon a pet peeve that Ms. Up-speak illustrated when she came into the audition room: singers who enter the audition space without having their music out and ready for the pianist. It's as simple as putting a finger between the pages of music or coming in with the music open. Instead, many singers come in, fumble through pages of their songbook, searching, wasting valuable time, and appearing disorganized. Do I really want to offer a salary to someone who can't get his or her act together? Only if that disorganized person is the final option after all other better options have been eliminated.

RUDE AUDITORS

Every actor has audition horror stories of auditors behaving rudely. An actress who sought my advice complained that at an audition she attended (not mine), one of the auditors got up, turned his back, walked to the rear of the room, and attended to paperwork just as the actress had slated and was about to begin her taped audition. She was devastated, and, because of the distraction, she gave a poor audition. My response to her was, "Yes, when it comes to your audition, no matter how much time and money invested, Linda Loman's cry in *Death of a Salesman* applies: 'Attention must be paid.'" But on the flip side I asked the flustered actress, "Why were you paying attention to the activity behind the table? The audition is about what you're presenting. Not about the auditor's movement."

Every actor with a similar complaint of audition distraction should ask him- or herself this question before entering the space: Where is my focus? The answer should be: on myself. Focus on your participation in the audition and what needs to be done to gain employment! Don't focus on the movements and reactions of the auditors. Screw them/us. We're just people with opinions who say yes or no to an actor. You the actor are the action to which we respond. Action comes before reaction, which is why you must be focused on yourself.

How secure are your inner resources as an actor if you let a distraction throw you and then hold the distracter responsible for the end result of your audition? If you can be rattled easily in an audition, our expectation for your survival during a live theatrical performance is minimal at best. A sneeze, a cough, a ringing cell phone, or a near bladder explosion by an audience member will not be put on hold to accommodate the focus of those onstage. When I attended the black-tie opening of *Chitty Chitty, Bang Bang* (three hours of my life lost), a woman behind me was eating Ruffles potato chips from a party-size bag during the performance. Her rustle, rustle, crunch, crunch was audible to the performers onstage. Rude and inappropriate as her personal opening night gala crunch and munch was, no one onstage appeared rattled. Not even the flying car.

On film and television stages, nearly all is calm except for the necessary activity of grips moving cables, assistants assisting, and script supervisors gnawing pencils. If minor audition distractions disturb you, God help you when you work on a project that is filmed out of doors. Nature will not go quiet for you as you strive for focus nirvana.

The auditors behind the table should let you know prior to your reading that at some point there may be unavoidable movement during your audition. An audition is a personal, intimate environment for which there should be respect and simple courtesy granted by all. Yes, in the best of all worlds, everyone watching you should be still, alert, and riveted on the actor at hand. But limited attention spans, stress, work, and our personal dramas may trump professionalism, creating white noise in our minds that blocks our concentration on the performer. We're (gasp!) mortal.

The distracter that pulled away from Ms. I. Rattle Easily's audition may have been an intern or assistant who was there as technical/clerical support and/or traffic control. If this were the case, the distracter's attention on actors auditioning was most likely not within his job description. Running errands for and serving at the pleasure of the production team behind the table is how interns/assistants remain employed. These interns and assistants work endless hours under great stress for wages far below the hourly rate paid to lethargic teens at Mickey D's.

Actors often encounter interns, assistants, or creative team members running noisy errands, or distractions made by auditors for which you'll never know the reason. When a distraction occurs, your best bet is to focus on yourself and what you're doing. You do have the option to stop the audition (it's your time, so take control) and ask to wait for the distraction to end. You never know—the distraction could be annoying others in the room as well. Simply pause, smile, and politely offer: "Pardon, I noticed that you were momentarily distracted. If you need some time to finish what you were doing, I don't mind pausing and then I can begin again." Your tone should be sincere, with never a hint of contempt or reprimand. Be humble. Even if you're in the right and the offender is a scurrilous swine unworthy of the last truffle known to hogs, be polite and humble. The swine could be the director or producer.

The Group of Eight on Rude Auditors

Bonnie Black, part of the Group of Eight, has one of several stories of rude auditor behavior. Hers involves encountering a social faux pas that sadly is now commonplace wherever a cell phone and its attached servant disturb silence and personal space. "I had an audition where one of several casting people behind the table answered a cell phone during my audition and continued a long conversation as I read," Black justifiably complained. "It was one of those moments where my mind split in half and I kept talking but one half of my mind was thinking, 'What should I do?' I was concerned that if I stopped I would insult her." Insult had already been tossed upon Black by the casting person. Unsure of protocol, Black pushed on. "I kept going. She finished her conversation, she didn't leave the room. It was an extremely disturbing experience. I think in retrospect I should have just stopped and maybe not even have taken the reins but just allow them to say what I should do. What concerns me more is that perhaps the artistic director or even the director of the play didn't jump to the fore and at least say, 'Let's start over.'"

James Rebhorn encountered a similar scenario. "A director, I don't recall who it was," Rebhorn reflected, "took a cell phone call during my audition. I just tried to ignore it and kept on going because obviously whatever I was doing had no impact anyway!" Rebhorn laughed off the experience, but it's one that is increasingly familiar for many actors in auditions.

Just as in the civilian world, cell phones have become an omnipresent necessity of communication within the industry and all too often are an audition interruption. If an unanswered cell phone's ringing interrupts the audition, do one of two things. Pray that it's not your cell phone, which you forgot to turn off before entering the room. If you are indeed the culprit, stop the audition, turn off the cell phone, apologize, and resume as if the interruption never occurred.

If an auditor answers a cell phone and a conversation ensues for more than thirty seconds while you're auditioning, pause and politely offer the cell phone servant an opportunity to finish the call. Unfortunately, once the rude auditor has taken the call everyone in the room including you will have focused on the intrusion rather than on you. Now, you may have an urge to throw the cell phone and its servant out the nearest window. I wouldn't recommend it; audition room windows are generally painted shut. Instead, stand open, *without* arms crossed or eyes glaring, and politely say in a nonthreatening manner, "Please take the call. I understand your time to do business is limited. I'll resume my audition from the beginning once you have finished."

A cell phone call taken by an auditor during her audition is not the only offsetting experience Black has encountered during her auditions. "I had an audition once where . . . ," Black recalled with regret, "and this I kick myself for . . . It was when Michelle Ortlip was still in New York, casting, and it was for *Dancing at Lughnasa*, and the damned reader started the scene before I was ready to start! And I allowed myself to be intimidated by her. I don't know what that was about, a hostile reader."

There's little an actor can do in response to a hostile reader or, as in most cases, a reader who is a bad actor. Hopefully the casting personnel will recognize that the reader *they* hired is not of benefit to the audition process. If not, the actor must push forward, be ever pleasant, and do his or her best. Why? Because once the actor lets the auditors know that the reader is destructive to the audition, casting no longer focuses on the actor as talent but as someone who complains. Justified as you may be in your complaint, it's best to ignore the situation, unless hired. If you get the job, then you can politely make a passing comment to casting such as, "I'm thankful you offered me the opportunity. I didn't feel comfortable or at my best because the reader didn't seem engaged in my audition." Say nothing more; let casting figure out on their own what "the reader didn't seem engaged" means. You, with tact and grace, raised a small red flag of warning, and that's all that is needed for the casting person to reevaluate whom they continue to use as an audition reader.

Just as an audition reader can gain a reputation among actors for being hostile or ineffective, so too can casting directors. I hear horror story after horror story from actors about rude and obnoxious casting directors. There are some (one of whom I worked for) for whose projects actors refuse to go in, no matter how high profile the show or film (and we're talking multimillion-dollar budgets). Michael Mastro spoke of one casting director whose reputation was less than stellar.

"There was a commercial casting director," Mastro began. "She's not casting anymore, she was, I think, not well. She would do things to completely undermine your audition. She had me in front of the camera one day, she was taking my Polaroid, she put the camera up to her face and then she lowered it and she looked at me and she said in the snidest, meanest possible way, 'What . . . are . . . you *wearing*? Did your agent tell you to wear *that*?' I said no, and then she just kind of rolled her eyes. I felt like my penis had been cut off. I don't remember that I was dressed inappropriately. I take care to look at least Banana Republic–level."

Mastro then spoke of the demise of the fashion-critical casting director. "Those kind of things happened enough with that casting director that my commercial agent had a list of clients who refused to go in for [her]," Mastro continued with contempt. "I remembered my agent called me one day: 'We have an audition for you for [this casting director].' I said, 'No. I don't go in for her anymore, and you have a list of people who won't go in for her anymore, don't you!?' And my agent said, 'Well . . . yes.' I said, 'There's a reason for that. She's a fucking sicko, and I'm not going to do that to myself. Put me on the list. I don't go in for her anymore.' A year later that agent told me, 'Look, several agents have had a talk with this casting director and she's promised to behave.' I said, 'No, I'm not going in for her anymore; she's not well.' I feel the rage, even now, as I talk about it. She finally had to stop casting because nobody would go in anymore."

Mastro's rage may have been justifiable, but other than refusing to go in for that casting director (which punished him and not the casting director) there's little an actor can do. Casting has "the power," unfortunately. It shouldn't be that way, but some people who are the gatekeepers to jobs for actors let their positions go to their heads. When overinflated casting egos happen, often it's the actors and art that suffer. But a veteran actor knows that he or she has to keep quiet. The business is small. People gossip.

When encountering casting gatekeepers who have bad manners, "Just zip the lip. Zip your fucking lip," Mastro wisely advised. "Leave. You don't know what's going on. You don't know the kinds of pressures that the casting director's under. Go to the gym and work it out. Call your friends, go out, and have a martini at eleven o'clock in the morning. I don't give a shit what you need to do. If still after two days something needs to be said, run it by your agent."

Mastro also suggested another way to vent frustration for being treated poorly by an auditor. "You could write a letter, work on the letter, make it a beautiful letter, even if it's rageful. Work on it, make it funny, get all your feelings out and then put the letter away for two days. Then after two days, take the letter out; if you still feel like this is something for your honor, that needs to be said, and you understand you'll be burning a bridge, and you've shown the letter to people to make sure that it's clear and isn't burning other bridges that don't need to be burned, then go ahead and send the letter. But blowing up in the moment is never really a good idea."

Charlotte Rae was part of an audition horror story scenario for which an actor would have no remedy. "Early on," Rae recalled, "when I was in New York, I was auditioning for a casting director at CBS, and I was doing some of my songs, and right in the middle of it . . . he left." Rae was left alone, singing to an assistant. Her embarrassment must have been horrendous, but to Rae's credit she kept on singing. One never knows, in entertainment, when or to where an assistant may be catapulted into a position of power.

Courtesy, respect, and good manners should always take precedence in an audition on both sides of the table. Apart from their grazing at the table because they have no time for a proper lunch break, thereby turning your audition into dinner theater, the auditors' poor behavior should not commandeer your audition. The audition is your time. Use it. Take control.

Mark Price knows how to control an audition that is permeated by auditor rudeness. He recalled an incident in which the auditor, a well-known pop artist legend, greeted him with arrogance. "I remember walking into an audition for the workshop and the writer requested a song from the '50s. When I went in, he said to me, 'What're you going to sing?' I said, 'I have "River Deep, Mountain High."' He said, 'Well, go ahead and sing it if you think you can.' What he said was actually great, because the only thing it did was piss me off. So I just went over to the accompanist and I said, 'Follow me, no matter what happens.' And I sang the shit out of it, and I booked the job."

The option to respond to inappropriate behavior or to stop your audition in response to an auditor causing a large distraction has to be used judiciously and only when appropriate. If you implement this option properly, you won't be thought of as high maintenance. But before charging into the fire, putting the brakes on your Bard, Bernstein, or Brecht, objectively—repeat, *objectively*—and quickly review the situation.

The examples that follow are of appropriate and inappropriate situations in which to stop your audition:

When to Stop an Audition

✓ Recommended	VS.	🚫 AT YOUR OWN RISK 🚫
✓ If there is cell phone call interruption behind the auditor table. (If auditors making cell phone calls occur with frequency during most if not all of your auditions, then return to your temping career and seriously investigate a permanent position in the civilian world. Preferably something secure. Healthcare related. Screw retail.)	VS.	If auditors seems to be stretching their legs by standing or pacing. (I had one director pace the back of the room during an entire audition process, and it drove the actors and me nuts. But that was the director's process in sleuthing talent. Every auditor you meet has the potential for having some form of physical action within his or her audition process that you may consider distracting. Deal with it. One of my clients has what I call earthquake knees; he shakes them vigorously during auditions. I've come to ignore his tremors.) 🚫
✓ If one or more person(s) at the table is reading a newspaper or magazine. (When this occurs, likely there's internal strife within the creative team. Best to finish the audition and move on to another project that will have less drama attached to it.)	VS.	If an auditor is searching, momentarily, 15–30 seconds for something. 🚫

OK ... there's an audition horror story that must be told, because it's reflective of one that happens often to actors. The basic stabbed-in-the-back theme—actor is given a promise, actor is denied that promise—is the same each time it occurs. Only the players differ. And ummm ... this time, I was one of the players. Yes, me. It's with shame that I admit to being an unwilling participant in an audition horror story for one of the Group of Eight, Phyllis Somerville. I say shame for two reasons. First being that despite my candid musings here in print, I'm basically shy, quiet, and wish no harm to anyone, especially an actor. But without having full knowledge of previous casting promises made but aware of present casting intentions, I became part of the machinery that brought hurt upon Phyllis. The second reason for said shame is that I have been a silent witness and participant in the gatekeeper process through which some colleagues have treated actors seeking employment with disrespect. One of the reasons for my writing this book was to shed light upon unacceptable, rude auditor behavior. And the behavior in the story of how I met Phyllis Somerville and a well-known TV star was beyond rude.

I was casting the annual marathon of short plays for the Ensemble Studio Theatre in New York. The EST Marathon was a high-profile industry celebration of the written word for the stage—twelve to sixteen one-acts crammed into several evenings. Notable playwrights such as Mamet, Durang, Howe, and Guare would have their newly written one-acts performed by the best of actors in a theatrical setting. The setting being a rancid black box theater in a dilapidated West Side tenement in which rats often crossed the stage during auditions.

With each EST Marathon, stars are a near requisite for some of the casting. The pay for actors (and casting), like the working conditions, was crap. But the event was an occasion of such great regard that actors and their agents fought each other to get an opportunity for the exposure. In the melee, actors often get hurt. Somerville was steamrolled.

One of the one-acts to be cast was a two-character relationship play about a mature man and a mature woman. The director had wanted to get Frances Conroy (of *Six Feet Under* fame) for the female role. In addition to his desire, and as is custom in casting, I submitted a list of actresses, both household and industry names, to be considered for this role. James Rebhorn had already been cast in the male role. He had done a studio reading of the play. Wait!? A studio reading . . . ? That must have meant there was an actress who originated the role. What of her? The actress was Somerville. My instructions were to pursue others, preferably Frances Conroy.

Somerville recalled the experience as she knew it. "It was all set up that Jim and I were gonna do it. Then I got a call from my agent: 'You gotta audition.' It was just, uh . . . I understand how EST is set up, but I worked there a lot before. I just thought it was a real . . ." Somerville, with dignity, did not finish the thought and went on. "I had heard of what was going on in the background. I just thought it was a lack of respect. Maybe I thought I hadn't earned it, but I thought it was a lack of respect. And then I came in [to audition] thinking it was going to be all right and then . . . when I'm in that kind of situation I can take pretty much anything but kindness, and Jim, who was at the audition, said, 'I know how hard it is . . .' and I just started to cry."

I recall her tears. The moment was awful and uncomfortable. We were in the darkened black box theater on a cold morning with no heat in the space. Phyllis, a smart woman of tough resolve, crumbled. Jim Rebhorn, gentleman that he is, held Phyllis, hugging her as she cried. He gave her assurance and comfort while the director and I stood off to the side like helpless fools.

Still to this day, I don't know why Phyllis was made to endure the disrespect of auditioning for a role that was to be hers. A lot of shit had gone down during the casting of that piece. Phyllis was not the only actress to be given such a slap. On my list of people to offer the role to was Sharon Gless, most remembered for her tough portrayal of detective Christine Cagney on CBS's *Cagney and Lacy*. Everyone in the Marathon casting process knew of Ms. Gless, but the director thought her too urban for the role. Despite that knowledge of who she was, and the director's uncertainty of her appropriateness, she was asked to come in and take a meeting. OK, a meet and greet is not too out of place. What was out of place was what happened at the meeting.

Quarters at EST were small, dirty, dilapidated, and cramped. The director and I met Ms. Gless in a space that could not remotely be considered a room by common third world standards. It was no larger than a tiny, tenement kitchen pantry (it probably once was). Ms. Gless was seated in a corner. Her chair occupied most of the available space. The director and I, merely inches from her, were blocking the opening to the windowless cubbyhole. She was trapped. The director and Ms. Gless spoke about the play. She was charming and earnest as she discussed her theatrical background. And then came the bomb. The director asked her to read—in effect, audition. He then turned to me and said, "You'll read with her." Fuck. I'm reading with Sharon Gless.

I had assured her representative that Ms. Gless would only be meeting with the director. There was to be no reading for the role. This was a job that didn't pay enough for two weeks' train fare. A low-rent job, at a studio theater, in a crumbling tenement that should have been condemned decades ago. Actors of Ms. Gless's stature don't read for dumpster-budget theater. But, Ms. Gless was the consummate professional. She did as asked and read. She didn't get the role. After much needless searching, auditions, and backstage bickering, the role went to the person who should have been cast in the first place: Phyllis Somerville. And she was wonderful!

Somerville later found joy in the results: "I loved that part. I don't feel that way about many parts. I wanted to do it with Jim. It was one of those amazing fits. I hate when actors do this, but I'll admit that every now and then you'll let something get to you and I let that [audition experience] get to me. I'm not proud if it. I'm not proud of it at all. I wish I had handled the situation better. But I got to do the role. And every night Jim and I would sit there and say, 'This is it. This is what it's about.' We were *very* happy doing that show."

The emotional hell Somerville was made to endure was not necessary and shouldn't have occurred. But . . . this is show business. We often eat our young and callously dispose of our respected elders.

Bonnie Black spoke of rude behavior by auditors: "Friends of mine, who are obviously actors, share similar stories with me. Stories about going to an audition and being kept waiting for an hour, with no apology as to why they're late, nowhere to sit down. It's either boiling hot or freezing cold, and you walk into the audition room and you're questioning 'How? How can I do my best for you?' It's very disheartening, because we want to work.

"Often we spend an inordinate, phenomenal amount of time preparing for an audition, hours upon hours upon hours of prep to walk into a room for three minutes. When you're greeted with cold aloofness, it's doubly disheartening. It's mysterious to me," Black pondered. "What I lament is that we're an industry that at its best defines itself as a people industry. Especially in film or television when the auditors will say, 'We want to see you. Don't act, we want to see *you*.' And yet you might come into one of these environments where you've been kept waiting *an hour* for a job that's two lines or a job that requires you to be at an emotional peak. And you think, 'What??' There seems to be no thought, on the part of some auditors, as to what actors are going through and how much we love what we do. The passion, commitment, and care that are being brought into the room by the actor, that can get submerged by a negative environment."

This business is tough, often beyond redemption; nothing new learned there. At its core, the scenario played out over and over in the world of entertainment feels like an ironic joke: Place highly sensitive, emotionally fragile psyches, for the most part, into a labyrinth of creative exploration that for survival requires cold, ruthless, insensitive behavior equal to the questionable humanity of loan officers, lawyers, and state agency employees (OK, I just offended a third of New Jersey and most of Southern California). And yet somehow, actors are expected to survive and thrive without losing their humanity.

Put up your walls, guard against assaults on sensitivity. Push forward and don't let the distractions detour your talent, ability, and desire. The nature of this game is not going to change much for the better. Play to win. Play with dignity. Play with respect.

AUDITION CATASTROPHE

There are times when the horror of an audition comes not from rude auditor behavior but from mistakes made by you, the actor. You're not perfect. Neither are auditors. And as much as it wounds my Virgo pride, I'm not perfect either. Having once been an actor I understand the trauma of auditioning. My first audition for *Les Miserables* (the original Broadway production) was a disaster. I was asked to sing my best sixteen bars. I knew I had this one aced for a callback. My best sixteen (a cutting from "They Call the Wind Maria") and I, we were a great pair and kicked ass together multiple times. We always got jobs and callbacks.

At the *Les Miz* audition the pianist played the short, two-chord intro. I took a breath, held my ground, looked straight at casting director Andy Zerman, opened my mouth, and . . . nothing. I forgot the first word! The first *fucking* word being *Maria*! It's in the damned title! Andy generously offered me a second attempt. Two chord intro, deep breath, mouth open, look at Andy, nothing. Again I forgot the first word!!! Arrggghhh! After the pianist dryly shot me the word that would lead me into the song's cutting, the third time was the charm. But by then I had lost all confidence as I sang. Andy, a gracious casting director, asked me how long I had been in New York. "Two weeks," I replied sheepishly. Liar. I'd been in New York for half a decade. I was so humiliated that I would rather Andy think I was green and new to New York than a veteran actor experiencing a brain fart.

Of the Group of Eight, one was brave in exposing past personal audition tragedies. Opening her audition catastrophe closet, Phyllis Somerville confessed to one that may have left the auditors confused. "This'll make me really look stupid," Somerville began. "I was auditioning for the original production of *Nine*." Somerville broke into laughter, recalling her foible. "This is so awful. I had done musicals, but I did not realize that when they said, 'Sing something in another language,' that that was code for German lieder, French art song, or an Italian aria. So I sang 'La Cucaracha'!" Somerville's hearty laughter exploded, rocking her body like summer sea waves rolling a boat. Her convulsive laughter filled the large audition studio in which we met. She caught her breath, shook her head, then mused about the auditors: "Oh what they must have thought!"

I witness similar mistakes from actors, due to misunderstandings or nervousness, when they audition for me. I appreciate and acknowledge that an audition is not going to be perfection. Communication of what is required of the actor often gets distorted as the instructions go from creatives to casting to agent to agent's assistant to actor's voicemail.

Many of my casting colleagues and I also understand that nerves wreak havoc on self-confidence. Placing yourself in front of auditors is the equivalent to standing before a firing squad, only instead of bullets, you face shots of raw opinion. Commend yourself for such bravery.

The healthiest emotional action you can take after every audition is to put the audition behind you. Walk away, forget the audition, good or bad, and move on to the next opportunity. If you fail miserably at an audition—forgetting a lyric, dropping lines, missing a note, not understanding what is being asked of you—appreciate the humanness of your error and know you're not the only actor who had an audition mishap in his or her career. Never beat yourself up after an audition that didn't go as perfectly as planned. The best you can do is to learn from the experience, pick yourself up, lick your wounds, laugh at the experience, and, in the words of Stephen Sondheim, "Move on . . ."

CALLBACK

Is there a way to win a callback? Just asking the question alone is both audacious and absurd. Why? Because other than your talent and appearance and how you present both, the actor has no control over someone's opinion of your audition. None. Nada. No-go. Some actors, especially new ones, may often have the fanciful, frustrated idea that there must be something simple that other actors do in auditions, each time, that gets them a callback or the job. Ditch the fantasy. Quick. I have seen actors give a brilliant audition and once finished I circle their names on my session sheet because I am certain that the audition that they just aced will elicit a callback from the creatives. Wrong. Another auditor or I say, "Thank you," from behind the audition table. The actor leaves the room hopeful, I turn to the creatives, they look at me with dead eyes and on a sigh say, "Next." Good actors doing great auditions and getting nothing back in response . . . it happens. Happens often. When it does I'll challenge the creative disinterest as far as I can push without losing them as a client. But it's the voice of the creatives—the decision-makers with final yes or no power—that determines if an actor will be pushed forward and win the job. Actor, agent, and casting can only promote, not control. You can lead an auditor to talent, but you can't force 'em to think. Same goes for getting a callback from creatives.

We've already covered what you can do to better your chances at being called back. Be prepared with the audition material—know it as well as you know your phone number, ATM pin, and location of your favorite pizza place. Other than being enormously talented, physically right, charming, and professional, the rest is up to the creatives as to whether you'll return.

For farts and giggles, I asked the Group of Eight, "What do you do that seems to work best for you in an audition? How do you win an opportunity for a callback?" I was expecting laughter accompanied by spittle spewed in my face followed by a response of, "Are you serious?!" The closest to that retort came from Robert LuPone, sans spittle and guffaw. His response was grounded deep in the reality that is the bedrock of entertainment: "You can't control how people think about you. What you do is you do the best work of the day. Which means you realize the obligation as defined by the director or the playwright."

Charlotte Rae has been required to audition, even after a successful television, film, and stage career. Rae reflected my earlier thoughts on being positive. She credits callbacks to her positive personality, her "positiveness and friendliness without being overly pushy." Rae also chimed that it was important to show that she was delighted to be at the audition. She felt that her gratitude at being called in would often be returned in kind.

Darrie Lawrence was also an advocate for staying upbeat. "Present a positive image of yourself as a person," Lawrence advised. "You want people to want you because you're obviously emotionally strong and your personality is strong and your technique is strong and that you're not gonna cause a lot of problems!" Being seen as low maintenance is definitely attractive to your potential employers. Lawrence also stated that *having* work will enhance your ability to *get* work. "Common thought is that you always audition best when you're working because you're confident and next month's rent isn't riding on whether or not you get this job. Try to free yourself of everything except enjoying doing the scene. Find in the audition process the same feelings that made you want to be an actor in the first place. Which in my case, and I think in many of us, is a kind of joy and pleasure in the process of creating that character."

James Rebhorn believed, like Rae and Lawrence, that being positive does wonders to win over auditors. He approaches the audition experience affably and with respect. "I try to be gracious in an audition. I try to go around and introduce myself to everybody in the room, even if there are six people there," Rebhorn offered. "I go around and shake everybody's hand, say hello, and make eye contact. To let us all know that we're human beings and that we're trying to solve a problem." Now, before you write me or stop me on the street about Rebhorn's shaking hands remark, I'm not changing my point of view on this issue. My clients and casting colleagues would love to put palm to palm with all who enter the audition room, but we'd rather not accept or give harmful germs that lead to colds and the like. So while I advise actors against this practice, if someone with Rebhorn's refreshing spirit for humanity and one-on-one connection offers a hand, I'd be a fool not to welcome the gesture.

Speaking of gestures . . . Michael Mastro (who gestured often and with passion during his interview) employs a more technical approach to winning a callback. "When I *really, really* have the time to prepare, when I prepare as if the role is mine, I've almost always gotten a callback or clearly made an impression that led to other things with that director or casting director." When a callback comes his way, Mastro's determination for winning the job intensifies. "If it's for something I really, really want I will prepare hard for the first audition and then I will prepare more for the callback. My feeling is if I get a callback I have to show them everything I showed them at the first audition, *plus* it's got to be deeper and richer now. It's got to be on the same track but show improvement. They have to see the actor always progressing toward something deeper and richer."

Mark Price is also one who believes that being well-prepared is what best helps secure a callback: "In hindsight, the times when I've had the most successful auditions are the ones where I've been the most prepared and I haven't had to think while I'm in the audition," Price acknowledged. Preparedness for the callback is also his path to success at winning the job: "I get a coach for my callback preparation. It puts me in the material and less on the page. I think going to an acting coach is another way of getting what's on the page off of the page and making it more three-dimensional, so that the next time you go into the room, you don't have to think about what you're doing; it's just second nature. "

THE CARDINAL SIN OF AUDITIONING

There is a cardinal sin of auditioning that an actor *must never* commit: auditioning for projects for which you have no intention of accepting employment if offered the job. Practice this once and you'll have done yourself in many times over. Auditioning without the intent to accept work is lying. Liars are not forgotten. Despite such warnings by auditors, sadly this awful behavior occurs often.

Acting academics often preach to impressionable students to audition for anything and everything possible; even if they're not right for the role or, worse, not available and willing to accept the employment. Acting academics can afford to give such misguided advice. Unlike their students, they have an income or tenure.

Selfish, rude, and conceited does not begin to describe the actor who auditions for a project without any intention of accepting the work if offered. The casting director and production team invest far too much time, money, and labor into the audition process to have that investment bankrupted by a false supplier. Also wasted is an opportunity for another actor to be seen for the project—an actor who could have been better suited for the role, an actor who *needs* the work to pay rent due and accumulate his or her health insurance weeks for the fiscal year.

The audition clock is relentless. Not everyone submitted can fit into the audition schedule. Be considerate of your fellow artists. If you're not right for a role, give the chance to someone who is. Live, learn, and deal with reality. If you're not ready, willing, and able to accept work, get the hell out of the way for the others who are. And if you're wondering, "How can a casting person tell I never wanted the job? I could always claim it was the money I passed on," I say, bullshit. Often the salary is specified upfront *before* the audition. And don't even think about trying to back out by saying the dates of the job are a conflict. Dates of employment are told upfront with every casting notice. So barring money and dates, there's very little else to pass on except ... you never intended to take the job if offered.

Once when I was casting an out-of-town project, a forty-something actress campaigned my office, her agent, and the production's director to be seen. After relentless badgering, she was allowed to audition. She made the callbacks, got an offer, and then passed. Her reason? Despite previously knowing the production commitments and money before auditioning, she decided that she'd rather focus on her film and TV career. What film and TV career? She lived in New York. It was summer, film casting for the season ended in April. She was forty-something, long in the tooth for starting a film and TV career (in which she had *no* credits).

I saw the lying actress two weeks later. She was warming up in my audition room when I arrived to begin auditions to fill the position she had passed on. I was confused. She told me she was auditioning in a nearby studio for an out-of-town theater project that was to take place during the same period as my project. With a smile and chuckle she said that she was just auditioning for the project in the nearby studio to keep herself in shape. I kicked her out of my room.

Auditions are what you make them. They can be hell or they can be fun. I prefer the fun. Remember, we're not sitting there to judge you (OK, OK . . . we are, but try to overlook that minor detail). We're sitting behind the audition table, or behind a camera, or in a darkened theater hoping that you'll be the person who will solve our casting puzzle, be better than what we've previously seen, and that you'll go beyond our wildest expectations. We hope that you'll do all of this and enjoy yourself while showing us the piece of the puzzle you have to offer. Forget about us "judging" and put your focus on you. For those few minutes you're before us, we're your audience. Reach out to us emotionally with your gift for storytelling. Draw us in through the way you craft the spoken or sung word. Capture us. Enthrall. Enjoy. For every audition:

✓ Be true to yourself.
✓ Be courteous, polite, and receptive.
✓ Be prepared.
✓ Be early.
✓ Ask questions.
✓ Have fun.

Having fun is the most important audition guideline of all. It's very hard for anyone to succeed in any endeavor approached with disdain and no joy. Revel in the joy.

CHAPTER TEN

NEGOTIATING THE CONTRACT

Get It On Paper

"We are one of the few professions where we are asked to work so hard for no money, so often . . . we're not working for a living wage. It shouldn't be that way."

Bonnie Black

Actress

"We'd like to offer you the role of . . ." is how it begins for the actor without representation. "You got an offer" is how it begins for the represented actor. What is *it*? Negotiating the contract. At first you're overjoyed and justly so. You've been accepted! *Yes!* People want you and your amazing talents. *About f-ing time!!* You're bouncing off the walls. Ready to call every actor friend because, *HA! You got a job and they didn't*. OK, we went a bit too far there with the enthusiasm. Let's be real. While you should be thrilled at being offered a job, be humble. Jobs don't come often, and soon you could be the unemployed actor receiving the "Boy howdy, I got a gig!" phone call. But for now . . . you got the job!

First thoughts on receiving an offer are reflections of gratitude. You're thankful that a noncivilian paycheck will replace your waitron pay stub. No more serving spicy beef satay and Amstel Light to drunken foodies from Connecticut (for as least as long as the new job will last). You're thankful that after months of creative job drought you'll be at the computer adding a new line to the résumé (each new credit is prized booty). You're grateful that you'll get to work with new or familiar colleagues. If a union actor you're happy—hopeful that you might be eligible for health insurance coverage (if the contract meets union health insurance requirements or you accrue more union work within the year). There's so much to be thankful for.

But then reality hits. It's an out-of-town gig. Three months away from home. One-third a year's rent paid for your soon-to-be empty, shoebox studio apartment. Quick, post a sublet ad online and set aside time to screen who'll be sleeping in your bed without you.

Then the thoughts of reality burst open like bulging floodgates. The pay, is it enough to cover expenses? Will it meet or exceed my civilian pay stub? What if I can't find a sublet? I have no car. How will I travel to my new job several state borders away? How will I travel locally once at the new job? Is ground transportation provided? What type of housing will I have? What are my "outs," options for leaving if a better job comes my way? Tootles, my little Persian purr machine, where will he go? Who will look after my furball and dutifully clean his litter box? Screw Tootles; time to put your interests as an actor first. Handle the puss later.

Many questions, many options—and everything is negotiable. *Everything* (including Tootles). By negotiable I don't mean that you'll get all that you wanted. I mean that you can *ask* for things you need or desire. Need and desire are two different realities. Know that and prioritize when going into a negotiation. Needs are things that you cannot live without in order to survive. Desires are things you want to live with for an orderly survival. But without asking for either, you'll never know what you could have gotten. Sometimes you'll be pleasantly surprised, while other times you'll ask and receive a firm no. While you may not get what you want, you can and should try for what you believe is fair. Compromise does happen. Tall willows do bend.

One of my clients has me handle the entire offer process between him and the talent or his or her representative. With me as middle man his "negotiating" is basically, "Here's the offer. It's take it or leave it." He rarely modifies a first offer. But sometimes when the actor or his or her agent ask for a modification he believes to be fair, the producer, my client, will compromise and allow me to say yes to the altered offer. Compromise and modifications of an offer by a producer depend on how fair the producer perceives the request to be and, more important, how much the producer (and director) desires the talent chosen. Plus, how much the budget will allow. If you don't ask, you pass on opportunity. Negotiating is asking followed by compromise. Ask.

Actors who are not represented (and some who are) often feel nervous or shy about asking for what they believe is fair and acceptable: a living wage, clean housing. Why? Because insecurity eats at self-worth, leaving actors afraid they'll lose job opportunities if they ask too many questions, knowing that many producers consider an actor's version of "fair" (housing that isn't destined for demolition, a private bathroom for nonunion accommodations, a private kitchen or above minimum monies for union actors) to be extravagant. Get past such doubt and fear. An actor will *not* lose an offer by asking questions. The offer will not vanish. It'll either be modified or stay the same. The only time an offer will vanish is when the producing entity, after a period of negotiating with the actor, places a deadline on the offer and both parties cannot come to an agreement (deadlines occur more with nonunion producing entities than in the union world of entertainment).

If an offer *is* withdrawn before the negotiating participants mutually agree to part (and that happened to me on one occasion *after* a deal was verbally agreed upon), then the producer who pulled the offer is not someone with whom you want to work. Their behavior displays a lack of regard for you as a person and as an artist. A producer pulling an offer shows disrespect and waves a red flag announcing his or her lack of integrity and professionalism.

Getting an offer is wonderful and glorious, but you must take great care to protect your best interests. Don't let your joy and excitement at having just landed a new job overshadow common sense. Common sense being that you don't immediately say yes. You listen. You ask questions. You deliberate. You decide.

When receiving an offer personally or through a talent rep, write or type the offer information, ask questions, and with great gratitude, politely end the conversation and say, "I'd like to review the offer for a bit. When is a convenient time for me to respond with follow-up questions or an answer?" After the giver of the offer responds, thank him or her, find a quiet place, and carefully review the offer. NEVER—repeat, NEVER—say yes immediately, even if the person presenting the offer wants an immediate answer (which is both bad form and a warning for you to flee from the offer). Review the offer information (alone, with peers or representation), deliberate, ask questions, review responses, and then decide. Your questions will lead to your acceptance or refusal of an offer.

What are those questions to ask? All union or nonunion offers of contracts require the recipient to ask the following basic questions: When? Where? How much?

Those three basic questions are the foundation for all offer negotiations. The medium (theater, film, television, or Internet) will alter or expand the basics. What follows are the primary questions that you as an actor should be concerned with upon receiving an offer. The questions (some with accompanying advisories) are placed into two categories: theater and film/television/webisode. The queries often apply to both the union and nonunion actor. Being that nearly all actors begin as nonunion artists an additional advisory section on nonunion offers appears later. First, we'll go through the offer questions that matter most to an actor (plus a few perks here and there, including care for your Tootles).

THEATRICAL OFFER QUESTIONS

The questions that follow are the basics an actor needs to be concerned with when considering a theatrical offer. Unless you're a star or being offered a contract for Broadway, national tour, or a first-class, sit-down production in a major city, billing, dressing room, photo approval, and personal perks are not appropriate negotiating points. If these latter concerns become your focus of negotiating during your early career then you're either one of two things: a reality-star, box-office draw who is catered to, or an egocentric, not based in reality, who believes all others should cater to you. Perks are nice and comforting, but place focus on where it needs to be: the work!

The following queries apply primarily to AEA contracts. These are accompanied (on occasion) by parallel questions for nonunion theatrical offers. While most actors begin in nonunion theater, the questions to ask upon receiving an AEA offer of employment can serve as a guide for either scenario.

I strongly recommend that in regard to AEA contract guidelines, terms, and contracts, actors should routinely contact the Actors' Equity Association for updates.

Length of Contract?

This question addresses the period from the first rehearsal to the last performance.

Two points pertaining to contract length have the potential to be negotiated. The first is the first day of your rehearsal. If you have a previous conflict and need to start a day or two later than the rest of the company you may be granted a belated start.

The second point is your "out." This term refers to how much notice an actor is permitted to give an employer should he or she have a better offer or must leave the employment for personal reasons. Most AEA contracts specify the out: four weeks, two weeks, less or more, depending on the contract the producing entity has with AEA.

The length of contract is generally not negotiable. If the producing entity is a Broadway or national tour producer, they will want you for however long they want you, be it a month (as a temporary replacement), six months, or a year. Regional theaters will generally hire an actor as a jobber (someone who comes in for one or several shows in a given season). The jobber will be needed for however long the shows are scheduled to run, along with their prior rehearsal period. Some theaters may invite you for an entire season (which saves them money in hiring and transporting jobbers). When a season is offered and you only desire to do one or several shows within its duration, it's unlikely that you'll be able to negotiate that point. Length of employment will either be take what is offered or pass.

For nonunion theater: Outs are foreign, because they generally are not in a nonunion contract or welcomed as topic for negotiation. Nonunion producers want you for as long as their contract stipulates. No exceptions. You can try to negotiate an out clause in a nonunion contract, but more than likely your inquiry will be met with this response: "You want the job or not?"

Role Assignment?

Don't assume that because you went in for a particular role that that's the role you'll be cast as. The casting decision-makers may have loved you but felt that you were more appropriate for another character found within the project, play, or a theater's season. Always ask for what role you're being hired.

Some nonunion theaters (mostly lesser-grade summer stock) are notorious for not assigning roles until the actors arrive at the theater, unpack their luggage, and sit down for the first read-through. That's crap! Before you arrive at the theater, be sure to get in writing what role you'll be performing. If you're hired for a season, or jobbed in for several shows, get at least one role on the contract.

Money?

Broadway principal salaries, above union minimum, are determined by compromise between actor and producer (generally with a talent rep as the go-between). Some Broadway producers are notoriously stingy/prudent (depending on which side of the table you're on) and will, as a rule, offer only principal union minimum as a salary. For Broadway ensemble offers, standard practice is that producers offer union minimum salaries. All minimums for Broadway and Broadway national tours (union) are agreed upon by AEA and the League of American Theatres and Producers. National tours, requiring actors to be away from home base, may pay a bit better than Broadway, but that extra cha-ching doesn't come in the salary; it's in the per diem.

For regional theater, actors might be able to raise the salary offered by 10 to 40 percent. Don't expect regional theater to pay you civilian-like wages that can be found in large cities like New York, Los Angeles, or London. Budgets for producing theater in the regions are limited. Don't expect to be making a fortune off of any single—or for that matter, any repeated—job in regional theater (unless you're a box office draw; then you might eke out several McMansion mortgage payments with your salary). Most theatrical producers want to pay actors their due worth, but financial resources limit producer generosity.

Additional AEA Contract Salary Questions:

✓ Favored Nations?

Favored Nations designates that all actors receive the same salary.

✓ Plus 10?

Plus 10 means that if you have talent representation, you're asking that the talent reps' 10 percent commission be added onto the salary instead of deducted. This is an option often requested when the contract remuneration is low—i.e. the money is barely living wage and taking any more out of the gross salary after federal, state, and local taxes, union dues, and talent rep commission would make the net salary near third world standards.

Additional Nonunion, Theatrical Salary Questions:

✓ Rehearsal salary?

Some nonunion jobs pay half of performance salary during rehearsal or no salary at all.

✓ Production/performance salary?

✓ Pay periods?

✓ Is there any withholding of salary that is then used as an end-of-term bonus?

Stay away from producers who use this end-of-term blackmail tactic; it signifies that actors previously hired departed early because of poor working conditions.

Transportation?

This question is crucial if the job is located beyond local travel distance from your home base.

For AEA theatrical employment outside of your home base region, some form of one-time, round-trip transportation (or reimbursement of your travel expenses) from your area of residence to/from the job site is provided.

Union-actor baggage receives a producer-paid ride. Unknown to many actors who travel to regional theater, producing members of LORT are to provide shipping of an actor's unaccompanied baggage (check AEA regulations for current guidelines). The traveling actor can ship ahead their favorite books, blankets, and cherished tchotchkes. The theater is required to pay for the bundled shipment between the actor's home residence and the actor's new, temporary housing. When the actor has completed his or her contract the theater is obligated to pay for the unaccompanied baggage's return trip.

Housing?

With nonunion theatrical housing, ask if a housing fee is charged or deducted from your salary. Personally, I'd stay away from nonunion producers who charge you to live where they have invited you to work temporarily. The actor should be treated as a guest not a tenant.

✓ What type of housing?

> Apartment, hotel, or a room in a private residence? AEA contracts stipulate that the producer must provide the AEA actor with a private room.

✓ Private or shared bathroom?

✓ Kitchen facilities?

> Are the kitchen facilities shared or private? Is the kitchen properly stocked with dishes, utensils, and cookware?

✓ How far is the housing from the production site/theater and the rehearsal space?

✓ How far is the housing from the nearest grocery store and/or restaurants?

✓ Bedding? Linens provided?

> This is a question that should be asked of the company manger *after* the deal has been closed.

On-Site Ground Transportation

✓ Is a personal or company car provided? What is the access to a company car? How many company cars are there?

✓ If the theater and/or rehearsal space is not within walking distance of the housing, is company ground transportation provided by the producer between the accommodations, the theater, and rehearsal space?

✓ If the nearest grocery store is not within walking distance of the housing, is company transportation provided between the accommodations and the grocery store? If so, how often?

✓ Parking?

> If you provide your own car, is free parking available?
> When working in densely populated urban areas, this is an important concern for the actor who has a car.

Per Diem?

Per diem is a payout, in addition to salary, to an actor based on a daily rate for daily expenses such as food and accommodations. For theatrical contracts, per diem is offered primarily for all AEA tours and *occasionally* for nonunion tours. For other union work on the boards (regional theater or first-class, sit-down productions; Broadway, L.A., Las Vegas, Chicago, and other large city-long runs) the actor, if not permanently based in or near the town of the production, and a talent of respected stature with either industry or audience, might be able to negotiate a per diem into his or her contract. For nonunion regional theater and summer stock, a per diem is as uncommon as it would be to find Karl Rove marching in a gay pride parade.

For all current per diem rates, which are mandated by AEA, check with the union.

Costume Rental?

AEA theaters must pay the actor a costume rental fee if the actor uses personal clothing as part of his or her costume wardrobe. AEA union designates the fee per item.

Extra Duties?

The actor receiving an offer for nonunion theatrical work cannot overlook one vital question, *the* most important inquiry (aside from pay): Ask if there is any technical, waitstaff, or other nonacting duties required of you as part of the employment. Many nonunion theaters (predominately the nonunion summer stocks and dinner theaters) that don't have generous budgets for a proper support staff require actors to build, shift, and strike scenery (and, if touring, load and unload scenery), sew costumes, clean public areas of the theater, help with theater administrative duties, or wait tables (if a dinner theater). Generally these additional duties are included without additional pay (except potential tips for waiting tables). Whether you want a job as an actor/set builder or actor/dinner-theater waiter is up to you.

FILM, TELEVISION, AND WEBISODE OFFER QUESTIONS

With film, television, and webisode offers, the questions become more involved and . . . well . . . more plentiful. You'll want to ask the basic questions asked for theater offers, such as the length of contract, role, money, transportation, and housing (the latter two points if the shoot is beyond your home base).

The film, television, and webisode contract negotiating queries that follow apply predominantly to SAG or AFTRA projects for principal and supporting players. Occasionally nonunion, principal screen work is addressed. None of the guidelines applies to extras, a.k.a. background actors. Union parameters for contracts often change. Contact the appropriate union, SAG or AFTRA, for current contract definitions, salaries, and terms.

Production Dates? When Does It Shoot?

This question should encompass first rehearsal, on-set work-throughs, and first shoot day all the way through to the last day of your shooting.

There are two terms that must be addressed: guarantee and drop/pick-up. Both are contract terms that deal with what the actor is paid and when and/or and how long he or she works.

Guarantee

Unless hired as a series regular (television) or for the run of the picture (for film, meaning you're a principal contracted from shoot start to finish), get a guarantee. What's a guarantee? It means that despite how long the production initially intends to work you (one day, a week, or three weeks), the production guarantees you'll be paid for a certain amount of time, regardless of how long you've actually worked on the set (prior to going beyond the guarantee). In film an actor is commonly contracted as a day or weekly player, but there is potential to work beyond the intended employment period. For example, an actor may be hired for one day of work on set at a SAG day rate, but the person giving the offer will mention that shooting for the actor may go for a week. Ask to be guaranteed (paid) for the full week. Having a guarantee can also be of benefit when shooting schedules run quicker than expected. If you're hired for three days of work on a film but shooting miraculously goes faster than anticipated, cutting your three days down to two, with a guarantee you get paid for the full three days.

Having a guarantee does not limit your pay for work that goes beyond the guarantee. If with a guarantee you work beyond your proposed shoot schedule, you will be paid for the extra time. On all film contracts, especially nonunion or the lower budget SAG contracts, where your time can be exploited, it's important that you fight for a guarantee. If your shooting goes beyond your contracted rate and you don't have a guarantee, you're screwed out of money that could have been rightly yours.

While on set, maintain a log of your days and hours worked. Occasionally errors may appear on your pay stub. If this becomes the case you then have a written record to present to the union should you need to go to arbitration to receive monies owed.

Drop/Pick-Up

Like the term suggests, this is when the actor is dropped, for a time, and then picked up again to resume work. You need to ask about drop/pick-up to know when you will and won't be working on a film or series. You may be hired to do several weeks of work on a project, but those several weeks could be spread over a period of three months. When your material is not shooting, you're dropped and may be put on hold. When your scenes shoot again, you're picked back up. Depending on the project and the present governing union regulations, you may or may not get paid for that period in which you're placed on hold.

If applicable to the project, hold pay can be negotiated, depending on the circumstance of shooting. If placed on hold and you're receiving monies from the production, you cannot work on another project during that period (refer to current SAG and AFTRA guidelines for updates).

Turnaround Time?

Turnaround time is the interval between the end of one day's work and your start of the next scheduled day of work on a single project. If the film or televised project or webisode is nonunion or is covered by a union contract that does not stipulate a minimum of hours for turnaround time, you must, to protect your well-being and sanity on set, negotiate turnaround time that will allow you to rest fully before the next day of work begins.

Budget?

You're not being nosy by asking about the project's budget. Rather, you're discovering if the project that you once auditioned for, which was a SAG Feature Film, remains a SAG feature or has since been reduced to a SAG Modified Low-Budget contract (or worse, a SAG Ultra-Low Budget).

Change happens quickly in film and television. Budgets are adjusted, cast sizes increase and decrease. Knowing the budget under which your contract will be drafted will inform you how much the producer can work you, the salary minimums/maximums, and other working conditions on set. If the project is under SAG or AFTRA jurisdiction, once you learn of the budget, refer to the union's guidelines and contracts.

Money?

✓ Does payment include Plus 10 percent (when the actor is represented by an agent, as noted in theatrical offer questions)?

✓ Is payment Favored Nations?

✓ Points?

If cast in a lead role or as a major supporting character, ask for points of the project's net or gross profits. When the film is then distributed you'll earn extra cha-ching from the project's profits. Gross points are straight off the top of the profits and given predominately to stars. Net is income after investors and expenses have been paid. Points on net income are easier to negotiate into a deal, but the returns are more difficult to track and lesser in value as compared to gross points.

✓ Looping/reshoot pay?

There will be times when recording your voice to previously shot scenes will be required (e.g., sound was originally distorted, dialogue has been changed) or when scenes need to be reshot.

Per Diem?

For most SAG film projects, the producer is required by the union to give a per diem to the principals who are working out of their town of hire (an industry term meaning the actor works far away from his or her residence). When the project is a series for television, and the hired principal must relocate to the city where the series will be shot, as standard practice, studios often offer the actor a relocation fee (for finding a new home) in lieu of a per diem.

For all per diem rates which are mandated by unions check with the appropriate union for current information.

Location of Shoot/Taping?

Ask for all locations of your shooting/taping to better understand and prepare for what your working conditions will be like: indoors, outdoor, in a muggy swamp, a cold meat processing plant, around the block, or several thousand miles away. By knowing where you need to be to work you can then begin to inform yourself as to how much travel time you'll need from your permanent or temporary residence to location, as well as what personal items (clothing, fluids, snacks, medications, and distractions) you may wish to bring with you. If you're curious about the bringing of "distractions," there's a lot of waiting time on the sets of screen productions.

Transportation?

✓ Stipulate preferred class and mode of long-distance transportation.

For SAG Feature Film contracts and similar union principal contracts for television: If a principal actor requires long-distance transport (air or train) from his or her home to the city or region in which the shoot takes place, the producer must provide first-class accommodations. Once on the ground, from home to airport, airport to hotel, studio, set, and back, the producer must continue to supply transportation for the actor.

For union contracts lower in grade (more modest budgets), the producer provides what transportation they can afford.

For student films covered by a SAG contract . . . you might, if lucky, get cab fare (once again, check with current SAG contract terms).

Hotel, House, or Apartment?

✓ Specify type and class of housing preferred.

This question is applicable when the shoot is to take place out of your home base area.

Most actors (day and weekly players) are placed into hotel accommodations. If you're to be on set for the run of the picture, you can negotiate an allowance for an apartment or private home. Sometimes (mostly for stars) you can have a home or penthouse apartment provided as part of the contract.

Meals?

Most SAG contracts have provisions for actor meals. Some SAG contracts and nearly all nonunion films do not. You are perfectly justified in negotiating for paid, catered meals. Because of demanding shoot schedules, there is little time given, when on set, for actors to fuel their bodies. If you have special dietary needs, they must be placed in the contract.

Wardrobe?

✓ Is wardrobe provided?

For larger budget SAG features or AFTRA projects you won't have to ask about wardrobe—it'll be provided. For the smaller budget union (and especially nonunion) films, "Is wardrobe provided?" is a customary inquiry. If wardrobe is not provided ask for a fee for the wardrobe you offer, as costume, to the production.

✓ Can wardrobe be purchased?

Occasionally you can ask that the wardrobe be provided to you permanently after the production has wrapped. As I wrote at the beginning of the chapter, everything is negotiable, including the designer gown or suit you wear on set. Before shooting begins and you sign your contract, ask for a wardrobe purchase clause.

Dressing Facilities?

This is the most heatedly fought-over term of film and television contracts. Dressing rooms are sometimes battled for more than the money. Why? Because actors spend most of their time in their dressing rooms (sometimes eight to ten hours) waiting to do a half a page of dialogue. That's a long while to be stuck in a small, cramped space. Most actors get placed into "honey wagons." Like the beehive it's appropriately named after, a honey wagon is a large tractor-trailer with four to six narrow dressing rooms crammed side-by-side the length of the trailer. The rooms (if you wish to give them that luxurious term) are no bigger than a Port-O-Potty. If not squeezed into a honey wagon, actors are bumped up to a "double banger," a trailer divided into two to three dressing rooms. Private trailers are for stars and run-of-picture players.

Billing

Billing, like dressing rooms, is another prized possession in negotiating a deal. Billing placement in the opening and end credits is just as important as the salary. I've witnessed deals made and crumble based on the billing clause alone. You have to request preference of billing. The better the placement, the better your value after the film's release or televised production's air date.

Size, type, and positioning of the billing are all points of negotiation. The preferred placement for billing is in the main titles (the titles that appear as the film/program begins) on a single card (i.e., your name appears alone). This is a placement reserved for stars and major principal characters. After single-card billing comes shared-card billing. Here, your name shares screen time with another actor's (or actors'). How many other actor names appear with yours is negotiable. The less clutter around your name, the better the deal.

Paid Ads

Paid ads are on-air and online commercials, print advertisements, and theater lobby posters ("one sheets"). Getting your name prominently printed on or voiced in the paid ad is as prized a possession as billing. The more your name appears for public consumption in font or voiceover, the more recognized you become and the greater your worth grows in the industry—all while marketing creates the public perception that you're a "somebody."

I've witnessed the phenomenon of marketing a relatively unknown actor to stardom via effective positioning in paid ads. Once upon a time there was an actor from the original Broadway company of *Rent* who found himself right in the middle of this Madison Avenue–meets–Hollywood fairy tale. For his first major film release, after his Broadway success, his name and face were touted in all television commercials for the film, alongside the names and faces of widely recognizable actresses. Talented he is, but those paid ads instantly helped catapult his career forward. His name? Taye Diggs.

Air Date? (Television Project)/Release Date? (Film Project)

You'll want to promote your upcoming work, which awaits its scheduled release. With all your actor marketing, herald the screen project name and its release. Plus, with your knowing the air date of your latest television project you hopefully won't forget to set your DVR to capture your work.

Copy of Tape? (Television Project)/DVD (Film)

Also ask for clips of your performance, before tape or DVD is released. Having the material sooner will allow you to add it promptly to your reel.

ADDITIONAL ADVISORY ON NONUNION OFFERS

For offers of employment on nonunion projects (film, cable, Internet, and theater) the nonunion actor (or scabbing union actor) is in freefall when it comes to negotiating a contract. There are no contract parameters previously set by a collective bargaining agent such as Equity, SAG, or AFTRA. There are no protections for the actor. No health benefits. No bond by employer to guarantee a salary. Either you get paid or you don't.

Housing and transportation covered in contracts under union jurisdiction are left to the whim of the nonunion producing entity and the demand of the actor. The actor must fend for his- or herself. To be treated in a fair manner, I suggest that when encountering a nonunion offer use the previous guidelines for offer questions and the publicly posted union contract guidelines (on the Web for each actor union) that match the medium. Let both resources for terms of employment be your roadmap for negotiating a nonunion offer.

The actor with a nonunion offer must be shrewd and vigilant so as not to be exploited. As with anything nonunion, start high with the expectation of what you require (as opposed to luxury you demand) and work your way down. You never know; you might hit upon one or two points in the negotiations that can be accommodated, like a comfortable hotel room at a Hampton Inn while on location. Far better than a cheap mom-and-pop roadside fleabag advertising "Beds almost like new" (driving in the Appalachian hills of southwest Virginia, I encountered a dirt-encrusted motor lodge heralding that amenity . . . my foot floored the gas pedal).

NEGOTIABLE PERKS AND SPECIAL CONSIDERATIONS

Perks (luxuries or needs outside of basic contract points) are generally granted by film and television producers more than they are by theatrical producers. Major studio projects have greater budgets and resources than do their theater counterparts. When asking for perks or special needs, don't go for extravagance. Request accommodations that can be considered reasonable to your day-to-day living. Try to get complimentary tickets or house seats built into your contract so that others can see you in performance. Some of the more acceptable perks and special considerations to ask for in film, television, webisode, or theater include the following:

- ✓ Local gym membership during run of contract
- ✓ Accommodations for specialized medical needs that may require breaks for rest or administration of medication(s)
- ✓ Quiet housing
- ✓ Fluids (water, tea, vitamin/mineral replenishment beverages) on the set or backstage
- ✓ Comps (set number of free tickets for the film screening or your theatrical performances)
- ✓ Opening-night gala party tickets
- ✓ Screening party tickets
- ✓ Press packet (containing reviews)

Including Your Pet as a Negotiation Point

Betcha thought I forgot about Tootles, huh? Everything is negotiable, including your pet: your Tootles, Fido, Fluffy, Tyler, Dorie, Murphy, or whatever moniker given. Work as an actor often takes you away from home, friends, and loved ones. While expense may prevent you (and the producer) from bringing along your spouse, partner, other half, the bed lump, or whatever name given, you can ask for the next best affordable thing: your pet.

Your right to have your pet live with you at your new, temporary away-from-home home base is negotiable. For screen projects where actors reside in apartments or hotels, ask for places that allow pets. For theatrical projects where the housing is often a cast house or apartment, and the producer is often the "landlord," the producer may charge the actor a fee for the pet to take up residence with the actor. Having worked out of town myself, without and with a pet, I'm a happier artist when having my fur ball familiar, Tyler, sleep with me at night in towns unfamiliar.

GET IT IN WRITING

Once an agreement on all terms of employment has been reached verbally, get the contract (and any riders) in writing *before* you begin rehearsal. If the contract is missing any of the agreed-upon terms, request that a new contract be drawn. Some producers/production managers will blow this off and tell actors not to worry about what is missing. Do not believe them. Get it in writing. They may also deflect your inquiries for a written contract by having an assistant give the excuse that the producer (or other executor of contracts) is not reachable before your arrival. Or because you're to begin work shortly there's not enough time for a contract to be delivered to you. Bullshit. With overnight mail services and instant telephonic and Internet communications, there is little reason for you not to receive a fully executed contract before you arrive at the job site.

Never begin a job without all verbally agreed-upon terms placed in writing with both your signature and the producing entity's signature inked onto the contract.

CHAPTER ELEVEN

REJECTION

"Thanks for coming in . . ."

"If I have a good audition and I don't get the job, that's not rejection, that's money in the bank because somewhere down the line that's gonna pay off. Either the producer, the director, or the casting director will think of me again because I had that good audition. If I'm rejected because I did a poor job, that's not rejection, that's my fault."

James Rebhorn

Actor

For nearly all actors it begins at the end of the audition with four words from the auditor, "Thanks for coming in." For some, it's a half-hearted mumbled: "Thanks . . ." For the less fortunate, it's an uncomfortable silence broken by the actor: "Is there anything else you'd like to see?"—a question often met by the reply, "No, that's all. Thanks."

Actors who have been around for some time will know the immediate indicators of not being wanted. Especially if "thanks for coming in," a seemingly pleasant phrase, is spoken without enthusiasm. "Thanks for coming in" is a polite entertainment euphemism for "You suck. Was that the best you could do?" On occasion there's actual gratitude behind it. It's the speaker's tone that'll indicate whether a call will be coming with an offer or whether the actor's phone will remain silent.

The actor who understands the euphemism moves on to the next audition, realizing that auditions come and go. But some miss the early indicators of rejection entirely. They torment themselves with a dangerous mix of hope and paranoia. Eventually they'll catch on, but until they do, these actors will worry themselves needlessly. They'll wait for the phone to ring, their number dialed by a person who'll announce a callback or offer. But the call never comes. The silence creates a frustration that opens the mind to uninvited, nagging voices of doubt about self-worth, talent, and ambitions—an internalized cacophony of criticisms, a continuous loop about the actor's last audition. Each demoralizing critique, chipping away at their self-esteem and security: "I'm no good. I'm a waste, talent-free. Maybe if I had pushed harder? Maybe I pushed too hard. Was it my shirt? I should have never gone with Abercrombie for a businessman. Why can't I get things right?! What the fuck else am I doing wrong? What's wrong with me?! Why am I still in this damned business?!" All are destructive thoughts, and obviously (from our present vantage point) not one of them is helpful.

This self-doubt, laced with anger, is followed by thoughts of suspicion, questioning every motive and move of the auditors. "'Thanks for coming in,' the director said. He thanked me for bringing in my best, shook my hand. That had to mean something. That had to mean that he liked me. Did he like me?? Maybe he was just being kind? The casting director liked me, kind of, I think. She smiled at me, but that was only after I smiled at her. Did I not smile enough? Was I not pleasant enough?? She was pleasant . . . well for the most part . . . maybe she was tired . . . maybe it was me, maybe I disappointed her? But she smiled and the director thanked me. That had to mean something!?" Yeah. It did. The director offering gratitude as you departed may have been expressing sincere thanks, or a repressed response so as not to give away that he *really* likes you as an actor and wants to hire you, or the words may have been a polite way of saying "thanks, but no thanks." If it was the latter, it won't be the first time you encounter the polite rejection or the last. Whether you're the actor who understands that the audition did not succeed as hoped or the actor who is blind to the indicators of rejection, you need to let each and every audition be part of your history and not baggage that you carry in your present and deliver to future auditions.

There's no escaping rejection. Actors face rejection throughout their careers more often than they will acceptance. It's a fact of the business. If being told no directly in silence or in code keeps you from growing both as a person and as an artist, get out of the business. Otherwise you'll be forever stalled in doubt, depression, and despair. There's no forward motion in despair. Continual despair is a well dug deep and one hard to escape. The best one can do is move on.

There was an actress who once wrote me that she had been auditioning for over a year and that her life that year had been summed up in one word: no. She asked me how much more rejection she should take before she quit. I told her to stop whining about opportunities lost, push forward, or call it quits because she was in for many more cold servings of rejection to be plated before her. Rejection happens. It happens to all actors.

The causes of rejection are plentiful. But in general an actor is rejected for one of the following, seven basic reasons:

I. The actor is not type-appropriate for the role.
2. The actor is not skilled enough for the demands of the role.
3. The actor gave a bad audition.
4. The actor gave bad personality.
5. The actor hired was better.
6. The actor hired previously worked with the director or a member of the creative team.
7. The actor, right for the role, gave a good audition, but the director had issues.

Except for giving a bad audition or being a walking personality-disorder reality show, you have little control over whether you are accepted. Particularly for the last of the seven basic reasons, the one in which the actor excelled but the director rejected him despite his talent and appropriateness.

WHEN REJECTION IS NOT ABOUT YOUR TALENT

Your audition performance alone doesn't necessarily determine whether you will be cast or rejected. Absurd reasoning by an auditor, based on past personal experience and tastes, can lead to a great actor failing to win a role. I once witnessed an actor who brilliantly captured the essence of a character in his audition lose the job because he reminded the director of a past failed love interest. There was nothing the actor could have done to avoid the director's rejection (other than undergo intense plastic surgery).

I've heard many an odd reaction from fellow auditors after witnessing actors ace their auditions. Some memorable brow-raising reasons for rejecting actors are:

"I'm too attracted. He's someone I'd rather fuck than hire."
"I don't like the bump in the nose." (The project was for a 5,000-seat amphitheater.)
"Her eyes are too blue for the role."
"The girl has a cellulite problem."
"Her body is too small" (for a character who was petite).
"I wish that he were taller."
"I don't like the way he pronounces his *ts*."
"The lip-liner killed it for me."
"He's a leading man, but not my kind of leading man."
"She's right for the role but not right enough."
"He's too right.
"Too pretty" (for a character who was pretty).
"Too gay" (for a role that was gay).
"Too straight" (for a character who was masculine).
"The nose hairs turned me off."

Sometimes the reason for rejection is far more ludicrous, bordering on the bizarre. There are two behind-the-scenes stories of my casting past that I often recount for actors to let them know that, "Hey, your not being hired has nothing to do with you. It's because of the bullshit going on behind the audition table."

The first comes from early in my casting career. I was casting a new Off-Broadway, Catskill-kitsch comedy relying on Jewish stereotypes for the hah-hahs. The material, on paper, was hah-deficient. It needed strong comic Jewish actors to lift the lifeless clichéd script to an acceptable comic quotient. I was required to bring in comedic actors who were either Jewish or could believably play Jewish. Simple. But the casting process manifested complications because of the director's insecurities.

The director became obsessed with the last names of the auditioning actors. If an actor's last name didn't sound or read Jewish, the actor failed to register on the director's Jew-dar. Didn't matter to the director if an actor was 100 percent Jewish by birth, fluent in Hebrew and/or Yiddish, plus, more important, was capable of translating the Catskill-kitsch material into intelligent humor. If the actor's last name was sans Stein or Berg barren, the actor was cut. The director (who was Jewish) repeatedly reasoned out loud, "I can't have in the playbill an actor with a name that doesn't sound Jewish. The reviewers will kill me." Upon running out of authentically funny Jewish actors, the director, in desperation, turned to me and seriously questioned, "Can Asians be Jewish?"

The second tale of actors being rejected for reasons beyond talent and type comes from a scenario I briefly touched upon in Chapter 9: internal strife within a project. Of the problems with this project, the main cause for many actors being turned away was an auditor's controlling behavior. A creative team member who either because of insecurity or an overwhelming need to dominate forgot that theater is a collaborative art form.

"The show that shall not be named," as it has now come to be known among some of its participants, was a new musical with an out-of-town tryout at a regional theater. The New York commercial producer had a cautious eye on bringing the family-fare musical into town. The New York commercial producer and the director repeatedly asked the creator-writer-conceiver (whom I'll tag as CWC) to restructure portions of the story to enhance clarity and flow. He declined. They persisted. He stood steadfast.

CWC's behavior continued into auditions. Knowing that there was the potential of a New York commercial run, I first brought in Broadway A-list talent. What was previously seen as problematic on the page was suddenly coming to life with the assist of the auditioning actors. But before the director could voice opinion on any actor, CWC would dismiss the auditionee.

CWC continued to reject the parade of A-list actors for reasons known only to him. We were a bit baffled and growing agitated by CWC's negative and unexplained reactions to actors who, before us, had made his written words vibrant.

After several days of this, anyone who walked into the audition studio observed frustration and tension among my fellow auditors toward CWC. At one point during the process, a co-producer began to read a newspaper as actors auditioned. He wasn't intentionally being rude to the actors; the co-producer realized early on that time was being wasted by CWC, and since serious considerations were not being made, scanning headlines about the president's recreation with an intern was time better spent amused.

I continued to shepherd in talent to be seen. The director sat quietly while CWC accepted, dismissed, or occasionally interrogated actors. One questioning of an actress (a friend of the choreographer) was especially vicious. We knew her to be a great dancer (an asset we needed) but a so-so singer. She could have been a lead dancer in the project. Her aptitude for singing was not relevant. After she finished her song, CWC dryly asked, "My dear, do you dance as well as you sing?" Despite her dance skills, and the choreographer's plea to hire, the young lady was rejected by CWC.

Eventually the show was cast; the majority of the decisions were made by CWC, not the director or producers. The chosen cast was fine—a talented grouping of good quality for the regional stage but not all strong enough to transfer the project into town and bear the scrutiny of New York. The show didn't fare well out of town, and there it died quietly.

Why weren't the more capable actors chosen? Was CWC intimidated by the thespians who made his words ring with wit, or did he believe his actions were best for the project? Unless he openly confides, we'll never know his reasoning. But one thing is certain: CWC refused to let his collaborators (director, choreographer, producers) collaborate. And many actors, sure that they had succeeded in their audition, were rejected.

So there may be times when you hit a homerun, get great response from the creative team, and feel that an offer is surely coming. Don't count on it. You never know what is going on behind that audition table. You'll never know what the director envisions, who may already be cast, what roles if any are actually available, if the project will see rehearsals and production . . . so many variables, so little to be sure of. I often say to friends and colleagues that no offer or potential for work is finally realized until the final credits roll or the closing performance curtain falls. Then and only then can I say, "I got a job." Facing so much insecurity and rejection in this business, I'd rather move forward with the thinking, "There's no time but the present. Tomorrow will be whatever it is depending on what happens today."

THE GROUP OF EIGHT ON REJECTION

The Group of Eight cumulatively has experienced nearly four hundred years of rejection (when you add up the collective number of career years). That's a *lot* of rejection! How have they dealt with it? For some of our working actor friends, rejection comes hard, like for Phyllis Somerville. "Sometimes it [rejection] just kills and doesn't get any better," Somerville confided. "Sometimes I'm OK and sometimes . . . it's just . . . a stab in the heart."

I asked Somerville how she dealt with the pain. She spoke of calling actor friends for support and other comforting distractions like reading a book or going to the movies, any activity that would divert attention from the loss of not getting a desired job. Bonnie Black also looks for comfort in things familiar when faced with rejection. "I talk to loved ones . . . I'll call my husband, call close friends for support and encouragement and reassurance that this one job not won is not the end," Black began. "Depending on the amount of devastation I just do something else to distract myself: go for a hike, garden with my plants indoors, or read a book or go to the movies, trying to get my mind off the rejection by being active with things that please me and make me happy."

Black doesn't only focus on distractions to make the pain of lost potential dissipate; she'll also heal by focusing on what's next. "I look forward to the next audition, and hopefully I have another audition lined up so that I start work on it immediately," Black said with optimism. "If I don't have another audition lined up, that may be a time when I'm turning on my radar to hear what's going on out in the world. I become proactive about my career and try to get it moving forward by contacting people I know who can help get me work."

Mark Price has a near cavalier spirit about not getting the job. "If they don't want me, they don't want me. It's really their call," Price offered, with great awareness for the end game that is the sport of casting. "The way I deal with rejection," Price continued, "is making sure that when I go into the audition I do the best job that I possibly can."

Robert LuPone appeared to be resistant to rejection-triggered self-doubt and disappointment. "It doesn't bother me anymore. It's part of the process. I get rejected all the time!" LuPone laughed. "I just get used to it. What you can't allow rejection to become is persecution. That's what happens with rejection, *years* of rejection. You can't allow that. You can't allow the negative self-image, you can't absorb the rejection. You can't personalize the rejection. Then you start drinking. Then you show up late. That's the downward spiral." But how much truth was behind LuPone's bravado? Did he believe in his own wise words? Or were they words he wished he could be faithful to? Earlier in his interview, when LuPone spoke of his youthful self, job hungry like any ambitious, young actor, with dreams of great achievements, he recounted an experience that displayed a chink in his emotional armor.

The recalled experience was of an audition, long ago, one that LuPone approached with great desire, ambition, and preparation. "I spent six months preparing my audition for *The Elephant Man*." LuPone spoke of the original Broadway production, a play that was highly celebrated and popular, receiving intense media and audience attention—a phenomenon rare for a play on the modern Broadway stage. LuPone was auditioning to go in as a replacement for the actor playing the true-life character of John Merrick. Merrick was a disfigured Englishman whose deformity was exploited in shocking sideshow entertainment. Later in life he became celebrated for his creativity, wit, and intelligence. "I loved that play," LuPone continued. "I spent six months working on that audition. I wanted that play desperately. I came in, and I got profound acceptance of my work in that audition and did not get the job." LuPone's voice retreated in quiet remorse, to a near whisper. "To this day, crushed. Crushed," LuPone reflected. "You learn . . . if you do your best work it doesn't mean anything. That's part of the equation to getting the job. To not have gotten that job, with the work I did, and I'm talking two to three hours a day exploring the word *the*. It was a character I related to *so* much. I would have done the bus and truck [tour] of it. But I didn't get it and it killed me. And I was somewhat of a realist. I knew I hit it. It wasn't that I was fantasizing . . . no, no, no, this was an in-*depth*, *dimensional* realization of the character that was profoundly significant in that audition. The stage manager told me. The director told me; he was very accommodating. I thought I had the job before I finished the audition, but it wasn't that at all. I didn't get the job."

FIRST AID FOR REJECTION

In our business of show with rejection creating a constant dread and an endurance test of patience (like those rambling holiday form letters from distant relatives), there's a tendency to let the rejection (and the cousin's boastful correspondence) diminish our success and love for what we do. We'll wallow in our wound of punctured pride. We'll question our worth. We'll doubt if we're contributing anything of emotional or artistic relevance to others around us. You'll notice I keep repeating "we." If ya haven't noticed it yet, you're not alone in experiencing the trauma that is rejection. There's comfort in knowing others, like you, have been on the gurney of near-despair. But rejection is only traumatic if you let a brush-off of your product profoundly wound you. Yes, being nixed is nasty. But don't let the negativity of being cut spread within and overpower you. Like an infection you must stave off rejection's side effects and heal so that you remain ambulatory in both your professional and personal lives.

Ten Thoughts for Accepting Rejection

✓ There will be many more audition opportunities to come.
✓ A rejection is not an assessment of your career.
✓ Every actor (famous or not) has been rejected.
✓ A rejection barring one opportunity makes you available for other opportunities.
✓ Auditors are human and can make errors in judgment.
✓ Actors are human and make errors in auditions.
✓ Rejection for a job does not mean you're unemployable as an actor.
✓ A bad audition does not make you a bad actor.
✓ Your mother will still be proud of you.
✓ Your other half will still think you're the hottest thing in bed.

Ten Tips for Dealing with the Pain of Rejection

✓ Forgive yourself for mistakes (imagined or real).
✓ Learn from failure; improve weaker skills.
✓ Forget what could have been.
✓ Move on to the next audition.
✓ Vent your frustrations to loved ones.
✓ Harbor no anger toward yourself.
✓ Harbor no anger toward the auditors.
✓ Send a thank-you note to the auditors.
✓ Indulge in enjoyable, safe, and healthy distractions.
✓ Buy yourself a present.

If there is a Supreme Being, he/she/it played a nasty game of mischief with the emotional foundation of actors. Most actors are, by nature, sensitive. This sensitivity is a great asset for an actor's craft but also the Achilles' heel when an actor is dealt the blow of rejection or must dominate, rising above others, to promote him- or herself. Although there are a number of Eve Harrington's out there with ferocious egos and ambition to match, those actors, with an overflow of self-centeredness, drown any vestige of sensitivity, for and to others, in their gene pool. They also happen to constitute a larger percentage of the players who survive the longest (and gain the most notoriety) at this game that is entertainment. But being ruthless isn't a prerequisite for keeping a career alive or successfully withstanding rejection. Even ruthless people cry.

To survive rejection silent or spoken, you must remember that it is often not about you as a person or even about you as an actor. Rejection or acceptance is an auditor's opinion based on his or her life experiences and emotional well-being. Those two elements stimulate his or her response. Not everyone is going to love the product you offer. Audition rejection doesn't mean that you're disliked as a person. It just means that your product is not presently what is being sought or desired. There's always another audition tomorrow to look forward to.

An actor who has been endowed with amazing talent but does not have resilience to withstand rejection, failure, and humiliation faces a career doomed to early extinction. How you, as an actor, accept the recurring offerings of "no" will determine your desire and ability to persevere at your career.

CHAPTER TWELVE

AGENTS

An Introduction

"There's really no one description of the job of an agent. On my consumer affairs certificate it says, 'employment agency.' I am part employment agency, part therapist, part accountant, part friend, part parent, and part assistant to the actor."

Jack Menashe
Agent/Agency Owner
Independent Artists Agency

Leeches, sharks, lawyers in suits, Shylocks, power mongers, talent pimps, money mavens, integrity-free artist-arbitrating whores—all also known as agents. Promoters of talent who are also the punch line of entertainment industry jokes. The thankless industry job against whom bias and barbs are considered justifiable by participants and onlookers. An agent is the least *genuinely* respected player in the entertainment industry (albeit a slight degree above ticket-taker on the industry respect-o-meter). An agent's job is neither easy nor glamorous. They are working for the actor as much as they are working for themselves. Agents survive by generating opportunities for actors. Creating those opportunities is a daunting task. A talent rep faces more defeats in a single hour than one actor does in a month.

What's missing from the previous litany of derogatory descriptions and perceptions is what an agent actually is: a champion of actors. An agent is the actor's cheerleader. Part of an actor's support system—a professional partner in guiding, advising, and promoting an actor's career. However, an agent is a *facilitator* of employment, not, as too many actors mistakenly believe, a *creator* of employment.

So many represented actors misguidedly bitch, "My agent doesn't get me work." *Bullshit!!!* Agents don't create work! Writers create work! Agents promote your interests and talents to the gatekeepers of employment opportunities. Work that has been written by a writer, picked up by a producer, and guided by a director. The agent's role in the process is to push for you to be seen, if you're the right type for the project. Once the agent has gotten the actor into the audition room, it's the actor who must do the work to get the work! Not the agent.

The agent doesn't audition. That's the actor's job!

Another misconception about agents is that they represent actors solely for the money. HA! Wrong!!! Agents are only 10 percent as rich as the clients they represent. If the clients are all living modestly, so is the agent. If the clients are all living luxuriously, then so is the agent. But most agents do not find themselves in the latter situation. Unless he or she is a Jaguar-convertible-as-fashion-accessory, power-breakfast player at a large corporate talent agency on Fifth Avenue or Sunset Boulevard, the average agent does not live extravagantly.

As there is not much wealth distribution among actors, it's certainly not money that keeps the majority of talent representatives at their desks, promoting talent. Agents do their jobs either out of their love for the art of storytelling, their love for the artists who bring the stories to life, or both. Or they're agents because that's where life has presently placed them. And even if some agents were in the business for the money, what's wrong with that? (Remember: An agent is not a creator, he or she is an administrator.) Do you think CPAs, factory workers, retail clerks, and gas station attendants have altruistic admiration for their work? *NO ONE* works because they *love* to work. We all work because life insists that in order to survive, paid employment must be had to offset the expenses that come with living, whether our budgets are modest or extravagant. Working in the arts does not make the participants loftier in ideals, morals, or values.

Agents once frightened me. Before having agents as representatives, working with agents as a casting director, and living with one for most of my adult life, I carried around fears and expectations of what an agent was, and my preconceptions were woefully misguided. The industry helped build my assumptions about agents. As an actor my only references to them were the stage and screen caricatures I had seen. Stage and screen agents were portrayed as loud, brash, obnoxious, soulless, money-driven creatures. I didn't want to encounter those monsters.

When I jumped the table as a casting intern, they scared me more so. I was new to this world of buyers (casting directors) and sellers (agents). I looked upon the sellers as people of power, a force to be feared. I, along with many actors, believed that if an agent happened to favor you (the actor) with his presence, you bowed, shuddered, and kissed the ring of His Grace. Wrong. Well, OK, there are a few agents out there who do think themselves to be an emperor or empress of the talent trade, but that's their insecurities waving red flags for therapy and a prescription for Prozac.

I've abandoned my fear of agents, and so should actors. Agents are not gods, just personalities in a job whose function is to enable an actor's career. During my time in the arts I've encountered many agent personalities. Just as in the general population, differing personalities abound. There is no cookie-cutter agent persona. There is no MFA program for aspiring agents to become agents, instructing them on behavior. Agents learn on the job, usually starting as an assistant or intern, working their way up to their own desk and roster of clients. They often emulate the agents who taught and trained them.

AGENT PERSONALITIES

The agent-actor relationship is a marriage. That marriage, like any partnership between two people, needs to be based on compatibility. That compatibility begins with personalities: yours and the agent's. You should work with an agent whose personality best matches yours or who has a personality that you can tolerate. Sometimes a personality opposite of our own is the best match. Only you will know what works for you.

The Mean Agent Personality

Mean agents do exist (but so do mean bank tellers and Department of Motor Vehicle employees). The Mean Agent is going to be a shrewd but caustic negotiator when working on deals on your behalf. He or she will have a thick skin and will not let anyone steamroll over him- or herself or you. While this may sound wonderful and to your best advantage, the Mean Agent's behavior can deter your advancement. Casting personnel may not want to contact an agent known for being rude, curt, or discourteous, and so casting may ignore that agent's client list. Casting colleagues and I have our short lists of abrasive agents we either ignore or try to circumvent by contacting their clients directly. But even if we contact the talent, that Mean Agent will eventually discover our going behind his or her back. The confrontation is often not worth the risk of reaching out to the actor.

Often the Mean Agent's abrasiveness will not only be directed at industry colleagues but at his or her clients as well. I know of several agents who continually lose clients because the clients cannot endure the abuse. Actors tell me stories of how their off-putting agent will speak directly to them in derogatory language regarding their talent, abilities, and/or physical features. I always respond with, "Why do you stay? Leave!" Eventually most, if not all, do.

The Ego-Agent Personality

This type of agent is focused on how many A-list people he or she can collect in his address book. The Ego Agent's job is not about representing artists but about wielding influence in the industry. In high school the Ego Agent was probably that kid who had the gossip on everyone and was mean-spirited about those who didn't meet his or her social standing. The Ego Agent views entertainment as a power game and wants to go home with all the marbles; his or her clients are just prized aggies in their booty. How does this benefit an actor? An Ego Agent's valued address book filled with high-profile names might get the actor into projects of greater visibility. The downside is that the Ego Agent, without the actor's knowledge, will ignore projects whose commission (or profile) doesn't garner him or her enough money to pay for a new pair of Prada shoes or an invite to a top industry-player-attended party, premiere, or opening.

The All-Business Agent Personality

Some agents have no clue as to what it is to be an artist. This variety includes those who have little or no background in the performing arts. They're all business and treat actors, casting directors, and projects in a cold, clinical manner. This behavior can benefit both them and their clients. They look at the bottom line and are not influenced by personalities or emotion. If this is the type of agent you're attracted to, don't hope for your agent to become your best bud or part-time therapist. It's all business to them, and maybe that's not such a bad thing.

The Respectful Agent Personality

The majority of agents respect the actor, the actor's craft, and the business in general. These agents treat clients and colleagues with equal professional regard. There are no power trips, no b.s., they listen to their clients' hopes and disappointments. They care to some degree about the actor's life but not so much as to forget that this is a business relationship. This is the kind of agent I like to work with and the agent personality I recommend to actor friends I assist in finding representation.

TOP TEN THINGS TO KNOW ABOUT AGENTS

1. An Agent Is Not Your Audition Bitch

Having an agent does not mean that you can sit on your ass and wait for the auditions. As an actor, you must still go out, on your own, and continue to find work. As previously mentioned, agents facilitate audition opportunities. They don't create the jobs. Go out and help yourself just as your agent is helping you.

Let your agent know when you get an audition or job on your own. Informing your agent is not about owing him money for potential work he didn't assist in accessing. By making the agent aware, you inform him about your availability for projects he is pursuing on your behalf. Plus it demonstrates that you're a wanted commodity.

2. Agents Are Governed by Actors' Equity, Screen Actor's Guild, and AFTRA

For an agent to represent a union performer and legally negotiate a union contract for employment on behalf of the union performer, the agent must be franchised. "Franchised" (or "french-fried" as some agents call it) means that the agent has been approved by a union to represent actors for employment within its membership. For each actor's union, the agent must be individually franchised. Contact the unions to verify an agent's franchise. If the talent representative is not franchised, they're not an agent. They're a modeling agency, events-marketing staffing agency, or a manager.

Managers

Managers are not agents, and the unions do not govern them. Managers are not allowed to submit clients for employment or negotiate contracts (but many do, as heads are consciously turned away). Managers can take whatever amount of commission agreed upon with their client. The normal commission is 15-20 percent of salary. Having both an agent and a manager is a personal decision. The thrifty actor chooses one. The needy actor or star has both. Later, we'll learn more about the role of the manager and how some agents view them.

Modeling Agencies

This is where the business of talent representation gets the biggest black eye. Strip mall modeling schools, weekend modeling "contests" held in hotel ballrooms, and online "talent scouts" are, 99 percent of the time, frauds that do not advance a career but grow rich taking money away from actors. The fraudulent modeling agencies charge pricey fees for the contests, impose expensive "makeover" sessions on the participants, and often require the model and actor wannabe to purchase an expensive portfolio photo-shoot session with a photographer of the agency's choosing. The photographer is often a close business associate, friend, or sometimes a relative of the agency and often their work is far from picture-perfect.

Legitimate modeling agencies or talent agencies with beauty departments *do not charge clients* for anything (this includes headshots, portfolios, hair, and makeup).

Marketing Staffing Agencies

Staffing agencies that hire actors for marketing promotions of national brands will often masquerade as modeling agencies. They are not modeling agencies or artist representation agencies of any kind. These businesses offering opportunities of temporary employment (predominantly to people who consider themselves actors) can be a good source for additional income, with hourly, daily, weekly, or flat-fee rates. Some are fly-by-night companies, while others are fairly well known and respected among actors. A marketing staffing agency hires warm bodies to hand out product samples or display products at trade shows and audience events and on the street. You'll find these companies advertising online for "brand ambassadors" or the much-abused term "promotional model." Many of the warm bodies are far from model material. Take it from me, I ain't a model but was hired many times to stand next to cars and pretend I was pretty.

3. An Agent Is Only Allowed to Receive a 10 Percent Commission

Ten percent commission, that's it. No more. The unions set the commission rate and determine if the project is commissionable (meaning the franchised agent can collect commission). Some union salaries are not commissionable as determined by the union that governs the contract. (Check with each union for current commission rates and applications.) Managers can collect commission on a noncommissionable project. Why? They're not governed by the unions and can commission whatever projects their clients participate in.

Occasionally, an agent is offered a flat fee in lieu of commission. This can occur on projects that are either union or nonunion. The flat fee is paid by the producing entity hiring the talent and *does not* come out of the actor's salary.

Agents cannot charge fees, beyond commission, of any kind. None. I once heard from an actor whose "agent" was allegedly charging clients twenty-five dollars per month for office expenses. Wrong. Not allowed.

If you're represented and get a job on your own (you got the job through a friend or an open call), pay your agent the commission. The agent works for you nearly 24/7, not just when they get you an audition. He or she deserves to be paid. It's called respect and being fair!

4. Agents/Agencies Are Only Allowed to Operate in Specific Geographical Areas as Determined by the Unions

If you live in the New York City area and have representation through an "agent's" office located beyond the borough of Manhattan and the person taking your commission claims to be an agent, *he or she is not an agent.* Run!

Franchised agents in the metro New York area are limited by the unions as to where they may have their offices. As of this writing, New York City franchised agencies must be on the isle of Manhattan. As ruled by the unions, the agency must have a waiting area for the actors, and the agency cannot be located in a residence, unless the residence has a commercial office with a separate entry to the office that is accessible from the street. Also, the agency office may not be located in or on the same floor as the office of a casting director. Geographic restrictions for franchised agencies beyond the metro New York area are less stringent. Check with union guidelines for updates.

5. Agents Cannot Sell Breakdowns to Their Clients

Breakdowns are audition notices, as published and distributed by Breakdown Services. Breakdown Services is a company that offers a subscription for these notices primarily to franchised agents and a few managers. To be eligible for a subscription, managers must meet standards as set by Breakdown Services.

There is a black market for breakdowns in which they are copied and sold by actors to actors, agents to managers, and, worst of all, talent reps to actors. I know of some actors who have been charged by less-than-reputable talent reps for access to breakdowns. One example is a manager who sold copies of his subscription to his clients, then gave his clients his company letterhead along with company return address labels. He instructed his clients to submit themselves for the projects announced in the breakdowns. If you encounter a talent rep who behaves similarly, my advice is to run. Seek new representation and contact Breakdown Services to report the inappropriate behavior. Copying and selling black market breakdowns, whether done so by talent reps or fellow actors, is illegal.

6. Agents Do Not Choose Your Headshot Photographer

Choice of photographer is at the actor's discretion, not the agent's. Agents can refer you to a photographer whose work they admire. They cannot require you to use a photographer of their preference. You're born with free will. Just like at Burger King: Have it your way.

7. Agents Predominantly Sign a Union Actor for Representation in All Major Unions

Most Legit (theater, TV, and film) agents will only sign a client for all three unions (meaning the agent represents you for projects under the jurisdiction of AEA, SAG, and AFTRA). Industry lingo for this is "signing across the board." When signing with an agency, the talent signs individual union contracts, issued by each of the unions to the agency even if the client is not a member of any of the unions. A client can be signed to an agency for one year with a renewal process in twelve months or signed for three years with a renewal process at the conclusion of the contracts. An actor hoping to break an agency contract during its term will need a mediator or court order.

Managers, being self-governed, issue their own form of contract to their clients with whatever terms the manger demands.

8. Agents Can and Do Sign Nonunion Talent

An actor does not need to be union to be represented by an agent. If the potential client is nonunion, the actor signs standard union contracts for representation that are issued by the unions to the agency, thus legally establishing the relationship. Signing union agency papers, however, does not make the actor a union member.

9. Agents Freelance Actors Who Freelance with Other Agents

Freelance means that the actor is not signed to any one agency but is represented by one or several agencies on a handshake agreement. The ability to freelance with more than one agency may appear wonderful. The idea of being championed by more than one agent has potential appeal. But freelancing does have limitations and liabilities.

Freelancers are often forgotten or intentionally overlooked. Freelancers are ignored as clients because submitting a freelancer on a project requires additional time and labor for the agent. An agent must repeatedly get clearance (approval) from the freelance client to submit that actor on individual projects. Clearance establishes that one agent, above any other agent with whom the actor is freelancing, receives the audition appointment (if there's one to be given) and commission (if the actor is hired) for the cleared project. This is frequently a headache for agents because, often, several or all of the freelancer's agents will simultaneously submit the actor on a single project. This happens because agents need to get submissions to casting as quickly as possible, before competing agencies bombard the casting director with other possibilities. Waiting for a return phone call or e-mail from a freelance actor delays the agent's submission. So better for the agent to send the submission off without a clearance and worry about potential consequences (if any) later.

When the casting director receives multiple agency submissions for one freelance actor in whom he or she is interested, there's confusion as to which agent is to be contacted with the appointment. The consequences have arrived. Bickering between the submitting agents begins, with the casting director in the middle, and often becomes a heated pissing match marking territory. Most agents want to avoid this free for all. So to steer clear of the spray of other agents, many will either refuse to have freelancers as clients or limit submitting free-lancers on projects.

10. Agents Are People

Treat them with the respect you expect others to bestow upon you. The agent doesn't have to be your best friend, but you should give him or her regard equal to that you give others you invite into your life.

MEET THE AGENTS: A QUORUM

I've worked with many agents: affable agents, asshole agents, considerate agents, careless agents, agents who were agents while looking for direction, and agents who found their calling early on and had been agents for most of their adult lives. When I pushed myself to write this book, I knew I would have to cast for agents. I wanted widely respected agents who were knowledgeable, affable, blunt advisors. I wanted people of candor. I wanted agents who had a passion for being champions of actors. I found four, a quorum. All are agents I've worked with repeatedly. Agents I knew to be more than their jobs. Agents with a respect for actors. Agents who focus more on the work than do Ego Agents, who concentrate on how many recognizable industry names they can acquire in their personal phone list. The Ego Agent is a personality that I *really* despise.

The quorum of agents—Philip Adelman of the Gage Group, Lynne Jebens of the Krasny Office, Cyd LeVin of Independent Artists Agency, and Jack Menashe, owner of Independent Artists Agency—does not contain a single ego-driven member. Selfless supporters of artists, dedicated to their clients, these four talent reps have, combined, over one hundred years of experience in the entertainment industry.

Philip Adelman

For over three decades Philip Adelman, a gregarious fellow, has been a dedicated servant to the arts. A self-described "kid from the Bronx," Adelman knew early on that he had an affin-ity for the arts, but he kept discreet about these desires. He attended the Bronx High School of Science because, as he joked, "It really wasn't appropriate for a Jewish kid growing up in the 1950s Bronx to do anything in the theater." Adelman later escaped the Bronx and majored in theater and music at New York University. After he graduated from college and became eligible for the draft, the Vietnam War threatened Adelman's aspirations for pursu-ing anything artistic. To avoid the jungle of Southeast Asia, Adelman taught elementary school music. He freely admitted that teaching was his Vietnam deferment. Music and teaching ironically returned Adelman to the Bronx, where he taught until he was twenty-six (past the age of being draftable). Adelman then began directing theater, which, as he reflected, "I think I was put on this earth to do," along with writing. And write he did. But not what he expected.

Adelman wrote songs for Captain Kangaroo, the jovial, mustached, early morning television friend of many young baby boomers like myself back in our now distant youth of the 1960s and early '70s. From writing songs for the Captain and Mr. Green Jeans, Adelman went on to writing questions for game shows, his most recognizable credit being the *Pyramid* game show franchise. Penning game-show clue topics like "Window Pains—things that cause window installers to scream in pain" may not have been Shakespeare or Simon, but it was steady and profitable. Eventually Adelman went on to be a composer/lyricist at the BMI workshop. He would later direct summer stock and stage club acts, which is how he met some of his former and current clients, like musical theater comedienne Mary Testa.

Adelman began his agenting career like most agents do, at the front desk, or as Adelman termed it, "Debbie at the desk." In August 1979, at the age of thirty-four, he met with the Gage Group agency owner, Martin Gage. "I didn't want the job." Adelman recalled, "but I figured I'd meet him because I needed an agent. So I met him and he wound up offering me the job. I figured I'd take it for a while so I would learn what happens on the other side of the door because I was such a babe and so ignorant. Six months later I was running the office. Twenty-seven years into it, I still come to work every day thinking 'When does this end?' and 'When do I go back to my life?'"

I sat down with Adelman in his midtown office on a cold, end-of-winter New York day. His office high-rise was across the street from Macy's Herald Square and overlooked bustling Penn Station and the neighboring iconic sports arena that is Madison Square Garden. During the interview I kept glancing at an orderly line of framed headshots that hung several feet above and behind Adelman. Unfamiliar headshots neatly placed in a position of prominence. The headshots didn't resemble any of his clients that I knew, nor did I recognize the names under each headshot. Odd names like Saul N. Rapp, Cherri Rimmer, Daniel Getzoff, Lila Gottoff, and Bum Suck. I was confused. Agents often proudly display on their office walls the 8 x 10s of their favorite or well-known clients, as though they were trophies. Bewildered and oddly intrigued, I continued stealing glances at them, realizing that each was less like a trophy than a side-show cartoon displayed on the billowing tent canvas of a back-road carnival, advertising oddities never before seen by man. At one point during the interview, Adelman calmly turned to the collection above his head and said, "That's my changing display up upon the wall of the more bizarre pictures I've received over the past twenty-seven years." My mouth dropped open. I asked him if that was his Freak Wall. He admitted to it and then pulled several folders from a nearby shelf. King-size-mattress thick, stuffed with more than two decades worth of odd and embarrassing pictures and résumés. Unintentional oddities sent to him by clueless actors. Adelman is a serious Freak File curator.

As an agent at Gage, a bicoastal agency, for over two-plus decades Adelman has also been curator of a great roster of clients. He's represented Bebe Neuwirth, Halle Berry, Woody Harrelson, Bill Pullman, Chris Cooper, Kim Basinger, Tim Robbins, Adam Sandler, and Leslie Uggams, to name a few. But not all famous names remain clients. Departure is different for each. Competing agencies lure some clients away with whispered promises of glory; others leave for reasons beyond anyone's control. Adelman recalled one painful departure. "I remember being angry with Geraldine Page when she died because she was my *star!*"

Adelman is not star-obsessed. He has no pretense as to what his role as an agent is. "At the base of it, we're an employment agency. We actually hold an employment agency license from the city of New York to do business as an agent. At the most simplistic level, I'm getting people jobs. What becomes more complicated, more rarified is, in order to *get* those people jobs there are a lot of things involved. First of all the relationship I need to maintain with the hirers, so that they have *trust* in me. So that if I call and suggest someone, they're going to take it on faith, perhaps, that they should pay attention. It is in their *interest* to pay attention because I'm helping them do their job better by helping them find the better people. So sometimes they're relying on agents, many instances relying on agents, to help them do that; to provide them with the proper talent pool. There's a kind of a prescreening, and the trusted agent can send the client list or a submission to a casting director and attention will be paid, because it's in the casting director's best interest."

I asked Adelman what kind of actor interests him most. He had been prompt with past responses to questions, but this one caused him to pause with great deliberation. He remained silent for nearly a quarter of a minute before answering. "It's hard for me to really quantify it because picking a client, for me, is almost like picking a friend, falling in love," Adelman finally ventured. "I think I just have to plain like a person . . . because I'm going to be spending a great amount of time, potentially, with them through their career; some wonderful times and some difficult times. And if I don't really just plain ole like somebody, it's just not fun for me to be in that marriage." But Adelman does have prerequisites beyond basic one-on-one compatibility.

He expressed the obvious, that the actor had to be "fiercely talented," as Adelman described. But there's a component beyond talent that actors often overlook about themselves. "I also like people with good self-knowledge," Adelman continued. "I have to feel that they are realistic about what they want and can attain with their expectations. My sense of what they're going to be getting or attaining needs to match theirs, so that we're on the same road together. Because if they're going to want something that I don't think is gettable, then all I can see is built-in disappointment and unhappiness. That spells a future that doesn't seem rosy to me."

Additionally, Adelman prizes self-reliance, as do many agents when considering potential clients. Adelman prefers actors with, "a good sense of smarts about the business. We're not hand holders. I don't want to have to tell somebody what to wear to an audition." Adelman likes self-starters, actors who don't require instruction for every decision encountered, and actors who don't come with a manager attached. "Managed people don't really appeal to me," Adelman scoffed. "People who need management are the people I don't generally like to agent for." With such a firm dislike for managed people, I asked, "What other kind of actors do you run away from?"

"Those who won't sleep with me, because that's very important," Adelman laughed. "You know it's very lonely in the middle." After a chuckle, his response turned sincere to the issue of actors he'd rather keep a distance from. "Egomaniacs. Difficult people. Unhappy people. People who are unrealistic about their own place in the world," Adelman said, once again hitting upon actor self-awareness. A point of great importance, for Adelman, as he highlighted in a past client relationship anecdote:

"There was a client that I had, very happily, because she was terrifically talented and I enjoyed working with her. She was fun, and during the course of several negotiations, it became clear to me that she had a different perception of herself and her level of stardom (or attainment in the industry) that I felt was not realistic. Certainly wasn't consistent with my perception of who she was. I felt that made her 'wants' during a negotiation unrealistic . . . things I felt uncomfortable asking for her because I didn't think there was an entitlement that she felt was there. So she was one of the four or five or six people during my twenty-seven years here that I've actually asked to leave. So that's the kind of person I run away from. And I liked her. She was very, very talented. I just didn't want to have to ever do a negotiation for her ever again."

Just as in negotiating, agents expect actors to be somewhat realistic about the preparation and training it takes to be an actor. Each agent's preference in actor training varies. I asked Adelman what type of training he preferred an actor to have.

"If I'm working with somebody who's coming out of a training institution," Adelman began, "it's easier for me to sell a Juilliard, NYU, or Yale kid than a kid from Otterbein because the designer label matters; makes it easier for me to get them seen. And the fact that their school showcases are so well attended means that in one shot the entire world of casting has seen them. So I don't have to do the 'sell' in quite the same way, it becomes easier."

But the industry-approved, "designer label" schools aren't the only institutions Adelman looks to for the well-trained actor. "There was a young man that I saw at the Alabama Shakespeare Festival showcase five years ago," Adelman recalled. "He was the most talented man I saw come out of any of the schools, and I was very pleased to take him on. He's in *Coast of Utopia* now and doing quite well. Talent is undeniable."

Adelman is correct that talent is inherent and thus can't be taught. But to grow the seed of talent planted within, an actor requires refinement, judicious editing, and a broadening of his or her ability. For Adelman, the hardiness of that seed, not the institution, sometimes determines whether the talent will blossom.

"I sometimes think that the quality of the actors that these institutions turn out," Adelman said, "has more to do with the quality of the actors who entered them than whatever they are taught in those two, three, or four years. The best ones *survive* the training, rather than get educated by the training. They come out more experienced for having done what they've done. I think you can get fine training at Alabama and bad training at Juilliard, sometimes, if you're the wrong match for the institution."

I agree with Adelman. At many of the graduating showcases of trained actors I sit through (where it can often feel as if we're at a fashion runway show), some of what gets trotted out before us is a mismatch of institution (fashion) to talent (model). Just as you wouldn't place an actor who cannot sing into a musical theater program, you wouldn't put fashion model and TV host Heidi Klum in apparel made specifically for Rosie O'Donnell.

As most in the entertainment business have had to pursue civilian jobs to supplement income, I asked each of the agents if there was another career they had ever been tempted to pursue. Adelman did not hesitate with his response.

"At this point I'd rather be anything else," Adelman laughed. It's a terrible job. Nice people shouldn't want to do this."

Lynne Jebens

Before e-mail became modus operandi between agent and casting director, the phone was how agents and casting directors communicated hourly throughout the workday. We never saw each other; all we knew were voices. Even at functions in which agents and casting directors mingled, no one would know who was who. It wasn't odd to see among the mingled a body lean into a conversation of others and attempt to recognize the voices of the chatterers.

Lynne Jebens's voice, sometimes raspy from colds or overwork, is warm, mature, and often maternal. I always looked forward to hearing, on the phone, her sincere sweetness, that sweetness a rarity among agents. Jebens, Midwestern born and raised, is one of my favorite agents. Jebens is candid, yet charming. She'll soundly put you in your place when you're wrong and then end the reprimanding conversation with her motherly, "Hugs and kisses, darling."

An agent for over thirty years, Jebens, like Philip Adelman, is a vanishing breed: the class act. Unlike younger agents who concentrate on acquiring high-profile acquaintances to raise their own profiles, Jebens focuses on her work and clients, scoffing at and refraining from social-ladder climbing. She doesn't have the desire or the time. She's busy with the things that matter most to her: her work, her life, and her numerous cats beyond the work.

As with most in the talent promotion trade, becoming an agent wasn't Jebens's first choice for a career. She began in the arts with ambition to be an actress. It was her friend and actor Wayne Knight (the nebbish Newman of *Seinfeld* fame) who suggested to Jebens that she would be a great agent. Immediately Jebens rejected the idea, reminding Knight that she was an actress. "But I was living in Baltimore at the time," Jebens recalled, "and the more I thought about it, I said to myself, 'Hey wait a minute. I'm a twenty-seven-year-old character actress, and all the things I played in college were the mothers and the grandmothers.'" Jebens had great self-awareness and knew she would not be immediately marketable at her young age.

"After I got out of school I knew that professionals were not going to cast me in these roles; these roles will go to people who are age appropriate," Jebens admitted. "I realized there were no young character-women parts. So I got to thinking about waiting tables until I hit my forties and that frightened me! So I thought, 'You know what, maybe Wayne's got an idea.' When I got to New York, instead of going after a waiting job I started writing letters to agencies and interviewing and it was two months without a job but I finally got one."

Jebens began at Ann Wright and stayed there for two years. She later went onto the Michael Hartig Agency (a twelve-year stint) and has been an agent with The Krasny Office for over fifteen years. Over the years and at different offices, Jebens has represented Steve

Root (*News Radio, The West Wing, King of the Hill, and Ice Age*), Barbara Luna, Kaye Ballard, Helen Gallagher, Earl Hindman, Martin Balsam, and Robert Reed (*the* Mr. Brady). As Jebens was recounting past and present clients during the interview, she named one that brought me instant shame and guilt. I didn't know the actor was presently her client, and it was someone I mentioned earlier in this book, someone who was in my column years prior and highlighted by me in not the most flattering light. The actor? Ron Palillo. I mention this because how she spoke of Mr. Palillo goes straight to the heart of who Jebens is as a person, the admiration and respect she has for actors and her disappointment for how the business can unfortunately mistreat people it once favored.

"I now have Ron Palillo," Jebens said. "He's a very sweet human being. He's an example of what the Hollywood machine does to human beings: It wreaks havoc on their personalities. Ron had a great deal of success early on, and he hasn't necessarily been able to repeat it. I can't imagine what that must be like." Nor can I, and no one should have to travel the path of the Ron Palillo's—actors once celebrated and then dismissed.

Jebens views her role of agent as that of an opportunity provider. "My job is to only open doors for my clients," Jebens remarked. "My job is to get them there prepared with the right material." But Jebens doesn't just look upon her role simply as an audition doorman, ushering in actors to opportunities. She also views herself as the actor's confidante and protector. "To be a conduit for them to vent frustration," Jebens continued on her job description, "to be a conduit to protect them when they are under contract and when others are misbehaving or my client is being treated badly. I'm very Mother Earth. I'm a Pisces. I'm typical maternal, Mother Earth Pisces. How scary is that? It's an asset on one level; it's also a liability because I do get attached to my clients, not all of them, not every one of them, but when something bad goes down or a client leaves, it can be very painful. Actors don't understand that."

With over thirty years experience in the business, Jebens has worked with many actors of varied personalities and skill. When I asked her about the type of actor that interests her most, Jebens quickly shot back, "A talented one." I nearly fell out of my chair with laughter at the obvious reply. Jebens in reaction to my Chris Matthews–like "Hah!" outburst followed up with, "Well it's the truth." She then paused and sighed heavily. "I can't say that I have any criteria, but I literally want someone who is transformational." She wants an actor who can change and adapt. When asked what kind of actor she runs away from, Jebens firmly replied, "The pushy. There's a fine line between confidence and egomania. I like an actor with confidence, but I don't like an actor who is over the top to where it becomes stupid. The confidence is not realistic." False confidence and egos that need to be straight-jacketed are not the only aspects Jebens finds unappealing in an actor. She, like many agents, prefers that an actor have realistic expectations of what an agent can do: "I don't want an actor who thinks that I'll be able to create miracles. I *can't*. I work hard, I work honestly, but I'm not a miracle worker."

Jebens is correct; actors must be realistic as to what the agent can do for them. But how much power *does* an agent have? "Agents walk a tightrope," Jebens began in response to my query on power. "On one hand they're balancing their actors, whom they have to service, whom they have to get auditions for. On the other hand they have their buyers. If those casting directors don't trust you, if you lead them to wrong material when they're casting, lie to them, or send them someone who is age-inappropriate, too old, too young, just wrong, then you're going to lose that casting director's trust. They won't bring your people in in the future. So the agent really has to establish honesty and trust with the casting director that if you say, 'Please meet this person,' they're going to do it because they believe you. They believe that you believe in your client and you can open that door for the client.

"But I have to say that I had a couple of actors who were musical theater performers, who I got the door open for down at *Law & Order*, and they had an audition, but I could never get them back in. Well what does that say? Probably that they didn't do a very good job if I can't get them back in. *They* didn't do a good job."

And part of doing a good job comes from audition skills and preparation, both of which are often learned in an actor's training. As with all the agents, I asked Jebens what type of training she favored for actors. "I'm a basic Stanislavski kind of girl myself," Jebens reflected. "I just want someone who comes out of a good teaching program. It doesn't necessarily have to be college. I think Bill [William] Esper is one of the best teachers in the business. He created Rutgers' program, and Rutgers has got a phenomenal program! I always like those kids coming out of Rutgers."

I mentioned that I knew her agency to sign a lot of "those Rutgers kids." Knowing that Jebens, like Rutgers' Mason-Gross theater students, wanted to be an actor herself, I wondered if there was any other career she'd would have liked to pursue.

"Oh Jesus, you wanna know what my game plan was?" Jebens began to confide with a long sigh. And then she recalled, without pause, how she would systematically proceed with her life. "I was going to be a successful Broadway actress; I would do that for a few years and then go to directing. Then, when I had sort of burned myself out on that, I was going to go back to college and get a degree in archeology and spend the end of my life at digs around the world."

I interrupted Jebens and commented that I could envision her happily digging and sifting through dirt and sand for artifacts. She agreed but quickly interjected, "Yeah, but I wanted to be a doctor originally. That's why I was going off to college. But me and blood and needles don't do so well, so it really wasn't going to be much of a success." Jebens laughed, and I let loose another "Hah!" And it's that sense of self-effacing humor that makes Jebens all the more valuable as an agent *and* as a person in this often cold business. The industry could use a few more Jebens.

Cyd LeVin

The first and most important thing to know about Cyd LeVin is, as LeVin would vehemently stress, she is *not* a he. When actors, who have not met or spoken with LeVin, send her letters of inquiry seeking representation, nine out of every ten received are mistakenly addressed. "I get Mr. LeVin," LeVin said testily, "which when I was younger and angrier made me want to call the actor up and say, 'How could you be so stupid? You want me to represent you and you don't even take the time to learn my sex?'" But gender identity is not the only mistaken address that gives her temptation to call actors. "Then there are the people who spell my name *Sid*. It makes me crazy. I feel like calling them and saying, 'I'm not a fat, old Jewish man with a stogie!'" LeVin, apart from her Jewish heritage, is quite the opposite. She's a firebrand in stilettos and miniskirts. Always fashion-forward. Always mindful of her appearance. She's also *my* agent.

When LeVin visited me at an opening of a show I directed, before meeting the producer at the opening-night gala, she pulled me aside for feedback on her hair. As always, she looked stunning and her concern for her appearance both amused and touched me. As my agent she wanted to look her best as she represented me, her client, to the man who signed my paycheck. That's Cyd LeVin. She places the representation of her clients first before her own needs and desires. Looking her best is not about vanity. Looking her best is about representing her clients in the most professional manner possible. "I *love* being an agent," LeVin spoke of her work. "I absolutely love being an agent. I help people get jobs that I can't do, which I have great envy for."

LeVin has been both an agent and the owner of an actor management company, Cyd LeVin and Associates. After fantastic success as a manager, LeVin took time off to be with her family. Eventually, her desire to be a part of the entertainment community pushed LeVin back into the business, and she happily returned as an agent with Independent Artists Agency. LeVin's past and current clients include Luke Perry, Marisa Tomei, John Leguizamo, Robert LuPone, and directors Walter Bobbie and Paul Lazarus. LeVin has also been a producer; she was the executive producer for the film *8 Seconds*, starring Luke Perry, James Rebhorn, and Stephen Baldwin, and an associate producer for the television movie *Invasion*, starring Kim Cattrall.

LeVin knew at age six that she wanted to be an agent. At first the desire came not so much from the job but from one of the tools vital to an agent's work: the phone. At first, for LeVin, being an agent was all about the phone: "I was a kid model for Sears, believe it or not. I had an agent . . . who was very flamboyant. She had two phones on her desk and I thought that was so fascinating! It looked like so much fun, what she was doing, and I hated being in front of the camera; I was shy. I said to myself at six years old, 'I'm gonna do what she does.'" And with a vision of a desk topped with an army of phones, LeVin went after her dream of being an agent. An agent with phones.

LeVin began her pursuit of a desk with phones in the big-hair days of 1984 New York City. "I came to New York in '84; I sent my résumé out to different agencies, not knowing anybody in the agency business. Nobody, not a single soul. I got two responses, one from William Morris and one from Don Buchwald. William Morris promised me the moon, the sun, the stars, and that I would get franchised, while Don Buchwald said, 'You can have a desk at reception and God knows when you'll be promoted.' I took Don Buchwald because I thought he was being honest with me."

Honesty is integral to LeVin's personality. It's prevalent in her work ethic and her preference of actors she represents. She strongly dislikes actors who are, in her words, "superficial. They're perky, they're bland. The ones that interest me the most are the ones who have an intelligence about the business, an intelligence about acting. They look at the business as a craft, and the craft is very important to them. That's the kind of actor walking through my door I can totally relate to."

Knowing LeVin's career history for being a recognized player in the industry both as the buyer (a producer) and seller (a respected representative of talent), I asked for her thoughts on how much power, if any, an agent has in getting her clients in for a project. "It's the power of the agent's ability to communicate and push an actor in front of a casting director and make the casting director see why the client should be seen," LeVin began. "Actors are out there thinking, 'Well, if I'm with agency A,' which is a bunch of lawyers masquerading as agents, 'they can get me into projects better than agency B,' which is just a few people in an office.' Absolutely not, absolutely not," LeVin vehemently disagreed with the popular actor assumption of brand name agencies wielding more power than mid-size or boutique agencies. "As a manager I was in business with twenty-six different agencies, and did CAA get the calls before Jack Menashe got the calls? Absolutely. But the idea of casting is to see as many different people as possible and to have as much diversity as possible. So it's in the casting director's best interest to talk to the Jack Menashes as well to the CAAs."

When I asked LeVin what type of training she preferred an actor to have, she answered, "I have had actors that have had the *traditional* type of education, where there was the university or the conservatory, and I've had actors who had very little, like Luke Perry. But one thing about Luke Perry, he didn't have formalized training, but he continued training throughout, whether it was with coaches, whether it was through books or even other actors, he kept training. That's important to me, very important to me, that an actor continue working on his craft and not take it for granted. The perfect clients are the ones that will not take it for granted, keep working at acting, keep finding the mystery of it. That's the perfect actor."

I asked LeVin if there was another career she would have liked to pursue. It was without hesitation that she answered, "No. I always wanted to be an agent or manager."

Jack Menashe

I've known Jack Menashe, the owner of Independent Artists Agency, since we met as actors in 1989, when we began rehearsals for a national tour of *Annie*. Well ... "national tour" was a gracious term and how the producer and our stiff-smiled televised commercials billed the production. The national tour consisted of three cities in Pennsylvania. Starting point? The depressed and isolated coal mining town of Hazelton. Since that national tour of Pennsylvania, Menashe and I have remained close companions.

I didn't like Menashe when I first met him. I thought he was a chatty Cathy and far too eager to make anyone in the company be his friend. I was wrong. His fortitude for placing himself jovially into a social situation, a trait I disliked because maybe it's one that I envy, is one of Menashe's plentiful and better attributes. His affability and deep concern for the well-being of others is what makes him an effective and respected agent and agency owner.

Menashe began his career in entertainment as a child actor, making the rounds to multiple commercial casting offices in New York. *Stand. Smile. Shoot the Polaroid. Read the copy. Here's some candy. Thanks for coming in.* Menashe realized early on his journey that being an actor didn't offer him the security he desired. "I always had a fascination with the other side of the table," Menashe began recounting, "even when I was acting or auditioning. I would always somehow envy the safety or the position of the people on the other side of the table and would think in the back of my head, when auditioning, 'How lucky are they, to be in their seat right now.'"

The sight of that supposed security and power was not the only marker that prompted Menashe to veer off the road of acting and exit to a place of safety. The requirements of being an actor weighed down Menashe. "I got to a point where I felt like I wasn't doing what I needed to do in order to get ahead in my career. I wasn't willing to. I couldn't afford to. I needed new headshots. I needed to take classes. I saw that all my friends were going into New York to audition, and to tell you the truth, I really felt put upon to do all this stuff. So I made a choice at that point just to get out of it all together." The final breaking point for Menashe was being a singing waiter. "I also needed money," Menashe bemoaned, "and I was tired of schlepping my ass onto a boat and singing in front of a bunch of people who didn't want to hear waiters sing every single night on the *Spirit of New Jersey!*"

Menashe looked to the other side of the table for refuge. He knew that an agent's assistant was an entry-level position, but as to which agency and how to knock on the door for entry, he wasn't quite sure. "I didn't know what agency I was going to approach; it was just a coincidence that a relative of mine in Los Angeles had a child in a play group with the significant other of an owner of a talent agency in Los Angeles. A bicoastal, Legit talent agency that was very highly revered at the time. The owner of the agency convinced his business partner in New York, who already had in mind someone for the assistant job, to take a meeting with me. She begrudgingly pushed the other person aside and had her associate meet me. They met me a second time and gave me the job. That's how I became an assistant. My first day, I knew it was what I was meant to be doing. I felt great. That first day I stayed at work until eight o'clock at night with my feet up on the desk and felt really important. I became an agent through many hard years of work as an assistant."

From agent's assistant to agent to agency owner, Menashe has represented many actors. Some past and current clients include Samuel L. Jackson, Taye Diggs, Edie Falco, Kevin Chamberlin, Idris Elba, Lois Smith, Charlotte Rae, Cheryl Freeman, Daniel von Bargen, and Maria Thayer. Menashe views his role as agent, like Adelman, Jebens, and LeVin, as being the person who facilitates opportunities. But being a facilitator is not Menashe's greatest joy as an agent and agency owner. "I absolutely adore giving an actor an offer," he told me. "I absolutely adore giving an actor great feedback or even having them enjoy their own growth and development in the business. I enjoy seeing people develop and watching their careers grow."

Menashe is most interested in "actors who are just very natural. I enjoy actors who don't look like they're acting." When asked, like the other agents in the quorum, about actors he'd run away from, Menashe quickly responded, "Self-indulgent performers. I don't like watching an actor's technique; I'd rather be lost in their performance than be aware of how brilliant somebody is. I like to see the character. I don't like to see the actor."

As to seeing the actor, I asked, how much power does an agent have in getting his client seen by casting? Menashe was very direct with his response. "I think agents have a lot of power getting their clients in for things. If an agency has a good client list or a hell of a lot of passion for [the actor], either one of those things is really going to help the actor get into the audition room. I think the true power, the best power and the most effective power comes from the actor having a really good audition."

When asked what training for an actor was relevant or important to Menashe, his answer was surprising: "I really don't care what type of training an actor has. It's not really important to me. MFA, BFA—they're all abbreviations for nothing. I look more at life's training than at a school's training. I think it's more about the person than the training." But then immediately contradicting himself, Menashe says he does feel that the focus of specialized training is important for an actor, depending on the actor's career interests and expectations. "Training really depends on where you're going in your career," Menashe added. "Obviously if you're somebody who has no desire to make it on the Shakespearean stage, you don't need to have eight years of Shakespeare or Chekhov on your résumé."

I disagree on this point with Menashe. If you as an actor ignore skills or education in areas of performance, like Shakespeare, then later when a director or casting director has interest in you for a film or stage adaptation of Shakespeare, you're screwed and more than likely will be passed over for an actor who is properly trained and experienced. It's a risky educational choice to ignore areas of performance, a choice in which avenues for potential work are closed off.

Having known Menashe for so long, I was surprised that in all the years that we've kept company I had never asked him if there was another career, besides acting, he wanted to pursue. I knew of his dabbling with a paint brush on canvases and clothing, but what other desire for work did he have?

"I have fantasies," Menashe confided. "I would love to travel the world . . . be a cruise ship director or flight attendant. If anything, I would probably dream to do something extremely brainless . . . because what I do is so stressful."

AGENTS ON MANAGERS

Does an actor *need* a manager? "No, no, no, no. And no," was Lynne Jebens's ardent reply. Jebens then bluntly vented her thoughts: "I think managers have become a waste of time. Anybody can hang a shingle out and call themselves a manager now.

"I think managers, like in the old days, should be with two types of actors. Either the actor is too big, a major star or industry name, to go through all the material that is being sent to the actor—then the actor needs a manager who'll weed through the material. *Or,* if you're a beginning actor and you can't get an agent, a manager is the only way to go."

Philip Adelman's view of an actor's need for a manager reflected that of Jebens. "If I were an actor who couldn't get an agent, I might seek out a manager to help me; to use them, to effect meetings with agents. If I were a star trying to choose between projects and have somebody to package a deal for me, perhaps I would want a manager. I can't imagine why anybody in the great middle would. I don't get it."

Managers have taken it upon themselves to change their role from being an actor's advisor and filterer of information to becoming producers and unlicensed talent employment agents. Franchised agents who must follow federal, state, and local laws, and who are regulated by the unions, take umbrage at the unlicensed encroachment upon their territory. Adelman, a past president of the National Association of Talent Representatives (NATR), has been at odds with the unions for years over trying to have managers regulated. "Managers functioning as agents," Adelman began, "has become an unfair business practice. Agents are franchised, we're licensed. I'm bonded, I've been fingerprinted. I have to sign actors to contracts that the unions hand us. I have to obey an inch-thick book of rules that the unions impose upon us. We sign on so that we have the right thereby to exclusively represent union members. We're regulated as to how much commission we can charge. Managers are not. We're regulated as to the length of time we can sign a client, and actors have generous outs that the unions provide them in our papers. Managers can do what they wish. They're submitting talent. They're negotiating. They're [acting as] agents. They're doing it without bonds, licenses, and franchise agreements. They're *supposed* to be advising. They're supposed to be doing everything short of soliciting employment and negotiating for their clients. That's unfair competition."

As Adelman noted, agents are held accountable to the unions. This accountability extends into the employment agents seek for their union clients. Managers are not accountable to anyone. "Perfect example of accountability," Jebens began. "If I send somebody in for a movie and I make them sign the contract and then they get to the set and they've never seen the script and it turns out it's a pornography movie. The client is going to call the union in a panic and say, 'Hey, my agent made me sign a contract for a porn movie and I didn't know it was a porn movie!' Well, the union is going to come after me. They are going to have my head on a pike in Times Square!! I could lose my franchise for conduct like that! Had it been a manager, the union's gonna say to the actor, 'Sorry, Charlie, you signed a contract. Nothing we can do.'"

Jack Menashe's disdain for managers is obvious. "Managers . . . really annoying," Menashe said with a smirk. "Most of the managers out there are out there because they want to work in their slippers." Menashe was referring to agents being required to have a standard business office while managers are free to work at home from their kitchen table. "They don't want to go and have to get licenses with the state," Menashe continued, "because they want to be able to produce, which agents are not allowed to do. Most of the managers have the title of 'Production' in their company name, yet they've never even produced gas."

Gaseous or not, modern managers and their present role as representatives baffles Menashe. "I don't understand the role of managers nowadays," Menashe said, shaking his head. "Years ago management was established because actors desired a sounding board, someone to go between the agent and production. Someone to help connect actors to projects, writers, directors, and others who could help the actor grow within the business. Throughout the years, *management* has become a synonym for "agency without a license." Most managers today call themselves "managers" because it's easier not to be tied down legally while collecting more money from their client."

Menashe does have respect for some managers, legitimate ones who are not fly-by-night operators. "I think there's a couple of good ones out there, and what I mean by good ones are managers that have truly connected themselves with writers and are knowledgeable of packaging. Packaging meaning bringing elements of a project such as director, writer, and actors they represent together to a studio or producer, and the studio or producer picks up that project based on the elements presented."

You might assume that Cyd LeVin, as a former manager herself, would be a proponent of managers. She is, sort of, with a caveat. "I don't believe in managers that never were agents in the past," LeVin cautioned. "I don't believe they have a handle on the business at all. I think that if managers are there helping the agent and actor get auditions, that's fabulous! If managers are helping an agent handle a difficult client, that's fabulous. What I don't love are managers that call me and are being a burden, pretending they're doing their job by calling to say, 'Did you see in the Breakdowns that so-and-so was perfect?' Actors don't always need a manager."

In my humble opinion, unless the actor is a star, or the actor cannot get an agent, the actor *does not* require a manager. If a working actor has a good agent, he or she doesn't need a manager. Managers are no longer good listeners and advisors; they're a mess of unproduced Web scripts and half-done deals.

Jebens was correct: Anyone can hang a shingle and be a manager. I get submissions from "managers" who are the actor's latest bed bumper or a relative or acquaintance of the actor. The actor foolishly believes he or she will favorably impress the casting director or agent by having someone else submit him or her for a project. No, it won't. Agents and casting know who are the legitimate, quality managers, and we can immediately recognize faux managers or instant managers—a.k.a., cockroach managers.

Faux and cockroach managers are people on the far fringe of the industry who possess little to no experience in the talent trade. They often have a middling interest in entertainment and a client list of two to three showcase-leech actors (actors who can only get showcases as work). Most of the cockroach manager's income is earned from waiting tables, temping at clerical jobs, or delivering pizza. Most don't have an office. They have a cell phone and that's it. No brick-and-mortar address, no landline, no letterhead, and no business papers filed with the government required to work as a representative of talent. To grow their client base they rely on the naiveté of inexperienced actors desperate for representation of any kind, even if that representation is a guy on a street corner with a cell phone and a telephone directory of agents and casting directors. The latter description is not an exaggeration; I've stumbled across such cockroach managers and ignored what little they had to offer. Cockroach managers don't last long. Eventually they die out of the profession for lack of experience, ability, recognition, and quality clients. My advice: Stay away. Find a reputable agent.

Having an agent is a tool. A tool that should be respected and implemented with great courtesy. The agent will not be a one-person solution to your actor marketing. You must continue marketing yourself relentlessly. Having an agent is not an excuse for an actor to become complacent, sitting and reading a Stephen King novel, playing video games, or drinking rum and Cokes all while waiting for your agent to call you with an audition. If you adopt this attitude once you have retained an agent, your career will not advance. Your career will come to a close faster than the curtain fell on the ill-conceived, pig-blood musical *Carrie*. And more than likely you'll lose your agent because he or she will feel that you're not being an equal partner in the relationship that is the actor-agent marriage. Assist your champion as he or she assists you. The better you play well with your agent, the better the results of having an agent as a tool to advance your career desires.

As we go further into the pages, we'll be getting more insight from our quorum of agents. Let's move on to some advice on finding an agent, keeping an agent, and agent pet peeves with respect to actor behavior.

CHAPTER THIRTEEN

AGENTS

Finding One

"It's important for an actor to know that an agent is a partner. That the new actor is seeking a mate as actively as the agent might be. So do not be cowed by the procedure because the actor is selecting as well. It is a partnership."

Philip Adelman

Agent

The Gage Group

Finding an agent is rarely a one-time occurrence in an actor's career. Agencies flourish then founder. Agents retire or life retires the agent. Actors become restless and drop an old agent for a fresh perspective. Actors are signed then dropped, either because of poor performance in getting jobs or poor behavior as a person. Whether it's the first agent, second, third, tenth, or last, the search is never easy. The actor is seeking a professional partner. The relationship must be mutually compatible as in a marriage.

This hunt is one that many actors tentatively approach with a fear of agents, an anxiety about individual compatibility, and a hope for finding mutual respect in a relationship with a professional partner. Actors would do themselves well to play more on the hope than the anxiety and fear. Agents are not deities to be placed on pedestals and revered. They're just people. People pushers with phones (like Cyd LeVin of Independent Artists). People with a strong desire to assist actors. Anyone who has a desire to assist others can't be all that bad . . . can he?

"You have to remember we're all just human beings," agent Lynne Jebens reflected about her representation colleagues. "There are so many diverse personalities when you talk about agents. There are some agents out there that I really adore and I think *are* wonderful individuals and are caring agents. And there are others that I realize are just ugly human beings. It's about *them*. It's about power. It isn't about the actor."

The best agent an actor can have is the one who is all about the actor. You want an agent who'll champion you before he champions himself. Our friends from the Group of Eight have all had to do the search for their champions. When asked what worked best for them individually in finding their first agent, most of the Group of Eight couldn't recall (what does *that* say about their feelings toward their first agent?!). For Robert LuPone, finding his first agent, like for most actors, was a struggle. "I tried any number of ways to get attention. 'Please?! Hello?' Knocking on doors, 'Hi! Nice to meet you, I'm available.' Any number of ways to try to get attention." When I asked if LuPone's approaches for attention were of benefit, he responded with a laugh: "Not at all."

What did work for LuPone was one of the common backdoor entries into an agency. "I bought my first agent," LuPone admitted. "I got a job as a dancer and I went to an agent and said, 'Here's my commission.' And he took it and I stayed with him for ten years." If you're an actor without representation, having a lucrative contract to be negotiated is the quickest way to get an agent. Money often speaks louder than talent. Like LuPone, I had a similar agent-finding journey. I was in search of representation for one of my creative careers and continually hit brick walls. When a contract for work came my way, and negotiation for monies was needed, within one hour of receiving the offer of employment, I had an agent.

For Darrie Lawrence, finding her first agent came from another common scenario: The agent saw her work. "My first agent had a number of clients at the Denver Center, where I was working," Lawrence recalled. "He came out to Denver to see the shows and saw me and was interested. He called me into his New York office, and I went in and he had me do a monologue. But actually the real story is he didn't follow up. I didn't put any pressure on him because I had a job at the Denver Center, so I wasn't too worried. I saw him on the street one day and he said, 'Oh, what are you doing? How're things?' I said, 'Great, I'm working out at the McCarter.' Then he said, 'Have I *signed* you!!?' I said, 'No.' He said, 'Well, that was a mistake. Come in and talk to me tomorrow!'" Lawrence's example is a perfect demonstration of how agents are not the personification of perfection or deities of talent. They're just people doing business. It's your business to connect to them.

NINE IMPORTANT CONSIDERATIONS WHEN LOOKING FOR AN AGENT

1. Matching Actor to Agency

Think of yourself and an agency in terms of product-brand matching. You're the product. The agency is the brand. The two must complement each other. Before doing a scattershot mailing of your P&R, followed by annoying postcards, shop the available talent reps in the agency market. Finding talent representation that's right for you and vice versa is like shopping the cereal aisle at the grocery store. Which brand of cereal matches your taste? The matching of your brand (you) and the agency isn't about the level of visibility for an actor or the agency. It's about matching two sensibilities: yours and the talent rep's. A good match will result in a successful relationship. You wouldn't match Weight Watchers with Dunkin' Donuts.

2. Brand Matching

Brand matching does not mean that you physically have to resemble the talent representative's clientele. In fact, that would harm you more than assist. Talent reps share a strong belief of less is more in client homogeneity.

Agents regard representing two or more people who fall into the same look and type as a cardinal sin. Actors, when approaching an agent for representation, often hear the response, "I like you, but I've got someone like you already." Sometimes the statement is true. Sometimes it's a polite white lie used to brush the actor off.

Branding of a client list can extend to physical type and age. Some agency client rosters maintain a twenty-something age range. Similar to the movie *Logan's Run*, when a person (client) reaches thirty, he or she is dead and gone. Forgotten. Young, fit, and attractive bring in the revenue from film and TV. But hope is not lost for the forty-plus-somethings. Some agencies prefer clients forty and beyond. With age comes an emotional maturity. Hopefully. Agents prefer emotional maturity in clients (of all ages) as opposed to the headaches brought upon by green, insecure, "Where's my TV series?" fame-driven actor-brats.

Branding for an agency is more than the look of the clients on the list. It also highlights what the office is best known for in regard to their clients' abilities. Some agencies gain a reputation for supporting a strong theater client base. Broadway and regional theater casting directors will target these agencies when casting, while TV and film casting directors will generally ignore them. There are agencies that are weak in theatrical clients but are strong with TV and film actors, and so the TV and film casting directors go to those agencies first when scheduling appointments. Not every agency can be pigeonholed. A number of them have strong client lists for all three mediums, theater, film, and TV.

When seeking an agency, look for those that excel in the medium of entertainment in which you get most of your work. Now you may be a theater actor who desires to expand into film or vice versa. Too many actors think they can jump between mediums. Cold water splash here: Only a small percentage of actors can successfully cross between work on stage to screen or screen to stage. Your talent, training, and the industry (the most significant influence) will determine the medium for your career. Your desires are of little relevance.

To get an understanding of agency brands, ask friends who have representation about their talent rep's client list. In many cases they won't know who else their agent represents. Agencies don't host client weekend Kumbaya campfires. There's little opportunity for a client list to join as one in peace, harmony, and s'mores. If you're fortunate enough to have developed personal or close working relationships with a casting director, ask for his or her opinions and recommendations as to what agencies would be a match for you.

And finally in the branding department there is the quietly referenced issue of an agency's standing within the industry, based in part on client list quality and agency power. When I worked with Mary Colquhoun on several films she had me separate agency submissions into three piles. Pile A for the designer name agencies (such as CAA, ICM, Morris, UTA, Gersh, and Innovative). Pile B for agencies respected by industry (and Mary) but which lacked designer name cache. And then Pile C, containing submissions that were rarely, if ever, opened. As Mary once said of an agency in pile C, "She gets her clients from the Port Authority Bus Terminal." You can get an idea of the type of talent/agencies that made up that particular stack.

This kind of attitude toward and recognition (or lack thereof) for agencies by industry remains prevalent today. However, there are occasions when the C agency talent can gain ground on the to-be-seen list. Not all agencies work on all projects being cast. Many agencies decide whether to respond to a casting call based on the project's prestige and/or money (actor's salary and the resulting commission). And so, often regional theater and lower salaried screen projects are ignored by the A agencies while casting receives a smattering of Bs and a whole lot of Cs. Suddenly Bs and Cs become As and Bs, respectively.

How you, as an actor, can discover the level of respect the industry has for the talent in an agency is to bluntly ask casting directors, as well as inquire of agents (when meeting) who some of their current clients are. Most important, ask your actor network about agency reputations for the offices you have an interest in. They may not know all or any of the clients on an agency's list, but actors who have been at their trade for a while are often aware of an agency's reputation within the industry.

3. Size

Yes, size does matter. Agency size should matter as to the level of attention you, as an actor, require. Small and medium-size agencies (of which there are As and Bs) can wield the same power with casting directors as do the large, law-firm-like monster agencies. If you prefer personal contact and attention, a smaller agency may be better for you. If you're into big name brand names like ICM, CAA, William Morris, and Gersh and have no qualms about being one among many, then the big agency is the way to go . . . if *they* want you.

Large-Size Agencies

The large, law-firm-like agencies invest only in talent that is instantly marketable and generates copious, continuous caravans of cash. If not a box office star or an audience-recognizable actor or a talented-beyond-belief, more gorgeous than any Greek god or goddess actor who just graduated from an industry-approved school, there's little to absolutely *no* hope of being with a monster agency like William Morris, CAA, or ICM. And if you're not a box office star, why would you want to be with the law-firm-like agency anyway? Hand-holding attention by agents is given only to those actors who produce multiple Mount Everest mounds of money. Whether you're the newly graduated, brilliant MFA actor or the sexier-than-a-magazine-cover actor, or the working actor, if the commission you generate for your agent in a year falls below what the agency desires or if you don't generate any commission, you will likely be dropped into the black hole that is the assistant agent's voicemail or . . . dropped from the roster. When an actor doesn't meet the large agency monetary expectations within six months to a year, that actor becomes a nonperson. Money (lots of it) generated by an actor earns fickle love and temporary devotion from an agent at a large agency.

Medium-Size Agencies

Medium-size agencies are the backbone of talent strength to the industry. They generally have great reputations while maintaining a client list that includes both the recognizable actor and the developing actor who is new to the business. Medium-size agencies often have offices on both coasts or affiliates. The level of personal attention agents give their clients is far better than at larger agencies, but don't expect your agent to be a chummy companion. He or she will be your champion, not your best friend. The actor-agent relationship is business with courtesy. If medium-size agencies were retail stores they would be Macy's. Respectable without the attitude and the high price of Gucci.

An actor will often get an appointment at a medium-size agency through a casting director's recommendation, or a referral by an actor already signed with that agency, or by an agent seeing him or her in a project featuring someone on the agency's talent roster. The odds of getting a meeting with an agent at a medium-size agency through an unsolicited P&R mailing are extremely low. Unless the résumé of the inquiring actor has credits that are high-level and recognizable, or the actor is a graduate of a great school (preferably industry-approved), or the actor is sexier than a '69 Ford Mustang, there are only two other ways to get into a medium-size agency through an unsolicited P&R. First, buy your way in like Robert LuPone or I did with a profitable contract that needed to be negotiated. The second way in is the back door. Agencies do have back doors; they're called the Commercial and Voice-Over departments. If you can get in as a signed or freelance client with one of those departments of a medium-size agency, then you may eventually be able to get into the Legit department. Getting into a commercial department of an agency is generally easier to get into than the Legit department, because commercial casting is primarily all about the look of the actor, not the talent.

Small-Size Agencies

The small-size agency, sometimes referred to as a "boutique agency," provides the best opportunity for an actor to get representation. The client list is generally filled with actors who work in regional theater, fill out the ensembles of Broadway and tours, and do the walk-ons in film and television projects. Small-size agencies welcome the new actor who displays promise and working actors who care more for the work than their visibility. The personal attention at small-size agencies is generally high and much greater than the agent-to-client relationship found at medium- and large-size agencies.

Small agencies are more willing to meet actors who send them unsolicited P&Rs. Their agents attend showcases and paid auditions and are willing to take greater chances with unknowns. All of this doesn't mean that small-size agency agents are easy targets or less discriminating. While a small-size agency will still provide challenges for the actor seeking representation, the opportunity to get a foot in the door will be far more available than at a medium- and large-size agency.

The small- and medium-size agencies develop and maintain an actor's career with loyalty. The larger agencies take the developed talent from the small- and medium-sized agencies.

When the talent is no longer profitable, the large, law-firm-like, big-name agencies toss the talent back out onto the street for the smaller agencies to pick over the remains. What a lovely business.

4. Mailings

Before spending lots of valuable time and money on a mass-mailing agent hunt, where a fair amount of earnings and much needed cash go to waste on misguided marketing, know to whom you're sending your materials and why. Be selective. Choose targets. Match the product (you) to the brand (the talent rep). Know *your* image and the image of the talent rep.

When sending out materials, keep everything looking sharp and clean. Clutter and amusement are your two worst enemies here. What follows are some reminders for mailings, including what to send and how:

Headshot

Send one, high-quality headshot that accurately reflects you at present. Don't overkill with the amount of photos you send. One headshot is plenty. You must look *exactly* like your headshot when going to agent interviews and auditions. This doesn't mean wearing the same clothing; it means your face, hair, and body match the picture. No exceptions.

Résumé

Always have your résumé stapled, not taped, to your headshot. Seems obvious right? No. Many agents I know receive résumés that are "pasted" to the headshot with toothpaste, or bubble gum. One sticky, malodorous substance I received in a mailing was near hazmat material.

The résumé should look clean and be easily readable. Leave white space. It's okay to have white space on your résumé. Ask any marketer with worth about their direct-mail-marketing skills and they will say that the eye needs open space to read content. Use the standard, three-column approach. Separate your areas of performance by Theater, Film, and Television.

Cover Letter

Always include a cover letter. Use clean letterhead. Clean lines. Keep it brief—four to five sentences or two *very* short paragraphs. Leave out the cute and humorous. Tell the facts. Give some history (less is more). Name-drop any names you know personally that the agent knows personally. Name-drop industry and box-office names with whom you've worked closely (appearing as a background actor for one scene in a Brad Pitt film does not equal a close working relationship about which you can boast).

Envelope

Use a white envelope. Rise above the millions of actors who use the standard Staples yellow envelope. Look professional and stand apart. Businesses use white. Don't use the clear envelopes. A clear envelope is rarely opened and usually tossed into the trash along with the unviewed contents.

When it comes to addressing the envelope, you have two choices: Use a label that you created through your database of agents, or brush up on your penmanship and make the outside address appear personal. Stay away from the preaddressed agent labels for sale online and at performing arts stores. Why? The information is not always up to date. Also, don't clutter the envelope with warnings like "Fragile," or "Do Not Bend." Seventy-five percent of the envelopes agents and casting directors receive with (or without) the insecurity warnings to the postal carrier land on industry desks in a toss-and-tumble condition.

VHS Tapes, CDs, and DVDs

Research, via *The Ross Reports*, if the agent/agency you wish to contact accepts or does not accept recorded material. Most don't. Why? Because the agents are extremely busy with current clients and have little time to stop and review the hundreds of examples of recorded material they receive. When an agent wants to "see your tape" he or she will let you know. Many of my agent and casting colleagues and I publish in *The Ross Reports* that we do not accept recorded material but still the items come, and into the trash they go without viewing. I used to feel guilty about this, but I have no room to keep the deluge of tapes, CDs, and DVDS. Nor do I have the money and time to send back material I didn't request.

Scope of the Mailing

Don't limit your mailing to just the agent. Send a mailing as well to the agent's assistant and associates. Why the assistant? Assistants often become franchised agents.

5. Film Agents

If your hopes are on an agency that works predominantly in film, then you had better have something on tape/DVD to back up your desires. Before presenting yourself to an agency known for film and TV clients, you'll need to be both young and hot or have experience in the screen media. If lacking experience, get involved in quality student films and low-budget independent features. With patience and persistence, your desires will begin to be fulfilled. If you're not young and hot, there's hope. Bea Arthur had a great career.

6. Paid Auditions

Paid auditions are an effective way to get attention, brief as your time is (three minutes or so) in front of your industry person of choice. Paying thirty-five to forty bucks to be seen by industry is worth the gamble that the person you're meeting with will like you and take an interest.

7. Showcases

I've said it before and I'll repeat my belief again: New York showcases, initially a good idea proposed by AEA as an outlet for member visibility, have become nothing greater than AEA's infamous version of really bad community theater. Agents rarely, if ever, attend a non-client showcase.

If you should be able to get a prospective champion of your talents to see you in action upon the stage in a showcase, make damn sure that the level of *all* production elements (you, your fellow castmates, the script, the direction, and design) are nothing less than stellar. Don't invite an agent, who has worked an exhausting ten-hour day, to a showcase that is an endurance test for both the audience and for those on stage. Before sending out that postcard trumpeting your latest showcase, ask yourself, "Would I subject my mother to this?"

8. Professionalism

Image. Image. Image. Finding representation should be near-parallel in mindset to seeking civilian employment at a *Fortune* 500 company. So be professional! Mailing gimmicks that you find fun and unique can be unnerving and foolish to the stranger who doesn't know you. Being relentless with an agent is not viewed as perseverance but as cause for a restraining order. If you want an agent's respect, then you must respect him or her and be both professional and dignified in seeking your professional partner and champion.

9. Being Positive

Be positive when meeting with prospective representatives of your talent. This doesn't mean you present the giddy exuberance of *Up with People*. God no; then you'll be quickly pushed out the door. When meeting with an agent, be honest, be yourself, be open. No pretense.

Don't bash or gossip about anyone during your interview with the talent rep. The warning might seem obvious, but once a person gets either nervous *or* comfortable, the filter on the mouth loosens. Censor yourself. The industry is small. Very small, near incestuous. If, during your meeting, you were negative about anyone, the talent rep you just met may phone or e-mail their friend whom you flamed out on. Then you're really screwed; you'll become known as a negative gossip.

Highlight and emphasize the industry associates who know you and your work, but don't be a braggart. One of the first questions asked by an agent in an interview is, "So tell me, what casting directors or directors know you?" And by "know," the agent means that the casting director or director has seen your work, knows your personality to some degree, and can recall your name without difficulty.

A talent rep is looking for honesty and marketability. Most important, talent reps seek someone who is well-adjusted as both a person and as an actor. To know if you're agent-ready, examine those three aspects of yourself (honesty, marketability, being well-adjusted) before reaching out for a champion of your talent.

AGENTS ON ACTORS FINDING AGENTS

Here's a rare opportunity: agents candidly offering insight into how actors can best approach an agent for representation. Our quorum of agents is also blunt as to what an actor should not do in seeking representation.

Before I interviewed the members of our agent foursome I approached over one hundred actors, asking them what questions about finding representation they would want to ask an agent. The actors replied with plentiful inquiries. What surprised me was that many of the actors approached didn't understand the actor-agent relationship, and many did not know what a talent agent *did*! There are a lot of uninformed, unrepresented actors *and* represented actors with mistaken assumptions or perceptions about agents. Our quorum of agents was eager to enlighten.

Contacting an Agent

What are some of the most effective ways actors have reached out to you in getting your attention for a meeting?

LYNNE JEBENS: What I pay attention to is when actors use someone's name as a recommendation, but it has to be a *true* recommendation. Because when an actor uses somebody's name, I call and check it out. It better be truthful, and it better be honest.

CYD LeVIN: It's hard to get a meeting with me. The biggest way an actor gets a meeting with me is through a casting director's recommendation, especially a casting director that I respect. The other way is through seeing the actor in a show. Work bequeaths work.

JACK MENASHE: I love when the actor lets me come to them instead of trying so hard to force me to like them. I feel that so much about this business is letting people get excited about you rather than begging to get excited about you. Nobody really wants to be begged.

When an actor contacts you for representation, what about the actor's picture and résumé peaks your interest so that you invite him or her in for a meeting? What makes you keep an unsolicited picture and résumé?

JEBENS: The first place I always look is the eyes. There has to be something active going on. The eyes are a reflection of who the actor can be as characters.

LeVIN: I'm not big on unsolicited pictures and résumés. I need to see the work. But if the picture and résumé is of somebody *really* attractive, because unfortunately this is a visual business, I may take a second look at that picture to see what that person's training is. What, if anything, they have done. I will give that person an extra chance.

MENASHE: If somebody is in a Broadway show or understudying in a Broadway show or has really good regional credits and has gotten all this work on their own plus a good, marketable look and a nice clean presentation, I will absolutely call them in for a meeting. I do look at the training if the actor doesn't have a lot of credits.

PHILIP ADELMAN: It's very rare that I will respond to ANY unsolicited headshot except if it's somebody I know or somebody remarkably beautiful. What I need, what I become interested in potentially in an actor, has so little to do with the two-dimensional info I get on a picture and résumé. Occasionally somebody will be so undeniably beautiful that really what they're selling *is* on that piece of paper, if this is going to be a soap opera boy or girl or some seventeen-year-old sitcom beauty that I know can help pay the rent. So that I can *afford* to agent for my scarily brilliant and virtually unmarketable forty-year-old, who is unlikely to get the good paying jobs but who enriches my soul for agenting. But somebody's got to pay the rent for me to do that, and sometimes that's the soap opera girl and sometimes I can tell that from a picture and résumé. I can't tell if she's an *actor* from that picture and résumé. So it's pretty difficult for me to meet somebody from a picture and résumé.

What causes you to trash an unsolicited picture and résumé?

JEBENS: I hate the word *trash*, honestly. I file those into the circular file, unfortunately, because I don't have the space to save them all. I did a panel once with some girl [agent] from one of the big agencies, and one of the comments she made was, "Well, we don't open pictures and résumés. We're beyond that!" And I thought, "Well, who died and made you God?"

I don't like résumés that are not cut to the size of the headshot. I don't like glitter coming out of envelopes. I'm not amused when the glitter is all over my desk and my floor. This is a business; treat it like a business.

Also, I personally think that the envelopes with the windows in them are bothersome and stupid. Reason being that if there's nothing appealing in the face, most people are just going to throw it away without opening the envelope. So here you think you're intriguing somebody with being able to see your face, but if the agent doesn't like your face, they don't open the envelope! So even if you have a recommendation, it ain't there because the agent has thrown it out with the rest of what you sent.

MENASHE: I throw away pictures and résumés that come with a messy cover letter, with bad grammar, or my name spelled incorrectly on the label or letter. I also throw away a picture that is confusing and doesn't convey to me that this person has an idea of what they're about. All these things tell me that the actor is not educated and doesn't have a lot of pride in what they do.

We get all kinds of freaky things in the mail. Composites with an actor wearing all kinds of different outfits from chef to a police officer holding a club to a Sumo wrestler; we don't need to know how you, as an actor, look in different clothes. I think that's part of our job, to get a sense of you. If we can't get who you are from one photo, we're certainly not going to get it from twelve. The only thing we're going to get is that you're fucking crazy.

The other mailings that I trash are from the actors who, I believe, have formed a cult that shares rainbow and star stickers and Hello Kitty stickers. Hello Kitty sticker-crazed actors put these on the outside of their envelope, all over. I'm really glad that they enjoy a Hello Kitty or two, but I really don't need to know that in order to open their envelope. Maybe they think I'm a Hello Kitty fan so I'll go to their envelope first. I have never called in anybody with a rainbow star or Hello Kitty sticker. It's not that I'm anti-sticker, it's just that I think the people who generally use the sticker as a draw are people who are freaky.

LeVIN: I throw a picture and résumé away because it's unsolicited.

How important is a cover letter when you're first contacted by talent?

MENASHE: It's extremely important. I think the cover letter is indicative of the personality or person.

JEBENS: The actor does have to have some kind of letter. I only pay attention to it as points of reference. Is there a name being thrown at me that I should pay attention to? Is there a new teacher or booking that hasn't made the résumé yet?

LeVIN: The cover letter, from actors who have been referred to me, can be what makes or breaks further interest. If it's aggressive or *salesman*-like, trying too hard to sell themselves, then it doesn't do anything. It turns me off.

What and how much information do you want in the cover letter?

JEBENS: It's a business letter. Write in a business-like manner. Don't be cavalier about what we do. Treat the professionals you're contacting as professional. "Hi, this is who I am. I'm directing this letter to you. I'd like to meet you." That's all I need to have.

LeVIN: You don't need that much in a cover letter. Tell me why I should represent you. Tell me about your training, and tell me what you've accomplished.

MENASHE: I think the cover letter should be short, to the point, and professional. I think the picture and résumé say 90 percent of what an actor is trying to convey, and a cover letter should be there to give an idea of what type of person this is.

The cover letter should say essentially who they were referred by, if anybody, what's included in the envelope, how to get in contact with them, and what, most importantly, is going on in their career at the moment, if anything at the moment.

Meeting with an Agent

What can an actor do in a first meeting that will inspire you to represent him or her?

ADELMAN: Who they are is what's going to make me respond to them or not. Not what they do. Be yourself. Be honest. Be comfortable.

JEBENS: I have to see some work first. You can get a sense in a meeting of who the actor is, but that's about it. I don't think there's anything [in a meeting] that's going to make me go, "I have to represent this person!"

LeVIN: Go into the meeting with one key thing in mind: "I want this person to represent me because I have this, this, and this to offer." You don't want a "briefcase actor" (this is somebody that totally turns me off). A briefcase actor is somebody that comes in with notes, they've got everything documented, and they're documenting the agent. And the agent is thinking, "OK it's gotta be more free-form than this."

MENASHE: I like the actor I'm first meeting to be somebody who doesn't try so hard to sell themselves and just lets their personality come through. Somebody who just talks to me rather than trying to impress me. I can't stand when someone is trying to sell me in a meeting because I can't possibly get to know who they are if they're working so hard at selling me.

I think that if an agent is going to like you, they're gonna like you. I don't think there's a whole lot an actor can do to make an agent, in a meeting, fall in love with you other than to just be yourself. It's either going to be a match or it's not going to be a match. We're professionals at getting the truth out of you. We're professional at getting to the bottom line and seeing you for who you are.

When meeting an actor, as a potential client, what are the three most important things you look for in him or her?

MENASHE: Intelligence, talent, and marketability.

ADELMAN: A self-knowledge along with confidence and a sense of humor.

LeVIN: The three things important to me are training, what they've done, and how they approach the business.

JEBENS: Confidence, a quiet confidence. Interest in me and how I work; everybody's office is run differently. And I want an actor who has respect for the craft. I want an actor who wants to come in and do everything. I don't want somebody walking in and saying to me, "I only want to do film and television." You know what I've started to say to people who say that? I say, "Move to L.A. You're in New

York, if you don't have theater, theater is not a part of who and what you want to be, then I don't have time for you."

What questions should a potential actor-client avoid *asking you when meeting you for the first time?*

JEBENS: "How many actors like me do you have?" We wouldn't be taking the meeting if we weren't *interested.* Who *cares* how many actors like you we have? Also, "How many clients do you have?" It's none of *your* business! Actors shouldn't care how many clients there are as long as they're getting serviced. There are offices that take on only thirty to forty actors. There are other offices that will handle hundreds of actors. As long as the actor is getting out, as long as you feel that you have contact with your agent, why do you care?"

MENASHE: I find that actors come in and ask questions they *think* they should ask. They're not really asking questions that they want answers for; they're asking questions because NYU or Rutgers told them to ask it. "How many actors like me do you have?" "What about me did you like when you saw me?" "How many clients do you have?" What do they want to *hear?* Do they want to hear that we have five hundred actors or do they want to hear they we have three?"

One question the quorum is collectively tired of hearing from actors during interviews: "'How do you see me?'" LeVin vented in frustration. "It makes me absolutely crazy! First of all, how does the actor see themselves? I'm not God. I'm not going to give the actor their identity; they should have their own identity!"

"'How do you see me?'" Menashe echoed the actor question that drives LeVin mad. "That's the one question that we shoot back with 'Well, how do you see yourself?' which really means absolutely kind of nothing except for that we don't want to answer that question because it's retarded."

"I don't like an actor asking how I see them," Adelman added to the quorum. "I feel that it's too early on to know the answer. If the actor is shallow enough to think that sitting across the desk from them I can assess their talent and know the range of the roles that are right for them, that speaks to the shallowness of the actor and how they view their own talent. The question teaches me about the actor in a negative way."

What are the questions that actors *should ask you?*

ADELMAN: The actor should ask about the agency, how we work, what I'm looking for potentially in an actor.

JEBENS: "How does this office work?" Do the individual agents have their own clients, or does the office work together with all clients?"

MENASHE: See, this is the problem, programming actors to ask certain questions. The actor should ask things that really matter to them! The actor should sit down, alone, and think about what they really want to know about the agency. I think most times actors are asking specific questions because they're being told they should. It's really annoying because they have to know that every other actor who is coming into our office is asking the same questions. The most important thing is to get to know the agent. No one's going to have a passion for you unless they relate to you.

LeVIN: I hate people who bring the notebooks to meetings. There are things that they should ask, but to bring out "the list" drives me absolutely crazy, because this business isn't that precise. If the actor is just trying to put the interview process into a little contained box, our business doesn't work that way.

Other than what is on his or her résumé, what are you looking for in an actor's conversation with you?

LeVIN: What they're doing to promote their career. What classes they're taking. What they're doing to better themselves and what they're doing to get their name out there. Are they doing the mailings? Are they doing the paid auditions? Are they going to EPAs? How are they marketing themselves? I don't want an actor who just sits there waiting for their phone to ring! I've never had an actor that did that, *never*.

MENASHE: I'm looking for someone to live in the moment when I'm having a conversation rather than them thinking of the next ten things they want to say. I just want to have a natural conversation to see how the chemistry is, because I know that without having that chemistry there's no way I can possibly serve this person. If I don't like a person and there's no chemistry, I have no interest in working for them. I just want to know if we can get along and that we have a sense of like for each other.

Dressing for an Interview with an Agent

How should an actor dress when he or she comes to meet you?

MENASHE: This is the problem; I think there's too much thorough examination by actors out there who are just trying too hard. I think that actors should just dress casual and dress so that they look really nice. They don't need to get dressed up and wear evening clothes. It's a business interview, but it's not a business interview with a noncreative entity. You should wear clothes that are flattering to you, your hair should look somewhat neat, and you need to have a defined look that matches your personality.

You have to consider that when a talent rep is meeting you for the first time, they have to get a clear picture of you. They've got to know that when you walk into an audition, you're going to present yourself properly. If somebody walks in a disheveled mess or doesn't have a sense of who the hell they are or a sense of style, based upon who they are, then the agent is not going to want to represent them.

ADELMAN: Well this is a kind of casual jeans and sneakers office ... if somebody gets too dressed up it kind of indicates to me that they don't really know the business. It's a casual business.

I like to see that somebody is tasteful, that they're wearing clothes that are well-chosen. And CLEAN. And that their appearance is important to them, which does not necessarily mean that they have to be fancy; this could be jeans and a shirt or a sweater. They should be comfortable, and in some way I want to be able to judge their body type.

If a young woman has an extraordinary body I don't want her to be wearing a sweater to be cut [really low] and skirt [up too high], but I want something that kind of allows me to understand that her body is part of the package. That's just smart merchandising. I want actors to be smart about merchandising themselves because they're going to be my partners in doing that.

JEBENS: Neat and clean. I've had people show up in holey jeans and sweaty T-shirts. I've had actors show up with stained clothing; that's TOO casual. I don't need a formal. I don't need a tux. I don't necessarily need evening clothes. I need actors who are neat, clean, and presentable.

LeVIN: What an actor wears to an interview should represent their identity, but it's amazing how ugly and sloppy actors dress when they come to meet an agent.

We have interviewed lots of smelly actors. OK, I know they're not making money, but it doesn't cost that much to smell and look nice. Guys can go to the Gap and get a plain white T-shirt or a plain black T-shirt and a pair of jeans and they'll look acceptable. You would be surprised how many people don't even look acceptable. Too slutty; with low-plunging shirt lines with too much breast going on. It serves no purpose.

Agents' Pet Peeves

What is your biggest pet peeve about actors who want you as their representative?

ADELMAN: If the actor I'm not interested in doesn't take a hint. It's very uncomfortable for me to just come out and say to an actor, "I don't like you. Go away. Stop bothering me. You're not talented. You're ugly." For me to say, "I can't help you at this time," is kind of a catchphrase that enables me in a kindly fashion to say all those things without having to actually say those words. I expect that the actor will take the implication and leave me alone. When they *don't* it becomes uncomfortable because then it forces me to say the uncomfortable things I'd hoped not to have to say to someone because it's cruel. And I don't believe that I have the right to say to an actor, "You shouldn't be an actor," "You don't have any talent," or "You don't belong in the business."

LeVIN: Badgering. When I lived in the city [New York], I used to be attacked all the time. I remember once I was buying underwear and this guy walked up to me and said, "Aren't you Cyd LeVin?" I said, "Yes." He said, "I really want you to represent me." I said, "Well, I'm sure as hell not gonna do it while I'm buying my underwear!" A similar incident happened a week later at a flea market. And I thought, "OK, is somebody putting my name on the bathroom walls?"

When I lived in L.A. it was just as bad. I would be in the grocery store and the guy bagging my groceries asked me if I was an agent. I was like, *yeah, not for you.* Actors have to use intelligence. They think they're being aggressive, but they're really being stupid.

MENASHE: Pushiness; being overly pursued by actors. Getting twelve e-mails from actors I didn't give out my e-mail to. If I don't seem interested, I'm *NOT* interested.

An actress met with me at a paid seminar. I asked her for her reel, she sent it to me, and I didn't call her after watching it. She sent me a follow-up e-mail (God only knows how she got my address). I responded by saying, "Thank you for your inquiry. I will get back to you if I am interested. I have your materials." And she sent me a reply saying that she just signed up for another paid seminar with me. I don't want to see her! I don't want her coming back to see me. I have her materials. I've looked at them, I've met her, and I'm not interested, I'd like her to save her thirty-five dollar fee to the seminar.

Agents on Paid Auditions

Paid auditions are the industry meet-and-greet toll system that provokes strong reaction, either support or disgust. All in the agent quorum do not share the same regard for paid auditions.

What are your views on paid auditions?

ADELMAN: I think it's unethical. I don't do the "classes" where they pay agents and casting directors because I think they are paid auditions. I did it occasionally before because I was really poor and I needed the extra money and I was always uncomfortable about it.

JEBENS: I have two views. One view (with an actor's head and heart in my body): I find paid auditions rather disgusting, that people have to *pay* to meet people like me. But part of me that's an agent says, "You know, I work really hard; forty plus hours a week. If somebody wants me to sit and watch actors do monologues for three hours, after work, my time is valuable. I have to be paid for it."

LeVIN: Before I returned to the business I thought that only desperate actors did paid auditions. That no good actors did them. But that's not true anymore. I've changed on this. I think they're becoming viable in a certain respect because I do see there continues to be more and more unknowns in this business and more and more people in this business. There are only so many unknowns casting directors and agents can get to know. These paid auditions allow the actor to go in front of us and show us *the work!* I don't see this as a bad thing.

MENASHE: Paid auditions are the most effective time and way for me to get to as many actors as possible in one shot.

Additional Advice from Agents

ADELMAN: A new actor is always feeling like the agent is so above them, so it might affect their ability to be natural and comfortable in a meeting. To the other end of the spectrum, the successful actor [believes he is] "hiring" an agent and uses that expression as if agents were the help. The healthy balance lies somewhere in the middle.

JEBENS: A general piece of advice. If you've been doing this for a while and in any capacity it's either not giving any satisfaction or you're not getting anywhere, look and see if there might be some other phase or facet of the business that you can go into that might give you satisfaction. Because I don't think there's anything sadder than to see actors who are sixty, seventy years old and lost, with nothing on their résumé, and unhappy and sad and poor. Have *a life*. If you can't make a life in this business, go have one somewhere else. As far as we know, this life is it. It's one shot. Don't turn around, be sixty-five years old, and say, "Oh my God, I've wasted my life!"

LeVIN: Learn how to sell yourself. Put your best foot forward. Dress appropriately. Talk about what you've done to succeed in this business.

MENASHE: Don't try to be someone else. If you're a raving bitch and you wouldn't pay attention to me if I had a flat tire and was dying on the side of the highway, don't act all friendly to me when you walk into my office, because I'll know you're that person who drove by me on death's bed. I can tell. We're not stupid. We deal with people twenty hours a day.

CHAPTER FOURTEEN

AGENTS

Keeping One

"Work smart. Treat your representation with respect. We don't make a dime unless you book a job. An agent is more likely to get you auditions when they feel motivated by your respect for them as a person and professional. So, let us enjoy working with you. Don't make us work for you.

Jack Menashe
Agent/Agency Owner
Independent Artists Agency

Working with agents (and living with one), I hear daily how clients make monumental professional and personal fuck-ups that jeopardize the actor's career, the actor's relationship with his or her agent, and sometimes the actor's relationship with industry beyond the agent's walls. Here's a slight sampling:

A stage actor in his forties, after receiving a Tony nomination and losing the award, felt less than appreciated and immediately auditioned for a new Broadway play. After three auditions, he got an offer to originate a role. He waited on giving an answer, and then, seconds before the offer deadline came due, he declined. The stage actor abstained from the opportunity of work because he mistakenly thought himself to be a viable and desired screen commodity. The actor, having passed on his last moment of appreciation, remained unemployed for a long time thereafter.

An actress sent out an enraged e-mail complaining that her agent was not getting her work and that he was ineffective and incompetent. She sent the mad missive to her friends and cc'd her agent. When the agent confronted her after receiving the e-mail, the actress claimed her champion received the carbon copy due to "operator error."

An actress, without auditioning, was offered the lead in a new, three-character play written by a world-famous playwright-director. The play would premiere at a prestigious regional theater that was a thirty-minute commute from her residence.

The actress would rehearse blocks from her home and sleep in her bed at night after rehearsals and performances. The producer would be providing transportation between the actor's home and the theater. The actress passed because she didn't want to work out of town. Out of town being a half-hour limo ride from her doorstep (oh, the horror).

An actor was shooting a movie; he was one of the leads. It was his first major studio film. He stood alongside stars and worked with an award-winning director. He had the script for months, had gone through rehearsals, and had started shooting his scenes. The actor, on set, then called his agent to drop out of the film because he found Jesus. He explained to his agent that Christ came to him in a dream, announcing that the language in the script was un-Christian, and the actor was to bolt from the film like the Jews from ancient Egypt.

These unfortunate and true stories all feature actors who were self-centered, shortsighted, and career-paralyzing. Except for the e-mail-enraged actress, the other inappropriate actions by actors pissed off a director, a writer, producers, and casting personnel. All the outlandish scenarios did severe relationship damage closer to home with the actor's champion: the agent. Actors who engage in such behavior *never* stop to think of potential consequences their actions cause beyond the clothing they wear. Many actors are that shortsighted!

Lynne Jebens spoke of the consequences she suffers due to some of her clients' inappropriate actions. "I don't like it when clients have had the material for a week and then they say to me the day before the audition, 'Oh I didn't like the piece, so I'm not going to go to the audition.' That puts me in a bad situation because then I'm gonna call the casting director, make up some excuse, or sometimes I'm just honest and say, 'My client didn't like it.' But then I've left the casting director with only twenty-four hours to fill a hole. Then you guys [casting directors] are going to get mad at me."

Casting personnel should never be forced to be angry with agents because their clients can't see further than they can see to piss in darkness. Which is effectively what the client is doing—pissing on the agent, pissing on a project, and pissing off all others involved! But many actors are very content to roam in darkness splashing their wee. And as they do, they bump, trip, stumble, fall, and often break valuables. Valuables like relationships. And the actor-agent relationship is one treasure an actor should want to protect and maintain with respect.

THE GROUP OF EIGHT ON AGENTS

I asked the Group of Eight what actors can do to maintain a healthy relationship with their agents. Bonnie Black was the most succinct: "Get work!" Black laughed. "A lot! Agents aren't in this for their health. They have to pay the light bill. I think on a practical level, if you are booking, that's always going to help your relationship. I think also the actor has to be understanding that an agent cannot create jobs. And that if things are slow, to understand that and be patient, and also realize that opportunities or lack thereof are cyclical."

Black also advised that represented actors should ask their agents about how they prefer to work with actors. "Ask if the agent feels all right with you calling up and asking about projects you've heard about, and for which you would like to be submitted," Black suggested. "Or do they prefer that you don't bug them? Understand that they're doing their job and submitting everything they think you're right for. This is a personal route that takes time and patience and some finesse to understand how you work together."

Darrie Lawrence suggested that an actor treat the agent like "a human being." She also believes that using the agent's time in an efficient businesslike manner keeps the actor-agent relationship at its optimal performance. "Being businesslike, meaning not taking up the agent's time," Lawrence declared. "Not wasting your agent's time with frivolous calls or whining. Attacks on what they can or cannot do or what they're not doing for you. I'm always hearing actors saying, 'Well I'm gonna call my agent and light a fire under them!' Attacking them is counterproductive. Usually they are working for you." Lawrence also stresses that the actor should support his or her support system with the needed tools. "Make sure that your agent has an ample supply of updated pictures and résumés," she urged. Lawrence added, "There's also telling your agent if you're going out of town and when you'll be back. Plus, being really prepared for your auditions. It's amazing how unprepared some people are. People come into auditions and they haven't even read the play! You need to be good at your part of the job, which is to go into the audition more than well-prepared."

Charlotte Rae also believes in actors supporting their agents. "I think the main thing is to support the agent as much as you can. Through relating to other people in the business and reading the *New York Times*. Even though I live in L.A. I get the *New York Times*, every day, and once I read that Encores! was doing *70, Girls, 70*, which I had done out here in L.A. I played Ida. So I told my agent about it. He got me an appointment, even though casting was not auditioning people at the time. I came to New York, I did a couple of numbers for Kathleen Marshall, the director and choreographer, and Jack Vertel [artistic director of Encores!], and they loved me. You can't expect to sit there like in a nunnery and expect everything to be coming to you from the agent. You have to do your footwork."

Robert LuPone believes above all else that an actor should "have a forthright and honest relationship with his agent. They're working for you (that's not known at twenty-something). Be honest with them. If you're not interested in a project, you're not interested. Don't go to an audition if you're not interested. Even if they want you to go, DON'T go if you're not interested."

Mark Price, like LuPone, believes in honesty. "I think when the communication dies, just like any relationship, whether it's with an agent, a partner, or business partner, that's when the relationship stops evolving.

"Maintaining that communication; being able to share your opinions with them," Price continued. "I used to make it a point every six months to a year to go into my agent's office when I was first starting out and say, 'OK, what am I lacking here? What can I improve upon?' or 'What would you suggest that I do that I'm not doing right now to make progress?' Basically it was a way of checking in with them, making sure that I was taking care of my part of the relationship. It worked for me and brought success in keeping communication open."

I also asked the Group of Eight, "What can an actor do to damage a relationship with an agent?" Bonnie Black cautioned, "Being completely insensitive to them as human beings. Understand that agents are under certain pressures and constraints. Never be abusive or rude. Plus, promptly return calls. Stay on top of getting back to the agent about auditions, let them know if you accept the audition or not."

Robert LuPone spoke of an actor attribute, near natural to most actors, that can cause the actor-agent relationship to turn sour. "Bother them. Bother them with telephone calls and neediness. Insecurity, anxiety, and neediness, which are part of the world of acting, can't be transferred to the people who support the career. Then you become like ...," LuPone caught himself, "people in this business, dare I say it, who have reputations?" LuPone then laughed, alluding to a thespian-singer extraordinaire with whom he was very familiar.

James Rebhorn believes an actor should have realistic expectations. "I think it's a huge mistake to blame your agent for the success or failure of your career," Rebhorn began. "Casting directors are more responsible for the success or failure of your career than an agent is, it seems to me." Casting directors are responsible? Well, gee thanks, James, for the God-like power you've bestowed, but personally, this casting director thinks that the person mostly responsible for the success or failure of an actor's career is the actor.

AGENTS ON ACTORS WORKING WITH AGENTS

Back to our quorum of agents. The people who have seen more actors as clients than Rosie O'Donnell has seen threats of lawsuits from Donald Trump. The Donald, Rosie, and actors are all personalities with egos and ambitions larger than a fleet of cargo ships. What they also have in common (The Donald, Rosie, actors) is that agents are at one time involved with each. And who better to talk about the actor-agent relationship and inflated egos than agents?

The Actor/Agent Relationship

How can an actor better work with his or her agent to maintain a healthy, mutually honest, trusting, positive relationship?

> PHILIP ADELMAN: They can be prepared for auditions, show up on time, get the job, and say thank you.

> LYNN JEBENS: They have to keep themselves *in shape!* Taking classes. Things that are gonna keep the machinery oiled. Seeing the plays that are out there. Knowing the literature. [Actors] are the product. They are what I sell.

> CYD LeVIN: This is like any other relationship; maybe because I've been married for twenty-three years it reminds me of a marriage. The actor has to have trust. The

actor has to have an understanding of what we do. Communicate, that's all. Not be needy. I wouldn't call my husband every single day and badger him about something.

JACK MENASHE: Trust your agent. Keep a clear line of communication. If you as the actor have a question, just ask it. There are some actors who are a little too careful with their agents, and there are other actors who avoid their agents altogether because they're scared to make a phone call, because they're "trying to be good." An actor has to be real about the relationship. You have to be organic. If you have something that's important, *call*.

If there's a breakdown in communication or issues that need to be resolved or there's a confrontation that needs to be had when things seem to not be going right, there needs to be a clear line of communication. The actor needs to confront the agent and not be afraid, rather than going around town and bad-mouthing their agent.

What are some of the worst things a client can do to harm the relationship between actor and talent rep?

ADELMAN: Get the Breakdowns ... and call us and harass us about whether you were submitted or not on projects. I feel that every time an actor does that, they're questioning my professionalism and my talent at what I do. I trust that my clients are professional. I expect similar respect back. If they're calling about the Breakdowns, I feel that I'm not getting that respect.

JEBENS: Being late for auditions or missing auditions on a constant basis. Being rude when they are at auditions. I had an actor years ago who was two and a half hours late for the audition, and the casting director by then had moved onto auditioning children who were to be in the show. The casting director apologized to my client that he could not audition him because the people who needed to be there for my client's audition had already gone. My former client actually chased the casting director around the room, demanding that he give him the audition. The casting director felt terribly threatened. That was the last time I saw that actor.

LeVIN: Lecturing the agent on what you as an agent are doing or not doing. Then there's the clients who sell themselves to us but have no clue as to who they are and what type of roles they are right for. We had a thirty-five-year-old who believed she could still play the roles of a sixteen-year-old. There was no way she could play sixteen. None of the casting directors who knew her wanted to see her for sixteen, but she was determined that they did want to see her. An actor has to realize who they are, what they're capable of, and what they're not capable of pulling off.

MENASHE: Going around town and badmouthing their agents. Not trusting us in anything we do. If an actor is not happy with their agent, the most important thing is to immediately address the situation.

Contacting Your Agent

How often should a client call you, and what's the best time and way to do so?

LeVIN: Nobody should ever call their agent in the morning. All agents do Breakdowns in the morning; it's not a secret. Calling later in the afternoon is best. I think clients should call, but they shouldn't make a nuisance of themselves with everyday calls, the calls with repetitive questions.

MENASHE: I really don't care how often a client calls me as long as they have a really good reason for doing so. It really just boils down to common sense. The best time to call is the hour before lunch and the one to three hours following lunch. The worst times to call are first thing in the morning and at the end of the day. Because we're doing Breakdowns in the morning and we're wrapping up business in the late afternoon.

If not returning a call, why should a client contact you?

JEBENS: I don't need for my clients to stay in touch. I want them to certainly feel free to call, but at the same time I need them to have a little trust in me. If the client needs to, certainly call or e-mail. E-mail's become a great way for agents and actors to communicate because it gives the agent time to look into what the actor is asking and then I can return the inquiry while I'm on the phone.

LeVIN: If the actor knows somebody involved in a project who has an edge [influence] to give me an appointment. That's valuable information.

MENASHE: We're helped a lot of times by actors when they get information on projects that we get later. It does help when an actor has information that we can really use. Phone calls about things that may be coming up for them, which have yet to be released on Breakdown Services, that they've been told about by a director or producer, writer, or choreographer are things that we need to know about. Those are the types of phone calls we need to have from the actor.

With what type of inquiry should a client NOT contact an agent?

ADELMAN: If it's every day calling about this project or that project, then they're nudging and I want to kill 'em and I want them to go away. It's a delicate line. Information sharing is good. The part that crosses the line and becomes nudging and that they're not trusting that I'm doing my job becomes difficult for me to take.

JEBENS: The "Just checking, I haven't heard from you in a while. Is there anything for me?" I give a little sass with my guys and I'll say, "Yes, there's been twenty auditions, and I didn't call you with any of them." I don't mind people reaching out. It's hard when you haven't heard from your agent in a little while, but think about how and why you're calling before dialing the phone. Just don't be stupid.

LeVIN: Calling about the obvious, like when a client calls saying, "I saw a Breakdown for a twenty-year-old male with blue eyes. I'm twenty-one and have blue eyes." Give me a break! I think I can read. Agents on the whole are very intelligent people. We're well-read, usually well-educated, have been in the arts for a long time; we get it. Yes, there are always exceptions to the rule, but on the whole you're dealing with an elite group, and I don't need the obvious spelled out to me. That's why you as the actor came to me. Again, it's about trust. The reason you wanted me to represent you is that you trusted I had your best interest at heart and that I'm going to be out there trying to get you jobs.

MENASHE: It's the "What's up?" phone call that really annoys me and nearly every agent in this business. The "What's up?" phone call is literally just that, you pick up the phone and it's John Smith. The agent says, "Hi, John! What's going on? What can I help you with?" and the actor replies, "Oh just calling to see what's up?" I'm left to reply, "What's up with what?" And then we get to the heart of the actor's call. They reply, "Well I haven't been getting out, I'm just calling to see what's going on?"

If the actor could put himself in my position, I've got ten lines ringing and employees bitching that they need things and I have this actor on the phone asking, "What's up?" What's up in film, TV, and theater to an agency owner who has three departments to cover and a total of two hundred and fifty projects to cover, the feeling is completely overwhelming when an actor calls and says, "What's up?" and you want to serve them—you just can't possibly answer that question. What I say to that phone call is, "Get specific. What do you mean 'What's up?' Are you calling to say hello, or are you calling to find out what you can go in for?" "I'm calling to find out what I can go in for," is usually what the actors say back. I respond, "Well why don't you do this, break it down, read some scripts, or ask me some specific questions about projects you want to get in for, not just 'What can I get in for?' or 'What's up?'"

Actors Pushing to Be Submitted

Actors are always talking to other actors about jobs and open roles. How should an actor best approach an agent with an open job they think they're right for? How do you feel about clients pushing themselves?

ADELMAN: If it happens occasionally, I'm going to pay attention. If it happens too often, that becomes the pain in the neck.

JEBENS: I hate calls from clients saying, "Oh my friend is going in on this movie, is there anything for me in it?" Clients can send me an e-mail if they are interested in something specific; they can let me know that way. But I don't like calls like, "Is there something for me." Either know there is or leave it alone. I would like to have the assumption that if I'm doing my job the client is going to have a little trust in me.

LeVIN: Sometimes clients who are friends with production designers and positions like that tell me about an upcoming film that's happening before casting directors are hired. *That's* valuable information. A client hearing that somebody fell out of a role and they would be right for it is valuable information. The client telling me that they saw in Breakdown Services the casting of a "role" is *not* valuable. I know what casting directors are casting in Breakdown Services.

MENASHE: I don't mind if clients push themselves, unless they do it far too often. And far too often is just when it's annoying or they're just pushing themselves on the wrong things. The actor network is the most dangerous network in the entire world, because my philosophy on actors telling other actors about auditions is that they're *not* generally looking out for their friends' best interest. They're rubbing in their faces the fact that they're going in for something. I find most of the time when a client calls me to tell me a friend of theirs has told them that they were right for something, their friend is completely wrong. I always tell actors who push themselves often to go get the script and read it before calling me.

When clients want to cross over into a medium in which they have little or no experience (such as a theater actor wanting to move into film and TV), how can they best help you in selling themselves?

JEBENS: Clients have to be studying in those areas, and they have to have credits for me to build that desire. Somebody who has *no* Shakespeare on their résumé: forget it! You're never going to get into The Public. Ain't gonna happen! You're not going to be seen for Nebraska Shakespeare or New Jersey Shakes! If you as an actor don't have it on your résumé—I don't care if you have studied it, you no have credits—they don't want to see ya. Period.

If you're a musical performer and that's where your forte is, and you want to make the crossover into straight theater, you need to get out there and make sure you're studying. Make sure you're auditioning for straight [plays] showcases. You as an actor need to work in those areas and build.

And in film and TV, I can't make promises in those areas. It's so much about things that are out of our control. It's looks; it's somebody else's opinion. It's the naturalness and believability. The actor has to be able to make that communication come out their eyes. You literally have to be able to do more communicating with your eyes in film and television than you do on stage.

LeVIN: A client who wants to cross over into television and film should take television and film classes. Also, they should go to the paid auditions for television and film casting directors so that they get feedback on how they're doing. And the biggest thing they can do is get a camera and a goddamn mirror, tape themselves doing television and film copy. It'll show the actor what they're doing.

Getting Audition Feedback via the Agent

How often should an actor inquire of the agent about audition feedback?

ADELMAN: If the client *really* thinks he or she booked a job and didn't hear anything ... I'm happy to make that call. But just, "How did I do?" feedback, I find it not useful. I'd rather spend that time trying to get my client another job.

JEBENS: Feedback is a callback. Or the next audition in that casting office is your feedback. By the time casting directors get done with auditions, everybody's already moved onto the next project. Does a Paul Russell want all 330 agents calling him and asking for feedback on his projects? I don't think so.

The kinds of feedback casting directors call us with are the kinds of feedback the actor won't want to hear. Casting directors call us to complain. They call us when the client's fucked up. Examples of "fucked up": being unprepared, attitudinal, wrong material, *late!* A casting director's more likely to call us on the negative than on the positive.

LeVIN: When we're in pilot season, the casting directors are not going to stop to give feedback. In theater the actor has a better chance of getting feedback than in television or film. In television or film the feedback is either you got the job or you stunk up the room. Only when you really stink up a room does a casting director tell you, "Listen, I gotta tell you, he was so off base it was unbelievable." Most of the time when an agent calls up for feedback for television or film we get, "Your client did a nice job, we went a different direction. We want a different look." So it's almost stupid calling for television and film feedback.

MENASHE: Inquiring for feedback is not always a good thing for the actor. A lot of actors don't realize that if an agent calls a casting director asking for feedback ... calling for feedback is a commentary on how the actor or agent thinks the actor did in the audition room. When an agent calls a casting director for feedback it reinforces how the client did in the room. If you sucked and the agent calls asking, "How'd they do?" that casting director, a lot of time, would have forgotten how badly you sucked, overlooked it, and forgiven the actor. But now with my calling, the casting director is reliving the audition in their head as they give the agent the feedback. The best feedback is a job.

To Be Bicoastal or Not to Be?

How important is it for an actor to have a bicoastal career, and why?

ADELMAN: It's not necessary to be bicoastal; it depends on the actor. There are some actors who are not going to work in California whether they went there or not. They just don't have a film or television part of their career that is going to happen.

JEBENS: If you don't have a career here [New York], why are you *even worried* about L.A.? If you don't have a career there, why are you worried about New York? So let's say an actor says, "Well I came to New York and did a couple of showcases. I think I'll go out to L.A. for a while." *With what?!* What are you selling to L.A.? To open those doors, you have to have something behind you. You either have to have credits or training in the genre or a really good agent to open those doors.

The people who are able to do bicoastal are the people who are working, unfortunately. It's only a handful of people who are ever able to do it.

LeVIN: I believe actors have to establish themselves on one coast first, whether it's New York or L.A., and build their roots in that one area before branching out to the other. I think eventually it's very important to have a bicoastal career.

MENASHE: I think it's most important for an actor to have a career that makes them happy and makes them money.

Does an actor need to have an agency with offices on both coasts?

JEBENS: Why??? We all have affiliates. It's more important that an actor finds *an agent* that they feel comfortable with.

LeVIN: Having an agency with offices on both coasts is not important when the actor is starting out, but they will eventually need agents on both coasts. The agents don't have to be with the same agency. Sometimes it's better than it's not. I had things go both ways for me as a manager; I had clients simultaneously with Gersh New York and Gersh L.A., and Gersh L.A. didn't even know who Gersh New York clients were. I had other people who were with Jack Menashe in New York and Ginny Raymond in L.A., and everybody loved them and everybody was working for them. So it really depends on the actor and the scenario, but I don't always believe that bicoastal agencies are the best way for an actor to go, unless *both coasts* are passionate about that actor.

Pet Peeves Agents Have About Clients

What are your biggest pet peeves about actors you have represented or currently represent?

Philip Adelman repeated his strong dislike for clients who call him, pushing themselves because they saw a project listed on Breakdown Services. It's an oft-taken action by actors that most, if not all, agents feel displays a lack of trust and respect. For the remainder of our quorum, their pet peeves about clients included these:

> JEBENS: My biggest one these days is I call an actor on his cell phone, he misses the call, and just immediately returns my call. Don't they know their voicemail has picked up and I've probably left all the information there? And now they call back and want me to repeat it? I make them call their cell phone.
>
> Also, taking a phone call from me without a paper and pen in hand. Or when returning a call to your agent, not having paper and pencil or something to write on and then saying to the agent, "Well, could you call in the information into my voicemail?" Or making the agent go through all the audition information and then they say, "Could you put that on my voicemail, I didn't have a paper and pencil."
>
> LeVIN: When I call a client and leave a message, I want them to call me back in a reasonable timeframe. I once called a client in the morning with an audition for ten o'clock the next morning. By six o'clock that night I still hadn't heard back from him! I left him another message and said, "This is not good. You need to check your messages more than once a day because what if I had an audition for you the same day?" Also another pet peeve is clients who are not prepared for an audition. That's death to me.
>
> MENASHE: One pet peeve I have is clients who send me laundry lists of things that they think they're right for. Things they haven't even read the scripts for. They have no clue as to whether or not they'd really be right, but they just heard through the grapevine. Or they see scripts around our office, sit down and read them, and then cast themselves with no idea whether or not they're really what the casting director sees for the role. They forget our business is to talk to the casting directors and to read Breakdowns and read scripts and sides and make determinations based on the information given to us.

AGENT-ACTOR/ACTOR-AGENT LOYALTY

Loyalty. It's a two-way street paved by bricks of respect, trust, and appreciation. Without any one of those elements, the street is pocked with holes of doubt, insecurity, and suspicion. As it's more than likely you're an actor reading this, you're probably thinking of loyalty in terms of an agent being loyal to you. If so, how short-sighted and selfish your thinking! Remember that professional partner of yours? The one who takes your calls on his cell phone during weekends, listens to your professional ambitions, consoles you about your personal traumas, and supports you despite never receiving a thank you? Your agent who is loyal to you? Remember that champion? How loyal are you to him or her? An actor can be disloyal to an agent in various ways. Most common forms of disloyalty include the client who does not pay commission, the client who bad-mouths the agent to others, and the client who abandons the agent (the biggest slap of disloyalty of all).

Actors drop agents quicker than agents drop actors. Why? Actors have less potential to see beyond themselves, while agents can see beyond the actor in the moment and look toward the actor's future career. Actors are focused on the tight shot, unable to see the panorama (that's why actors are actors and not directors or agents). Agents will invest in an actor more so than an actor will invest in the agent. Most agents want to serve the best interests of the actor, their client. Too many actors want to serve themselves. And actors want that service quicker than yesterday has passed. Actors' impatience and their inability to understand that the journey takes time are the biggest reasons actors drop agents.

An agent is willing to be at the actor's side for the entire journey of the actor's career, not to be just a way station. Agents see the union of actor and agent as a marriage. Actors look at agents as dating stepping stones. It's as if the actor is single at a cruisy bar, looking and hooking onto something they like at the moment but thinking, "Oh this one is cute . . . for now . . . but someone better will walk through the door, and that someone better is gonna be mine." Actors have got to stop this mentality and the practice that follows the thought. But actors won't. Actors will continue disposing of or abusing agents like worn welcome mats. Not caring for the agent's efforts in getting the actor into new doors of opportunity. Forgetting the agent was an emotional support when old doors were closed. Forgetting the agent was/is a person who believed in the actor's potential when others didn't.

James Rebhorn, from the Group of Eight, is one of the few actors in general who has a proper grip on this issue. "I tend to be very loyal to agents," Rebhorn admitted. "If somebody shows an interest and some respect for me, I return it and stay with them.

"A lot of actors say, 'I gotta change agents 'cause my career is going nowhere.' I've never bought into that . . . my feeling is most of your career is because of what people see you in, not what your agent submits you for. If you've done the work and you're out there, your agent put your name out there, but they're not gonna get you the job. You're gonna get the job because of what people have seen you do. I'd much rather be with a small agency that knows me than be in a large stable of people and end up way in the back of the room."

Agents on Actor Loyalty

I asked the members of our agent quorum their thoughts on client-to-agent loyalty. It's the exposed nerve of every agent, no matter if the agent is a one-person operation or part of a worldwide entertainment representation conglomerate. Every agent has been cut raw by a disloyal client.

ADELMAN: It's very seductive for someone to come along from another agency and lure clients away from us, with great promises. In a way, if I were an actor, happy with my agent but somebody else was whispering in my ear, "You know your agent's wonderful but they can't get you A, B, C, or D that you've been dying to get. You need to be with agent X to get that"—it's very seductive for an actor.

The actor doesn't seem to be trusting enough or comfortable enough to come in and say, "This is what is being whispered in my ear. I'm happy. I'm loyal. I'm wavering because this is what I'm hearing. Help me with your view of it, and what are the facts?" I think the actor may be too embarrassed or feel it's too hurtful to have that conversation with the agent.

JEBENS: Client loyalty is very important to me. Because if I'm going to put all this time and effort into a client I'd like to feel that there's some loyalty. I actually lost a friend many years ago in a handshake arena. He got a job on his own and didn't think he should have turned it over to me to negotiate. And so I said to him, "All those *other* jobs that you *didn't get*. All the time and effort I put into getting you those auditions. You don't think that's worth something?" I said, "Fine, take a hike. Have a nice life."

Another instance: I had an actor, same situation and again a very good personal friend of mine. I've always said to my friends when I've worked with them, "We work on two levels here. We have friendship and we have business. You can screw me on one and the other one can still exist; screw me on both and it's over! So I had this friend I was working with and I thought it was really weird that he hadn't got-ten a callback from an audition. They had called me about his interest. As far as I knew he went to the audition, he's interested. Well then the fucking theater called him directly to negotiate! Rather than him telling the theater to call me, he tried to negotiate it himself and then he turned the job down. I called the theater, not knowing any of this. The theater said my client turned it down, and I said, "What do you mean he turned it down?" They said, "Well, we tried to negotiate it with him." You know this client should have told the theater to call me! I was the agent. I set him up with the audition! What was that? So as a friend, he slapped me in the face. As a professional, he slapped me in the face. And I asked him, "When were you going to tell me all of this?" and found out that it had happened two weeks before. I said, "Enough. Out of my life. This was the most insulting thing you could've done. Go away."

It was very hard because he was part of my immediate "family" here in New York. Finally four years after this had happened, when he was doing a show at the Shakespeare Theatre in Washington DC, he called me and said, "I'm coming up on Monday; could we talk?" I said, "No." He said, "Please, I need to talk to you. I realize I made a huge mistake." And so I met him for a drink, and he apologized profusely. He said, "I don't know what I was thinking. It was self-centered. I made a huge mistake, and I realize that now."

I had one actor call me at home and say, "I'm leaving the agency and I wanted you to know. I'm going somewhere else, and I wanted you to be happy for me." I said, "Would you like to explain how I'm going to be able to do that? Tell me how I'm supposed to do that?"

LeVIN: Loyalty means everything to me. Fortunately, I was very blessed for a lot of years. The ones who stuck by me are the ones I would kill for. It's devastating when a client leaves you, especially when you feel they're not justified in leaving, but it is a beast of the business. Clients do leave. Actors think the grass is always greener, that somebody else has something that's better.

MENASHE: I've learned not to be in this business for loyalty because a manager friend of mine told me something that is so true: "The only thing you can count on in this business as a talent rep is that actors will leave you."

I had a client sitting at lunch with me who looked at me and said, "I'll never leave you." I said, "Yeah, ya probably will, and it's OK, get over it. Do you need some salsa for your chips?" and I laughed. He said, "No, no, no I'll never leave you." I said again, "You probably will, and it's OK. Will you stop saying it, because if you *do* leave me it's going to be that much harder to look back and remember that you said this to me."

Agent Disloyalty to the Client

Now, my soapbox rambling on loyalty is not going to be all actor-bashing. Remember, I did say loyalty was a two-way street. Along with the hardworking and honorable talent representatives are instances of questionable ethics and morals. Some agents are disloyal to actors. I've witnessed it far too often.

One of the Group of Eight was the victim of an agent's disloyalty, to which I was witness and participant. I often tell actors this cautionary tale of agent deceit. The mistreated thespian involved has always asked that I never reveal his/her identity or the identity of the disloyal agent. For this telling, I'll call the thespian "Nancy." Her agent will be "G. G." and I'll still be me.

Once as I was casting for a regional Shakespeare company, Nancy, who I've known personally for years, called to ask if I felt she would be right for any of the available roles. I refuse to favor friends. I favor talent over relationship. Nancy's talent triumphed friendship, and that talent lent itself to several roles within the season.

Her agent, G. G., had not made a submission on the Shakespeare project as he had done previously with regularity. Possibly this was because the industry was going through a lean period (shortly after 9/11) and G. G. was holding out for a project with a larger commission return. But lean period or not, if a client of G. G.'s were to be booked for the Shakespeare project, the client would have been paid $1,000 per week and G. G. would have received a weekly commission of $100 for seven weeks, totaling $700. That $700 would have paid his assistant's salary for a week or two. Imagine if G. G. had two or more clients book the project? More cha-ching for the agency. No matter, it seemed any single or multiple amount of commission from the Shakespeare project was not enough of a cha-ching and motive for G. G. to submit his clients. I had called him to ask for a submission and none came.

To Nancy, G. G.'s lack of interest for this Shakespeare project paralleled a deepening malaise with which he had treated her over the past several years. It had been a very, *very* long time since she received any calls from his office. I suggested that the lack of activity could be due in part to the production slowdown that followed 9/11 and the accompanying sluggish economy. Also, her age range was not industry vogue. I suggested that she might have a false perception of agent apathy. This project offered a wonderful opportunity to venture into an investigation of her suspicions, if she was willing. Nancy was up for the risk.

After penciling Nancy into my Shakespeare audition schedule, I advised her to do the following: Call G. G., not divulge to G. G. our conversation or the appointment I had given her, and ask to be submitted by phone for the Shakespeare festival. To help Nancy persuade G. G. into making a cold call, I nudged her to emphasize our friendship. Nancy phoned, and G. G. replied that he would ring my office that same day. Nancy and I waited.

One day went by. No call to my office from G. G. I called him. Voicemail. Two days passed. Nothing. The auditions were less than a week away. Three days passed. Nada. Four days. Zip. Five. I called Nancy.

I asked her if she had any further contact with G. G. since the initial call. She hadn't. Not good. I asked how much more of a journey she was willing to take in discovering the truth about her agent's loyalty and belief in her. Nancy was invested for full disclosure. I asked her to call G. G. again, follow up, and inquire about the result of her submission request.

G. G. informed Nancy that a phone call had been placed to my office; a message was left with my assistant and went unreturned. Message? Assistant? Odd. I had *no* assistant on the Shakespeare project. I was answering my own phone at the time. The lie was unsettling for both of us. More so for Nancy. I've grown accustomed to this inexcusable example of asinine agent behavior.

Shortly thereafter she dropped G. G. and I arranged a meeting between Nancy and another agency. They signed her. She has seen more auditions and work come her way from her new agents than what she had gotten via G. G.'s office. To this day we have never revealed to G. G. our deception aimed at discovering his deception.

Investigating the Support, Trust, and Loyalty of Your Agent

So what can you, as an actor, do to find out if you're being represented properly and being championed for opportunities that equally match your desire and talent? If you have a close and trusted friendship with a casting director like Nancy did, you're lucky and can follow her path of discovery. Otherwise if you're going through a slowdown, an audition famine, examine yourself, your abilities, and casting activity before accusing your talent representation of not meeting your ambitions.

Investigate Time of Year vs. Audition Activity

Before giving into agent abandonment panic, consider the time of year. Is it one of those periods when auditions and work perennially slow down? As a reminder, slowdowns occur from late March to early April, May to early August, and mid-December to the first week of January.

Investigate audition activity versus industry activity. Begin seeking audition-activity information from actors you know who match your abilities, look, and personality. Ask those who are type-identical to you if they are getting called in for anything (ask that they reply honestly without fabricating auditions for pride). Actors cannot take audition-activity information from those who bear no resemblance to them. If you do, you will wind up misinformed, and you'll attribute your own career momentum (or lack thereof) to this incorrect information. This is a path to self-destruction.

That same actor will then go raging in a phone call to his or her own talent rep, "Why am I not being seen for such-and-such. My friend Lea DeLaria was called in. Why wasn't I seen?" Usually the agent will reply with something such as, "Well . . . Lea is of the opposite sex. You're not. She has a sense of humor. You don't. And oh, by the by, Lea has an industry name that will sell tickets; she matches the character breakdown and *is* what the director is seeking. You aren't! Any other questions before I hang up and continue seeking sincere opportunities for you?"

The actor-friends to ask about activity are the actors you've grown to know socially because you see each other repeatedly in the audition halls and waiting rooms as you both await to be seen for the same roles. Gauge your activity against that of actors of similar type. Know your type.

Is your current type market-friendly?

Does your type (age, physicality, and character) suit the current market (casting, creatives, and audience)? Objectively know how you're perceived in our eyes before taunting a talent rep with the "Why am I not being seen, because my friends are being seen?" phone call.

Your maturing age and changing body also may be the cause of your audition activity slowdown. Have you come to the point in your life where now you're being called in for the mother or father instead of the son or daughter? Those wrinkles and crinkles on the neck and face aging you are postcards from your youthful summers under the sun when the tanning mantra was "darker is better." The harsh entertainment reality on age is, the older we get, the less we're needed. Age is not the only body factor to cause a slowdown in auditions. Diet can be a factor. Were you once the young lead but now the young lead's fat best friend? Another harsh entertainment reality. Slender is sexy. Sex sells. Slough rarely does.

How you treat your body can affect audition activity. A persistent glossy, glazed look in the eyes is a reminder from your liver of all the rum and Cokes it had to endure each weekend between the Miller Lites. Are your teeth teetering toward the blackened tiles of the Lincoln Tunnel? Smoking truly does bring more to your life, but not an extension. Hair thinning? Just how much coloring can one scalp stand before the follicles resign en mass so as not to endure another bleaching?

What has your mental state been of late?

Your auditions are intermittent, but the industry is going full force. Could you be hindered by a negative or defeatist disposition within yourself, subliminal or obvious to others? When you're mentally positive the world comes to you. Other people can pick up signals of your true emotional state. Some creatives and people in casting, like me, have a strong sensitivity to the mental-state signatures of others. The sensitivity goes to the reaches of often seeing an actor's aura as they audition. Witnessing the body of those who audition be silhouetted by an ethereal light can be beautiful or extremely unnerving.

Is your agent the cause of your audition slowdown?

Ok, so your slowdown for receiving auditions does not match an audition slowdown period on the calendar. You seem positive with or without the aid of Zoloft. You're a jaw-dropping, walking ad of success for Bally's gym. Actors you replaced in shows, or vice versa, or those who have been in consideration for the same role as you are getting a large number of auditions during a period while you're still waiting on table eleven at TGIF or handing out free samples of gum in Times Square. If the aforementioned are true, *then* it's time to examine two vital aspects of your career seriously: First, your talent. That's kind of an important factor. Second, your relationship with your talent representation.

If you're not getting calls after matching all the previous criteria (and assuming you're talented), begin speaking cautiously with actors you know who share your representation. I say cautiously because they may have wonderful one-to-one relationships with the agent and agency. Invite the actor(s) you target out for drinks, coffee, or Krispy Kremes on the pretense of something unrelated to the business. Go out to have fun . . . and learn.

During your latte slurping or doughnut downing, casually move the conversation into how they're doing with auditions. The frequency? The quality and organization from the agent/agency when getting an appointment? Do they speak to the agent or are they always relegated to the agent's assistant or worse . . . voicemail? What's their perception of manner and tone with which the agency treats them on both a personal and professional level? Don't interrogate. Make the conversation light and seem less than interested (that's when people have their guard down and talk without a filter).

If the answers and replies are Hallmark cards of endearments, don't take everything yet at face value. Is this informant (actor), who shares your agency, someone who would persist in being a politically and socially correct boob even if he or she were being cattle prodded? Or does the informant really share honest views and opinions without a Paula Abdul, everything-is-beautiful filter? Listen and watch closely, without giving yourself away. Is the body language comfortable or rigid, inward or dramatic?

If the answers and replies begin to mirror your dissatisfaction, and the source is not a high-maintenance person of drama, it's the agent or agency and not you. Begin to look for another champion of your abilities.

ADDITIONAL ADVICE FROM AGENTS

ADELMAN: I think clients should get report cards and graded [on how] well they work with others. One needs to work well with others, which is basically giving respect.

JEBENS: Here's my final comment for actors. If you only want to be a star . . . *get out!* Only 2 to 3 percent of this industry becomes stars. You should want to be an actor. You should want to be an artist, a craftsman. Somebody who is interested in the history of what we do. If you're not, then *get out* 'cause you're going to be very sad at the outcome.

LeVIN: Trust that your agents are doing their job, that they have your best interest at heart. That if you contact the agent it should be to add *something*, not just to question or threaten. If you have valuable information, call your agent. Use common sense.

Last, there's the best advice for an actor maintaining a healthy relationship with his or her agent. It's also the hardest for an actor to fulfill. In the sage words of agency owner Jack Menashe: "Get jobs."

CHAPTER FIFTEEN

EXIT LINES

Parting Advice

"If you still continue to want to be an actor so badly, you should really try for it. A career is like a roulette wheel: You never know where it's going to land."

Charlotte Rae

Actress

I hope that you've gained new insight into what it means to be a professional working actor. I haven't been easy on you as you've turned these pages. Nor have some of the people interviewed been tactful in their candor. The blunt commentary may have seemed, at times, as if members of the Group of Eight, agents in the quorum, and I were trying to dissuade you from either becoming or continuing as an actor. That assumption would be false. The honest objective of this actor handbook-with-a-bit-of-bite is to help actors be better than their potential. The candor expressed was motivated by frustration, a head-shaking frustration that comes from continually encountering actors who approach the business as a hobby or recreation. For the working actor, it can be neither of those. Acting is a profession.

"Entertainment is such a hard business" has been often said, but does anybody with an ambition for storytelling ever truly listen? And I'm not talking about listening just to the cautionary phrase itself but also to the warning advisor (whoever it may be). *Listening*, that's the key to success at being a professional, working actor. Listening in training, listening in the rehearsal studio, listening to the script, listening to the director, listening to audience reaction, and most important, listening to colleagues you meet along the journey. All that listening is *learning*.

Before parting ways with you, the Group of Eight has a few exit lines of wisdom . . .

THE GROUP OF EIGHT'S EXIT LINES OF WISDOM FOR ASPIRING ACTORS

Robert LuPone

"My recommendation to anyone who aspires to be an actor is to not get *sucked* into your immaturity and the fame game. Recognize the true value of art and what artistry is in terms of acting. The aspiration to that, to me, is the only reason to be an actor. Don't let anybody or anything take you off that course. Taking on the great roles and communicating to the public the significance of what it means to be a human being—there's nothing better. There's no better life. There's no better pain. There's no better insecurity. There's no better confidence. There's no better absolute. There is nothing better.

"Acting is a worthy, noble profession and deserves the attention of people who have talent and want to express themselves that way. And there's no support for it. None. Your parents aren't going to like ya. Your parents are going to be upset about it. Society says, 'Thank you very much'; they're only going to like you when you're royalty, or if you make a million or 20 million dollars a film. The rest of the time it's, 'Oh, you're an actor. Where do you work in the restaurant?'

"Why do *this*? Why subject yourself to [being an actor]? Forget fame and fortune, because 97 percent of the union is unemployed. So if you're lucky to have fame and fortune, God bless. What's interesting is everybody who gets into this business wants to be of that 3 percent that work because they're 'special.' They've been told that since they were seven years old. They're all 'special.' You're 'special, special, special.' So there's already a fantasy coming into the business, that you're special. The only thing you have to overcome is what's happening on the other side of the [audition] table. Once you overcome that, you'll be that star. But that formula sucks. It's not a true formula."

Bonnie Black

"If you don't wake up thinking about acting and go to sleep thinking about it, think about doing something else. If you choose to do this, have a support system. Maintain your physical and mental health. This business is brutal and incredibly difficult. You've got to have the hide of a rhinoceros and the soul of a child.

"Sit down with yourself and ask, 'What do I want?' If you want movies and television, get yourself to L.A. immediately and capitalize on your youth and beauty. If you want to do theater, New York is the place to be, or look into regional theater work. There are still some regional theaters and smaller hubs like Chicago, Philadelphia-Baltimore-Washington, and the Florida-North Carolina-Virginia circuit. There are places in this country where you can go where you will be a part of a smaller pool of actors, and there is the potential that you can work more than if you come and be a very small fish in a very large pond like New York or L.A. Nobody can make you any guarantees. There are some places that still have [acting] companies like the Oregon Shakespeare Festival, Alabama Shakespeare, and Barter that hire an actor for a season of work. You will be working. You may not be advancing your career to be the next cutest thing in shoe leather on a pilot, but you'll be working. Decide if you want to work or if you want a career; they are two very different things.

"If you're looking for a 'Daddy,' if you're looking for somebody to constantly tell you you're great, you're not going to find it. You're choosing an incredibly competitive, brutal industry. If you want to come into this industry, bend at the knees and gird your loins and stay as mentally and physically healthy as possible. Be ready to have a hell of a lot of competition and find your way through that."

Michael Mastro

"I have parents, all the time, coming up to me with their sixteen-year-olds and telling me, 'She wants to be an actress. Tell her no. Tell her how hard it is!' I'm like, No, I'm not going to tell her that. They continue, 'She doesn't want to go to college.' OK, then she shouldn't go to college. She can go to college when she's twenty, thirty, forty, or fifty years old. College isn't going anywhere. I know of a woman who is fifty years old and got into grad school. If an aspiring actress is absolutely dead-set against going to college and what she wants to do is come to New York right now and just jump in, then maybe that is what she needs to do. She needs to follow that path and find out what she's going to discover on the path.

"Follow your heart and do everything you can to *not* cater to your fear. If I have one regret, looking back, it's that I still, *still* far too often cater to my fear. Instead of just picking myself up and saying, 'Just be afraid and do it anyway.'"

Darrie Lawrence

"You never know when you're auditioning. I was the understudy for the Manhattan Theater Club's *For the Other Side* with Rosemary Harris. The reason I got the job was that they had asked me to be the reader when they were casting the young man in the play. And then there was casting about for an understudy and they just called me. So that is one piece of advice: Be a reader. Also always be nice to everybody because you never know who you're going to meet on the way up that you pass on the way down."

Mark Price

"Something that I always tell myself is there's always something to be gained. There's always more that you can learn. Which is one of the reasons that I always like working with people who are better than me. And taking class, class never really ends. I read an article about Patrick Dempsey (*Grey's Anatomy*) and how for years people thought he was a big joke because he did all those teen movies. The article went on to talk about how this affected him psychologically until he had to step back for a while, step out of the business, and go back to acting class. Then he was very able to approach his craft in a new way. I think his experience spoke volumes about how you have to go back to basics.

"I always think of Laura Linney when she was nominated for *You Can Count on Me* and people asked her, 'How did you do that?' and she said, 'I went back to basics. For each scene I broke it down and I figured out how, when, why, what am I doing?' Acting is always going back to the basics. I think in this business it's easy to get ahead of yourself or to develop an ego, and those are the most dangerous things you can do."

Charlotte Rae

"You really have to realize that the competition is enormous and that rejection is part of the whole experience. Swoosie Kurtz, in *Actors' Equity* magazine, said that, 'It's a life filled with rejection.' I'm sure that even Meryl Streep gets rejected for a part she wants. I know that some people have read, tried to get parts, and haven't gotten them, and they're big names. You have to be prepared for that, but it doesn't mean that you shouldn't go ahead for it. You can't just be like a nun in a convent expecting the agent to call you. You really have to be active. Study. Get a network of fellow actors so you all know what's going on. I remember Charlie Durning saying to me, 'I never get a job from my agent; I find out about it from my friends.'

"Being an actor is not just studying and working. I hope that you know how to drive a cab or you can wait on tables or work in an office. You need some way to supplement or support yourself until you get into a position where the most thrilling thing in the world is to be able to say, 'I had a lifetime in the theater and in television and in film and I've earned it all through my work.'"

James Rebhorn

"Nobody should squelch your dream, but you have to really want to [be an actor]. You also have to think that you really don't want to make money. If you want to make money, you're in the wrong business because only a handful of us ever make any money, make a living at it. So you have to want to do it and not be concerned about material wealth and well-being because it's not a business that encourages that kind of thing. A lot of people think stars make a pile of money; well, that's the wrong attitude. You have to want to act because it's important to you and you think it's important to the world. If everything falls into place, then you're very fortunate, you're very lucky. I have been very, very lucky."

Phyllis Somerville

"Either be a really good businessperson or really have a fire in your belly, because it's not an easy business."

THE GROUP OF EIGHT'S EXIT LINES OF WISDOM FOR FELLOW WORKING ACTORS

All but James Rebhorn and Phyllis Somerville had advice for fellow working actors. Somerville couldn't think of any at the time, and Rebhorn replied, "I think it would be presumptuous of me to give them any tips. We each have our own burdens to bear." The remaining working actors in the Group of Eight wanted to impart upon other thespians these following, final lines of wisdom.

Robert LuPone

"The director Tom O'Horgan once said to me, 'You start out as a human being and you become the asshole, depending on how big you go up in the business.'"

Bonnie Black

"Never lose your sensitivity to those around you, as a professional actor and as a human being. Never be rude or cruel to anyone, especially younger people and the people who are breaking their backs as stagehands and dressers. There is no hierarchy. Everyone is completely equal, from the doorman to the director. Always demonstrate the kind of behavior, both onstage and off, that you want demonstrated toward yourself."

Michael Mastro

"Define for yourself, 'What is a rich life?' What does that mean to you? Get really specific about the actions you need to take and the goals you need to set for yourself, writing them down. Then find ways to keep yourself focused and passionate, in terms of achieving those goals. Take responsibility for the way you're using your mind. The quality of our lives is not dependent upon our circumstance; it's really dependent upon what we're doing, with the way we're thinking about how we're going to take what life is giving us and use it. I create my life by the way I think. We know as actors that we use our imagination to change our emotional state to prepare for a scene. If we can use our mind, imagination, and creativity to take ourselves into the dark place we need to go to play Hamlet, then we can use the same tools to take ourselves into the places we need to go to be effective for the rest of our lives. It has a huge, *huge* effect on your experience of your life, your experience of what's going on inside you, and *that* has a huge effect on how the world responds to you.

"Also, you should always be working on your craft. Your voice can always be better. Your grasp of dialect can always be better. Your knowledge of yourself can always be better. Your exercising of the muscle of courage can always be better, and that may mean going into an acting class and working on a scene that scares the shit out of you. It may also mean going out hiking and doing something you've never done before, like learning karate, doing something that frightens you. Whenever you can, nudge yourself out of your comfort zone. That may mean getting into a relationship because you're someone who thinks you can't do relationships. That may mean walking down a different street you've never walked down before. You may find a café or store that you never knew was there and you're like, 'Oh wow!'"

Darrie Lawrence

"Unless you're fantastically talented or very, very lucky and a star immediately, you need to protect your reputation. Not just as an actor but as a person. And news travels. There are people who really enjoy gossiping. There are people who do it inadvertently, and I've known directors do it to each other and I have had directors call me, who are friends, and ask me about a particular actor. And there is one, who shall remain nameless, whom I tell people is horrible. Not necessarily as an actor but as a person. I've worked with difficult people, mostly in regional theater, who were a little bit big for their britches."

Mark Price

"Find hobbies, just to keep you sane. It's a self-obsessed business to begin with, which I've always had a problem with and I really don't like, but it's just the nature of what it is. For me, the only way that I've been able to make it work is to have other interests and to have a life outside of it. If you live in New York City, there's a lot this city has to offer that has nothing to do with being an actor."

Charlotte Rae

"Be a generous human being and relate to each other on stage."

Ms. Rae's advice for being "a generous human being" is probably the most needed guidance in our business of entertainment but is also the most often ignored. All of us involved in this industry have lapses where we fail to treat our colleagues and peers with generosity and respect. In these moments, we approach survival, ambitions, and success with a singular focus. We stop listening to those around us who support and encourage our goals.

Writing this book took several years. I had never wanted to write a book for actors because, honestly, I *hate* actor handbooks. How's that for irony? But as I moved from actor to casting director to director, I grew increasingly aware that actors were making serious career mistakes. Many times upon witnessing the errors, I wanted to shout "STOP! You're doing yourself more harm than good. Shut up and listen!" But yelling doesn't get a message across properly. Look at what screaming did to Howard Dean's presidential aspirations in 2004 (if you're asking "who?" I've more than made my point).

What began as an eight-page booklet used in classes I taught or at lectures I was graciously invited to give became this nasty little monster. During its lengthy gestation, one of the first champions of this work suddenly passed, titles came and went, and I survived cancer (I had a book to finish, damn it!). Occasionally I'd question myself, "Do we really need another fucking, actor how-to book?" I knew in my heart the answer. Yes. Because I wasn't giving you, the reader, the saccharine sunshine bullshit of authors past, who wrote with Pollyanna prose on how to be an actor. With an assist from the Group of Eight and the quorum of agents, I wanted to give you straight talk as to how you can be a *better* actor. And I know you will be a stronger actor now than you were when you first opened these pages. Stronger how? That's up to you. For as I noted in the beginning, "Everything I say is right. Everything I say is wrong. There are many conflicting opinions in this industry. Don't take one person's words as gospel, including mine. Take what works for you."

And finally, my parting exit line before you venture on with your journey. With great respect and admiration for your bravery to be an actor, I suggest that as you take the journey, you listen, explore, have fun, and, with every aspect of acting, make it your business.

Now go kick some ass with your new skills and talent.

ACKNOWLEDGMENTS

No journey is ever truly taken alone. One person may trek forward on a path, but it's often others who give direction that leads the traveler to his destination. The writing of this book is one such journey. I am deeply grateful to the following for their guidance, support, and criticism and for helping me get out of my head, onto paper, and to my goal of helping others. Thank you:

Philip Adelman, Misha Angelovskiy, Lisa Barnett (in memoriam), Mark Baron, the company and staff at Barter Theatre, Bonnie Black, Bruce Clough, Victoria Craven, Michael Giorgio, Matt Greenbaum, Darrie Lawrence, James LaRosa, Chris Lucas, Cyd LeVin, Robert LuPone, Lynne Jebens, Brad Malow, Michael Mastro, Jack Menashe, Brian O'Neil (this is all your fault; thanks for the push), Bob Nirkind, Mark Price, Charlotte Rae, James Rebhorn, Diane Riley, Richard Rose, Phyllis Somerville, Martin Thompson, and Danny Vaccaro.

A big hug of thanks to my literary agent, Mitch Douglas. Thank you to my publisher for believing in this work. A gracious nod and bow to my editor, Gary Sunshine. I will be forever grateful for your insightful guidance and compassionate support.

And a special thank you to my immediate family—Dorie, Tyler, and Snuggles—for putting up with my multiple Jack Torrance (*The Shining*) "All work and no play" moments. The work is done. Time for play.

APPENDIX

COMBINED REGIONAL AUDITIONS

There are many metropolitan-area, statewide, and regional combined auditions in the United States. What follows are the more popular, producer-attended, combined auditions. Registration for an audition appointment at each combine audition is generally several months prior to the actual audition. Most combines require a fee. Contact each audition host organization for fee and registration details.

Organization	Audition Calendar	Audition Location	Notes
National Dinner Theatre Association (NDTA) www.ndta.com National Dinner Theatre Association PO Box 726 Marshall, MI 49068 (616) 781-7859	March	Each year a producing member of NDTA hosts the auditions with the location of auditions changing year to year.	Founded in 1978, the NDTA membership includes some of the top dinner theater producers in the country including Equity and non-Equity theaters.
New England Theatre Conference (NETC) www.netconline.org New England Theatre Conference 215 Knob Hill Drive Hamden, CT 06518 (617) 851-8535	March	Boston area	The annual NETC theater auditions provide a service whereby producers and directors of New England and theaters from throughout the country meet to audition candidates for positions as performers in summer and year-round professional theaters. An average of sixty companies are represented at the auditions annually, including Equity and non-Equity theaters.
New Jersey Theatre Alliance (NJTA) njtheatrealliance.com New Jersey Theatre Alliance 163 Madison Avenue, Suite 500 Morristown, NJ 07960 (973) 540-0515	August	New Brunswick, NJ	With over two dozen professional theaters, the NJTA producing membership includes nationally recognized theaters: George Street Playhouse, McCarter Theatre, Paper Mill Playhouse, Surflight Theater, The Shakespeare Theatre of New Jersey, and Two River Theatre Company. Union and non-union performers are seen at the annual auditions.
Southeastern Theatre Conference (SETC) www.setc.org Southeastern Theatre Conference P.O. Box 9868 Greensboro, NC 27429 (336) 272-3645	Spring and Fall	A different southeastern city in the United States is chosen for each audition conference.	SETC sponsors auditions every Spring and Fall for actors, singers, and dancers. At the Spring Convention, over eighty-five companies seek performers for both summer and year-round employment. The Fall Professional Auditions in September offer employment opportunities at over thirty theater companies.

Organization	Audition Calendar	Audition Location	Notes
StrawHat Auditions strawhat-auditions.com StrawHat Auditions #315 1771 Post Road East Westport, CT 06880 (212) 346-1133	March	New York City	New York casting offices, forty-plus theaters (mostly summer stock), entertainment companies, and some TV shows have used the StrawHat Auditions as a part of their casting efforts.
Theatre Bay Area (TBA) www.theatrebayarea.org 870 Market Street # 375 San Francisco, CA 94102 (415) 430-1140	Several audition periods are held throughout the year.	San Francisco Bay area	The San Francisco Bay area is the third largest theater center in the country, with more than 400 companies in eleven counties. The region boasts more theater companies per capita than almost any other metropolitan area in the United States and is home to the third largest community of Equity (union) actors, following New York City and Chicago.
Unified Professional Theatre Auditions (UPTAs) www.upta.org Unified Professional Theatre Auditions 51 South Cooper Memphis, TN 38104 (901) 725-0776	Spring	Memphis, TN	UPTAs attract over one hundred employers of talent, both union and non-union. UPTAs attract major regional theaters, national tours, New York and Los Angeles casting directors, dinner theaters, and national and international theme park entertainment casting.
University Resident Theatre Association (URTA) www.urta.com 1560 Broadway Suite 712 New York, NY 10036 (212) 221-1130	Winter	New York City, Chicago, and San Francisco	These auditions are designed for graduating degree candidates who are seeking advanced study through graduate school. Several hundred positions are offered annually, primarily through acceptance in MFA graduate programs. Casting opportunities are also available in Shakespeare festivals, resident theater companies, both on and off campus, and various seasonal activities.

PAID AUDITIONS

As the popularity of paid auditions increases, so too does the number of outlets for paid auditions. What follows are the more well-known paid auditions attended by industry and performers.

ACTORS CONNECTION

www.actorsconnection.com

New York

> 630 Ninth Avenue
>
> Suite 1410
>
> New York, NY 10036
>
> (212) 977-6666

Los Angeles

> Annual actor-industry seminars/auditions are held in L.A. Contact Actors Connection for details.

ONE ON ONE PRODUCTIONS

www.oneononenyc.com

> 126 West 23rd Street
>
> New York, NY 10011
>
> 212-691-6000

THE NETWORK

www.thenetworknyc.com

New York

> 312 West 36th Street
>
> 4th Floor, Studio 4C
>
> New York, NY 10018
>
> (212) 239-3198; (212) 239-3203

THE NETWORK STUDIO

www.thenetworkstudioeast.com

New York

> (917) 549-1986

Los Angeles

> 14542 Ventura Boulevard
>
> Suite 209
>
> Sherman Oaks, CA 91403
>
> (818) 788-2075

TVI ACTORS STUDIO

www.tvistudios.com

New York

165 West 46th Street
Suite 509
New York, NY 10036
212-302-1900

Los Angeles

14429 Ventura Boulevard
Suite 118
Sherman Oaks, CA 91423
(818) 784-6500

Chicago

116 West Illinois Street
Suite 3E
Chicago, IL 60610
(312) 828-0053

WEIST-BARRON

www.weistbarron.com

New York

35 West 45th Street
6th Floor
New York, NY 10036
(212) 840-7025

Los Angeles

Weist-Barron-Hill
4300 West Magnolia
Burbank, CA 91505
(818) 846-5595

PERFORMING ARTIST UNIONS (NORTH AMERICA)

Theater

ACTORS' EQUITY ASSOCIATION (AEA)

www.actorsequity.org

National Headquarters
    165 West 46th Street
    New York, NY 10036
    (212) 869-8530

Orlando
    10319 Orangewood Boulevard
    Orlando, FL 32821
    (407) 345-8600

Central Region / Chicago
    125 S. Clark Street
    Suite 1500
    Chicago, IL 60603
    (312) 641-0393

Western Region / Los Angeles
    Museum Square
    5757 Wilshire Boulevard
    Suite One
    Los Angeles, CA 90036
    (323) 634-1750

San Francisco
    350 Sansome Street
    Suite 900
    San Francisco, CA 94104
    (415) 391-3838

AMERICAN GUILD OF VARIETY ARTISTS (AGVA)

AGVA did not have an Internet presence at the time of this printing.

National Office
    American Guild of Variety Artists
    184 Fifth Avenue
    6th floor
    New York, NY 10010
    (212) 675-1003

The American Guild of Variety Artists (AGVA) is an actors union that represents certain performers (predominately actors with unique skills such as actor/musician or actor/acrobat) in Broadway, Off-Broadway, and cabaret productions, as well as live performers in variety shows, touring productions, and theme parks.

CANADIAN ACTORS' EQUITY ASSOCIATION (CAEA)

www.caea.com

National Office

44 Victoria Street, 12th Floor

Toronto, ON M5C 3C4

TEL: (416) 867-9165

FAX: (416) 867-9246

Western Office

505-321 Water Street

Vancouver, BC V6B 1B8

(604) 682-6173

Film and Television

AMERICAN FEDERATION OF TELEVISION & RADIO ARTISTS (AFTRA)

www.aftra.com

National Office–Los Angeles

5757 Wilshire Boulevard, 9th Fl.

Los Angeles CA 90036-0800

(323) 634-8100

National Office–New York

260 Madison Avenue

New York NY 10016-2401

(212) 532-0800

SCREEN ACTORS' GUILD (SAG)

www.sag.org

National Headquarters–Hollywood

5757 Wilshire Blvd., 7th Floor

Los Angeles, CA 90036-3600

(323) 954-1600; TTY/TTD: (323) 549-6648 (for deaf performers only); 1-800-SAG-0767 for SAG members outside Los Angeles

New York

360 Madison Avenue, 12th Floor

New York, NY 10017

(212) 944-1030; TTY/TTD: (212) 944-6715 (for deaf performers only)

ONLINE AUDITION RESOURCES

A cautionary note: Many audition websites copy audition information from the trade papers, Breakdown Services, or other websites and then charge actors for that information. Sometimes the audition information is outdated or completely bogus. There are hundreds of audition sites, both credible and suspect. Finding trustworthy online resources takes patience and investigation. Below are links to sites I have used in the past for extending my outreach. Most offer free services to the actor and/or have had a respectable reputation.

ACTORSACCESS.COM

Breakdown Services' subscription service for actors. Actors receive the same breakdowns as the agents and can submit themselves on projects. Fees are required for various service options.

ACTORSLIFE.COM

Free-access website created by an actor that includes industry interviews, audition notices, and actor-tool resource information.

BACKSTAGE.COM

The online presence of the industry trade paper that most actors utilize as their main source of industry information. Features include articles on actor life, work and survival, audition notices, and contacts to actor training, photographers, headshot reproduction services, and many actor-related services. Fees are required for various service options.

CASTINGNEWYORK.COM

Free-access website created for actors, which includes audition notices, industry interviews, union news, and actor-tools resource information.

CRAIGSLIST.ORG

The free bulletin board for everything from auditions to apartments to anonymous sex. Casting directors and studios DO use Cragslist.org to expand their outreach. Caution: Some of the "casting notices" are for less-than-respectable projects and/or producers. Be judicious when responding with your electronic picture and résumé.

NYCASTINGS.COM

A casting wire service and job information website for actors and production personnel.

PLAYBILL.COM

As the name suggests, this is the website from the producers of the classic yellow header playbills given out at nearly every Broadway, Off-Broadway, and touring production. Site resources include audition information (free to readers), industry articles, ticket sales to theatrical productions in New York and across the country, and information on regional theater seasons.

WWW.TCG.ORG

The Internet home to the Theatre Communications Group (TCG). TCG is the publisher of *American Theatre* magazine and *ARTSEARCH*, both valuable trade resources for seeking employment in the arts and the latest information in the theater arts.

WWW.VARIETY.COM

The Internet home of the fabled periodical that gives the Hollywood dish on everything from box-office receipts to which studio exec is being canned, and from what's going into production to what's hot at the moment. This site is more useful for industry gab and insight than as a trade resource for audition information.

INDEX

ABOUT THE AUTHOR

PAUL RUSSELL, casting director, director, and former actor, has nearly thirty years of experience in entertainment including film, TV, and Broadway. He has been involved with the casting of films for 20th Century Fox and HBO and the feature *Following Bliss*. He has also done casting for TV shows such as *Cosby*, *Murphy Brown*, and *ER* and for New York theater productions of *Disney's Beauty and the Beast*, *Cobb*, *Woody Guthrie's American Song*, and *Pera Palas*. Paul has also worked with the Ensemble Studio Theatre and the Lark Theatre in New York and with the touring production of *Keep on the Sunny Side*—plus over two hundred plays, musicals, classical works, and premieres for numerous, acclaimed regional theaters.

A member of the Society of Stage Directors and Choreographers, Paul has staged national tours, regional productions, and premieres in New York. When not behind an audition table or guiding actors in a rehearsal, Paul can be found on a distant road exploring places both new and familiar—preferably on his way to the Pine Barrens of South Jersey or to the nearest roller coaster. Paul lives in a small Jersey town with many trees, quiet streets, and his two rambunctious cats that he parents with his partner.

Paul can be contacted via his website at PaulRussell.net.